AN INTRODUCTION TO
The Counseling Profession

AN
INTRODUCTION
TO

The Counseling Profession

MICHAEL D. LEWIS
Governors State University

RICHARD L. HAYES
Bradley University

JUDITH A. LEWIS
Governors State University

 F.E. PEACOCK PUBLISHERS, INC. ITASCA, ILLINOIS 60143

BF
637
.C6
I54
1986

Copyright © 1986
F.E. Peacock Publishers, Inc.
All rights reserved
Library of Congress Catalog
Card Number 85-063211
ISBN 0-87581-316-X
Printed in the U.S.A.

CONTENTS

Preface   vii

Chapter 1. The Professionalization of Counseling   1
Roger F. Aubrey

Chapter 2. Human Growth and Development   36
Richard L. Hayes

Chapter 3. The Helping Relationship   96
DeWayne J. Kurpius

Chapter 4. Groups   130
John C. Dagley
George M. Gazda
M. Carole Pistole

Chapter 5. Life-Style and Career Development   167
Edwin L. Herr

Chapter 6. Social and Cultural Foundations   215
Clemmont E. Vontress

Chapter 7. Appraisal of the Individual   251
Lawrence Litwack

Chapter 8. Research and Evaluation   278
Leo Goldman

Chapter 9. Professional Orientation   301
Joe P. Wittmer
Larry C. Loesch

Epilogue   331

Appendices   334

A. Ethical Standards of the American Association for Counseling and Development

B. Ethical Guidelines for Group Leaders of the Association for Specialists in Group Work

C. Code of Ethics for Certified Clinical Mental Health Counselors of the American Mental Health Counselors Association

D. Responsibilities of Users of Standardized Tests of the American Association for Counseling and Development

E. Credentialing Information

F. Counseling-related Organizations

G. Relevant Professional Publications

H. Public Law 94-142 and Section 504—Understanding What They Are and Are Not

I. Commonly Used Assessment Tools & Test Publishers

Index   399

PREFACE

In recent years the counseling profession has expanded rapidly, not just in numbers but in knowledge and ideas. Counselors now work in a greater variety of settings than anyone could have foreseen, using technologies that were nonexistent just a decade ago. Amidst all this change, the profession itself—its preparation standards, its continuing education requirements, its accreditation and certification thrusts—has kept pace. Counselor education programs have changed to meet the needs of students who will assume unprecedented roles in unfamiliar milieus. The Council for the Accreditation of Counseling and Related Educational Programs (CACREP) and the National Board for Certified Counselors (NBCC) have developed standards appropriate for the training and certification of these practitioners. Counselors, whether experienced or newly trained, have come to perceive themselves as professionals.

All these developments have led to the need for a text that provides a detailed overview of the counseling profession as it is today. This book addresses that challenge. The fact that our outline conforms to the areas of study prescribed by CACREP and by NBCC makes the text appropriate both for an introductory survey course and for an experienced counselor's review.

We have attempted to make this book a state-of-the-art overview of the field, both by addressing each major area of professional concern and by selecting as authors for the various chapters recognized experts in their respective fields. All the chapters that follow have been prepared by individuals who have written extensively in the field and who have, in many cases, held national office in professional counseling organizations. Each chapter represents a fresh synthesis of the developments in a special area of the profession by one or more of its most knowledgeable participants.

In Chapter 1 Roger F. Aubrey provides an introduction to the field of counseling based on an examination of its historical background. Chapter 2 by Richard L. Hayes reviews the assumptions that underlie human development theories. Behavioral, maturational, and structural approaches are presented, with attention focused on the nature and needs of individuals at all developmental levels. Chapter 3 by DeWayne J. Kurpius continues the analysis with an introduction to the theory and practice of the helping relationship. John C. Dagley, George M. Gazda, and M. Carole Pistole add to the examination of core skills and theory with a discussion of group practices and methods in Chapter 4.

Chapter 5 by Edwin L. Herr presents an overview of vocational choice theory and approaches to career development. Clemmont E. Vontress in Chapter 6 discusses the social and cultural issues that cut across all counseling methods and approaches.

In Chapter 7 Lawrence Litwack develops a framework for understanding the individual, including methods of data gathering and interpretation, individual and group testing, and the study of individual differences. Chapter 8 by Leo Goldman provides a discussion of the counseling professional's use of research, with attention to innovative approaches to program development and evaluation.

The final chapter by Joe P. Wittmer and Larry C. Loesch provides a detailed analysis of the basic elements inherent in a professional orientation to counseling. Included are the goals and objectives of professional organizations, standards of preparation, certification, licensing, and the role identity of counselors. In an epilogue to the text the editors build on the preceding chapters to envision the role and characteristics of the counselor of the future.

The number of individuals to whom we are indebted in the preparation of this book is beyond the scope of this preface. In particular, we owe our gratitude to the authors of the respective chapters for their willingness to be a part of this project and their professionalism in completing tasks thoroughly and on time. In addition, we appreciate the support of our respective universities, Governors State University and Bradley University. The secretarial staffs, including Mariana Thompson, Mari Burnett, Betty Metcalf, and Wilhelminia Moore, have been very helpful in manuscript preparation. We would also like to thank our family members, Keith, Bree, Jon, Ali, Jessica, Gillian, and Barry B. for their understanding and support throughout this project. Finally, Ted Peacock and the outstanding staff at F. E. Peacock Publishers saw the potential of this idea and provided immediate and enthusiastic support.

CONTRIBUTORS

Roger F. Aubrey, Ed.D., Professor, Department of Human Resources, Vanderbilt University, Nashville, TN.

John C. Dagley, Ph.D., Associate Professor, Counseling and Human Development Services, University of Georgia, Athens, GA.

George M. Gazda, Ed.D., Professor and Director, Counseling Psychology Program, and Associate Dean for Research, College of Education, University of Georgia, Athens, GA.

Leo Goldman, Ph.D., Professor, School of Education at Lincoln Center, Fordham University, New York, NY.

Richard L. Hayes, Ed.D., Associate Professor, College of Education and Health Sciences, Bradley University, Peoria, IL. (Editor)

Edwin L. Herr, Ed.D., Professor and Head, Division of Counseling and Educational Psychology, The Pennsylvania State University, University Park, PA.

DeWayne J. Kurpius, Ed.D., Professor and Program Area Head, Department of Counseling and Educational Psychology, Indiana University, Bloomington, IN.

Judith A. Lewis, Ph.D., Professor, Division of Health and Human Services, College of Health Professions, Governors State University, University Park, IL. (Editor)

Michael D. Lewis, Ph.D., Professor, Division of Psychology and Counseling, College of Education, Governors State University, University Park, IL. (Editor)

Lawrence Litwack, Ed.D., Professor and Chairperson, Department of Counseling Psychology, Rehabilitation, and Special Education, Northeastern University, Boston, MA.

Larry C. Loesch, Ph.D., Professor, Department of Counselor Education, University of Florida, Gainesville, FL.

M. Carole Pistole, M.A., Research Associate, Counseling and Human Development Services, University of Georgia, Athens, GA.

Clemmont E. Vontress, Ph.D., Department of Education, George Washington University, Washington, DC.

Joe P. Wittmer, Ph.D., Professor and Chairperson, Department of Counselor Education, University of Florida, Gainesville, FL.

CHAPTER 1
THE PROFESSIONALIZATION OF COUNSELING

Roger F. Aubrey

Counseling is not a long-established profession. In fact, in many ways counseling is just emerging from being an occupation to being a fullfledged profession. This chapter will trace its evolution and those persons and events most significant in the creation of the profession of counseling.

Just as shamans, medicine men, and healers were not called doctors in the early days of medicine, the first counselors were not addressed by that title. In this country, the precursors to counselors were such people as the women deans and advisors who were employed shortly after the Civil War to watch over young women entering college. This group would also include settlement house workers concerned about the millions of confused immigrants entering this country in the late 1800s. There were also employees in schools who aided young people directly in classrooms through guidance programs and who gave informal "counseling" when needed. In addition, there were individuals such as the "Father of Guidance," Frank Parsons, who attempted to set up community centers to aid people in search of work. Finally, scores of people in the early 1900s were collectively called social reformers. Many of these were similar to modern-day counselors in their concern for the well-being of the clientele they served.

Historically there have always been individuals who assumed the roles of counselors. Granted, these individuals did not possess college degrees, specialized knowledge, or a code of ethics; they did not belong to a professional organization or graduate from a particular preparatory program. Instead, what they had in common with counselors was a willingness to assist people in need by providing a helping relationship or needed resources.

These people, who early on assumed counselor roles, Robert Kegan (1982) refers to as "natural therapists" and relegates today's professional counselors to roles as "secondary therapists." Kegan believes that mothers and fathers, friends, the peer group, clergy, and others have always been available as helpers and support groups for the troubled. Only in recent times has there been a need for what we now call a professional counselor.

A SOCIETY IN TURMOIL

Imagine for a moment what America was like one hundred years ago. Look at the landscape and you can see millions of farms and small villages. You would not see many large cities, but you would notice an increasing number of railroad lines coming and going from newly built factories. In time, large cities would spring up due to the growth of factories, mines, ports, railroads, and mills.

Look at the people at this time. Families still produced many of the necessities of life including food, clothing, furniture, and tools. These same families were together much of the time and lived in close proximity to their nearest relatives. The family often worked as a unit, and children were around much of the time because they attended school for only six or seven years, and it was a short school year.

Much of their time was spent in work aimed at satisfying Maslow's (see Chapter 2) lower-order needs of obtaining food, shelter, protection, and the like. There were no dishwashers, radios, television sets, vacuum cleaners, washing machines, dryers, automobiles, or microwave ovens. A great deal of time therefore was consumed in taking care of one's dwelling, preparing food, repairing utensils, sewing clothes, growing food, transporting goods and food, bartering for necessities, and earning money. Leisure time for many was hard to come by and frequently revolved around the local religious group. People did entertain themselves with music, storytelling, food gatherings, weddings and socials, ethnic games, and small talk. When in trouble, they would first turn to family members—if this failed, they might go to a neighbor, the local clergy, or the family doctor if one existed.

Improvements in tools dramatically changed the landscape of the late 1800s. As the Industrial Revolution picked up momentum, large factories sprang up like mushrooms throughout the North and South. Assembly lines and power machinery quickly put out of business women and men who labored at home with their hands to grow food and make family products such as clothing and furniture. In turn, in order to earn food for survival, families were forced to move from farms and small villages. Millions migrated to growing cities and metropolitan areas where the jobs were.

The upheaval of families meant the loss of familiar faces and support systems. It meant a drastic adjustment to a life where one could not be self-sufficient or rely on the land and family and friends. Instead, individuals were now forced to negotiate many new systems of living and to find and maintain employment for the wage earners in the family, who often included children before the enactment of child labor laws.

If life was difficult for those leaving the farms and villages, it was even worse for the millions of immigrants. These people were entering the United States to avoid famine, chronic unemployment, military conscription, wars, religious persecution, and intolerable conditions in their homelands. They were often hampered by an inability to speak English and many had little money. Their hopes centered on finding shelter and permanent employment. More often than not, they would end up initially working in factories, mines, ports, mills, railroads, or menial jobs.

The tapestry of America in the early 1900s was a patchwork quilt of southerners moving to the large cities of the North, of immigrants moving wherever jobs were to be found, of railroads spreading across the nation, of factories belching smoke night and day, wagons and carriages hauling goods, canals and rivers crowded with boats and barges, cities sprawling with a constant need for more buildings and dwellings, and the hope that industrialization would benefit the great mass of people.

INDUSTRIALIZATION AND MENTAL HEALTH

The industrialization of America did not benefit everyone. There were many losers in the not-so-gradual transition from an agrarian and small village society to one of industrialization and metropolitan living (remember, no suburbs as we know them today at this time in history). Among the losers were individuals who previously had taken pride in making clothing, furniture, utensils, and tools by hand. Many now found themselves on assembly lines, putting together pieces stamped by machinery. Instead of creating their own products from beginning to end, they now complemented machinery in boring and tedious hourly routines.

In addition to a loss of pride in their work, individuals also lost a sense of security and familiarity as people moved from long-established ties in one region or country to a new setting hundreds or thousands of miles away. This meant giving up family history and tradition and starting anew in a setting with unfamiliar norms and customs.

The mental health of individuals was also affected by a loss of friends, relatives, and support systems. These "buffers" against stress and emotional concerns were taken for granted for generations. Their removal due to geographic moves meant adjustments that often tore at the roots of family cohesiveness. The replacement of these "buffers" was no easier in those days than it is today with families on the move.

Although life on farms and in small villages was arduous and routine, individuals had some say in what tasks they would do and when they would do them. It was a major adjustment, therefore, for individuals to find their lives suddenly highly regulated by time clocks, the need to travel to a place of employment, the loss of family mealtimes, insensitive supervisors, dangerous working conditions, and job uncertainty. In particular, an unwelcome regimentation of much of one's waking hours led to a dehumanization of spirit and a loss of personal initiative. In terms of mental health, the combination of a loss of support systems and "natural therapists," in addition to a loss of self-esteem in one's work and manner of living and a growing feeling of powerlessness in coping with the external environment could hardly contribute to individual mental health. Indeed, it was a time when masses of people needed advocates, individuals who would intervene on their behalf and in their best interest.

GUIDANCE AND SOCIAL REFORM MOVEMENTS

There were advocates in many shapes and forms as the twentieth century began. Counselors were not among these ranks in name but certainly were recognizable in spirit and effort. Guidance would be the term best characterizing the work and role of early "counselors."

Guidance arose in the dawning twentieth century as one of several movements answering the upheaval and turmoil created by the nineteenth-century Industrial Revolution. Other reformers would look at abuses in the use of child labor, in the selling of tainted food, the dispensing of narcotics, dangerous conditions in mines and factories, lack of compulsory school attendance laws, absence of curbs on ambitious politicians, and so on. In general, all social reformers were linked in common battle against the increased exploitation of many segments of the American population by unscrupulous hucksters and entrepreneurs.

The injustice and suffering wrought by massive technological change would shape the early destiny of guidance. The leaders of this emerging profession would come essentially from the front ranks of idealistic and committed reformers. Their primary clientele would be children and adolescents, and schools would be the agent for rectifying the existing ills of society. What audience could be better attended than "the great armies of child laborers who were leaving the public schools to become wage earners under unfavorable conditions" (Miller, 1964, p. 7)?

Today, for those entering the counseling profession, it may seem odd that early guidance workers thought they could accomplish sweeping changes in children and adolescents without the tools of counseling. Prior to 1931, however, the word "counseling" was rarely used, and guidance was an umbrella term for functions associated with educational and vocational guidance. Not until the publication of *Workbook in Vocations* by Proctor, Benefield, and Wrenn (1931), which supplemented Proctor's earlier *Educational and Vocational Guidance* (1925), was the concept of counseling as a psychological process first delineated. Therefore, counseling was viewed initially as an adjunct process to assist in the presentation of guidance information regarding work and in educational planning.

ORIGINS OF GUIDANCE

Guidance began in the United States in the large industrial centers of the Midwest and on the Eastern Seaboard, where hordes of people came in search of work and the good life. Unfortunately, jobs were not always steady or even available. The work that did exist was often demeaning and dangerous, and although a few profited greatly, one historian has noted that "the human beings whose labor made these achievements possible were crippled and killed almost as fast as they would have been on a battlefield" (Mumford, 1961, p. 446).

Early guidance leaders were ambitious and idealistic. They were linked to other social reformers, and their weapons at this time were attempts at legislation, consciousness-raising, publicity, fund-raising, and the use of education. Significantly, the technology and "hardware" of today's mental health practitioners was nonexistent. At this point in history, Freud's work (see Chapter 2) was in the pioneer stage. Measurement and assessment were in their infancy with the work of Binet and Simon (see Chapter 7). There were no pharmacological prescriptions for clients. In brief, the focus of early reformers was not on the individual *qua* individual, but rather on the environment as both cause and cure of all societal problems. Caring and concern for individuals was not disregarded, but the ultimate remedy for personal travail was seen in societal transformation, not interpersonal alteration. Cremin (1961) sums this up by noting, "These young reformers came to their work convinced that the real curse of industrialization lay not so much in its physical blight as in its shattering of historic human associations . . . their ultimate goal was the humanizing of industrial civilization" (p. 60).

In schools, reform through guidance began much like any other subject. It was viewed initially as something that could be presented by a teacher in a classroom to large numbers of students. Furthermore, guidance was seen as a series of learning experiences enhancing the existing curriculum by specifically addressing areas and topics previously ignored or neglected.

Educational historians generally credit Jesse B. Davis with the first effort to systematize guidance into the accepted school curriculum (Brewer, 1942; Miller, 1961). As a school administrator in the rapidly growing industrial city of Detroit between 1889 and 1907, Davis was concerned with the vocational and social problems of his students. He carried this concern with him when he accepted the principalship of the Grand Rapids, Michigan, High School in 1907.

Interestingly, Davis selected English composition as the area best suited to what he termed "vocational and moral guidance," and one period a week was set aside for this lesson. For Davis (1914), the definition and objectives of guidance at this time were nothing less than the

> pupil's better understanding of his own character; it means an awakening of the moral consciousness that will lead him to emulate the character of the good and great who have gone before; it means a conception of himself as a social being in some future occupation, and from this viewpoint the appreciation of his duty and obligation toward his business associates, toward his neighbors, and toward the law. (p. 17)

At the same time that Davis recognized the need for planned guidance programs for young people in expanding industrial centers, another guidance pioneer arose in an industrial complex on the Eastern Seaboard. Frank Parsons, the "Father of Guidance," did not begin his career or work in public schools. Instead, Parsons was a versatile individual who worked as an engineer, college professor, and later as a social worker in Boston where he established a settlement house for young adults already employed in industry or in need of jobs.

Although the early work of Parsons was focused on out-of-school young people, his hopes centered on a time when vocational guidance would "become part of the public school system in every community" (Lasch, 1965, p. 157). To accomplish this end, Parsons established the

Vocation Bureau in Civic Service House in Boston in 1908. The founding of the Vocation Bureau was a major breakthrough because it represented the first "institutionalization of vocational guidance" (Ginzberg, 1971, p. 23). A year later, Parsons's volume on *Choosing a Vocation* (1909) was published posthumously, and in 1910 Parsons's contribution to guidance was recognized when Boston was selected as the site for the first conference on vocational guidance. This conference resulted in the founding of the National Vocational Guidance Association (NVGA) in 1913 in Grand Rapids, Michigan. The link between the pioneer work of Jesse Davis and Frank Parsons is obvious and led in 1915 to the first publication of the NVGA journal, *The Vocational Guidance Bulletin*.

EARLY USE OF COUNSELING IN VOCATIONAL GUIDANCE

Although the formal recognition of counseling did not occur until after almost three decades of vocational guidance, this acknowledgment was long overdue. Even a cursory reading of such early guidance leaders as Parsons (1909), Bloomfield (1915), or Kitson (1915) reveals traces of what later was to be called counseling. Furthermore, counseling as a psychological process is apparent in much of the legacy of the early mental health movement, the work of G. Stanley Hall and his disciples in the child-study movement, the introduction of psychoanalysis to this country in 1909 by Freud's lectures at Clark University, and in the application of psychometrics during and following World War I.

The early inception of counseling was highly dependent on the existing scheme of guidance. As such, counseling was viewed simply and solely as an adjunct technique in accomplishing limited vocational guidance outcomes. The first application of this method would be labeled trait-and-factor counseling (see Chapter 2). Its antecedents would owe a great deal to Parsons (1909), who in 1908 said that the wise choice of a vocation involved three major considerations. These three factors could also be employed by "counselors" in leading individuals through the process of decision making (see Chapter 5).

Trait-and-factor counseling has also been traced to early beginnings in French and German concepts of faculty psychology (Williamson, 1965). It also owes a debt to the work of Hugo Munsterberg (1913), the German founder of American industrial and applied psychology.

The early use of trait-and-factor counseling was simple and essentially a one-step operation. Counseling would be employed to enhance the three-factor model of Parsons, especially the third and final phase. Just as psychometrics had been employed earlier to give rigor and respectability to the first and diagnostic phase of the Parsonian model, so would counseling now be used in the final phase to match the individual with a suitable job. In so doing, the techniques of testing and counseling would give a scientific flavor to vocational guidance. Advances in psychometrics and experimental psychology would also enhance validity and predictability. In time, this combination would allow trait-and-factor counseling to dominate "the academic landscape of vocational guidance almost from its beginning until the end of World War II" (Ginzberg, 1971, p. 32).

The trait-and-factor approach to counseling in time was known as the model of directive or counselor-centered counseling. A prime leader in this area was E. G. Williamson (1965; Williamson & Foley, 1949). The model developed by Williamson and others reflected the exactitude and precision of the ambitious vocational guidance movement and placed counselors in a role not unlike teachers. The counselor possessed greater maturity than the student as well as skills and knowledge of benefit to the individual. As a consequence, the counselor was seen as the key figure in the counseling process, and this figure would take the responsibility for leading the client in areas and directions deemed most helpful.

In retrospect, it is easy to criticize trait-and-factor approaches as overly directive, rigid, counselor-centered, and single-minded in purpose. This approach, however, was fully in keeping with a historical period of general rigidity and authoritarianism. This would be reinforced time and again by nationwide conditions from the end of World War I through the early 1940s. Only after World War II would alternative models and approaches put directive counseling to the test.

ROLE OF BEHAVIORISM AND PSYCHOMETRICS IN EARLY COUNSELING

The psychology undergirding directive counseling was behavioral. The early beginnings of behaviorism (see Chapter 2) can be traced to the founding of the first psychological laboratory in Leipzig, Germany, by Wilhelm Wundt in 1879. Wundt's laboratory was based on the belief that human behavior is orderly and predictable and can be studied by use of the scientific method. This view would later reach America, and behavioral psychology would dominate attempts to understand human behavior for a number of decades. Even though Freud presented a series of lectures at Clark University in 1909, it would be a number of years before psychoanalytic psychology (see Chapter 2) could vie with behaviorism for respectability or popularity.

The school of behavioral psychology made its first major impact on counseling through the study of psychometrics (see Chapter 7). This field of study was important in the evolution of counseling because it provided early counselors with a scientific means of studying human behavior. Crude beginnings in this area came as early as 1890 in this country. At that time James Cattel (see Chapter 2) tried to relate scores on mental tests of reaction time to school marks. In France, the pioneer work of Alfred Binet and Théodore Simon on intelligence testing was also a seminal work, and collectively, psychological measurement by 1920 would be a powerful force. It received a tremendous boost in popularity from the first construction of group tests during World War I for screening military recruits. Known as the Army Alpha and Army Beta tests, these first standardized group tests would be the forerunners of hundreds by the mid-1920s (see Chapter 7).

Without behavioral psychology, and especially a psychological support base in psychometrics, it is unlikely that counseling and vocational guidance could have survived in their formative years. Before World War I, leaders in vocational guidance had rested their case largely on an indictment of the existing ills of society and the promise of guidance in matching a potential worker with a suitable vocation. The promise, however, was predicated on the ability of the potential worker and the counselor helper to determine the future worker's interests, capabilities, strengths, and limitations. Armed with this information, the potential worker would study various jobs and occupations and then confer with the counselor helper to analyze the relationship between worker occupations and future choice. Lacking a scientific means to justify the first step of individual assessment, it is unlikely that counseling and vocational guidance would have been received so widely.

Testing and the adoption of trait-and-factor psychology gave early counselors and the vocational guidance movement respectability, credentials, and a firm foothold in public institutions. The price of this newfound acceptance, however, would be an overdependency on testing and information giving as bases for counseling or guidance intervention. In turn, the overreliance on the Parsonian triad of diagnosis, information, and placement would effectively curtail the extension of counseling and guidance as a process encompassing the entire course of an individual's life. Furthermore, psychological measurement blinded guidance and counseling to many significant advancements in other areas of the behavioral sciences that resulted from the study of social class, motivation, ethnicity, longitudinal development, and values.

In retrospect, it seems unfortunate that early counselors and the vocational guidance movement became so "hooked" on tests and measurement. In the words of Ginzberg (1971), "Vocational guidance became first attracted to and then addicted to testing" (p. 3). Sadly, most of the tools adopted by counseling and vocational guidance did not fulfill the hopes and aspirations of its early founders. If anything, these techniques worked against the very individuals they sought to help by rigidly labeling, classifying, categorizing, and sorting individuals instead of aiding them in arriving at greater self-determination and human dignity.

COUNSELING FROM 1920 THROUGH WORLD WAR II

The 1920s and 1930s would see counselors working in schools as guidance helpers and teacher counselors, in colleges as various types of student personnel workers, in state and local employment settings as job counselors, in some industrial and building complexes as personnel workers, and in clinics and hospitals as rehabilitation counselors. By today's standards, there were not many counselors, and there were few professional associations. The methods of these early counselors included psychometrics, child and case study, directive counseling, and group guidance/information giving. The psychological foundation was essentially behavioral psychology.

World War II would change the face of counseling in the United States significantly. Changes came during the period of American involvement from 1941 to 1945 and especially immediately following the war. The war itself strengthened psychiatry as a profession. Prior to World War II, "Psychiatry was not a strong or prestigeful part of medical schools and medical centers" (Sarason, 1981, p. 828). The war would put unusual demands on psychiatry, however, with thousands of veterans in need of treatment. In turn, the psychiatric community was unable to deal with the sheer number of veterans with their traditional Freudian model and an inadequate number of professionals. Therefore, they turned to psychiatrically trained social workers and the new field of clinical psychology.

Historically, the most important breakthrough for the counseling profession at this time was the publication in 1942 of Carl Rogers's *Counseling and Psychotherapy*. This book would usher in an era of client-centered counseling and sweep aside existing models of trait-and-factor and directive counseling. In fact, the eventual impact of Rogers and his followers was so enveloping and unquestioned that Super (1964) believed the influence inimical to the profession as a whole. For Super, counseling and guidance theory at that time was simply too weak to assimilate and integrate the theory and research of Rogers without a resultant bandwagon effect. Nevertheless, Super believed that guidance and counseling theory "should reach a state of development at which it can assimilate useful ideas and modify itself in the light of newly discovered facts rather than be swept by them as it was by Rogerian theory" (p. 156).

World War II spawned another phenomenon following the cessation of fighting: a tremendous increase in the Veterans Administration and facilities for returning veterans. This, too, affected the counseling profession as monies were appropriated for research in counseling and psychotherapy and the training of psychiatrists and psychologists.

Seymour Sarason has called the post–World War II years the Age of Psychotherapy (1981, p. 830). He points out that it was not just veterans who needed counseling following the war. In addition, after almost five years of wartime stress, the civilian population also required help. Many had faced years of family disruption, geographic moves, and war-related deaths or disabilities. Suddenly, peacetime came, but with it arose uncertainties about the future and anxieties about massive social and economic change.

AN AGE OF MENTAL HEALTH

In the post–World War II years, client-centered counseling prospered. Overnight, by the mid-1950s counseling replaced testing as the key guidance function. In turn, counseling would rise to such eminence in the next few years that it would compete and contend with all traditional guidance functions in regard to the use and overall purpose of counseling and guidance. What began as an adjunct tool of guidance would now raise a challenge for ascendancy in its own right.

The influence of Carl Rogers on the profession of counseling in and out of schools can hardly be overestimated. In regard to public schools, the literature pertaining to the practice of counseling and guidance would change dramatically. Before Rogers, this literature was very practical and dealt with such topics as testing, cumulative records, orientation procedures, vocations, placement functions, and so on. In addition, this early literature would deal extensively with the goals and purpose of *guidance*. With Rogers there was a sudden new emphasis on the techniques and methods of counseling, research and refinement of counseling technique, selection and training of future counselors, and the goals and purpose of *counseling*. Guidance in schools for all intents and purposes would suddenly disappear as a major consideration in the bulk of the literature and be replaced by a decade or more of concentration on counseling.

Outside schools, the impact of Rogers and client-centered counseling was also felt. The work of Rogers and his colleagues at the University of Wisconsin and at the University of Chicago was marked by careful research, rigorous training, and creative theory building. This work and the writings of Rogers (1942, 1951, 1961; Rogers & Dymond, 1954) continued as the major force in counseling and psychotherapy throughout the 1950s.

Another factor in the Age of Mental Health (a term coined by Sarason, 1981) was humanistic psychology (see Chapter 2). This school of psychology has also been called existential, phenomenological, and third-force psychology. Abraham Maslow (1968, 1970) used this latter term in contrasting humanistic psychology with the earlier schools of behaviorism and psychoanalytic psychology. He and others (Frankl, 1963, 1965; May, 1953, 1961; Van Kaam, 1967) believed counselors needed a choice between the rigid and mechanistic-deterministic base of earlier systems and newer, more holistic models of self-determination. Shaffer (cited in Corey, 1982) has identified five themes within humanistic psychology that seem central to this belief:

1. The starting point for psychology in general is conscious experience. Humanistic psychology in particular emphasizes subjective reality, or the uniqueness of each person's experience.
2. The here and now—the immediate experiencing of the present moment—is an experiential approach that is stressed along with the wholeness and integrity of human behavior.
3. Humanistic psychology grants that humans are limited by both biological and environmental factors; and yet, within the framework of these limitations, human freedom is insisted upon.
4. This approach also contends that humans cannot be reduced to drives, need satisfactions, or unconscious determinants.
5. Humanistic psychology, based on existential philosophy, maintains that humans can never be defined as a product or as an entity; humans are continually in the process of self-definition. (p. 63)

The post–World War II years also saw a number of other developments in the social and behavioral sciences. These advancements in developmental psychology, learning theory, psychiatry, and sociology (Erikson, 1950; Havighurst, 1952; Hollingshead, 1949; Inhelder & Piaget, 1958; Lynd & Lynd, 1954; Piaget, 1952; Riesman, 1950; Sullivan, 1953; Warner, Meeker, & Ells, 1949; White, 1953) paved the way for significant gains in counseling theory. Also, bulwarked by Super's (1953, 1955, 1956) pioneering work, vocational guidance became transformed into career development. This dramatic change was enhanced by the addition of self-concept theory (Combs & Snygg, 1949) and furthered by the work of other career theorists (Bordin, Nachman, & Segal, 1963; Ginzberg, Ginsburg, Axelrod, & Herma, 1951; Holland, 1959; Roe, 1956).

PROFESSIONAL ORGANIZATIONS AND COUNSELING

As counseling expanded in scope and purpose in the early 1950s, it became evident that there was a need for a professional organization to unify the diverse concerns of counselors. This certainly could not be the American Psychological Association (APA) because many practicing counselors were not psychologists, nor were they eligible for membership in APA. Also, at a fateful conference in 1950 at Boulder, Colorado, clinical psychology had closely aligned itself with the psychiatric community. This meant a close and almost exclusive focus on returning veterans and the use of a medical model (see Chapter 2), which proved to be too narrow a focus for the vast majority of practicing counselors in the 1950s.

An attempt to create a guidance organization had been made in 1934. At that time, a loose association was formed called the Council of Guidance and Personnel Associations. After eighteen years, however, it had not succeeded in bringing together the range of groups it sought to influence. As a consequence, in July 1952, the American Personnel and Guidance Association (APGA) was formed. It represented a merger of the National Vocational Guidance Association (now called the National Career Development Association) and the American College Personnel Association with the cooperation of the National Association of Guidance and Counseling Trainers (now called the Association for Counselor Education and Supervision) and the Student Personnel Association for Teacher Education (now called the Association for Humanistic Education and Development). One year later, in 1953, the American School Counselor Association would join APGA. Since then, eight other divisions have been accepted into APGA. These divisions and the years of acceptance are as follows: American Rehabilitation Counseling Association (1958); Association for Measurement and Evaluation in Guidance (1965) (now called the Association for Measurement and Evaluation in Counseling and Development); National Employment Counselors Association (1966); Association for Non-

White Concerns in Personnel and Guidance (1972) (now called the Association for Multicultural Counseling and Development); Association for Religious and Values Issues in Counseling (formerly the National Catholic Guidance Conference) (1973); Association for Specialists in Group Work (1973); Public Offender Counselor Association (1974), and the American Mental Health Counselors Association (1978).

In July 1983, the Board of Directors of APGA, following a mail ballot by the membership, voted a name change. Today, APGA is known as the American Association for Counseling and Development (AACD). It also has a new organizational affiliate seeking eventual divisional status in the Military Educators and Counselors Association.

1950S: A DECADE OF MAJOR BREAKTHROUGHS

If one decade in history had to be singled out for the most profound impact on counselors, it would be the 1950s. Seven major events mark this decade. First, the counseling profession was introduced to new and more dynamic models of counseling, especially Rogers's client-centered. This caused an immediate shift from earlier directive counseling models and encouraged counseling professionals to consider other innovative means of dealing with clients.

Second, counseling associations were formed and became vehicles for working counselors and for those in universities. The Boulder conference would set the tone for clinical psychologists as a group and heavily influence the yet-to-come counseling psychologists. Also, the creation of the American Personnel and Guidance Association in 1952 would provide a home for thousands of counselors not eligible for or desirous of affiliation with psychologists.

Third, humanistic psychology would give mental health professionals a new vista. It would provide a breath of fresh air to the determinism, pessimism, and rigidity of behavioral and psychoanalytic psychology. Furthermore, it gave mental health professionals a holistic and optimistic picture of the individual. The person or self was not viewed as simply a mass of instincts or drives or a stimulus-response organism. Instead, in humanistic psychology individuals were viewed as essentially healthy, capable of making choices and decisions, and eventually mastering their environment.

Fourth, vocationalism as a subject and practice was replaced by career development (Barry & Wolf, 1962). For years, vocational guidance had operated without a defensible theory or research base (Ginzberg, Ginsburg, Axelrod, & Herma, 1951; Super, 1956). The work of Super (1955, 1956, 1957) and others, aided by developmental and self-concept theory, would strengthen and expand this earlier movement. The notion of career as a concept engulfing all of one's life would also enlarge the scope of counselors' work.

Fifth, lifespan developmental theory began to emerge as a field of study (see Chapter 2). From early beginnings in Europe with Charlotte Buhler (1935) and Jean Piaget (1952), the 1950s would see Americans eagerly embrace this field. As early as 1942, Donald Super would use developmental theory in formulating his conception of careers, which culminated in 1953. In addition, 1950 would see the publication of Erik Erikson's monumental book, *Childhood and Society*. A few years later, Robert Havighurst (1952) would write his classic book, *Developmental Tasks and Education*. Lawrence Kohlberg (1958) would also begin his research on moral development at this time. In the field of counseling, Robert Mathewson (1949) would incorporate a developmental perspective in his powerful book titled *Guidance Policy and Practice*. The flurry of work on life-span development, however, would not touch the counseling profession significantly until the 1960s.

A sixth major event of the 1950s was a comprehensive study of American schools by James Conant (1959, 1961). The results of Conant's work focused the public on deficiencies in America's schools and resulted in many changes in school structure, organization, teacher training, and curriculum.

A seventh and most potent event in the 1950s did not even occur in the United States. Instead, it occurred in Russia in 1957 with the launching of the space satellite *Sputnik*. The concern in this country over the technological lag between the USA and the Soviet Union prompted passage of the National Defense Education Act (NDEA) of 1958. Within a few years, the number of counselors in schools would quadruple, and the ratio of counselors to students would decrease from one to 960 in 1958–1959, to one to 450 by 1966–1967 (Shertzer & Stone, 1971, p. 120). The number of universities and counselor educators engaged in the training of counselors would also show tremendous gains during this period.

1960S: A TIME OF PROMISE AND UNREST

As counseling entered the 1960s, the future was promising. The rapid rise in the number of practicing counselors and those in training led many to believe that the profession was now entering an era when counseling could be available to all. Further, the infusion of self-concept theory and numerous variations by stage theorists who viewed life as a series of developmental milestones extended the audiences and aspirations of the counseling profession. This belief was clearly articulated in the early 1960s by the publication of the APGA-sponsored book, *The Counselor in a Changing World* (Wrenn, 1962). In this publication, Gilbert Wrenn expressed one of the central tenets of many prominent counseling figures by urging

> that primary emphasis in counseling students be placed on the developmental needs and decision points in the lives of the total range of students rather than upon the remedial needs and the crises points in the lives of a few students. (p. 109)

The renewed hope that a time in history had come when counseling would be available to large segments of the American population was bolstered in the early 1960s by a number of contributions from the behavioral sciences. In particular, writers in the areas of education, psychology, sociology, anthropology, and economics (Allinsmith & Goethals, 1962; Allport, 1960; Arendt, 1961; Bloom, 1964; Bruner, 1960; Coleman, 1962; Conant, 1961; Davis, 1960; Erikson, 1959; Gardner, 1961; Goodman, 1960; Harrington, 1962; Hunt, 1961; Kohlberg, 1963; Maslow, 1968; McClelland, 1961; Peck & Havighurst, 1960; White, 1960; Wylie, 1961) would enhance the work of counselors through serious questioning of existing practices in education and the behavioral sciences. In turn, their reformulations would strengthen the position of counseling by forcing attention on the total development of individuals and ways that this development could be furthered by systematic forms of human intervention.

The help extended to the counseling profession through the behavioral sciences was not fully used in the 1960s. The opportunity for a solid epistemological foundation in the social and behavioral sciences was only entertained on a limited scale (Blocher, 1966; Katz, 1969; Kehas, 1966; Mathewson, 1962; Super, 1964). What the profession needed at this time were unifying principles and common objectives to join together the wide array of individuals calling themselves counselors. It settled for much less.

The counseling profession in the 1960s faced a number of serious questions and challenges. One of these problems centered on clientele. Should the profession deal exclusively with the normal developmental concerns (and their ups and downs) of individuals, or should it tend to the psychological problems of a smaller and needier portion of the population? On the surface, this dilemma seemed clear and amenable to resolution. Events in the 1960s, however, would blur this simple dichotomy by suddenly expanding the potential counseling audiences to include minority groups, dissenters to the war in Vietnam, returning veterans, alienated hippie and youth movements, experimenters and advocates of the new drug culture, disenchanted students in high schools and colleges, victims of urban and rural poverty, and disenfranchised women.

A second problem confronting the profession at this time was related to counseling methodology. Commencing with Carl Rogers, the field of counseling would be open territory for numerous advocates of counseling, ranging from such diverse fields as psychiatry, clinical psychology, psychoanalysis, learning theory, and pastoral counseling. Collectively, the supporters of these approaches offered to counselors a bonanza of tools and techniques. As a totality, however, they added little to the professional identity or aims of counseling. If anything, they further segmented an already helter-skelter profession.

The cornucopia of competing counseling methodologies presented to counselors reached an all-time high in the late 1960s. Through university training programs, professional workshops, in-service training, or their own professional organizations counselors could choose from a virtual cafeteria of counseling methodologies including behavioral counseling (Krumboltz, 1966; Krumboltz & Thoresen, 1969; Michael & Meyerson, 1965); existential counseling (May, 1961; Van Kaam, 1968), reciprocal inhibition (Wolpe, 1958), reality therapy (Glasser, 1965), gestalt therapy (Perls, 1969), rational-emotive therapy (Ellis, 1967), Carkhuffian beginnings (Carkhuff, 1967), and various psychoanalytic adaptations (Hummel, 1962; King, 1965) (see Chapters 2 and 3). This inundation of methodologies became so profuse that those techniques intended to achieve broad counseling objectives competed with these very objectives as new ideologies in their own right. At the very least, competing and contending schools of counseling led to a confusion of means and ends and added to counselor identity diffusion as counselors lost a common perspective. At the same time, an overfascination with methodology increased counselor specialization and widened the gap between areas of possible commonality of purpose.

A third and related problem in the 1960s for the counseling profession was overall destination and direction. As a profession, counseling seemed adrift and was best characterized by Glanz's (1964) observation that the field increasingly resembled so much "flotsam and jetsam." In a similar vein, Tiedeman and Field (1965) questioned whether the recent overemphasis on methodology had not diverted the profession from a common sense of purpose. What did appear evident was that as counseling became a highly skilled technology with a primary emphasis on its method(s), "counseling" restricted its focus to areas amenable to this technology. This meant that as the counseling profession paid more and more attention to the enhancement of technological *means,* it paid less and less attention to inquiry about acknowledged *ends.* This narrowing of focus may explain why the counseling profession was so late in responding to the momentous social, political, and economic upheavals of the 1960s.

The 1960s were a time of unrest for scores of people. Counselors were caught off guard during this era, and the profession's response was tentative and diffident. In retrospect, this was understandable. The orientation of counselors at this time was toward intrapsychic issues, those concerns of a personal and individual nature. How then were counselors to respond to such social-cultural-political matters as Vietnam, civil rights, countercultures, drugs, women's rights, and so on? These matters were not amenable to the newly found dynamic counseling techniques. Instead, they begged for a perspective of earlier times when societal factors were identified as the essential causative factors in individual maladaptation. Unfortunately, the focus of counselors in the 1960s was on the person as a psychological being, not on the social environment as a countervailing force deserving equal attention.

DEVELOPMENTAL PSYCHOLOGY AND COUNSELING

To this point, the influence of three contemporary schools of psychology on the profession of counseling have been identified. These are behavioral, psychoanalytic, and humanistic psychology. A fourth school, developmental psychology, would also have an impact on counseling (see Chapter 2). It would particularly emerge in the 1960s as both an epistemological base for counseling intervention and as a philosophical position for unifying counseling methodologies.

One of the first authors to use a developmental framework in counseling and guidance was Robert Mathewson (1949). Even prior to the writings of Erikson (1950), Havighurst (1952), Piaget (1952), and others, Mathewson stressed the key concept of development as the essential principle in organizing and implementing programs of guidance. As early as 1949, Mathewson had written, "As an important phase of education, the guidance process moves with the individual in a developmental sequence up to the age of maturity, helping him gain self-understanding as well as perspective on his surroundings" (p. 29).

Over a period of years, Mathewson would refine and expand this notion of counseling as a process involved in monitoring and aiding human development. He would seriously question the posture that counselors can passively observe the process of development with no active intervention except when this development is arrested or interrupted by external circumstances.

Mathewson would also seek to influence American education through a developmental focus. In particular, he believed school counselors through systematic programs of guidance could further and enhance individual maturation. In his words,

> Of crucial importance in this stage of cultural development in American democracy is the question of whether we can any longer depend solely upon the individual's natural motivation for such essentials as civic responsibility, effectiveness in human relations, congruent matching of talents and tasks, and, in sum, the maximum development of a natural and common experiential sort. (1962, p. 40)

The dynamic concept of development adopted by Mathewson was a far cry from the early Darwinian notion of development as a sequential expansion and growth or the later Freudian notion of development as a series of stages dominated by a particular area or zone of the body. By Mathewson's time, the concept of development had been elaborated to include not only the specific tasks or problems at a given stage or level, but also the major epistemological correlates to successful mastery of developmental processes. Thus, the concept of development was transformed from the Freudian view of a series of potentially traumatic encounters to development as a process allowing for direct intervention and stimulation through recognition of desirable experiences at key positions leading to maturation.

Mathewson's work drew heavily on ego psychology and modern conceptualizations of numerous stage theorists (see Chapter 2). In positing individual development as the keystone in theory building and research, however, Mathewson was well aware of the lag between theory and practice, propagation and acceptance. A few voices at this time would extol the counseling and guidance professions to take heed of development as a key concept, but these utterances were few and largely ignored (Ausubel, 1959; Barry & Wolf, 1957; Little & Chapman, 1953; Peters & Farwell, 1959; Strang, 1955). What little enthusiasm the counseling profession generated for developmental psychology as a dynamic and guiding principle during this era of the late 1940s and 1950s was largely channeled to the expanding field of career development and not counseling (see Chapter 5).

The conditions for the receptivity of developmental counseling improved in the 1960s. At this time, the first book bearing the title *Developmental Counseling* (1966) was written by Donald Blocher. In addition to Blocher, other writers in the field of counseling began paying attention to life-span development as a basis for theory building and counseling intervention. Although these writers would differ in emphasis and prominence, all their models would have in common at least five common properties. All would begin with a clear acknowledgment that counseling has its roots and mainspring within the behavioral sciences.

The second common property of these developmental models was a desire to influence the ethics and values of individuals directly. This desire ran counter to many conceptualizations of counseling in the 1960s and especially to the prevailing model of counseling, Rogerian client-centered counseling.

The third common element in these models was a concern and commitment for all individuals. Developmental counseling would reject any and all notions of counseling for only the sick, disturbed, deprived, or distressed. Instead, all models of developmental counseling would embrace a holistic and wellness concept appropriate for all segments of the population.

A fourth commonality of developmental models would be a heavy debt to ego psychology and/or self-concept theory. All models of developmental counseling seemed to possess a connecting thread running from the work of such pioneers in self-theory as Mead (1934) and Allport (1937) to that of field theorists such as Lewin (1935) to self-concept theory in Combs and Snygg (1949), and to such theoreticians in the 1950s as Bordin (1955), Erikson (1959), Kelly (1955), and Maslow (1954).

The final common element in all developmental counseling models would be a deliberate effort to tie together the connecting threads from ego psychology and/or self-concept theory to a view of the person based on developmental unfolding. The particular school or stage theorist undergirding these models might range from Piaget (1952) to Erikson (1950) to Havighurst (1952) to Sullivan (1953) and others. Nonetheless, the underlying core would be a conscious linkup between a psychology of the person and a scheme of constant growth and unfolding.

INADEQUACY OF COUNSELING MODELS IN THE 1960S: TRANSITION TO THE 1970S

In the 1960s, the counseling profession was overwhelmed by many social and political upheavals. Counselors of that era had been educated in theories and models of a psychological nature, oriented to intrapsychic functioning. These models were incapable of dealing with the host of societal problems emerging from issues such as civil rights, Vietnam, the women's liberation movement, countercultures, drugs, and so on. The audiences generated by these issues required something more than methodologies designed for intrapsychic dysfunctioning and personal adjustment. Sadly, this was about all the counseling profession could offer.

For those educated as counselors in the 1950s and 1960s the dynamic theories of Carl Rogers and others were appealing. They gave counselors a singular technique with wide application that largely eschewed the laborious tasks of assessment and diagnosis. After all, most presenting problems were assumed to emanate from a single source, so why waste time with tests and the like? Also, much of dynamic and nondirective counseling was based on self-disclosure and self-responsibility. As a consequence, clients had to reveal and deal with the unresolved interpersonal concerns that brought them to the counselor's office. The counselor's role was to facilitate this process by providing the proper atmosphere and using reflection of feeling and similar techniques as the process evolved.

The inadequacies of counseling in the 1960s can be traced to their origin. Many of these counseling models were created and refined during and after World War II. They were tried out on soldiers and veterans suffering from fear, guilt, depression, and anxiety. A wider application was later made to other populations and with a great deal of success. Like penicillin, these models were highly effective within a delineated domain. But they were not a panacea with universal applicability.

The new and dynamic models failed in both perspective and application. The perspective was myopic, concentrating on intrapsychic functioning to the exclusion of environmental influences. In turn, applications focused on individual self-discovery and insight when, for many, this process failed to alleviate the presenting condition. What seemed to be needed was both a broadening of perspective and a wider array of intervention techniques.

The broadening of counseling perspective in the 1960s and early 1970s was accomplished largely through direct pressure by those seeking help. Many of these individuals sought help from those proclaiming to have skills in counseling and psychotherapy. Counselors, psychiatrists, social workers, psychologists, pastoral counselors—all were approached as potential helpers. Few of the potential helpers, however, were able to satisfy these individuals. Numerous help seekers, in fact, found more relief within their own groups (Alcoholics Anonymous, Synanon, Daytop, women's and other self-help groups) than they did from professional counselors.

Counselors' and others' lack of attention to causative factors within their clients' environments was understandable but disappointing. It was understandable in terms of history and the state of the profession.

After all, counseling and counseling psychology really began in earnest in the late 1940s. In the space of two decades one could hardly hope to have the sophisticated technology to deal with all human conditions. Consider though that as early as 1951, Kurt Lewin had made a strong case for $B = f(P,E)$, where behavior (B) is a function (f) of the interaction between the person (P) and his or her environment (E). This powerful explanatory principle was largely ignored by those who were developing models of counseling and therapy in the 1950s and 1960s.

In characterizing counseling models in operation in the 1960s, at least seven factors seem most descriptive:

1. Counseling was practiced largely in a one-to-one context.
2. Clients usually came to the office or setting of the counselor/therapist for help.
3. Clients were assumed to have an internalized problem that they were encouraged to share as part of the process of resolution.
4. Counseling techniques required some verbal facileness on the client's part (many techniques demanded some modicum of both verbal ability and education or intelligence).
5. The objective of counseling was largely personal adjustment or restoration to an earlier and "better" form of coping.
6. The environment and social context of the client were not considered alterable through the counselor's action.
7. The skills of the counselor/therapist were not viewed as something to "give away" or share with the client.

1970S: THE EXPANSION OF COUNSELING TECHNOLOGY AND CLIENTELE

Those coming to counselors twenty years ago were vocal and needy. They included minorities fed up with myriad forms of discrimination, women upset with sexual inequities, students bored and angry with indifferent teachers and administrators, drug-dependent individuals desperate and despondent, veterans with alternating moods of depression and bitterness, parents with young people swallowed up in communal living and countercultures, and those always living on the brink of disaster, the poor in our cities and countryside. How did the counseling profession react to this groundswell for their services? For one thing, counselors discovered group work (see Chapter 4).

In light of its usefulness and popularity today, it may seem strange that counselors did not discover group work until twenty years ago. This is even more surprising when considering that Freud (1955) himself wrote on this subject as early as 1921. Moreno (1946) would later do pioneer work on groups, and the late 1940s also saw the founding of the National Training Laboratory (NTL) in Bethel, Maine. Nonetheless, group work lay dormant for many years until fully used by counselors in the late 1960s.

The shift from individual counseling to work with groups began as people with similar problems and issues banded together. Initially these groups centered on alcohol or drugs, women's concerns, minority and veterans' grievances, parenting, and the like. Some were led by professionals and some by group members themselves. What seemed most important in this shift from individual to group work was a growing realization that one-to-one counseling was inefficient and ineffective for many audiences seeking the help of counselors.

The late 1960s and 1970s ushered in a host of counseling interventions that today are the stock and trade of professional counselors. Closely allied with group counseling were numerous self-help groups, many using live-in arrangements and sheltered workshops. This era would also see counselors attempting to give away to their clients skills hitherto the sole province of professionals. These activities would range from assertiveness training (Alberti & Emmons, 1974; Lazarus, 1971) to teacher/parent effectiveness (Gordon, 1970, 1975) to skill training (Carkhuff, 1972a, 1972b). Counselors at this time also expanded their use of individual counseling through telephone "hot lines," behavioral contracting, behavior modification, and biofeedback.

A final intervention emerging at this time was education. Like group counseling, educational interventions allowed counseling professionals to reach large numbers of people in dispensing information and in skill training. Some of these efforts were targeted to groups in need of career and vocational assistance. Other populations included those requiring attitudinal or behavioral support. The needs of this latter audience resulted in educational interventions such as deliberate psychological education (Mosher & Sprinthall, 1970), values clarification (Simon, Howe, & Kirschenbaum, 1972), moral education (Kohlberg, 1968; Kohlberg & Turiel, 1971), and variations of humanistic education (Alschuler, 1973; Bessell, 1969; Dinkmeyer, 1970).

The expansion of counseling technology that had begun some twenty years earlier broadened the perspective of counseling professionals and greatly increased the audiences that counselors serve. Initially, these new audiences thrust counselors out of familiar settings (schools, colleges, employment offices) and into strange territory (community mental health centers, hospitals, criminal justice systems, religious institutions, housing projects, drug and alcohol treatment centers, halfway houses, and the streets). Over time, counselors adapted quite well to these unaccustomed surroundings, and today they thrive on this diversity.

As counselors first moved into new areas, they were welcomed not only by their new clients but also by fellow professionals in areas such as clinical psychology, social work, and psychiatry. This may seem difficult to believe today when all these groups are engaged in professional protectionism approaching paranoia. Nonetheless, at that period in history, fewer mental health professionals were available, and the economy was healthier. These factors, along with the large numbers of new clients, minimized the friction that is so apparent today among contending mental health providers.

PROFESSIONALISM IN THE 1970S AND 1980S

Professionally, the 1970s saw a flurry of activity within counseling organizations. Earlier, both the American Psychological Association (1963) and the American Personnel and Guidance Association (1961) had developed and adopted ethical standards for practicing psychologists and counselors. The need for each organization to create separate ethical standards was brought about when APA refused to credential master's-level clinical psychologists or counselors. Nonetheless, both professions early on realized their dual obligations to both clients and society. As growing professions, each organization also recognized the necessity for strict standards of conduct for professional members practicing psychology and counseling.

Another set of standards was developed by the Association for Counselor Education and Supervision (ACES) and endorsed by the membership of ACES in 1973. These standards also furthered the profession of counseling by setting up criteria for university programs educating and training counselors. The first set of standards endorsed by ACES in 1973 dealt with entry-level (master's degree) preparation for counselors. Later, in 1977, ACES would also adopt standards for the preparation of advanced (doctoral-level) counseling degrees. In the early 1980s, the American Personnel and Guidance Association would adopt the standards created by ACES and apply them to all counseling programs preparing counselors. In 1981 APGA would also create the Council for Accreditation of Counseling and Related Education Programs (CACREP). The purpose of CACREP was to review any of the almost six hundred university programs (Hollis & Wantz, 1980) preparing counselors to see if they were adhering to the standards of APGA. As of 1985, nearly thirty university programs have been favorably reviewed, and a growing number are applying for review (see Chapter 9).

The Association for Counselor Education and Supervision was instrumental in dealing with issues related to professional credentialing. These efforts culminated in licensure and registry guidelines. In turn, just as with program accreditation, the American Personnel and Guidance Association (now the American Association for Counseling and Development) would pick up the work of ACES on licensure and registry and adopt their efforts for the total membership.

The credentialing of professional counselors was also aided in 1983 by APGA's creation of the National Board for Certified Counselors (NBCC). The purpose of NBCC was to evaluate counselor credentials and give examinations to determine professional counselor competencies. Successful counselors are then declared *national certified counselors,* and their names are placed in a registry published by AACD and NBCC.

Specialty groups within the American Association for Counseling and Development also deal with the credentialing of counselors. For example, in 1984, the National Vocational Guidance Association created a national council for the purpose of certifying career counselors. In addition, the American Mental Health Counselors Association in the late 1970s founded the National Academy of Certified Clinical Mental Health Counselors (NACCMHC) to certify counselors in community and agency work. Similarly, the American Rehabilitation Counseling Association has a Commission on Rehabilitation Counselor Certification.

State-level licensure is another movement that came into being in the 1970s. Efforts in this direction were largely forced on counselors as the professions of psychiatry, psychology, and social work attempted to "freeze out" counselors from private practice and third-party payments. As early as 1975 the state of Virginia enacted a counselor licensure law. Since that time, sixteen states have enacted separate licensure laws for practicing counselors. Another fourteen states are also in the process of seeking legislation toward this end. With a membership currently approaching 50,000 persons, AACD is in a position to further the professional credentialing of counselors in a host of directions.

COUNSELING COMES OF AGE: THE 1980S

Although the 1970s and 1980s produced a flurry of activity within professional counseling associations, other events were also shaping the profession. Early in the 1970s the Vietnam War came to a close, and the rash of assassinations begun in the 1960s continued to plague this country. The NDEA legislation eventually came to an end, and the beginnings of our present financial plight were felt. The scandal of

Watergate weakened an already wavering confidence by the public in political figures and social establishments. In the 1980s this pessimism spread to public education as it reached a low ebb. Concomitantly, America became mired in hard economic times with high unemployment and high interest rates. The pressures of women, minorities, and the disadvantaged did not abate, and counselors were kept busy with demands for their time and services.

The public that counselors face today is frequently one characterized by apathy, rootlessness, fear, and despair. This is understandable because many adults today have experienced tumultuous times over the past three decades. They have seen a steady challenge to family structure, an ever-increasing divorce rate, two futile wars, an increase in the possibility of nuclear annihilation, drug abuse on an unprecedented scale, a rapid rise in street crime, excessive political transgressions, erosions in our economic system coupled with high unemployment, the spectrum of high technology forcing people out of work or into lower-paying jobs, an increase in school dropouts for the first time in two decades, and new forms of media that bring instantaneous change to one's attention around the clock.

As social issues have caused stress and sent more and newer clienteles to counselors, intervention methods have also increased. Hot lines, group work, halfway homes, and the training of volunteers and paraprofessionals were unknown twenty-five years ago. Similarly, the concept of community counseling was introduced only in the late 1970s and required time in which to put its underlying principles into operation (Lewis & Lewis, 1977; Lewis, 1981).

Today, as counselors face the last part of the 1980s and the impending 1990s, the profession of counseling has come a long way. Both the clientele and intervention techniques and strategies available to counselors have shown tremendous growth, in decided contrast to two or three decades ago when only one methodology prevailed, namely, one-to-one, verbal counseling concentrating on intrapsychic functioning and aimed toward individual "adjustment." Because this method proved inadequate to meet new and pressing demands for service, additional models had to be developed. In a time that was stressful for counselors, professionals chose growth rather than stagnation. Counselors met their crisis and survived.

Yet, from the perspective of the 1980s, what seemed to be a major evolutionary leap appears to be as yet incomplete. Counselors have learned to feel comfortable dealing with groups as well as with individuals. They have also come to regard training as a natural ally of counseling. They have ventured into new settings and dealt with new audiences. Despite this increase in the number and focus of interventions, the basic perspective of counselors has not changed to the extent one might expect. Counselors still tend to overlook the impact of environmental factors on individual functioning, to distrust the efficacy of preventive interventions, and to narrow the scope of their attention to the individual psyche. If anything, a careful observer can begin to see the return of trends away from "giving skills away" and toward professional protectiveness, away from educational approaches and toward the traditional concept of therapy vis-à-vis the medical model. As difficult economic times threaten survival, counselors, like many other mental health professionals, seem to be falling back on the methods that seem safe and familiar.

Many today believe the profession of counseling is facing an identity crisis. This term was first coined and defined by Erik Erikson (1958).

> It occurs in that period of the life cycle when each youth must forge for himself some central perspective and direction, some working unity, out of the effective remnants of his childhood and the hopes of his anticipated adulthood; he must detect some meaningful resemblance between what he has come to see in himself and what his sharpened awareness tells him others judge and expect him to be. (p. 14)

Developmentally, a case can be made that the profession of counseling is experiencing an identity crisis (Hayes, 1984). Certainly the profession is currently manifesting the signs of someone in the midst of this exigency. In many equally important ways, however, it seems to be more a matter of what is better termed a developmental arrestment or lag.

A lag or arrestment in development implies that the timetable or sequence of development has temporarily plateaued or stabilized. This seems to describe the counseling profession, not only at the present time, but for the past two decades. Counseling reached its "adolescence" in the early 1960s and achieved a central perspective and direction. Identity achieved in adolescence, however, is only beneficial for that period of development. The counseling profession is now being deluged by forces calling for a more mature response than in an adolescent period. In fact, this is without doubt the central issue for the counseling profession today—that is, how do we best maintain hard-fought gains while developing further?

SUMMARY

Is counseling a profession today in America? Yes, it is if we judge counseling as we would any other profession. The counseling profession has a body of specialized knowledge that extends back nearly a hundred years with the publication in 1909 of Frank Parsons's *Choosing a Career.* Counseling has evolved to a point in time where it is recognized by the public as a unique competency and service. Further, the counseling profession has codes of professional ethics as well as professional standards. The counseling profession also has a number of active professional organizations. Among these associations, such as the American Association for Counseling and Development, there are procedures and vehicles linked to licensure, registry, credentialing, and university program accreditation. Finally, nearly six hundred colleges and universities are actively engaged in training and educating professional counselors. Indeed, counseling is a full-fledged profession with all the aspirations and problems of other professions. The remainder of this book will give you a fuller and more comprehensive picture of the profession of counseling.

REFERENCES

Alberti, R. E., & Emmons, M. L. (1974). *Your perfect right: A guide to assertive behavior.* San Luis Obispo, CA: Impact Press.

Allinsmith, W., & Goethals, G. (1962). *The role of the schools in mental health.* New York: Basic Books.

Allport, G. W. (1937). *Personality: A psychological interpretation.* New York: Holt.

Allport, G. W. (1960). *Personality and social encounter.* Boston: Beacon.

Alschuler, A. (1973). *Developing achievement motivation in adolescents: Education for human growth.* Englewood Cliffs, NJ: Educational Technology Publications.

American Personnel and Guidance Association. (1961). Ethical standards. *Personnel and Guidance Journal, 40,* 206–209.

American Psychological Association. (1963). Ethical standards of psychologists. *American Psychologist, 18,* 56–60.

Arendt, H. (1961). *Between past and future.* New York: Viking.

Ausubel, D. P. (1959). Developmental issues in child guidance: Plasticity, direction and conformity. *Journal of the National Association of Women Deans and Counselors, 22,* 103–10.

Barry, R., & Wolf, B. (1957). *Modern issues in guidance-personnel work.* New York: Teachers College Press.

Barry, R., & Wolf, B. (1962). *Epitaph for vocational guidance.* New York: Bureau of Publications, Teachers College, Columbia University.

Bessell, H. (1969). *Human development program: Activity guide, level B.* El Cajon, CA: Human Development Training Institute.

Blocher, D. (1966). *Developmental counseling.* New York: Ronald Press.

Bloom, B. (1964). *Stability and change in human characteristics.* New York: John Wiley.

Bloomfield, M. (1915). *Readings in vocational guidance.* Boston: Ginn.

Bordin, E. S. (1955). *Psychological counseling.* New York: Appleton-Century-Crofts.

Bordin, E. S., Nachmann, B., & Segal, S. J. (1963). An articulated framework for vocational development. *Journal of Counseling Psychology, 10,* 107–117.

Brewer, J. M. (1942). *History of vocational guidance.* New York: Harper.

Bruner, J. S. (1960). *The process of education.* Cambridge, MA: Harvard University Press.

Buhler, C. (1935). *From birth to maturity.* London: Kegan, Paul, Trench, Trubner & Co., Ltd.

Carkhuff, R. (1967). *The counselor's contribution to facilitative processes.* Urbana, IL: Parkinson.

Carkhuff, R. (1972a). *The art of helping.* Amherst, MA: Human Resource Development Press.

Carkhuff, R. (1972b). The development of systematic human resource development models. *Counseling Psychologist, 3,* 4–30.

Coleman, J. S. (1962). *The adolescent society.* New York: Free Press.

Combs, S., & Snygg, D. (1949). *Individual behavior.* New York: Harper.

Conant, J. B. (1959). *The American high school today.* New York: McGraw-Hill.

Conant, J. B. (1961). *Slums and suburbs.* New York: McGraw-Hill.

Corey, J. (1982). *Theory and practice of counseling and psychotherapy.* Monterey, CA: Brooks/Cole.

Cremin, L. (1961). *The transformation of the school.* New York: Alfred Knopf.

Davis, A. (1960). *Psychology of the child in the middle class.* Pittsburgh, PA: University of Pittsburgh Press.

Davis, J. (1914). *Vocational and moral guidance.* Boston: Ginn.

Dinkmeyer, D. (1970). *Developing understanding of self and others.* Circle Pines, MN: American Guidance Service.

Ellis, A. (1967). Rational-emotive psychotherapy. In D. S. Arbuckle (Ed.), *Counseling and psychotherapy* (pp. 173–192). New York: McGraw-Hill.

Erikson, E. (1950). *Childhood and society.* New York: W. W. Norton.

Erikson, E. (1958). *Young man Luther.* New York: W. W. Norton.

Erikson, E. (1959). Identity and the life cycle. *Psychological issues* (Monograph 1). New York: International Universities Press.

Frankl, V. (1963). *Man's search for meaning.* New York: Washington Square Press.

Frankl, V. (1965). *The doctor and the soul.* New York: Bantam.

Freud, S. (1955). *Group psychology and the analysis of the ego.* London: Hogarth Press.

Gardner, J. (1961). *Excellence.* New York: Harper.

Ginzberg, E. (1971). *Career guidance.* New York: McGraw-Hill.

Ginzberg, E., Ginsburg, S., Axelrod, S., & Herma, J. (1951). *Occupational choice: An approach to a general theory.* New York: Columbia University Press.

Glanz, E. (1964). *Foundations and principles of guidance.* Boston: Allyn & Bacon.

Glasser, W. (1965). *Reality therapy.* New York: Harper.

Goodman, P. (1960). *Growing up absurd.* New York: Random House.

Gordon, T. (1970). *Parent effectiveness training.* New York: Peter Wyden.

Gordon, T. (1975). *Teacher effectiveness training.* New York: Peter Wyden.

Harrington, M. (1962). *The other America.* Baltimore, MD: Penguin.

Havighurst, R. (1952). *Developmental tasks and education.* New York: Longmans Green.

Hayes, R. (1984). An alternative to rearranging our prejudice. In G. Walz and L. Benjamin (Eds.), *Shaping counselor education programs in the next five years: An experimental prototype for the counselor of tomorrow* (pp. 107–120). Ann Arbor, MI: ERIC/CAPS.

Holland, J. L. (1959). A theory of vocational choice. *Journal of Counseling Psychology, 6,* 35–45.

Hollingshead, A. B. (1949). *Elmtown's youth.* New York: John Wiley.

Hollis, J., & Wantz, R. (1980). *Counselor preparation 1980: Programs, personnel, trends.* Muncie, IN: Accelerated Development.

Hummel, R. (1962). Ego counseling in guidance: Concept and method. *Harvard Educational Review, 32,* 463–482.

Hunt, J. (1961). *Intelligence and experience.* New York: Roland Press.

Inhelder, B., & Piaget, J. (1958). *The growth of logical thinking from childhood to adolescence.* New York: Basic Books.

Katz, M. (1969). Theoretical foundations of guidance. *Review of Educational Research, 39,* 127–140.

Kegan, R. (1982). *The evolving self.* Cambridge, MA: Harvard University Press.

Kehas, C. (1966). Theoretical formulations and related research. *Review of Educational Research, 36,* 207–218.

Kelly, G. A. (1955). *The psychology of personal constructs.* New York: W. W. Norton.

King, P. T. (1965). Psychoanalytic adaptations. In B. Stefflre (Ed.), *Theories of counseling* (pp. 91–139). New York: McGraw-Hill.

Kitson, H. D. (1915). Suggestions toward a tenable theory of vocational guidance. In M. Bloomfield (Ed.), *Readings in vocational guidance* (pp. 103–108). Boston: Ginn.

Kohlberg, L. (1958). *The development of modes of thinking and choices in years ten to sixteen.* Doctoral dissertation, University of Chicago.

Kohlberg, L. (1963). Moral development and identification. In *62nd*

Yearbook of the National Society for the Study of Education (pp. 277–332). Chicago: University of Chicago Press.

Kohlberg, L. (1968). Early education: A cognitive-developmental view. *Child Development, 39,* 1013–1062.

Kohlberg, L., & Turiel, E. (1971). Moral development and moral education. In G. Lesser (Ed.), *Psychology and educational practice* (pp. 410–465). Chicago: Scott, Foresman.

Krumboltz, J. (Ed.). (1966). *Revolution in counseling.* Boston: Houghton Mifflin.

Krumboltz, J., & Thoresen, C. E. (1969). *Behavioral counseling: Cases and techniques.* New York: Holt, Rinehart & Winston.

Lasch, C. (1965). *The new radicalism in America.* New York: Vintage Books.

Lazarus, A. A. (1971). *Behavior therapy and beyond.* New York: McGraw-Hill.

Lewin, K. (1935). *Dynamic theory of personality.* New York: McGraw-Hill.

Lewin, K. (1951). *Field theory in social science.* New York: Harper & Row.

Lewis, J. A. (1981). Transition: From school to community mental health counseling. *Counseling and Human Development, 14,* 1–8.

Lewis, J. A., & Lewis, M. D. (1977). *Community counseling: A human services approach.* New York: John Wiley.

Little, W., & Chapman, A. (1953). *Developmental guidance in secondary schools.* New York: McGraw-Hill.

Lynd, R. J., & Lynd, H. M. (1954). *Middletown.* New York: Harcourt & Brace.

Maslow, A. (1954). *Motivation and personality.* New York: Harper.

Maslow, A. (1968). *Toward a psychology of being.* New York: Van Nostrand.

Maslow, A. (1970). *Motivation and personality* (rev. ed.). New York: Harper & Row.

Mathewson, R. (1949). *Guidance policy and practice.* New York: Harper & Row.

Mathewson, R. (1962). *Guidance policy and practice* (rev. ed.). New York: Harper & Row.

May, R. (1953). *Man's search for himself.* New York: Dell.

May, R. (Ed.). (1961). *Existential psychology.* New York: Random House.

McClelland, D. (1961). *The achieving society.* Princeton, NJ: D. Van Nostrand.

Mead, G. H. (1934). *Mind, self and society.* Chicago: University of Chicago Press.

Michael, J., & Meyerson, L. (1965). A behavioral approach to counseling and guidance. In R. L. Mosher, R. F. Carle, & C. D. Kehas (Eds.), *Guidance: An examination* (pp. 24–48). New York: Harcourt, Brace & World.

Miller, C. H. (1961). *Foundations of guidance.* New York: Harper.

Miller, C. H. (1964). Vocational guidance in the perspective of cultural change. In H. Borow (Ed.), *Man in a world of work* (Chapter 1). Boston: Houghton Mifflin.

Moreno, J. L. (1946). Psychodrama and group psychotherapy. *Sociometry, 9,* 249–253.

Mosher, R. L., & Sprinthall, N. A. (1970). Psychological education in secondary schools: A program to promote individual and human development. *American Psychologist, 25,* 911–924.

Mumford, L. (1961). *The city in history.* New York: Harcourt, Brace & World.

Munsterberg, H. (1913). *Psychology and industrial efficiency.* Boston: Houghton Mifflin.

Parsons, F. (1909). *Choosing a vocation.* Boston: Houghton Mifflin.

Peck, R. F., & Havighurst, R. J. (1960). *The psychology of character development.* New York: John Wiley.

Perls, F. (1969). *Gestalt therapy.* Lafayette, CA: Real People Press.

Peters, H., & Farwell, G. (1967). *Guidance: A developmental approach.* Chicago: Rand McNally.

Piaget, J. (1952). *The origins of intelligence in children.* New York: International Universities Press.

Proctor, W. M. (1925). *Educational and vocational guidance.* Boston: Houghton Mifflin.

Proctor, W. M., Benefield, W., & Wrenn, C. G. (1931). *Workbook in vocations.* Boston: Houghton Mifflin.

Riesman, D. (1950). *The lonely crowd.* New Haven, CT: Yale University Press.

Roe, A. (1956). *The psychology of occupations.* New York: John Wiley.

Rogers, C. R. (1942). *Counseling and psychotherapy.* Boston: Houghton Mifflin.

Rogers, C. R. (1951). *Client-centered therapy.* Boston: Houghton Mifflin.

Rogers, C. R. (1961). *On becoming a person.* Boston: Houghton Mifflin.

Rogers, C. R., & Dymond, R. F. (Eds.). (1954). *Psychotherapy and personality change.* Chicago: University of Chicago Press.

Sarason, S. (1981). An asocial psychology and a misdirected clinical psychology. *American Psychologist, 36,* 827–836.

Shaffer, B. P. (1978). *Humanistic psychology.* Englewood Cliffs, NJ: Prentice-Hall.

Shertzer, B., & Stone, S. C. (1971). *Fundamentals of guidance.* Boston: Houghton Mifflin.

Simon, S. B., Howe, L. W., & Kirschenbaum, H. (1972). *Values clarification: A handbook of practical strategies for teachers and students.* New York: Hart.

Strang, R. (1955). Guidance: Its larger responsibilities. *Teachers College Record, 56,* 367–373.

Sullivan, H. S. (1953). *The interpersonal theory of psychiatry.* New York: W. W. Norton.

Super, D. E. (1942). *The dynamics of vocational development.* New York: Harper.

Super, D. E. (1953). A theory of vocational development. *American Psychologist, 8,* 185–190.

Super, D. E. (1955). Transition: From vocational guidance to counseling psychology. *Journal of Counseling Psychology, 2,* 3–9.

Super, D. E. (1956). Vocational development: The process of compromise or synthesis. *Journal of Counseling Psychology, 3,* 249–253.

Super, D. E. (1957). *The psychology of careers.* New York: Harper & Row.

Super, D. E. (1964). Guidance in American education: Its status and its future. In E. Landy and P. A. Perry (Eds.), *Guidance in American education* (pp. 151–161). Cambridge, MA: Harvard University Press.

Tiedeman, D. V., & Field, F. L. (1965). Guidance: The science of purposeful action applied through education. In R. L. Mosher, R. F. Carle, & C. D. Kehas (Eds.), *Guidance: An examination* (pp. 192–213). New York: Harcourt, Brace & World.

Van Kaam, A. (1967). Counseling and psychotherapy from the viewpoint of existential psychology. In D. Arbuckle (Ed.), *Counseling and psychotherapy: An overview* (pp. 207–241). New York: McGraw-Hill.

Van Kaam, A. (1968). *The art of existential counseling.* Wilkes-Barre, PA: Dimension Books.

Warner, W. L., Meeker, M., & Ells, K. (1949). *Social class in America.* Chicago: Science Research Associates.

White, R. W. (1953). *Lives in progress.* New York: Dryden Press.

White, R. W. (1960). Competence and the psychosexual stages of development. In M. Jones (Ed.), *Nebraska Symposium on Motivation* (pp. 97–141). Lincoln, NE: University of Nebraska Press.

Williamson, E. G. (1965). *Vocational counseling.* New York: McGraw-Hill.

Williamson, E. G., & Foley, J. D. (1949). *Counseling and discipline.* New York: John Wiley.

Wolpe, J. (1958). *Psychotherapy by reciprocal inhibition.* Stanford, CA: Stanford University Press.

Wrenn, C. G. (1962). *The counselor in a changing world.* Washington, DC: American Personnel and Guidance Association.

Wylie, R. C. (1961). *The self concept.* Lincoln, NE: University of Nebraska Press.

CHAPTER 2
HUMAN GROWTH AND DEVELOPMENT

Richard L. Hayes

Clients often come to counselors to change their lives in some way, such as to become more assertive. As likely, clients seek counseling as a result of some change, perhaps a death or different working conditions. Clients often find themselves in the midst of some change they don't understand or over which they have little control. In its most general form, counseling provides a context for such change. How to explain any change, how to assess its direction or to predict its effects, and how to understand the meaning any change may have for the client are questions the effective counselor must ask.

The counselor relies on the concepts of human development to assess the client's level of functioning and uses different developmental theories as lenses through which to view the client. The professional counselor appreciates that people are different but uses knowledge of developmental theory to understand these differences within the context of a universal human process.

Because so much of their work involves making decisions related to human development, counselors need to understand the assumptions upon which such decisions are made. In this chapter, the issues common to all developmental theories will be discussed, the major positions will be outlined, and representative theorists will be presented to illustrate how developmental theories are applied to counseling.

DICHOTOMIES OF DEVELOPMENT

Developmental psychology is the study of the mental changes that take place over the human life cycle. The basic goals of this study are to *describe* systematically the ways in which people develop, to *explain* how and why they develop as they do, and to *predict* the ways in which they will develop (Fischer & Lazerson, 1984, p. 48). Although change and development both refer to transformations that take place over time and in some space, there has been some controversy about how to define development and how to differentiate it from mere change (Reese & Overton, 1970). At the heart of the controversy are several dichotomies that all developmental theories have attempted to resolve.

Active or Passive

All developmental theories take a position on whether humans are active or passive participants in their own development. Counselors make this distinction when they talk of "making" a client do something or when they leave clients free to decide for themselves. The active view depicts people as engaged in self-initiated activities that result from inborn capacities to be active. The passive view depicts people as inherently malleable objects that respond automatically to the demands of the environment.

Nature or Nurture

A second question revolves around whether development is a natural outcome of inborn tendencies or the result of some nurturing by elements in the environment. When people lament, "That's just the way Juan is," for example, they are speaking on the nature side of this dichotomy. When they argue, "If Chuck had had a better home life, things would have been different," they are speaking on the nurture side. This dichotomy always makes a distinction between the person or the environment as the source of development.

All contemporary theories acknowledge the contributions of both heredity and environment, but they disagree on the relative emphasis to be placed on each and upon the relationship that exists between the two. Anastasi (1958) pointed out that the issue is not so much *which* (heredity or environment) causes behavior or *how much* of each is needed for a given behavior, but rather *how* nature and nurture interact to produce development. For counselors, this means understanding that different conditions affect different people in different ways.

Continuity or Discontinuity

One side of this issue is expressed by the belief that development reflects a sequence of continuous changes and that developmental changes can only be separated arbitrarily. Those who hold this view contend that adulthood is best characterized as an ongoing response to changing life circumstances. On the other side, the notion of discontinuity in development implies that certain abilities or behaviors may be grouped together during a period of time. This notion of discontinuous functioning from one period to another is expressed in the idea that adults pass through a series of developmental crises on their way to old age.

Qualitative or Quantitative

Generally, qualitative change refers to a change in structure or organization, while quantitative change refers to a change in number, frequency, or degree. A related issue raises a distinction between *structure* and *content,* where the former refers to organizational aspects and the latter refers to that which is organized. This quantity-quality distinction in learning often prompts educators to ask whether *more* is necessarily *better.*

Growth or Development

Growth refers to changes that are quantitative, whatever the state of the system, and to functional continuity in a system of action (Langer, 1969). As a result of some training experience, for example, clients may speak of "relating to others" with a more "open and honest awareness of their feelings." Changes in vocabulary, however, may be nothing more than an increase in word usage without an accompanying change in self-understanding and therefore, would not be considered to be development. On the other hand, functional discontinuity of a system of action is qualitative and results from either the "coming-to-be" of a new system or the "passing-away" of an existing system (Langer, 1969, p. 3).

Another form of change consists of qualitative alterations in the existing system, such as the transformation of the child's language system from babbling to naming objects. Rarely, of course, do growth and development appear in isolation from one another. Changes in the neuromuscular system and experience in comparing their own vocalizations with the spoken words of others contribute to children's abilities to talk.

Phases or Stages

The continuity-discontinuity and quality-quantity issues rest on the question of whether or not there are stages of development. The appearance of similar behaviors, abilities, traits, and the like during the same period of time often lead a theorist to infer that the individual is in a particular stage. The idea of stages is the basis for dividing the life cycle into infancy, childhood, adolescence, adulthood, and old age.

This notion of stage implies that there is a qualitative change in the structure of some system, so that the system itself is preserved while its structure is changed. In effect, the individual is presumed to be organized into different levels of development. Phases, however, generally refer to periods of the life cycle, where the distinction between one phase and another is arbitrary.

In reviewing these dichotomies, a consistent pattern of relationships begins to emerge. For example, theorists who accept the active organism model logically accept that the individual is organized into levels, which leads to the concept of stage. What kind or type of stage is further qualified by still other dimensions of the particular theory. Although the combinations may seem endless, two positions that consistently relate these dichotomies have persisted throughout the history of science.

TWO OPPOSING VIEWS

For some theorists, development refers to nothing more than a quantitative description of changes in individual or group behavior. Theorists who adopt this position are usually referred to as *empiricists,* after the Greek word *empeiria,* meaning experience. In the alternative position, the *organismic,* development is conceptualized as a qualitative property of the organism itself, where the changes are directed toward some goal or end state. To be called development from this perspective, any change must represent a change in the organism itself and not reflect merely a change in behavior. In effect, the empiricist views development as a descriptive phenomenon, while the organicist views it as more theoretical.

Given that these two positions are irreconcilable in the extreme (see Reese & Overton, 1970), whatever view counselors adopt will have important implications for the way counselors intervene to help their clients. For instance, a thirteen-year-old may say that one should keep a promise "Because if you don't, it causes a loss of faith in the promiser and often a disappointment of expectations," while an eight-year-old may argue that promises should be kept "Because you don't get what was promised, and I will be disappointed." Can we say properly that one child has developed more than the other? And if so, in what way? And how might you prove or assess the levels of the children's development in this area? And as a counselor, how might you stimulate such development if you wanted to?

This empiricist-organicist distinction is rarely as clear-cut as it may appear here. In fact, developmental theorists generally agree about the basic issues in human development and to an extent about the important issues to be investigated. Their disagreement arises from fundamental differences in the assumptions each makes about the nature of development itself.

THREE APPROACHES TO HUMAN DEVELOPMENT

Three fundamental world views dominate contemporary approaches to the study of human development (Allport, 1962; Gardner, 1978; Gibbs, 1979; Hempel, 1966; Kohlberg & Mayer, 1973; Langer, 1969; Maslow, 1970; Reese & Overton, 1970; Snarey, Kohlberg, & Noam, 1983). These approaches differ primarily in the emphasis they place on this or that pole of the dichotomies presented above. T. S. Kuhn (1962) has called this entire constellation of beliefs, values, and techniques, which form the shared assumptions of a given community of scholars, a *paradigm*.

The first of these three paradigms, the *behavioral,* derives from the empiricist view of development, while the remaining two, the *maturational* and the *structural,* rely on organismic approaches. Each of these paradigms is distinguished by a particular emphasis upon the role of environmental or organismic factors on development, the nature-nurture controversy referred to above.

As might be expected, the behavioral paradigm focuses on behavior and explains development in terms of learning, which is believed to be controlled by environmental conditions. Intrapersonal characteristics are recognized but minimized in accounting for individual differences in behavior. Because development is viewed as continuous and as having no particular preferred direction, age is an irrelevant concept. Stages are viewed as arbitrary conveniences of the theorist, used to organize the data.

The maturational paradigm attributes the change process to growth and differentiation. Environmental effects are recognized, but only as placing limits on individual development, not as directing its course. Maturational explanations depend upon age per se, while development is described typically as a continuous sequence of discontinuous stages.

In the third paradigm, individuals are believed to produce their own development through active interaction with the environment. Development is the product of an interaction between maturational, social, and physical factors that are more or less in equilibrium with one another. Because most contemporary theorists view development as interactional, the more restrictive term structural is used to call attention to the importance attached to the unity and self-constructive nature of the individual implied in this third perspective.

ULTIMATE SOURCES OF KNOWLEDGE

Understanding how people obtain knowledge helps the counselor to appreciate the client's reality and to make better predictions about the course and direction for counseling. Each of the three developmental paradigms makes distinctively different assumptions about the basic mental structure. The behaviorist believes that knowledge is the result of an association between external events; the maturationist believes that knowledge is the consequence of innate patterning; and the structuralist conceives of it as resulting from interactions between certain structuring tendencies of the organism and its environment. How each paradigm explains the origin of knowledge has important implications for understanding the relationship between development and counseling.

Behaviorism

From the behavioral view, the newborn comes into the world with little, if any, specific knowledge. People are basically passive, having minds that operate like machines, into which the environment puts energy or information and from which the organism emits predictable behaviors in response.

Central to this thesis is the view that a person "grows to be what he [or she] is made to be by his [or her] environment" (Langer, 1969, p. 4). The human mind is like a *tabula rasa,* a blank page upon which experience writes or, in a more contemporary view, a computer into which data are fed and stored, and from which they are retrieved. Whatever the analogy, the mind receives environmental input and emits behavioral output. Because of its reliance upon direct observation of experience, the behavioral position is identified with empiricism and has been the dominant tradition in psychological research, especially related to counseling (Hayes & Kenney, 1983).

For the behaviorist, reality is a priori, existing outside the individual, who in the course of development internalizes some copy of reality through elementary impressions that are made on the mind. Associations are then made to this copy, and so on as the individual builds up images of various elements through lengthy exposure to the real world. Which associations take place is determined by external conditions that reinforce the repetition of specific behaviors. Development is defined as the "continuous quantitative accumulation of behavior" (Langer, 1969, p. 55). To promote development and to predict the individual's behavior, therefore, one need only know the history of past responses and determine relevant present environmental conditions.

The ultimate goal for the behaviorist is to predict and to control human behavior. Behaviorally oriented counselors attempt to discover the environmental determinants of behavior so that they can *extinguish* inappropriate or maladaptive behaviors and *reinforce* new and socially more acceptable ones. The emphasis in behavioral counseling is on training, or skill development, where success is measured by the client's ability to exhibit desired behaviors. Behaviorally oriented counselors emphasize empirical validation by making baseline observations of behavior, establishing observable goals, and evaluating progress toward these goals. Because all behavior is presumed to result from learning, the general therapeutic goal is to create new conditions for learning.

Maturationism

For the maturationist, the development of the mind is much like the physical growth of a plant or an animal. Children are born with what they need to know already prewired into the brain as specific information or as rules or structures for attaining knowledge. Development is an inherent part of being, while the environment provides the nutrients necessary for the individual's natural growth. The underlying assumption of this perspective is that the individual "is a conflicted being who is driven to action and growth by his [or her] own passions or instincts and by external demands" (Langer, 1969, p. 10).

Development is characterized by the unfolding of prepatterned stages that are genetically limited, if not determined. Differential rates of development are inborn, while the environment serves to frustrate, enhance, or fixate developmental progress. The nature of one's experience is determined by the conflict between the demands of the instincts and the limitations of the environment in which one finds oneself. In promoting development, therefore, the maturationist aims at the freest and fullest expression of the instincts and at increased self-control over those instincts that are negative and self-destructive.

Maturationally oriented counselors help clients to relive earlier experiences and to work through any conflicts. Their goal is to allow the client the fullest expression of innate abilities and drives. In effect, freedom is presumed to lead to growth. This freedom is realized by removing blocks to continued development and by providing a therapeutic environment that encourages self-discovery and promotes self-awareness. The outcome of counseling is freedom of choice and responsibility for the direction of one's life.

Structuralism

This system-oriented paradigm offers a dialectical synthesis of the organism-environment dichotomy. Structuralists believe that people are active and that the basic mental structures are reorganized and redefined through exercise and confrontation by opposing ideas. The structuralists' guiding metaphor is that the individual "develops to be what he [or she] makes himself [or herself] to be by his [or her] own actions" (Langer, 1969, p. 7). This metaphor is neither wholly behavioral nor wholly maturational, but rejects the dichotomy in favor of an interactional perspective.

Inherent in human nature are certain structuring tendencies, which attempt to make sense of people's experiences within themselves and of the world in which they live. The process of knowing emerges in the light of interaction between the organism and the environment. A key element of this position is that knowledge is actually constructed by the individual independent of the environment. Thus person and world are not separate, nor even in interaction, but rather are inextricably linked in *trans*actions with one another. Reality is constructed from experience and represents a relationship between the self and the world. Underlying this transactive notion of the origin of basic mental structures is the concept of *cognition*.

Cognitions represent internally organized systems of relations, which comprise a set of rules for processing information or connecting events in the person's experience. Cognitive thinking, then, is actively relating events. At the heart of the argument lies the assumption that knowledge is the *sine qua non* for psychological change, a position stated succinctly by I. A. Richards as "knowledge is growledge" (Langer, 1969, p. 111).

The idea of transactions going on between people and their environments leads to the notion of cognitive *stages*. Each stage is a more differentiated, comprehensive, and integrated structure than the one before it. Each succeeding stage represents the capacity to make sense of a greater variety of experiences in a more adequate way. As expressed in Werner's statement of the orthogenetic law of development: "The development of biological forms is expressed in an *increasing differentiation* of parts and an *increasing subordination,* or *hierarchization.* Such a process of hierarchization means for any organic structure the organization of the differentiated parts for a closed totality, an ordering and grouping of parts in terms of the whole organism" (Werner, 1940/1973, p. 41).

The fundamental reason for movement from one stage to the next, therefore, is that a later stage is more adequate in some universal sense than an earlier stage. The basic notion of this stage concept leads to the conceptualization of development as a movement toward greater adaptation, differentiation, and integration of distinct modes of thought in a universal, invariant, and hierarchical developmental sequence (Kohlberg, 1969).

Structurally oriented counselors try to understand how the client makes sense of personal experience, that is, the client's meaning-making system. Universal stages of psychological development provide a blueprint and a theoretical rationale for intervention in the lives of clients for whom the "*natural* facilitation of development has somehow and for some reason broken down" (Kegan, 1982, p. 256). Structurally oriented counselors focus on the interaction between clients and their environments. The counselor attempts to provide an environment that will facilitate the client's development by acknowledging the client's reality and supporting the client's efforts to restore some balance to the world *as the client knows it.*

OVERVIEW

Developmental theories help the counselor to describe and explain individual differences by providing methods for collecting and organizing the data of human development. Each theory must deal with four recurring dichotomies: Is it human nature to be active or passive? Does heredity or environment contribute more to development? Is development continuous or discontinuous? Is development qualitative or quantitative? Answers to these questions characteristically take one of two positions, either the empirical or the organismic. Three theoretical approaches, which are derived from these two positions, dominate contemporary study: behaviorism, maturationism, and structuralism. The major theories representing each of these approaches will be explored in the remainder of this chapter (see also Chapter 3).

THE BEHAVIORISTS

Clients who come to counseling usually find themselves in some problematic situation. To the behaviorally oriented counselor, this situation means that the client is likely to engage in one or more *problematic behaviors.* Problematic behavior, according to Egan (1982):

> (1) prevents an individual from attaining some goal (for instance, having a close relationship with a person of the other sex), (2) causes the individual significant personal pain or discomfort (for instance, Tess is making it through school but she is always extremely harried and anxious), and/or (3) results in undesirable consequences for others (for instance, Jamie's failure to control his temper causes suffering for his wife and children). (pp. 78–79)

The role that problematic behavior plays in understanding human development can be understood best through the A-B-C model. The problematic situation, sometimes referred to as the *presenting problem,* consists minimally of the antecedents (A) and the consequences (C) of some problematic behavior (B) represented sequentially as shown in Figure 2-1.

Antecedents ----→Behavior ----→Consequences.

FIGURE 2-1

For instance, imagine that Jon becomes interested in a television show and stays up beyond his usual time to go to bed (A). The next morning he oversleeps (B) and misses the school bus, so that he is late for his first period class (C).

Antecedents refer to all significant factors that precede the behavior. Consequences refer to events that follow and are associated with the behavior such that they either increase *(reinforce)* or decrease *(punish)* the likelihood of it occurring again. Antecedents contribute to the control of behavior by signaling that a given behavior is likely to occur. Ali, for example, knows that when she is worried (A), she is likely to have minor accidents (B), and so she takes precautions to avoid handling fragile items at such times. Consequences help to control behavior by satisfying desired outcomes. For instance, Jessica enjoys playing the piano (B) because it brings her recognition from her teachers and her peers (C). Gillian, on the other hand, hates to go to work (B) because she believes that she is not being paid what she is worth (C).

Behavioral approaches to counseling help the counselor to identify the antecedents and consequences that control a client's problematic behavior and to collaborate with the client in identifying and learning new behaviors. Although the specific techniques used in behaviorally oriented counseling vary from one therapeutic approach to another, all these approaches share the assumptions basic to two systems that dominate contemporary learning theory: *classical* and *operant conditioning.*

Classical Conditioning

Counselors who use the classical conditioning model of learning attempt to explain behavior by discovering its antecedents. In so doing, they are concerned with the relationship between A and B in the A-B-C model. Because classical conditioning is attributed to the pioneering work of the Russian physiologist, Ivan Pavlov (1849–1936), it is often referred to as Pavlovian conditioning.

While studying the digestive process in dogs, Pavlov (1927) discovered that after a time his dogs would salivate at the mere sight or smell of the meat powder he fed them. Furthermore, he discovered that ringing a bell repeatedly, for instance just prior to presenting the meat powder, eventually resulted in the dog salivating at the sound of the bell alone. This *new* behavior, salivating in response to the bell, was said by Pavlov to be "conditional" upon the presentation of the meat powder, hence the term *conditioning.* In translation, the term became "conditioned," which is most commonly used as a synonym for "learned."

Pavlov proposed that the responses of the mind and the body could be explained by a common element, the *reflex.* He believed this automatic behavior resulted from some *stimulus,* which represented some physical change. Because of the focus on behavioral responses, classical conditioning is also referred to as *respondent* or *reflexive conditioning.*

Basically, classical conditioning involves the pairing of two stimuli in such a way that the presentation of one evokes behaviors previously evoked only by the other. In more formal terms, an *unconditioned stimulus* (UCS), which evokes an *unconditioned response* (UR), is repeatedly paired, or *reinforced,* with a previously *neutral* stimulus until it *elicits* a response similar to the UCR. The resulting behavior is said to have been conditioned and is called the *conditioned response* (CR). The neutral stimulus, which is neutral only in the sense that it does not ordinarily elicit the UR, is now referred to as the *conditioned stimulus* (CS) (see Figure 2-2).

Pavlov also noticed that once the relationship between the CS and CR had been established, the relationship would weaken if the CS were not paired occasionally with the US. This gradual disappearance of the CR following the presentation of the CS is called *extinction.* The dis-

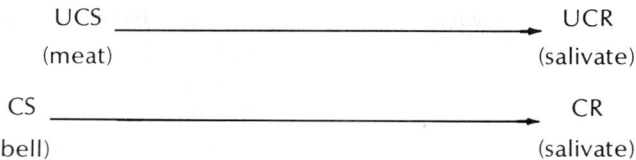

UCS = Unconditioned Stimulus UCR = Unconditioned Response
CS = Conditioned Stimulus CR = Conditioned Response
Note: The UCS is paired with the CS such that it is presented immediately BEFORE the UCS.

FIGURE 2-2 Design for classical conditioning

appearance of the CS does not happen all at once but disappears slowly over an often lengthy period.

In fact, Pavlov found that, following an intervening rest period, a weak CR would reoccur following the presentation of the CS. This *spontaneous recovery* of a previously extinguished response led Pavlov to conclude that previous learning was not forgotten but only *inhibited.* Thus, during the rest period there was an increase in *disinhibition.* This notion of inhibition-disinhibition is at the heart of counseling applications for classical conditioning.

Frequently, once a particular response has been conditioned, stimuli that are similar to the CS will elicit the CR without the CS present. This process of *stimulus generalization,* as it is called, is at work when a client behaves toward the counselor on the basis of similarities to other persons in the client's life. The ability to tell one stimulus from another, on the other hand, is called *stimulus discrimination* and is essentially the opposite of stimulus generalization. Stimulus discrimination is established through a combination of selective reinforcement and extinction.

In applying classical conditioning theory to counseling, remember that classically conditioned responses are innate, reflex behaviors that are mediated by the *autonomic nervous system.* Because reflexes are not under voluntary control, classically conditioned responses can be established in infants or even clients who are drugged or unconscious. Rather than involving the learning of new responses, classical conditioning involves the conditioning of new stimuli to existing responses.

James B. Watson (1878–1958). Generally regarded as the founder of American behaviorism, Watson (1919) coined the term "behaviorism" in 1912. In a series of well-known and highly controversial experiments, Watson and an assistant (Watson & Rayner, 1920) successfully conditioned a young boy named Albert B. to fear not only a white rat, but also a rabbit, fur coats, a Santa Claus mask, and even cotton.

Consistent with classical conditioning theory, Watson reasoned that Albert's uncontrollable fear, like all phobias, was a learned behavior. Consequently, Watson outlined a comprehensive plan to reverse Albert's phobia that anticipated the field of behavior therapy today. Unfortunately, Albert was released from the hospital where Watson was working before Watson could put his program into action. As a result of these and similar studies, Watson (1927) issued his most famous dictum to "Give me the baby," and he could shape it through conditioning into whatever was desired, concluding that "Men are built, not born."

Joseph Wolpe (1915–). A pioneer in the field of behavior therapy, Wolpe (1958) is best known for his work in applying Pavlovian conditioning principles to psychotherapy. Reasoning that "neuroses are persistent unadaptive habits that have been conditioned, . . . the fundamental overcoming of a neurosis *can* consist of nothing but deconditioning—or undoing the relevant habit patterns . . . the most characteristic and common feature of [which] is anxiety" (Wolpe, 1966, p. 9). Wolpe believes that almost all maladaptive behaviors are learned responses that result in the client reacting persistently with anxiety to situations that, objectively, are not dangerous.

To eliminate anxiety, Wolpe believes that the client must unlearn the undesirable learned behavior. He proposed the principle of *reciprocal inhibition,* which states that "if a response inhibitory of anxiety can be made to occur in the presence of anxiety-evoking stimuli it will weaken the bond between these stimuli and the anxiety" (Wolpe, 1966, p. 10). In practice, this technique substitutes one of three responses for the anxiety response: assertiveness, deep muscle relaxation, or sexual arousal.

Assertiveness training is often indicated when the client's anxiety arises from an inability to express feelings or opinions in interpersonal relationships. Using procedures first developed by Salter (1949), the counselor helps the client to develop more assertive responses, which enhance the client's self-esteem by reciprocally inhibiting the anxiety response. Such techniques include modeling, role-playing, or behavioral rehearsal in which clients act out the desired behavior in simulations of the anxiety-evoking situation.

Relaxation responses are the most commonly used reciprocal inhibition techniques known to have effects opposite to those of anxiety. In an adaptation of procedures first developed by Jacobson (1939), Wolpe's *systematic desensitization* technique involves the systematic tensing and relaxing of the major muscle groups of the body. After teaching the client deep muscle relaxation, which is paired with some cue such as "relax" or a deep breath, the client is instructed to imagine the weakest form of the anxiety-evoking stimulus for a few seconds. As the response reduces to zero upon repeated presentations of the stimulus, the client progresses up a previously established *anxiety hierarchy* from the least to the most anxiety-provoking event.

Sexual arousal is used to inhibit anxiety responses that result in sexual dysfunction. Using a process of *sensate focus* Masters and Johnson (1970) ask client couples to avoid intercourse in favor of nonerotic touching. Proceeding through a series of progressive stages until successful sexual intercourse is achieved, clients are conditioned to a new set of responses in the presence of the anxiety-evoking stimuli.

Aversive counterconditioning, although not directly attributable to Wolpe, represents a technique that is a direct application of the stimulus-response paradigm. A noxious unconditioned stimulus (US) is repeatedly paired with an undesirable conditioned stimulus (CS), so that the pairing results in avoidance (CR) in the presence of the CS alone. Perhaps the best known clinical application of this technique is the use of Antabuse in controlling alcoholic behavior. The nausea-inducing drug is mixed with alcohol and ingested by the client. With sufficient pairings, the presence of alcohol alone is sufficient to produce discomfort.

Operant Conditioning

While Pavlov was studying learning in dogs, the American psychologist, Edward L. Thorndike (1874–1948), was studying problem-solving behavior in cats. Thorndike believed that learning was accomplished essentially through trial and error and that the human mind was a machine no different from the mind of an animal.

Based on his studies, Thorndike (1913) formulated the Law of Effect, which states that when an S-R connection is followed by satisfaction (reward), the connection is strengthened. Conversely, if the connection is followed by annoyance (punishment), it is weakened. Thorndike later revised the Law of Effect to suggest that punishment does not actually weaken the S-R connection; rather it increases the variability of behavior. Thus, undesired behaviors are not unlearned; instead new behaviors are learned in their place.

B. F. Skinner (1904 –). No person is more identified with behaviorism than its most prominent contemporary spokesperson, Burrhus Frederic Skinner. The underlying principles of Skinner's work can be traced directly to Thorndike's law, which Skinner (1953) renamed the "principle of reinforcement." According to this principle, the social environment provides a wide variety of consequences that help to shape human behavior, so that people come to display or inhibit behaviors that they otherwise produce quite spontaneously.

Because the individual actively operates or acts on the environment in order to achieve some goal, Skinner called this type of learning *operant conditioning.* Referring to the A-B-C model, it can be seen that operant conditioning theory is concerned more with the consequences (C) than with the antecedents (A) of specific behaviors (B).

More technically, the individual freely *emits* a behavior *(operant),* which is associated with some consequence that either increases *(reinforcement)* or decreases *(punishment)* the likelihood that the behavior will reoccur. If the consequence is added, it is said to be *positive,* while if it is withdrawn, it is said to be *negative.*

A behavior that is attended by consequences that increase the likelihood of the behavior reoccurring by their addition is said to be *positively reinforced.* For instance, clients are more likely to self-disclose when their honest presentations are met with an understanding response. A behavior that is less likely to reoccur as a consequence of something aversive being added is said to be *positively punished.* For example, through a procedure called *overcorrection,* a student who repeatedly clutters the work space with trash might be required to clean the entire classroom after each offense.

When the frequency of an emitted behavior increases as the result of the removal of some aversive consequence, the behavior is said to be *negatively reinforced.* A common application of this principle occurs when a child cleans up the room to stop a parent's nagging. Because the desired behavior often results in removing the individual from the aversive event, the result of negative reinforcement is often called *escape behavior.*

Finally, the suppression in frequency of a behavior through the removal of consequences is called *negative punishment.* The most common clinical application of this principle is a procedure called *time-out* ("time-out for positive reinforcement"), in which the client is removed from the reinforcing environment or the environment is removed. For example, a child who is disrupting the family dinner may be removed to a quiet place for twenty minutes.

Many of the terms used previously with classical conditioning have their own meaning in the context of operant conditioning. For instance, reinforcement refers to a desirable consequence rather than a pairing trial, while extinction refers to the withholding of reinforcement rather than the absence of an unconditioned stimulus. In classical conditioning, the symbols "S" and "R" mean stimulus and response, respectively, and appear in the order S-R, where the "—" is read "elicits." In operant conditioning, they refer to the target behavior and its consequences, respectively, and appear in the order R-S, where the "—" is read "emits." The terms discrimination and generalization generally refer to the same processes, but with one major difference: In classical conditioning the US is presented after the CS, no matter what the participant does. In operant conditioning, the participant must respond in a particular way in order to obtain the reinforcer.

The most important difference between the two systems, however, lies in their respective approaches to conditioning the desired behavior. Where classical conditioning pairs new stimuli with existing responses in reinforcement trials, operant conditioning *shapes* new behavioral responses through the reinforcement of *successive approximations* to the desired or target behavior.

The maintenance of a particular target behavior depends upon its *schedule of reinforcement,* which may vary according to the frequency with which the reinforcement is provided. For example, when trying to establish a new behavior, the fastest method is to reinforce after each emission of the desired behavior *(continuous reinforcement).* Once the behavior is established, it is best to switch to a schedule that reinforces only occasionally *(variable reinforcement)* to ensure a higher resistance to extinction. This process of changing schedules is referred to as *thinning.*

Applications to Counseling. The application of operant conditioning principles to counseling is generally intended to change behavior *(behavior modification)* or to eliminate it altogether *(extinction therapy).* In addition to the specific techniques of behavior modification, such as time-out, positive reinforcement, shaping, and the like, counselors use *programmed instruction* to present small units of information to clients, who are then reinforced for their responses. The use of *computer-assisted instruction* (CAI) by counselors in vocational settings is rapidly increasing.

A most promising application of operant conditioning to counseling is the development of *biofeedback.* In essence, the client is taught to recognize physical symptoms of underlying physiological conditions and to bring these under control. In the simplest of examples, clients may be taught to monitor their heartbeats, so that they may rest rather than become angry in stressful situations.

Various techniques have been developed to eliminate undesired behaviors through extinction. Although they go by different names, for example, *implosion therapy, flooding,* or *paradoxical intention,* these therapies are all designed to eliminate avoidance behaviors in the presence of the anxiety-producing stimuli.

Social Learning Theory

Albert Bandura (1925–   ) and his colleagues (1977) have developed a theory of learning that is based upon principles of modeling and imitation. Based on his research with children who became more aggressive when exposed to adult models who attacked inflated Bobo dolls, Bandura concluded that learning could occur without reinforcement.

Growth and development from this perspective simply reflect differences in the child's repertoire of responses. Through *vicarious reinforcement,* the child learns what to do to achieve desired goals by watching others. Sex roles, for example, are explained as the learned result of watching how other males or females behave and how they are treated as a consequence. The use of books, especially autobiographies, to provide models for learning appropriate behaviors has been developed into a counseling approach called *bibliotherapy* (Rubin, 1978). The study of models and their characteristics, such as warmth, similarity to the observer, and relative power, has been an important area of study from this perspective.

Significantly, researchers (Strong & Dixon, 1971) report that modeling by the counselor enhances the effectiveness of other techniques to produce the desired behavior. In addition, the study of social reinforcers has provided valuable information for counselors in developing programs of peer and self-support (Hosford, 1980). A third area of study has explored the relationship between learning theory and maturation. The work of Dollard and Miller (1950), for example, attempts to rework Freudian psychoanalysis (see next section) into a social learning framework based on the premise that personality is learned.

Mediation and Cognition

During the past decade, researchers have become increasingly interested in the role that cognition plays in human behavior. Theorists have inferred that thinking is really the association of a series of S-R connections that go on inside the individual and that *mediate* between environmental stimuli and organismic responses. With age, the person's behavior is explained more and more by this mediational learning.

Within counseling, cognitive behavior therapists such as Aaron Beck (1967), Albert Ellis (1962), and Donald Meichenbaum (1977) have proposed that changes in thinking may alter behavior. The general assumption is that early experiences have contributed to the development of certain irrational beliefs that result in anxiety and depression. Therapy is directed toward the acknowledgment of these erroneous thoughts and the rehearsal of new and more appropriate beliefs.

Lev Vygotsky (1896–1934). Unlike the other behaviorally oriented theorists discussed to this point, the Russian psychologist Vygotsky was critical of approaches that focused primarily on individual functioning and that assumed that collective functioning was a derivative of it. Instead, he argued for the study of "how the individual response emerges from the form of collective life" (1981, p. 165).

Vygotsky (1956) believed that people not only are acted upon by environmental stimuli, but that they also act upon their surroundings to create new ones. Development consists of mastering external communicative signs that are internalized and become higher-order regulatory systems for the voluntary control of behavior. These thoughts, a kind of internal speech, become the primary mediators of human behavior.

The unit of analysis for Vygotsky's work was the meaning of the spoken word. Vygotsky (1962) believed that "every idea contains a transmuted affective attitude toward the bit of reality to which it refers" (p. 8.). Language and thought are thus related in such a way that the meanings of words are generalized concepts, which are the acts of thought. Vygotsky believed this generalizing process in which humans become aware of their own thoughts is consciousness.

Although thought and word develop by different processes, they become united in consciousness, so that

> the relation of thought to word undergoes changes which themselves may be regarded as development in the functional sense. Thought is not merely expressed in words; it comes into existence through them. Every thought tends to connect something with something else, to establish a relationship between things. Every thought moves, grows and develops, fulfills a function, solves a problem. (Vygotsky, 1962, p. 125)

Vygotsky's interest in the mechanisms of development and his emphasis on interaction move him beyond classification as a behaviorist only. His view of development as proceeding through qualitatively different stages of meaning-making moves his work in the direction of the structuralists.

The implications of Vygotsky's work for counseling are only beginning to become clear. Accepting that counselors use words more than any other medium, his work on the role of language in development provides an important link between the rapidly expanding field of behavior therapy and counseling's renewed interest in human development.

Nowhere is the potential of Vygotsky's work clearer than in the study of what he called *the zone of proximal development,* defined as "the distance between the actual developmental level as determined by independent problem solving and the level of potential development as determined through problem solving under adult guidance or in collaboration with more capable peers" (Vygotsky, 1978, p. 86). In this zone the counselor works as a mediator in the client's development. Although Vygotsky died before describing the events necessary for "problem solving under adult guidance or in collaboration with more capable peers," extensions of this work are being carried out (see Rogoff & Wertsch, 1984) that promise important changes in our current understanding of social interaction.

THE MATURATIONISTS

When counselors think of development, most are likely to imagine a predictable sequence of changes unfolding over time. This chronological-phase explanation of development has been so omnipresent in counseling theory that many counselors assume that maturation is synonymous with developmental theory. Despite the overwhelming popularity of behavioral approaches, particularly in American society which clamors for a democratic science, maturational theories of development have been especially useful in spelling out the *normal* or expected course of human development.

Maturational theories may be grouped along a continuum of factors from evolution to culture. The difference is not so much one of kind as it is of emphasis, with one extreme emphasizing evolutionary and biological determinants of the species and the other extreme focusing more on the unfolding of biologically limited characteristics within a social context.

Ethological Approaches

Derived from Darwin's evolutionary plan by the European zoologists, Niko Tinbergen (1951) and Konrad Lorenz (1937), ethology is concerned with the close fit that exists between the behavior of a species and its natural surroundings. Adapted to psychology, the ethological approach has been useful in identifying *species-specific behaviors* that serve as analogues to human behavior. Although the application of concepts from animal research to human behavior is risky, some of the basic concepts derived from this research have particular significance for counselors.

Fixed Action Patterns. When studying species-specific behavior, ethologists often encounter frequently repeated, ritualistic behavior patterns that show little variation from one member of a species to another. Related to these *fixed action patterns* are patterns of sensory stimulation called *sign stimuli* that reliably elicit these patterns of behavior.

In human infants, the human face brings a smile, a touch to the lips encourages sucking, and an object on the palm elicits grasping. Studies by Bowlby (1969), Spitz (1945), and Harlow and Harlow (1962) on the development of attachment demonstrate the importance of touch and vocalization by a caretaker upon the infant's subsequent development.

Behavioral Systems. Species-specific behaviors may be grouped into sets of related behaviors that may be expressed differently from one member or group of members of a species to another. Human examples of such systems can be found in the common use of language existing in hundreds of forms, in the common use of tools of many different kinds, and in the common occurrence of social hierarchies defined by different social values. The study of commonly occurring behavioral systems across different cultures gives the counselor important insights into the nature of the human condition as experienced and as expressed.

Critical Periods. Perhaps the most important notion to be borrowed from ethology is the idea that certain developmental events depend upon the exposure of the animal to specific stimuli during a restricted period of time. During this period, the animal is highly sensitive to these conditions, which are *critical* to the development of specific behaviors. Failure to be exposed to the requisite stimuli during this brief period results in a diminished capacity to respond in the appropriate way.

The most widely known example of this phenomenon is *imprinting,* which is a learning mechanism that helps young goslings to recognize their relatives. Although there is little evidence of such brief, dramatic periods in humans, they do experience broad, somewhat flexible periods during which they are especially *sensitive* to learning certain behaviors. For example, the first eighteen months of life seem to be particularly important for the development of attachment (Bowlby, 1969), while the years between two and twelve appear critical to the development of language (Lenneberg, 1969).

For the counselor, the concept of critical periods raises some questions: When and what intervention is appropriate? What will happen if I do or don't intervene? Is this particular problem behavior in response to some developmental crisis, or does it represent some more pathological disturbance? How each counselor answers these questions is determined, in part, by which theory one uses.

Genetic Factors

Estimates of *heritability,* the extent to which a given trait can be attributed to genetic conditions, help the counselor to understand certain mental and physical disorders. *Huntington's chorea,* for example, is a genetically transmitted disorder that first appears between ages thirty and forty and is characterized by a progressive deterioration of physical and mental abilities. *Phenylketonuria* (PKU) is an enzyme deficiency that results in damage to the nervous system. Unlike Huntington's chorea, PKU can be diagnosed and treated early, helping the person to live a normal life.

Klinefelter's syndrome and *Down's syndrome* both result from irregularities in the genetic makeup and result in mental retardation. Genetic factors have also been indicated in the development of certain abnormal behaviors such as schizophrenia and depression. The possibility that certain maladaptive behaviors may have related organic causes makes it vital that counselors consult with qualified medical personnel when physical symptoms are present.

The most controversial topic related to hereditability, however, concerns the nature of intelligence. Evidence from intelligence tests shows that people who are more closely related are more similar in intelligence, but the relationship is sufficiently imperfect, even in identical twins, to suggest that environment plays an important role. To complicate matters further, there is considerable debate about whether or not an *intelligence quotient* (IQ) is an accurate measure of intelligence or simply what an intelligence test measures (Richardson & Spears, 1972; Sattler, 1974).

Psychoanalysis

Without question, the most significant figure in the history of psychology is Sigmund Freud (1856–1939). Trained as a physician and neurologist, Freud was a man of such vision and personal power that he revolutionized the very way in which we think of human nature today. What makes Freud so difficult to understand, in part, is the breadth of his study. Even into his seventies, he was making major revisions in a theory that fills twenty-four volumes of his published works.

Dynamics of Personality. Freud believed that all behaviors have a cause and that human nature could be explained by the laws of chemistry and physics. His theory is a dynamic one, focused on the transformation and exchange of energy within the personality. This *psychic energy* originates in biological drives or *instincts* that make demands on the mind called *needs*. Human behavior results from efforts to satisfy needs, the two most basic of which are self-preservation *(Eros)* and self-destruction. The psychic energy that serves the needs of the life as opposed to the death instinct Freud called *libido,* a force he believed to be primarily sexual. Freud believed the function of the instincts was to return the system to a state of quiescence that existed prior to some disturbance. The direction of instinctual activity, therefore, is regressive, proceeding from excitation to relief through the release of psychic energy to reduce tension.

Structure of the Personality. The instincts reside in a substructure of the personality Freud called *das Es* (literally, "the it"), which is commonly translated in English as the *id* (Loevinger, 1976, pp. 368–369). As the main source of energy, the id acts to reduce tension by investing psychic energy in either reflex activity or by creating an image of the desired object, a process called *wish-fulfillment.* This investment of energy, referred to as *displacement,* is so fluid that the id can jump back and forth from image to image to reflex and so on in its efforts to obtain the desired object. Blocking the direction of this flow forces the id to seek other outlets, which often results in mistakes or accidents and, in the extreme, in a loss of touch with reality.

The inability of the id to produce the desired object through fantasy, leads to the development of the *ego.* As Freud (1939/1964) put it, "Where id was, there ego shall be" (p. 80). Where the id is dedicated to satisfaction *(the pleasure principle),* the ego is dedicated to survival *(the reality principle).*

Because the *primary-process thought* of the id cannot distinguish between real and imagined objects, a system of thought must be developed that can mediate between the demands of the inner world of the instincts and the outer world of reality. This *secondary-process thought* of the ego, which is rational and more logical than primary-process thought, includes the intellectual activities of memory, problem solving, judgment, and reasoning.

The ego has no energy of its own, but borrows it instead from the id in small amounts through the process of *identification.* As the ego develops, it acquires more and more energy and becomes more adept in using secondary-process thought to delay the discharge of energy in satisfying the demands of the reality principle. Satisfaction can come through finding objects in the real world following a delay or temporarily through dreaming or hallucinating. Although secondary-process thought does not replace primary process thought, it characterizes greater portions of thought as development proceeds. As the ego becomes stronger, an *identity* develops, hence the origin of Freud's term for the ego, *das Ich,* literally meaning "the I" (Loevinger, 1976, pp. 368–369).

Faced with the excessive and irrational demands of the id and the realities of an external world that threatens it with annihilation, the ego defends itself from the anxiety such situations create. Under the best of circumstances, the reality principle is adequate to the task, especially in dealing with external demands. When the threat is so great as to destroy the ego from within, however, it protects itself through *defense mechanisms* that control and alleviate anxiety through the distortion of reality (see A. Freud, 1936/1946). To illustrate how they work, two of these defense mechanisms are presented: *repression* (denying or forgetting the threat) and *regression* (returning to an earlier form of behavior).

Repression prevents a threatening thought from coming into awareness, or what Freud referred to as the *conscious.* Some of these thoughts, like incest, are inherited and so never become conscious. Other threatening thoughts may be perceptions, ideas, or memories that arouse painful feelings, such as guilt or frustration, or that threaten the ego's sense of control. These are driven out of the conscious into the *unconscious* through the act of repression. Ideas that exist just out of awareness, "on the tip of the tongue," are said to be *preconscious.* Although repression is a necessary part of normal development, some persons rely heavily upon repression and become withdrawn or inaccessible *(repressed).* Providing the conditions necessary to help clients gain access to their repressed thoughts forms an important part of the work of psychoanalysis.

Regression refers to the retreat to an earlier level of development out of fear. Drinking to excess, playing practical jokes, smoking, coming down with a cold, in short, "acting like a kid" are common ways in which normal adults retreat temporarily from the demands of a "world gone mad." Carried to its extreme, however, regression results in more permanent flights from reality, so that counseling may be required. Identifying the object of the defense mechanism helps the client to function more fully. (For a discussion of two other defense mechanisms, transference and countertransference, see Chapters 3 and 6.)

The *superego* is the last component of the personality to develop and is made up of two parts: the *conscience* and the *ego ideal.* In general, the conscience acts as an internalized set of parents that hands out punishments in the form of guilt feelings. The ego ideal, on the other hand, serves as an idealized set of standards toward which the child strives.

Stages of Development. Reminiscent of the ethologists, Freud believed that both normal and abnormal behavior have their origins in the early life experiences of the child. How the child handles the changing demands of the instincts determines the basic character of the adult personality. Based on discussions with his adult patients, Freud constructed a sequence of four developmental stages interrupted by a period of latency.

Although the aim of the sexual instinct, Eros, remains constant throughout life, its source moves from one area of bodily excitation *(erogenous zone)* to another due to biological maturation. Any failure to handle the demands of one stage lives on in attempts to deal with issues in the next stage. The three principal erogenous zones, mouth, anus, and genitals, serve as the center of interest during the various stages of development.

The oral stage is characterized by a preoccupation with the mouth and lasts through the first year of life. Pleasure is derived by sucking, chewing, eating, and biting in the relief of sexual tension. As well. the child encounters frustration and anxiety when the presentation of desired objects is delayed or when stimulation becomes excessive without release. The child's responses to these demands set the course for prototypical behaviors in adulthood. Just as the child incorporates food, so the adult takes in knowledge. Drinking to excess, smoking, sarcasm, and gossip all serve their purpose in reducing the anxieties of adult life. Because the mother has served traditionally as the source of satisfaction for many of the child's needs, Freud believed that this relationship served as the prototype for all future love relationships.

The *anal stage,* which occupies the second and third years, initiates struggles that are acted out in attempts to control a recurring cycle of retention and elimination. For example, the anxiety that attends the retention of accumulated wastes turns to pleasure with the elimination of the feces. How children respond to the demands of toilet training, therefore, influences their relationships to authority and determines their orientation to personal hygiene as adults.

The *anal retentive* child becomes the frugal and obstinate Scrooge of Dickens' "A Christmas Carol." The *anal eliminative* child becomes a giving and generous adult. Explosive and uncontrolled elimination leads to the uncontrolled spontaneity of the unkempt Oscar Madison, while constipation leads to the overcontrolled, compulsively neat existence of Felix Unger. The child who is successful in finding a balance between the demands of the body for expression and the social environment for control is prepared to take on the challenges of the stages that lie ahead.

The *phallic stage,* so called because of the child's heightened interest in the absence or presence of a penis, takes place over the period roughly between ages three and six. The sexual pleasure derived from manipulating the genitals is redirected to a desire for the parent of the opposite sex. This situation is called the *Oedipus complex* after the Greek tragedy in which Oedipus unknowingly kills his father and marries his mother.

For the male, the desire to possess the mother is offset by a fear of castration by a retaliatory father. To resolve the conflict, the boy represses his desire for the mother and his fear of the father through an *identification with the aggressor.* Freud believed that the Oedipus complex was not only inevitable, but that its successful resolution was necessary for the development of the superego and of a healthy identification with the same-sex parent. He believed homosexuality to be a maladaptive solution to this problem.

For the female, the realization of being without a penis leads to envy of the father's prized possession and resentment of the mother for sending her into the world so ill equipped. Because she believes that castration has already occurred, the girl has less to fear, and so her identification with the same-sex parent and, thereby, her conscience are weaker by comparison (Freud, 1925/1961).

As the most controversial aspect of Freud's theory, the Oedipus complex raises the issue of whether or not the identity development of children is necessarily traumatic and whether or not the course of development for males and females is necessarily different. The effect of Freud's (1925/1961) conclusion that women "are less ready to submit to the great exigencies of life, that they are more often influenced in their judgments by feelings of affection or hostility" (p. 258) was to provide "scientific proof" of the inferiority of women's development. The work of Gilligan (1982) provides a striking alternative to this explanation.

A period of latency marks the time between the age of about six and the onset of puberty. During this period, the child's sexual urges are repressed, and sexual energies are channeled into school and social activities with same-sex peers. The repression of the sexual trauma experienced in early childhood Freud believed accounted for the inability to remember the events of the first few years of life.

The genital stage witnesses the reappearance of the sexual drive in adolescence. Spurred by the physiological changes of puberty, the sexual drive is directed toward reproduction rather than the *narcissistic* self-manipulation of the pregenital period. *Object-choice* reflects the resolution of earlier conflicts as reflected in the familiar refrain: "I want a girl just like the girl that married dear old Dad."

The longest of Freud's stages, the genital stage lasts from puberty through old age, when there is a regression to pregenital levels of functioning. Freud believed that adult life is developmentally uneventful, occupied instead with acting out the predispositions of earlier periods in an effort to balance the two most important tasks of life: love and work.

Neo-Psychoanalytic Theories

Although he worked alone for many years, Freud was successful in gathering around him a select group of intellectuals who did much to expand and revise his ideas. The works of three of these people, Carl Jung, Alfred Adler, and Erik Erikson, are having a profound effect upon the practice of counseling today.

Carl G. Jung (1875–1961). During most of his thirties, Jung was a leading disciple of Freud and at the forefront of the newly forming psychoanalytic movement. Jung's association with Freud started in 1906 through an exchange of letters regarding Freud's dream analysis technique. The friendship lasted until 1914 when Jung withdrew from the International Psychoanalysts Association, eventually forming his own school, Analytic Psychology.

There are several theories explaining why Jung broke with Freud, but the most general centers on Jung's dissatisfaction with Freud's negative view of the nature of humankind. In particular, Jung (1928) believed that personality was more the result of striving for self-realization than tension reduction, as Freud believed. In addition, Jung disagreed with Freud on the notion that libido is primarily sexual in nature, viewing it as a generalized life force instead.

Of greatest significance for counselors are Jung's emphases upon adult development and upon the role of sociological factors in development. Considered by some to be the "father of the modern study of adult development" (Levinson, 1978, p. 4), Jung believed that the personality continues to take shape well into mid-life. Jung's (1933) idea that personality differences can be categorized by personality types forms the basis for the Myers-Briggs Type Indicator (MBTI), the use of which has brought renewed interest in Jung's work (Evans, Benner, & Hayes, 1985). Present-day notions about the distinction between *introversion* and *extraversion,* about the process of *individuation,* or the idea of a *collective unconscious* trace their origins to Jung's work.

Alfred Adler (1870–1937). Adler resigned as president of the Vienna Psychoanalytic Society in 1911 over disputes with Freud about the role of social forces in the development of neuroses. Adler (1926/1972) rejected the division of mind and body, arguing instead for a view of the individual as holistic and *becoming.* His Individual Psychology (Adler, 1963) holds that humans are motivated primarily by *social interest* to become members of the group. Pushed by the need to overcome *feelings of inferiority* and pulled by the *striving for superiority,* each person develops a unique *life-style* that directs the selection of goals to follow. The meanings individuals attribute to life determine their behavior, because they act as if their perceptions are true.

Many of Adler's original ideas have been retained in the theories of his contemporaries and have found their way into the common language of counseling theory today. *Birth order, life tasks, the inferiority complex, self-ideal,* and *life-style* are all common psychological constructs that originated with Adler. The importance of social interest within the Adlerian scheme led to an interest in group methods (see Chapter 4), which led in turn to the founding of one of the earliest child guidance clinics (in 1922) and the introduction of family therapy (Dinkmeyer, Pew, & Dinkmeyer, 1979).

Adler's student, Rudolph Dreikurs (1959), was the first to describe the use of group psychotherapy in private practice and was influential in introducing Adlerian methods into the treatment of children in schools. The existential psychologies of Erich Fromm (1941) and Victor Frankl (1963), the rational-emotive therapy of Albert Ellis (1962), the transactional analysis of Eric Berne (1964), and the humanistic psychology of Abraham Maslow (1962) all are derived in part from Adler's work (see Mosak, 1979).

Erik Erikson (1902–). While a young artist in Vienna, Erikson was called upon to paint the portraits of the children of Sigmund Freud. So began the career of the man who has had perhaps the greatest influence on counseling and education of all the maturationists except Freud himself. Although he still believes himself to be true to Freud's theory, Erikson (1950) made major expansions if not revisions in the basic psychoanalytic approach.

First, Erikson sees the ego as being far more independent than does Freud, who saw it in constant tension with the id and superego. Concerned more with the ego's independence and its development, Erikson views the healthy personality as one in which the ego is essentially in charge, with the id and superego serving as allies. The most significant innovation in Erikson's theory, however, is his emphasis upon the role of society in psychological development. For Erikson, developmental crises are predominantly psycho*social* as opposed to psycho*sexual*, as Freud saw them. In addition, Erikson believes that development continues throughout life.

Borrowing the principle of *epigenesis* from embryology, Erikson believes that personality development proceeds "according to steps predetermined in the human organism's readiness to be driven toward, to be aware of, and to interact with a widening radius of significant individuals and institutions" (Erikson, 1968a, p. 93). Erikson proposed eight stages that extend over the course of the lifespan. During each a component of the personality has its "time of special ascendancy" (Erikson, 1968a, p. 92) and meets its particular crisis.

Thus, each stage is characterized by a *psychosocial crisis* that represents a major encounter between the individual and the social environment. Each crisis is not so much a catastrophe as a turning point in the development of the ego. The mature ego is able to face the challenge presented by new social requirements and to seize upon new opportunities. Each crisis is described in terms of two opposing characteristics (see Table 2-1).

Too many readers of Erikson misunderstand him to believe that positive development consists of picking the correct option of two polar opposites. Instead, he argues for favorable "ratios" (Erikson, 1968a, p. 325) and the development of a series of alternative basic attitudes. Normal development, therefore, consists of navigating the distance between the two extremes in the development of a secure identity.

TABLE 2-1 FREUD'S AND ERIKSON'S STAGES COMPARED

Approximate Age	Freud Psychosexual Stages	Erikson Nuclear Conflicts
0—1	Oral	Trust and mistrust
1—3	Anal	Autonomy and shame, doubt
3—7	Phallic	Initiative and guilt
7—12	Latency	Industry and inferiority
12—18	Genital	Identity and identity confusion
18—30	Genital	Intimacy and isolation
30—60	Genital	Generativity and stagnation
60—		Integrity and despair

This sense of an *ego identity* has had a great impact upon counseling practice because it refers to the very nature of the individual's sense of self and of who he or she wants to be. Although the mature identity is first formulated in adolescence, how one resolves the balance required in previous conflicts imposes lasting limitations on the individual's abilities to resolve present and future conflicts.

Clients who come to counseling often find themselves in the throes of an *identity crisis,* wondering "Who am I?" "Where am I going in life?" "What will I become?" Understanding that such questioning represents the *normative,* or expected, course of human development helps the counselor to be more responsive to the client's very real concerns. Counselors can use Erikson's life-phase model as a map to design new learnings in which clients can become informed about previously unknown normal developmental changes in oneself or the environment.

Erikson has had an enormous impact upon the humanities, psychology, and the social sciences. Working primarily as a therapist and writing as a humanist, he has pioneered work in children's play therapy, given coherence and meaning to the psychological struggles of adolescents, advanced the field of psychohistory with his analyses of the lives of such men as Martin Luther and Mahatma Gandhi (Erikson, 1968b, 1969), and provided the framework for the first modern theory of adult development. The direct effect of his theory also can be seen in Havighurst's (1976) *Developmental Tasks and Education* and in Levinson's (1978) *Season's of a Man's Life,* both of which are influencing the practice of counselors today.

Harry Stack Sullivan (1892–1949). Like Erikson, Sullivan (1953) was profoundly influenced by Freud's work and sought to extend it in his own clinical practice. The core of Sullivan's thought can be found in his *psychiatry of interpersonal relations,* which is really the study of communication between persons. He believed that a large part of a client's problems arise from inadequate communication that results from some disruption created by anxiety.

The *self-system* emerges through efforts to manage and to avoid anxiety. Anxiety arises when security needs are not satisfied. As needs change over time, especially in interpersonal relationships, the self-system evolves new processes to deal with new realities that can be represented as successive stages in a sequence of self-other systems (see Table 2-2).

In effect, the self-system is an incorporation of the individual's world view of self in an interplay of three elements: the *good-me,* the *bad-me,* and the *not-me.* Information that is discordant with this view gives rise to anxiety. Ever vigilant to such incongruities, the self-system acts through the process of *selective inattention* to screen out or distort the unwanted observation in attempts to obtain satisfaction from an essentially irrational society. Sullivan's notion of an organized personality, set in the context of an interpersonal field, anticipated the work of the structuralists, especially Loevinger (1976).

Trait Theory

In its simplest form, a trait is a personality characteristic that predisposes the individual to behave in a particular way. As such, it can be used to predict how a person is more or less likely to behave under a given set of circumstances and to classify people on the basis of the degree to which they possess a given trait. Traits, which may be inherited or learned, both initiate and guide behavior.

Gordon Allport (1897–1967). Rejecting the Freudian notion of unconscious motivation, Allport (1961) set out to study what he viewed as the more proactive and changing nature of human motivation. In his view, selfhood develops through a series of seven stages in a continuing process of "becoming." Allport used the notion of traits as a means to understanding the organization of the individual personality, believing that "if you knew a few central things about an individual, you'd be able to predict most of his [or her] behavior" (cited in Evans, 1970, p. 28). Although the number of individual traits that characterize a given individual is rarely only one, usually five to ten is sufficient to describe a person with reasonable accuracy.

Allport also rejected a strict S-R psychology, arguing instead for a more dynamic view of personality in which the organism plays a major

TABLE 2-2 SULLIVAN'S INTERPERSONAL PHASES*

Phase	Primary Self-System	Primary Other-System	Communication
Infancy	Good-me, bad-me, not-me	Good-mother,[1] bad-mother	Crying, babbling, smiling, grasping, sucking
Childhood	My body	My mother, my father	Words, dramatizations, imitations
Juvenile (school years)	Myself	Peers (groups of friends)	Language, consensus, cooperation, compromise, competition, stereotypes
Preadolescence	Self-consciousness	Chum (one or two friends)	Reciprocity, valuing of other, love, loneliness
Adolescence	Genital, sexual self	Partner of opposite sex	Security, intimacy, lust
Adulthood	Integrated self	All of the above	Fully human repertoire of relating

*Each new state should be considered as *added on* to what has come before.
[1]Mother is the "mothering one" who is intimate with the child's needs, not necessarily the biological mother.
Source: From "Making Use of Human Development Theories in Counseling" by Polly Young-Eisendrath, 1985, *Counseling and Human Development,* 17 (5), p. 11. Copyright 1985 by Love Publishing Company. Reprinted by permission.

role in intervening between any stimulus and the organism's response. The individual not only tries to establish equilibrium between competing tensions, but under some circumstances actually seeks out disequilibrium. In essence, Allport saw the individual as self-determinate.

Allport's work in trait theory, a term he abandoned in later years, was very appealing to a test-and-measurement-hungry profession in search of a scientific means to sort the citizens of a democratic society (see Chapter 1). Allport's emphasis upon the ability to predict individual behavior was redirected to the analysis and prediction of the behavior of groups of people. All that was needed was a statistical procedure that would permit the analysis of a large set of characteristics, or variables, into a small number of traits, or factors (see Chapter 5 for a continuation of this discussion). Interested in developing an empirically based theory of personality, Cattell (1946) used *factor analysis* to reduce Allport's list of traits to identify what he believed to be "the primary source traits of personality" (cited in Anastasi, 1968, p. 450). After twenty years of such research, Cattell and his colleagues constructed a number of personality inventories, of which the most widely known is the Sixteen Personality Factor Questionnaire (16PF).

Humanistic Psychology

Less a theory of human development than a philosophical approach, humanistic psychology was organized in 1960 as a protest movement against the prevailing behavioral approach to research and the near domination of clinical practice by psychoanalysis. Some of its leaders, Abraham Maslow (1962), Carl Rogers (1961), Sidney Jourard (1971), Charlotte Buhler (Buhler & Allen, 1972), and Viktor Frankl (1963) are among the most familiar names in the field of counseling (see Welch, Tate, & Richards, 1978).

The emphasis of humanistic psychology is upon conscious rather than unconscious determinants of behavior, immediate rather than past experience, free will rather than tension reduction, individual uniqueness rather than determinism, motivation toward self-actualization rather than tension reduction, and most importantly, the basic goodness of the individual. The ideas of two of its founders, in particular, continue to exert great influence on the practice of counseling today.

Abraham Maslow (1908–1970). In a startling simple reversal of psychoanalytic tradition, Maslow (1962) interviewed the *best* people he could find to determine the characteristics of people who had escaped what he referred to as "the psychopathology of the average" (p. 16).

These *self-actualized* people are characterized by a realistic view of themselves and others, a capacity to tolerate ambiguity, even a welcoming of it, a need for solitude, spontaneity, acceptance of self and others, autonomy, a capacity for deeply emotional love relationships, inner-directedness and a resistance to conformity, creativity, and democratic attitudes and values. These qualities Maslow believed to be the developmental end point toward which the individual is motivated to grow.

Basic to his personality theory, is the *hierarchy of needs* through which the individual must pass in efforts to become self-actualized (see Table 2-3). Maslow believed that all human needs are grouped into two categories: lower-order needs (physiological and safety needs) and higher-order needs (belongingness and love, self-esteem, and self-actualization). Only when lower-order needs are satisfied can one move on to the satisfaction of higher-order needs. In the final revision of his hierarchy, Maslow added a level beyond self-actualization, called *transcendence,* or a surrender into an expanded sense of self. Maslow foresaw a "transpersonal world view which transcends ego boundaries, sees all parts as being equal in the whole, all humans as having the same needs, feelings, and potentials" (Hendricks & Weinhold, 1982, pp. 5–7).

Maslow's theory has not stood up well to experimental analysis (Fox, 1982). Nonetheless, the basic notion of a growth force inherent in the individual that moves development forward toward the maximization

TABLE 2-3 ERIKSON'S AND MASLOW'S SCHEMES COMPARED

Developmental Period	Erikson Nuclear Conflict	Maslow Need Hierarchy
Infancy	Trust & mistrust	Physiological
Childhood	Autonomy & shame, doubt Initiative & guilt Industry & inferiority	Safety Belongingness
Adolescence	Identity & identity confusion	
		Affectional/Love
Adulthood	Intimacy & isolation Generativity & stagnation Integrity & despair	Self-esteem Self-actualization

of human potential has proven to be a powerful metaphor for counseling. Indeed, much of counseling theory from a humanistic perspective has been devoted to liberating just these tendencies in the individual.

Carl R. Rogers (1902–). No single individual since Freud has had as all-encompassing an effect upon the counseling profession as Carl Rogers and his *client-centered therapy* (Rogers, 1951). According to Rogers (1961), the primary motivation for development comes from an *actualizing tendency*. This tendency causes the individual to experience life in ways that are consistent with one's *self-concept,* which is the constellation of self-perceptions of *I* and *me*. Maladjustment arises when the individual experiences a discrepancy between the self-concept and the *ideal self,* which is the self the person would like to be. This actualizing tendency motivates the person not only to remove the discrepancies in life but also to develop the self to its greatest potential.

The human potential movement, which has been such a powerful force in counseling over the past twenty-five years, is a direct expression of Rogers's developmental psychology. If people have an inherent capacity to move toward health and away from maladjustment, then counselors should shift the responsibility for therapy to their clients. In order to effect change, counselors must be as genuine and integrated as possible ("be *congruent*"), must demonstrate high degrees of nonpossessive caring for their clients ("show *unconditional positive regard*"), and must achieve a sense of personal identification with their clients' subjective experiences ("express *accurate empathic understanding*"). The experience of counseling helps clients to move in the direction of being less defensive and more trusting of their own experiences. The result is believed to be freer individuals who can take greater responsibility for managing their own lives.

THE STRUCTURALISTS

The existence of universal stages of psychological development provides the structuralist with a theoretical framework for counseling intervention, the purpose of which is to stimulate development to the next higher stage of development. Unlike the passage of phases more representative of most maturationist accounts of the life cycle, the structuralist reserves the term *stage* to refer to qualitative differences in the way the individual thinks about or resolves a particular conflict. Each of these stages provides a "structured whole" (Piaget, 1960, p. 14) that represents an individual world view or frame of reference for meaning-making.

Cognitive Development

At an age when most young children are pursuing more care-free interests, eleven-year-old Jean Piaget (1896–1980) published his first scientific paper. After a career that produced more than thirty volumes during a span of more than seventy years, Piaget has come to be recognized as *the* child psychologist, despite his never having undergone formal training or having earned a degree in psychology.

Dynamics of Development. Piaget (1936/1952, 1937/1954, 1960) believed that as biological organisms, humans inherit two basic functions: *organization* and *adaptation*. Organization refers to the *tendency* for all living things to attempt to order their processes; in effect, organisms organize. The second aspect of general functioning is the *tendency* of the organism to make modifications in response to changing environmental conditions. This process of adaptation is actually comprised of two complementary processes: *assimilation* and *accommodation*.

Assimilation involves the modification of relevant environmental events so that they may be incorporated into the individual's existing organizational structure. Much as a meal must be broken down by digestion into its component proteins, fats, carbohydrates, and minerals for use by the human body, information must be modified to fit existing mental structures. In effect, assimilation makes experience significant by making it coherent with what the person already knows. Incompatible situations are either distorted to conform to prior expectations or they are ignored, a process analogous to what Sullivan called *selective inattention* and Adler called *tendentious apperception*. Play may be thought of as the ultimate assimilative activity.

Accommodation, on the other hand, involves modifications in the organization of the individual in response to environmental demands. Just as the stomach and intestines tend to change in response to demands made upon the body through the ingestion of food, so too existing mental structures tend to be modified to suit the demands of the environment. In its extreme, accommodation is essentially imitation.

The individual's actions on and experience of the environment result in what Piaget called *schemes*. These regulated patterns of behavior represent forms of action that have structure, that structure experience, and that are self-structuring in the sense that they organize interests and attitudes. Schemes are the raw materials out of which knowledge is made at each stage of development; it is accepted that later schemes grow out of earlier ones.

Because assimilation and accommodation are complementary processes that occur simultaneously, they must necessarily be in some kind of balance if adaptation is to occur. In the process of organizing one's experience, the individual must simultaneously assimilate novel experiences into preexisting structures and accommodate preexisting structures to meet the demands presented by new environmental conditions. Although Piaget believed that achieving such a balance was a theoretical end point for development, he nonetheless believed that humans possess a natural tendency to strive toward such a balance or *equilibrium*.

The individual's self-regulating systems emerge as a consequence of new states of equilibrium that were created by the previous self-regulatory system. Therefore, disequilibration serves as a stimulus to development, while equilibration is its goal. Development can be seen from this view as the natural outcome of the individual's attempts to make stable sense of a changing world. In effect, the individual must change in order to remain the same. As a result of this recurring cycle of equilibration-disequilibration-equilibration, development takes a path that may best be described by a spiral, the outer turns of which are analogous to the individual's attempts at the integration of novel experiences to existing structures, while in each turn, the spiral moves to a new level of organization analogous to the movement to a higher stage (Langer, 1969, pp. 95–96).

For the counselor, the most important aspect of Piaget's view of development is that experience is the necessary condition for stage progression, although experience itself is not enough. Because individuals tend both to adapt and to organize, they must necessarily be in interaction with their environment. Thus, experience must be of a kind that presents genuine cognitive conflict for the individual, that is, a discrepancy to some optimal extent between the individual's existing mental structures and his or her present experience.

Stages of Development. Piaget identified four major stages or *periods* of development, which represent general changes in the child's way of knowing (see Table 2-4). *The sensorimotor period* occupies approximately the first two years of life. During this period, the child's reflexive behavior, such as sucking and grasping, are generalized, strengthened, and differentiated. The child's interactions with the environment are characterized by *actions on objects* and involve sensory and motor movements. Objects are assimilated to developing schemes of *things to suck, things to grasp,* and so forth.

A significant outcome of this period is the development of the concept of *objective permanence*, which refers to the ability to recognize that objects continue to exist outside of the child's presence. Thus the child now misses the primary caretaker who has until now come and gone

TABLE 2-4 PIAGET'S COGNITIVE STAGES

Age	Period
0–2	Sensorimotor
2–7	Intuitive or preoperational
7–12	Concrete operational
12–16	Formal operational

without notice. The end of this period is marked by the beginnings of *representational thought* in which the child can think about an object that is not actually present. The child can now dream or search in several places for an object that has been hidden in different places in sequence.

Evidence of the rudiments of sensorimotor thinking appears in adult life when people describe a spiral staircase by circling their fingers in the air, or when they open and close two fingers against one another while searching for a pair of lost scissors. Much of the nonverbal behavior or physiological symptoms experienced by clients in counseling are the expression of thoughts at a sensorimotor level.

The preoperational period, which extends from approximately age two through seven, is marked by the development of language and the *symbolic function.* The child's interactions involve *actions on symbols,* which permit representational interactions. Brooms can become horses, teddy bears can carry on conversations, and most importantly, words can be used to create language. In contrast to Vygotsky, Piaget argues that thought actually precedes language, which is the expression of thoughts already imagined by the child.

Piaget refers to this period with the prefix *pre-* because it is characterized by the absence of so many things of which the child will be capable in the next period. In particular, the child is not yet capable of reversible mental operations. Preoperational children cannot distinguish between internal mental states and external reality, they display an inability to take another's point of view *(egocentrism)*, and they have a rigidity of thought that is best exemplified by *centration,* the tendency to focus on only one salient feature of an object and to ignore other features.

The outcomes of this period include the notion of cause-effect relationships, a movement between different viewpoints, and the notion that an object has its own *identity* despite changes in its appearance. Examples of preoperational thought in adults include wishful or magical thinking, superstitious behavior, or the recurrent though illogical belief that our bad thoughts or neglect may have caused the death of a loved one.

The concrete operational period extends from approximately age seven through age twelve. Its distinguishing feature, and hence its name, is the development of operational thought. An *operation* is an internalized action that is part of an organized structure, while interactions during this period involve *operations upon objects.* The development of operational thought permits the child to classify objects, to seriate objects or events in their proper order, such as small to large or first to last, and to understand part-whole relationships, as in bigger or smaller.

Perhaps the most important development of this period is *conservation,* the ability to maintain relationships between objects despite their physical manipulation. The child who believed during the previous stage that a pizza cut into eight pieces was larger than one cut into only six, now understands that cutting does not change the amount of pizza; it only changes the number and size of the pieces. The ability to conserve permits the child to perceive a certain stability about the world and to make plans for the future.

For counselors, the most important implication of this period is the emergence of more mature forms of role-taking in which the thoughts and intentions of others are taken into account in communications and relationships. Thought is now decentered, dynamic, and reversible. Individuals who are concrete operational thinkers can appreciate a certain lawful nature in the events of the world, which is now in equilibrium with their own system of logic. Just as each new stage is liberating, however, it is also limiting. Piaget has referred to the thinking of this period as concrete operational because it can only be applied to concrete objects that are either mentally or physically present. In effect, the thinking of this period is bound to the concrete reality of what *is* rather than to the abstract reality of what *could be.*

The formal operational period does not typically begin before age twelve. Only in this period does the individual begin to exhibit true abstract thought and the kind of systematic approach to problem solving that represents hypothetico-deductive reasoning. Thinking involves *operations on symbols* and thus is concerned with the *form* of thought itself. During this period thought becomes truly logical, allowing the individual to consider the full range of dimensions to a problem, recognizing reality as only one of many alternative potential solutions.

Possibilities are considered alongside realities as the individual considers what *may be,* no longer limited to what *is.*

Researchers have suggested that an increase in the use of formal thought by adolescents accounts for their idealism and egocentric behavior as characterized by their increased self-consciousness (Inhelder & Piaget, 1958; Kohlberg & Gilligan, 1971). Although full formal operations may represent a developmental advancement achieved by less than half of American adults (Dulit, 1972), few adolescents or adults use concrete operational thought exclusively. Instead, many adolescents are capable of partial formal operations, while most adults are at the higher levels of formal reasoning (Kuhn, Langer, Kohlberg, & Haan, 1977).

Clearly, counselors should be at least at the same stage as their clients if they are to understand fully the nature of the client's problem *as the client understands it.* Moreover, counselors should be capable of formal operational thought if they are to be most effective in helping clients to consider alternative solutions to their current life questions.

Moral, Ethical, and Ego Development

Cognitive development of the kind Piaget described is only a prerequisite to other forms of structural development. Advances in moral, ethical, and ego development all appear to be dependent upon advances in logical development (Kohlberg, 1981, pp. 133–139; Loevinger, 1976, pp. 40–45), so that logical reasoning is a necessary but not sufficient condition for stage advancement in the other constructs. For example, many people are at a higher logical stage than the parallel moral stage, but essentially none are at a higher moral stage than their logical stage (Walker, 1980).

Lawrence Kohlberg (1927–). Kohlberg (1981, 1984) set out to extend into adolescence Piaget's (1932/1965) pioneering investigation of the moral development of children. Instead, he has spent the past thirty years developing his own theory of what he calls "a rational reconstruction of the ontogenesis of justice reasoning" (Kohlberg, 1984, p. 212). In effect, Kohlberg is interested in the development of the reasoning process by which individuals determine what is right or fair in resolving moral conflicts, which are really conflicts of perspective or interest.

As a cognitive-developmental theory of moral development, Kohlberg's theory accepts the Piagetian notion of the structural nature of stages, which occur in an invariant sequence, with each stage arising from and being more cognitively complex than the previous stage. Using a structured interview format in which a series of moral dilemma stories are presented, Kohlberg determines an individual's stage of justice reasoning by assessing how solutions for resolving the moral conflict are justified. How one reasons about the choice defines the *structure* of one's moral judgment, while the particular choice one makes defines the *content* of one's moral judgment. Moral stages, therefore, are structures of moral judgment or of moral reasoning about justice.

Kohlberg's model of moral development (see Table 2-5) consists of three levels, each of which may be thought of as a different orientation or type of relationship between oneself and the expectations of society. Each level consists of two stages. The first five of Kohlberg's stages have been demonstrated empirically, while the sixth stage is "a matter of theoretical and philosophical speculation and further empirical data collection" (Kohlberg, 1984, p. 215).

Level I, the *preconventional level,* is the level of most children under the age of nine and of some adolescents. For individuals at this level, rules and social expectations are outside the self. Recognizing that *conventions* are essentially socially agreed upon and individually accepted rules or expectations, this level represents a period before which the individual is capable of conceiving of such a generalized society, hence the prefix *pre-*. As an alternative, one might as well think of the individual at Level I as *presocial.*

Level II, *the conventional level,* is the level of most adolescents and adults in American society. At this level the self is identified with and conforms to the perceived expectations of others, especially authorities.

At Level III, *the postconventional,* the individual understands and generally accepts society's rules, but this acceptance is based upon an understanding and acceptance of the moral principles that underlie these rules. Because individuals at this level make decisions based on principles rather than rules, they exhibit a *prior-to-society perspective,* which, nonetheless, arises developmentally after they have emerged from the conventional level, hence the term *postconventional.* This level is reached by a minority of adults and usually only after age twenty.

Kohlberg's theory has generated a lot of interest in psychology and philosophy, but its most important contribution has been in its application to problems in education and counseling, wherein Kohlberg has argued for a view of "development as the aim of education" (Kohlberg & Mayer, 1973). Interventions based on Kohlberg's view of moral development (see Erickson & Whiteley, 1980; Kohlberg & Wasserman, 1980; Mosher & Sprinthall, 1970; Reimer, Paolitto, & Hersh, 1983; Sprinthall & Mosher, 1978) stress the following three principles: (1) knowledge of the individual's current level of development; (2) arousal of genuine cognitive conflict about problematic situations, especially

TABLE 2-5 KOHLBERG'S MORAL STAGES

Level and Stage	What is Right	Reasons for Doing Right	Social Perspective of Stage
LEVEL I—PRECONVENTIONAL			
Stage 1—Heteronomous Morality	To avoid breaking rules backed by punishment, obedience for its own sake, and avoiding physical damage to persons and property.	Avoidance of punishment, and the superior power of authorities.	*Egocentric point of view.* Doesn't consider the interests of others or recognize that they differ from the actor's; doesn't relate two points of view. Actions are considered physically rather than in terms of psychological interests of others. Confusion of authority's perspective with one's own.
Stage 2—Individualism, Instrumental Purpose, and Exchange	Following rules only when it is to someone's immediate interest; acting to meet one's own interests and needs and letting others do the same. Right is also what's fair, what's an equal exchange, a deal, an agreement.	To serve one's own needs or interests in a world where you have to recognize that other people have their interests, too.	*Concrete individualistic perspective.* Aware that everybody has his or her own interest to pursue and these conflict, so that right is relative (in the concrete individualistic sense).

LEVEL II—CONVENTIONAL

Stage 3—Mutual Interpersonal Expectations, Relationships, and Interpersonal Conformity	Living up to what is expected by people close to you or what people generally expect of people in your role as son, brother, friend, etc. "Being good" is important and means having good motives, showing concern about others. It also means keeping mutual relationships, such as trust, loyalty, respect and gratitude.	The need to be a good person in your own eyes and those of others. Your caring for others. Belief in the Golden Rule. Desire to maintain rules and authority which support stereotypical good behavior.	*Perspective of the individual in relationships with other individuals.* Aware of shared feelings, agreements, and expectations which take primacy over individual interests. Relates points of view through the concrete Golden Rule, putting yourself in the other guy's shoes. Does not yet consider generalized system perspective.
Stage 4—Social System and Conscience	Fulfilling the actual duties to which you have agreed. Laws are to be upheld except in extreme cases where they conflict with other fixed social duties. Right is also contributing to society, the group, or institution.	To keep the institution going as a whole, to avoid the breakdown in the system "if everyone did it," or the imperative of conscience to meet one's defined obligations.	*Differentiates societal points of view from interpersonal agreement or motives.* Takes the point of view of the system that defines roles and rules. Considers individual relations in terms of place in the system.

	LEVEL III—POSTCONVENTIONAL, or PRINCIPLED		
Stage 5—Social Contract or Utility and Individual Rights	Being aware that people hold a variety of values and opinions, that most values and rules are relative to your group. These relative rules should usually be upheld, however, in the interest of impartiality and because they are the social contract. Some nonrelative values and rights like *life* and *liberty*, however, must be upheld in any society and regardless of majority opinion.	A sense of obligation to law because of one's social contract to make and abide by laws for the welfare of all and for the protection of all people's rights. A feeling of contractual commitment, freely entered upon, to family, friendship, trust, and work obligations. Concern that laws and duties be based on rational calculation of overall utility, "the greatest good for the greatest number."	*Prior-to-society perspective.* Perspective of a rational individual aware of values and rights prior to social attachments and contracts. Integrates perspectives by formal mechanisms of agreement, contract, objective impartiality, and due process. Considers moral and legal points of view; recognizes that they sometimes conflict and finds it difficult to integrate them.
Stage 6—Universal Ethical Principles	Following self-chosen ethical principles. Particular laws or social agreements are usually valid because they rest on such principles. When laws violate these principles, one acts in accordance with the principle. Principles are universal principles of justice: the equality of human rights and respect for the dignity of human beings as individual persons.	The belief as a rational person in the validity of universal moral principles, and a sense of personal commitment to them.	*Perspective of a moral point of view* from which social arrangements derive. Perspective is that of any rational individual recognizing the nature of morality or the fact that persons are ends in themselves and must be treated as such.

Source: From *Essays on Moral Development* (Vol. 2): *The Psychology of Moral Development* (pp. 174-176) by Lawrence Kohlberg, 1984, New York: Harper & Row. Copyright 1984 by Lawrence Kohlberg. Reprinted by permission.

moral ones; and (3) presentation of modes of thought one stage above the person's own. In particular, Kohlberg and his associates (Kohlberg, Kauffman, Scharf, & Hickey, 1974) have delineated six conditions for moral change that have been adapted by Hayes (1985) for use in counseling: (1) considerations of fairness and morality, (2) exposure to cognitive conflict, (3) role-taking opportunities, (4) active participation in decision making, (5) exposure to higher levels of thinking, and (6) intellectual stimulation.

Jane Loevinger (1918–). Loevinger (1966) combined Harry Stack Sullivan's construct of interpersonal maturity and Piaget's structural aspects of hierarchical development in a study of the ego and its development. For Loevinger, the ego is a process much like a gyroscope, which orients the self to the world as the ego strives to master, to integrate, and to make sense of experience. After more than twenty-five years of research using a sentence completion questionnaire (Loevinger & Wessler, 1970), Loevinger has provided a blueprint for the sequential development of conceptions of self, having derived a sequence of milestones for ego development.

Loevinger has described seven stages and two transitions between stages that form a continuum, which closely parallels that presented by Kohlberg (Lambert, 1972), although they are in disagreement about the nature of that relationship (Kohlberg, 1984, pp. 397–401; Loevinger, 1976, p. 441; see Table 2-6). Each stage is a characterology within an age cohort that presents an abstraction the actions of which can be described but which itself cannot be observed directly. Loevinger's highest stage, *Integrated,* is similar to Kohlberg's universal, ethical principles orientation (Stage 6) and to Maslow's self-actualized person and is believed to be reached by only about 1 percent of adults (Loevinger, 1976). As in Kohlberg's scheme, movement to the higher levels of ego development is not inevitable.

Ego level has been shown to be related positively to the ability to be empathic (Kagan & Schneider, 1977) and negatively to dogmatism and external locus of control as they relate to the ability of counselor trainees to respond in a facilitative manner (Carlozzi, Campbell, & Ward, 1982). Swensen (1980) has suggested that clients should be matched with counselors who are one stage above them for therapy to be maximally effective. This allows the counselor to serve as a *pacer* (Dember, 1965) for the client, who attempts to master the complexity presented by the counselor's novel behavior, thus enhancing the client's own complexity (see D'Andrea, 1984).

TABLE 2-6 LOEVINGER'S MILESTONES OF EGO DEVELOPMENT

Stage	Code	Impulse Control, Character Development	Interpersonal Style	Conscious Preoccupations	Cognitive Style
Presocial			Autistic		
Symbiotic	I-1		Symbiotic	Self vs. non-self	
Impulsive	I-2	Impulsive, fear of retaliation	Receiving, dependent, exploitative	Bodily feelings, especially sexual and aggressive	Stereotyping, conceptual confusion
Self-Protective	Δ	Fear of being caught, externalizing blame, opportunistic	Wary, manipulative, exploitative	Self-protection, trouble, wishes, things, advantage, control	
Conformist	I-3	Conformity to external rules, shame, guilt for breaking rules	Belonging, superficial niceness	Appearance, social acceptability, banal feelings, behavior	Conceptual simplicity, stereotypes, cliches
Conscientious-conformist	I-3/4	Differentiation of norms, goals	Aware of self in relation to group, helping	Adjustment, problems, reasons, opportunities (vague)	Multiplicity
Conscientious	I-4	Self-evaluated standards, self-criticism, guilt for consequences, long-term goals and ideals	Intensive, responsible, mutual, concern for communication	Differentiated feelings, motives for behavior, self-respect, achievements, traits, expression	Conceptual complexity, idea of patterning
Individualistic	I-4/5	Add: Respect for individuality	Add: Dependence as an emotional problem	Add: Development, social problems, differentiation of inner life from outer	Add: Distinction of process and outcome
Autonomous	I-5	Add: Coping with conflicting inner needs, toleration	Add: Respect for autonomy, interdependence	Vividly conveyed feelings, integration of physiological and psychological causation of behavior, role conception, self-fulfillment, self in social context	Increased conceptual complexity, complex patterns, toleration for ambiguity, broad scope, objectivity
Integrated	I-6	Add: Reconciling inner conflicts, renunciation of unattainable	Add: Cherishing of individuality	Add: Identity	

NOTE: "Add" means in addition to the description applying to the previous level.
Source: From *Ego Development: Conceptions and Theories* (pp. 24-25) by Jane Loevinger, with the assistance of Augusto Blasi, 1976, San Francisco: Jossey-Bass. Copyright 1976 by Jossey-Bass. Reprinted by permission.

Swensen (1980) has proposed that there may be a decreasing influence of environmental factors on personal decision making as individuals advance to higher levels of ego development. Thus organic and manipulative therapies may be more effective at lower levels, while more insight-oriented therapies may be effective at higher levels. Young-Eisendrath (1985) proposed that the relative success of behaviorally oriented therapies with children and the mentally retarded and the success of psychoanalysis with wealthier and better educated clients may be due, in part, to a proper matching of the therapy with the appropriate client by ego level.

William Perry (1913–). Based on interviews with college undergraduates conducted over a fourteen-year period, Perry and his associates (Perry, 1970) identified changes in students' intellectual and ethical development during the college years. Each of the nine positions in Perry's scheme represents a mode of intellectual development in a cognitive-developmental sequences of stages that moves from a simplistic, categorical to a complex, pluralistic view of knowledge and values (see Tables 2-7 and 2-8). The nine positions may be grouped into three general categories: *dualism, relativism,* and *commitment.*

Dualism. The first three positions represent a dualistic mode of thinking that is used to classify all things into right or wrong. Right Answers exist in the Absolute and are known to Authority, whose job it is to give the Answer to the student. Learning is a matter of finding and mastering the Right Answer. Development through the three positions of this category involves a greater tolerance of ambiguity, which is believed to be a gray area where Authority has not yet found the Answer. In counseling, the dualistic person may accept that certain areas like feelings or advice on child management are areas where nobody really knows the answers although career guidance may be viewed as based on "scientific information" (Young-Eisendrath, 1985, p. 8).

Relativism. The absolute right or wrong conception of knowledge and values of the first three positions gives way in the next three positions to a more relativistic view. Uncertainty becomes legitimate, and everyone is recognized as having a right to an opinion. This view is set up against the view of a limited Authority that recognizes quantitative or scientific knowledge as different but legitimate. Clients at this stage are likely to question the counselor's authority vis-à-vis the authority of other, more scientific helpers such as physicians or possibly psychiatrists.

With position five emerges a capacity to think abstractly, where

TABLE 2-7 PERRY'S SCHEME OF INTELLECTUAL AND ETHICAL DEVELOPMENT

		Labels
Position 1	Authorities know, and if we work hard, read every word, and learn Right Answers, all will be well.	Basic duality
Transition	But what about those Others I hear about? And different opinions? And Uncertainties? Some of our own Authorities disagree with each other or don't seem to know, and some give us problems instead of Answers.	
Position 2	True Authorities must be Right, the others are frauds. We remain Right. Others must be different and Wrong. Good Authorities give us problems so we can learn to find the Right Answer by our own independent thought.	Multiplicity prelegitimate
Transition	But even Good Authorities admit they don't know all the answers *yet!*	
Position 3	Then some uncertainties and different opinions are real and legitimate *temporarily*, even for Authorities. They're working on them to get to the Truth.	Multiplicity subordinate
Transition	But there are *so many* things they don't know the Answers to! And they won't for a long time.	
Position 4a	Where Authorities don't know the Right Answers, everyone has a right to his own opinion; no one is wrong!	Multiplicity (solipsism) coordinate
Transition (and/or)	But some of my friends ask me to support my opinions with facts and reasons.	
Transition	Then what right have They to grade us? About what?	
Position 4b	In certain courses Authorities are not asking for the Right Answer; They want us to *think* about things in a certain way, *supporting* opinion with data. That's what they grade us on.	Relativism subordinate
Transition	But this "way" seems to *work* in most courses, and even outside them.	
Position 5	Then *all* my thinking must be like this, even for Them. Everything is relative but not equally valid. You have to understand how each context works. Theories are not Truth but metaphors to interpret data with. You have to think about your thinking.	Relativism (contextual) generalized
Transition	But if everything is relative, am I relative too? How can I know I'm making the Right Choice?	

Dualism modified ⟶

Relativism discovered ⟶

Position 6	I see I'm going to have to make my own decisions in an uncertain world with no one to tell me I'm Right.	
Transition	I'm lost if I don't. When I decide on my career (or marriage or values), everything will straighten out.	— Commitment foreseen
Position 7	Well, I've made my first Commitment!	— Initial commitment
Transition	Why didn't that settle everything?	
Position 8	I've made several commitments. I've got to balance them—how many, how deep? How certain, how tentative?	— Orientation in commitments
Transition	Things are getting contradictory. I can't make logical sense out of life's dilemmas.	
Position 9	This is how life will be. I must be wholehearted while tentative, fight for my values yet respect others, believe my deepest values right yet be ready to learn. I see that I shall be retracing this whole journey over and over—but, I hope, more wisely.	— Evolving commitments

Commitments in relativism developed ⟶

Source: From "Cognitive and Ethical Growth: The Making of Meaning" by William G. Perry in A. Chickering (Ed.), *The Modern American College* (p. 79), 1981, San Francisco: Jossey-Bass. Copyright 1981 by Jossey-Bass. Reprinted by permission.

TABLE 2-8 KOHLBERG, LOEVINGER, AND PERRY COMPARED

Kohlberg Moral Orientation	Loevinger Ego Level	Perry Intellectual- Ethical Level
	Prosocial	
Punishment and obedience	Impulsive	
Naive instrumental hedonism	Self-protective	Duality
Good relations and approval	Conformist	Multiplicity prelegitimate
Law and order	Conscientious-conformist	Multiplicity
Democratic contract	Conscientious	Relativism
Universal ethical principles	Individualistic	
	Autonomous Integrated	Commitment

Source: From *Ego Development: Conceptions and Theories* (p. 109) by Jane Loevinger, with the assistance of Augusto Blasi, 1976, San Francisco: Jossey-Bass. Copyright 1976 by Jossey-Bass. Adapted by permission.

all knowledge and Authority are now seen to be relative, with neither humanists nor scientists having the Truth. The ability to think about one's own thoughts permits the relativist to contemplate how one is to live if there are no Right or Wrong Answers. This period closes as the student becomes aware of the necessity to form some kind of personal Commitment to resolve this dilemma.

Commitment in relativism. The last three of Perry's stages are more affective than structural. Relativism is accepted, but the student gradually accepts the responsibility to live in a pluralistic world. An initial Commitment in some area provides opportunities to explore the dimensions of multiple responsibilities as the student comes to accept Commitment as an ongoing process through which to express one's personal life-style. Clients who approach counseling at this level recognize that different treatments arise out of different contexts and that the counselor's authority derives from training and experience in matching the client to the appropriate treatment.

Although Perry's scheme has required some adjustment to correct for the discontinuity between earlier and later stages (see Kitchener & King, 1981), his theory is having a broad impact on curriculum development in higher education (Mentkowski, Moeser, & Strait, 1983), career development (Knefelkamp & Slepitza, 1976), and the stimulation of intellectual and ethical development among college students (Stephenson & Hunt, 1980). In counseling, Young-Eisendrath (1985) has used

Perry's scheme to anticipate authority issues in the counselor-client relationship.

Robert Kegan (1946–). For Kegan (1982), the activity of being a person is the activity of meaning-making. "The most fundamental thing that we do with what happens to us is organize it. We literally make sense" (p. 11). For counselors who want to understand their clients, cognition must be recognized as more than what the client knows, however irrational or misinformed that may appear. To understand a client is to enter that region "*between* an event and a reaction to it—the place where it actually *becomes* an event for that person" (Kegan, 1982, p. 2). It is in this *zone of mediation* that counselors will help clients better to make meaning of their experience.

Kegan's developmental scheme presents six stages (see Table 2-9), each of which represents *an evolutionary truce in the natural emergence of the self.* His is a lifespan developmental approach to the study of object relations, which he views as relations to that which some motion has made separate from the self. This motion involves the construction of meaning itself through an evolutionary process whereby objects are differentiated from the self and integrated with the self simultaneously.

Subject-object relations emerge from a lifetime of successive, qualitative differentiations of the self from the world. Thus development describes the course of a person's attempts to emerge from an embeddedness in objects unrecognized to a world of objects to which to relate. As a result, "emergence from embeddedness involves a kind of repudiation, an evolutionary re-cognition that what before was me is not-me" (Kegan, 1982, p. 82).

The most profound implications to be drawn from Kegan's work are in the conscious application of his theory to the practice of counseling. In Kegan's view counseling provides a second-best means of support for a system in which the *natural* facilitation of development has broken down. If personality development is essentially the universal, ongoing process of meaning-making, then the developmental counselor should focus not so much on the stages of development as on the process and its experience by the client. Counseling provides a *holding environment* for the client's efforts to make meaning in the face of crisis, which *is* the transformation of meaning and a movement toward growth. Counseling, like development, involves the loss of the old self and "the dying of a way to know the world which no longer works . . . [from which emerges] a *new* balance . . . a new integration, a new direction" (Kegan, 1982, p. 267).

TABLE 2-9 BALANCES OF SUBJECT AND OBJECT IN KEGAN COMPARED TO SEVERAL DEVELOPMENTAL SCHEMES

	Stage 0 Incorporative	Stage 1 Impulsive	Stage 2 Imperial	Stage 3 Interpersonal	Stage 4 Institutional	Stage 5 Interindividual
Underlying structure (subject vs. object)	S—Reflexes, (sensing, moving) O—None	S—Impulses, perceptions O—Reflexes (sensing, moving)	S—Needs, interests, wishes O—Impulses, perceptions	S—The interpersonal, mutuality O—Needs, interests, wishes	S—Authorship, identity, psychic administration, ideology O—The interpersonal, mutuality	S—Interindividuality, interpenetrability of self systems O—Authorship, identity, psychic administration, ideology
Piaget	Sensorimotor	Preoperational	Concrete operational	Early formal operational	Full formal operational	Post-formal[b] Dialectical?
Kohlberg	—	Punishment and obedience orientation	Instrumental orientation	Interpersonal concordance orientation	Societal orientation	Principled orientation
Loevinger	Presocial	Impulsive	Opportunistic	Conformist	Conscientious	Autonomous
Maslow	Physiological survival orientation	Physiological satisfaction orientation	Safety orientation	Love, affection, belongingness orientation	Esteem and self-esteem orientation	Self-actualization
Erikson	—	Initiative vs. guilt	Industry vs. inferiority	Affiliation vs. abandonment?[a]	Identity vs. identity diffusion	—

[a] I believe Erikson's theory misses a stage between "industry" and "identity." His identity stage—with its orientation to *the self alone*, "who am I?", time, achievement, ideology, self-certainty, and so on—captures something of late adolescence or early adulthood, but it does not really address the period of connection, inclusion, and highly invested mutuality which comes between the more independence-oriented periods of latency and (early adult) identity-formation. [b] Piaget does not posit a post-formal stage. These are my own hunches about where their models point.

Source: From *The Evolving Self: Problem and Process in Human Development* (pp. 86-87) by Robert Kegan, 1982, Cambridge, MA: Harvard University Press. Copyright 1982 by The President and Fellows of Harvard College. Adapted by permission.

PERSISTENT QUESTIONS

Because no one theory satisfactorily explains development in its entirety, the counselor must be familiar with a variety of theories, their methods, their underlying assumptions, and their limitations. Developmental theories help the counselor to describe and explain individual differences that arise when considering the dichotomies of human development. Whether theorists can overcome the biases inherent in their separate approaches to the study of human development remains to be seen (Brabeck & Welfel, 1985). For the present, counselors appear to pick and choose their theory on the basis of what works.

Despite these differences, there seems to be a search within the counseling profession for a unifying method or theory (Hayes, 1984). In the future, counselors "will be searching for a logical consistency in their procedures, and as this consistency evolves, eclecticism, which now ranks as the theory of choice for most counselors, will lose favor to more systematic metatheoretical approaches that provide a rationale for what one is doing" (Ivey, 1980, p. 119). How a single theory can incorporate an affective, cognitive, behavioral approach to individual lifespan development within the context of a changing social environment remains to be seen (see Aubrey, 1980). In the meantime, counselors should be familiar with the assumptions that underlie existing approaches in their efforts to understand and promote their clients' growth and development.

REFERENCES

Adler, A. (1963). *The practice and theory of individual psychology.* Paterson, NJ: Littlefield, Adams.

Adler, A. (1972). *The neurotic constitution.* Freeport, NY: Books for Libraries Press. (Original work published in 1926)

Allport, G. (1961). *Pattern and growth in personality.* New York: Holt, Rinehart & Winston.

Allport, G. (1962). Psychological models for guidance. *Harvard Educational Review, 34,* 373–381.

Anastasi, A. (1958). Heredity, environment, and the question "How?" *Psychological Review, 65,* 197–208.

Anastasi, A. (1968). *Psychological testing* (3rd ed.). New York: Macmillan.

Aubrey, R. (Ed.). (1980). Counseling and the behavioral sciences [Special issue]. *Personnel and Guidance Journal, 58.*

Bandura, A. (1977). *Social learning theory.* Englewood Cliffs, NJ: Prentice-Hall.

Beck, A. (1967). *Depression: Causes and treatment.* Philadelphia: University of Pennsylvania Press.

Berne, E. (1964). *Games people play.* New York: Random House.

Bowlby, J. (1969). *Attachment and loss* (Vol. 1): *Attachment.* New York: Basic Books.

Brabeck, M., & Welfel, E. (1985). Counseling theory: Understanding the trend toward eclecticism from a developmental perspective. *Journal of Counseling and Development, 63,* 343–348.

Buhler, C., & Allen, M. (1972). *Introduction to humanistic psychology.* Monterey, CA: Brooks/Cole.

Carlozzi, A., Campbell, N., & Ward, G. (1982). Dogmatism and externality in locus of control as related to counselor trainee skill in facilitative responding. *Counselor Education and Supervision, 21,* 227–236.

Cattell, R. (1946). *Description and measurement of personality.* Yonkers, NY: World Book Co.

D'Andrea, M. (1984, February). The counselor as pacer. *Counseling and Human Development, 16,* 1–15.

Dember, W. N. (1965). The new look in motivation. *American Scientist, 53,* 409–427.

Dinkmeyer, D., Pew, W., & Dinkmeyer, D., Jr. (1979). *Adlerian counseling and psychotherapy.* Monterey, CA: Brooks/Cole.

Dollard, J., & Miller, N. (1950). *Personality and psychotherapy.* New York: McGraw-Hill.

Dreikurs, R. (1959). Early experiments with group psychotherapy. *American Journal of Psychotherapy, 13,* 882–891.

Dulit, E. (1972). Adolescent thinking a la Piaget. *Journal of Youth and Adolescence, 1,* 281–301.

Egan, G. (1982). *The skilled helper* (2nd ed.). Monterey, CA: Brooks/Cole.

Ellis, A. (1962). *Reason and emotion in psychotherapy.* New York: Lyle Stuart.

Erickson, V. L., & Whiteley, J. (Eds.). (1980). *Developmental counseling and teaching.* Monterey, CA: Brooks/Cole.

Erikson, E. (1950). *Childhood and society.* New York: W. W. Norton.

Erikson, E. (1968a). *Identity: Youth and crisis.* New York: W. W. Norton.

Erikson, E. (1968b). *Young man Luther.* New York: W. W. Norton.

Erikson, E. (1969). *Gandhi's truth.* New York: W. W. Norton.

Evans, H., Benner, H., & Hayes, R. (1985, March). Understanding personality differences using the Myers-Briggs Type Indicator. *Counseling and Human Development, 17,* 1–12.

Evans, R. (1970). *Gordon Allport: The man and his ideas.* New York: E. P. Dutton.

Fischer, K., & Lazerson, A. (1984). *Human development.* New York: W. H. Freeman.

Fox, W. M. (1982). Why we should abandon Maslow's need hierarchy theory. *Journal of Humanistic Education and Development, 21,* 29–32.

Frankl, V. (1963). *Man's search for meaning.* New York: Washington Square Press.

Freud, A. (1946). *The ego and the mechanisms of defense.* New York: International Universities Press. (Original work published 1936)

Freud, S. (1961). Some psychical consequences of the anatomical distinction between the sexes. In J. Strachey (Ed. and Trans.), *The standard edition of the complete psychological works of Sigmund Freud* (Vol. 19). London: Hogarth Press. (Original work published 1925)

Freud, S. (1964). *Moses and monotheism: Standard edition* (Vol. 23). London: Hogarth Press. (Original work published 1939)

Fromm, E. (1941). *Escape from freedom.* New York: Farrar, Straus & Giroux.

Gardner, H. (1978). *Developmental psychology.* Boston: Little, Brown.

Gibbs, J. (1979). The meaning of ecologically oriented inquiry in contemporary psychology. *American Psychologist, 34,* 127–140.

Gilligan, C. (1982). *In a different voice.* Cambridge, MA: Harvard University Press.

Harlow, H., & Harlow, M. (1962, November). Social deprivation in monkeys. *Scientific American, 207,* 136–146.

Havighurst, R. (1976). *Developmental tasks and education* (4th ed.). New York: David McKay.

Hayes, R. (1984). An alternative to rearranging our prejudice. In G. Walz and L. Benjamin (Eds.), *Shaping counselor education programs in the next five years: An experimental prototype for the counselor of tomorrow* (pp. 107–120). Ann Arbor, MI: ERIC/CAPS.

Hayes, R. (1985). Making meaning: Expanding the "C" in BASIC ID. *The Journal of Humanistic Education and Development, 23,* 146–155.

Hayes, R., & Kenney, J. (1983). Search for a system: Developmental paradigms, counseling research, and the *Journal of Counseling Psychology. Journal of Counseling Psychology, 30,* 438–442.

Hempel, C. (1966). *Philosophy of natural science.* Englewood Cliffs, NJ: Prentice-Hall.

Hendricks, G., & Weinhold, B. (1982). *Transpersonal approaches to counseling and psychotherapy.* Denver, CO: Love.

Hosford, R. E. (1980). The Cubberly Conference and the evolution of observational learning strategies. *Personnel and Guidance Journal, 58,* 467–472.

Inhelder, B., & Piaget, J. (1958). *The growth of logical thinking from childhood to adolescence.* New York: Basic Books.

Ivey, A. E. (1980). Counseling 2000: Time to take charge! In J. M. Whiteley & B. R. Fretz (Eds.), *The present and future of counseling psychology* (pp. 113–123). Monterey, CA: Brooks/Cole.

Jacobson, E. (1939). *Progressive relaxation.* Chicago: University of Chicago Press.

Jourard, S. (1971). *The transparent self* (rev. ed.). New York: Van Nostrand.

Jung, C. (1928). *Contributions to analytic psychology.* New York: Harcourt.

Jung, C. (1933). *Psychological types.* New York: Harcourt.

Kagan, N., & Schneider, J. (1977). *Affective sensitivity scale, Form E-A-2.* Ann Arbor, MI: Mason Media.

Kegan, R. (1982). *The evolving self: Problem and process in human development.* Cambridge, MA: Harvard University Press.

Kitchener, K., & King, P. (1981). Concepts of justification and their relationship to age and education. *Journal of Applied Developmental Psychology, 2,* 89–116.

Knefelkamp, L., & Slepitza, R. (1976). A cognitive-developmental model of career development: An adaptation of the Perry scheme. *The Counseling Psychologist, 6,* 53–58.

Kohlberg, L. (1969). Stage and sequence: The cognitive-developmental approach to socialization. In D. Goslin (Ed.), *Handbook of socialization theory and research* (pp. 347–480). New York: Rand McNally.

Kohlberg, L. (1981). *Essays on moral development.* (Vol. 1): *The philosophy of moral development.* San Francisco: Harper & Row.

Kohlberg, L. (1984). *Essays on moral development.* (Vol. 2): *The psychology of moral development.* San Francisco: Harper & Row.

Kohlberg, L., & Gilligan, C. (1971). The adolescent as a philosopher: The discovery of the self in a postconventional world. *Daedalus, 100,* 1051–1086.

Kohlberg, L., Kauffman, K., Scharf, P., & Hickey, J. (1974). *The just community approach to corrections: A manual* (Part I). Cambridge, MA: Moral Education Research Foundation.

Kohlberg, L., & Mayer, R. (1973). Development as the aim of education. *Harvard Educational Review, 43,* 449–496.

Kohlberg, L., & Wasserman, E. (1980). The cognitive-developmental approach and the practicing counselor: An opportunity for counselors to rethink their roles. *Personnel and Guidance Journal, 58,* 559–567.

Kuhn, D., Langer, J., Kohlberg, L., & Haan, N. (1977). The development of formal operations in logical and moral judgment. *Genetic Psychology Monographs, 95,* 97–188.

Kuhn, T. S. (1962). *The structure of scientific revolutions.* Chicago: University of Chicago Press.

Lambert, H. (1972). *A comparison of Jane Loevinger's theory of ego development and Lawrence Kohlberg's theory of moral development.* Unpublished doctoral dissertation, University of Chicago.

Langer, J. (1969). *Theories of development.* New York: Holt, Rinehart & Winston.

Lenneberg, E. (1969). On explaining language. *Science, 164,* 635–643.

Levinson, D. (1978). *The seasons of a man's life.* New York: Ballantine.

Loevinger, J. (1966). The meaning and measurement of ego development. *American Psychologist, 21,* 195–217.

Loevinger, J. (1976). *Ego development: Conceptions and theories.* San Francisco: Jossey-Bass.

Loevinger, J., & Wessler, R. (1970). *Measuring ego development I: Construction and use of a sentence completion test.* San Francisco: Jossey-Bass.

Lorenz, K. (1937). The companion in the bird's world. *Auk, 54,* 245–273.

Maslow, A. (1962). *Toward a psychology of being.* New York: Van Nostrand.

Maslow, A. (1970). *Motivation and personality* (rev. ed.). New York: Harper & Row.

Masters, W., & Johnson, V. (1970). *Human sexual response.* Boston: Little, Brown.

Meichenbaum, D. (1977). *Cognitive behavior therapy.* New York: Plenum.

Mentkowski, M., Moeser, M., & Strait, M. (1983, April). *Using the Perry scheme of intellectual and ethical development as a college outcomes measure: A process and criteria for judging student performance* (Vols. 1 and 2). Paper presented at the meeting of the American Educational Research Association, Montreal.

Mosak, H. (1979). Adlerian psychotherapy. In R. Corsini (Ed.), *Current psychotherapies* (2nd ed., pp. 44–94). Itasca, IL: F. E. Peacock.

Mosher, R., & Sprinthall, N. (1970). Psychological education in the secondary schools: A program to promote individual and human development. *American Psychologist, 25,* 911–924.

Pavlov, I. (1927). *Conditioned reflexes.* New York: Dover.

Perry, W. G., Jr. (1970). *Forms of intellectual and ethical development in the college years.* New York: Holt, Rinehart & Winston.

Piaget, J. (1952). *The origins of intelligence in children.* New York: International Universities Press. (Original work published 1936)

Piaget, J. (1954). *The construction of reality in the child.* New York: Basic Books. (Original work published 1937)

Piaget, J. (1960). The general problems of the psychobiological development of the child. In J. M. Tanner & B. Inhelder (Eds.), *Discussions on child development: Proceedings of the World Health Organization study group on the psychobiological development of the child* (Vol. 1, pp. 3–27). New York: International Universities Press.

Piaget, J. (1965). *The moral judgment of the child.* Glencoe, IL: The Free Press. (Original work published 1932)

Reese, H. W., & Overton, W. F. (1970). Models of development and theories of development. In L. R. Goulet & P. B. Baltes (Eds.), *Life-span developmental psychology: Research and theory* (pp. 115–145). New York: Academic Press.

Reimer, J., Paolitto, D., & Hersh, R. (1983). *Promoting moral growth* (2nd ed.). New York: Longman.

Richardson, K., & Spears, D. (1972). *Race and intelligence.* Baltimore, MD: Penguin.

Rogers, C. (1951). *Client-centered therapy.* Boston: Houghton Mifflin.

Rogers, C. (1961). *On becoming a person.* Boston: Houghton Mifflin.

Rogoff, B., & Wertsch, J. (Eds.). (1984, March). Children's learning in the "zone of proximal development." *New Directions for Child Development, 23.*

Rubin, R. (1978). *Using bibliotherapy: A guide to theory and practice.* Phoenix, AZ: Oryx.

Salter, A. (1949). *Conditioned reflex therapy.* New York: Farrar, Straus.

Sattler, J. M. (1974). *Assessment of children's intelligence.* Philadelphia: W. B. Saunders.

Skinner, B. F. (1953). *Science and human behavior.* New York: Macmillan.

Snarey, J., Kohlberg, L., & Noam, G. (1983). Ego development in perspective: Structural stage, functional phase, and cultural-age periods models. *Developmental Review, 3,* 303–338.

Spitz, R. (1945). Hospitalism: An inquiry into the genesis of psychiatric conditions in early childhood. *Psychoanalytic Study of the Child, 1,* 53–74.

Sprinthall, N., & Mosher, R. (Eds.). (1978). *Value development as the aim of education.* Schenectady, NY: Character Research Press.

Stephenson, B., & Hunt, C. (1980). Intellectual and ethical development: A dualistic curriculum intervention for college students. In V. L. Erickson & J. M. Whiteley (Eds.), *Developmental counseling and teaching* (pp. 200–208). Monterey, CA: Brooks/Cole.

Strong, S. R., & Dixon, D. N. (1971). Expertness, attractiveness, and influence in counseling. *Journal of Counseling Psychology, 18,* 562–570.

Sullivan, H. S. (1953). *The interpersonal theory of psychiatry.* New York: W. W. Norton.

Swensen, C. H. (1980). Ego development and a general model for counseling and psychotherapy. *Personnel and Guidance Journal, 58,* 382–388.

Thorndike, E. L. (1913). *Educational psychology.* New York: Columbia University Press.

Tinbergen, N. (1951). *The study of instinct.* London: Oxford University Press.

Vygotsky, L. (1956). *Selected psychological investigations.* Moscow: Izdstel'sto Pedagogicheskikh Nauk SSSR.

Vygotsky, L. (1962). *Thought and language.* Cambridge, MA: MIT Press.

Vygotsky, L. (1978). *Mind in society: The development of higher psychological properties.* Cambridge, MA: Harvard University Press.

Vygotsky, L. (1981). The genesis of higher mental functions. In J. Wertsch (Ed.), *The concept of activity in Soviet psychology* (p. 165). Armonk, NY: Sharpe.

Walker, L. (1980). Cognitive and perspective-taking prerequisites for moral development. *Child Development, 51,* 131–140.

Watson, J. B. (1919). *Psychology from the standpoint of a behaviorist.* Philadelphia: J. B. Lippincott.

Watson, J. B. (1927, July). The behaviorist looks at instincts. *Harper's Magazine,* p. 233.

Watson, J. B., & Rayner, R. (1920). Conditioned emotional reactions. *Journal of Experimental Psychology, 3,* 1–14.

Welch, I., Tate, R., & Richards, F. (1978). *Humanistic psychology: A sourcebook.* Buffalo, NY: Prometheus.

Werner, H. (1973). *The comparative psychology of mental development* (2nd ed.). New York: International Universities Press. (Original work published 1940)

Wolpe, J. (1958). *Psychotherapy by reciprocal inhibition.* Stanford, CA: Stanford University Press.

Wolpe, J. (1966). The comparative clinical status of conditioning therapies and psychoanalysis. In J. Wolpe, A. Salter, & L. Reyna (Eds.), *The conditioning therapies* (pp. 5–20). New York: Holt, Rinehart & Winston.

Young-Eisendrath, P. (1985, January). Making use of human development theories in counseling. *Counseling and Human Development, 17,* 1–12.

CHAPTER 3
THE HELPING RELATIONSHIP

DeWayne J. Kurpius

Practitioners, theorists, and researchers alike have found that the quality of the helping relationship is a primary factor in determining the effects of helping clients achieve the changes they desire. Kanfer and Goldstein (1980) state,

> There now exists a wide variety of research evidence, from several different types of two-person interactions, to indicate that the quality of the helper-client relationship can serve as a powerful influence upon communication, openness, persuasibility and, ultimately, positive change in the client. (p. 19)

Given that the quality of the counselor-client relationship is so powerful and influential, what makes for a quality relationship? For the counselor, the foremost element is caring. Caring implies a desire to be helpful that comes from within counselors themselves. The caring attitude becomes communicated to the client through the behaviors of the counselor, both verbal and nonverbal. The communication process leads to the second element of a quality relationship, the reciprocal interpersonal nature of helping and being helped. Both counselor and client give of themselves in the helping relationship, establishing an interdependence through caring and reciprocity.

True, some people seem to establish such a helping relationship almost naturally, but for most of us, professional skill training and supervision are needed. Thus, the interdependent part of the counselor, client, and situation equation, which is paramount in order to provide change in the client, is influenced by the attributes, training, and performance of the counselor.

Although we are only beginning to understand some personal characteristics that may be related significantly to an effective helping relationship, we know that some of these characteristics are part of the basic core of a person while others are peripheral to this core. Some basic elements or areas of counselor beliefs that researchers have found essential to effective helping are reported by Kanfer and Goldstein (1980) as: (1) attribution or beliefs about people, (2) a phenomenological view, (3) social power or the helper's feeling about self, (4) the purposes of the helper, and (5) the authenticity of the helper. Carkhuff (1969, vol. 2) summarizes basic helping into what he calls the four R's: "the *right* of the individual to intervene in another person's life, the *responsibility* he must assume when he does intervene, and the *role* he plays in the process of helping . . . and the *realization* of his own resources" (p. xi). Carkhuff considers these four R's basic for counselors engaged in helping.

A more global way to look at counselor characteristics that contribute to a positive helping relationship is to classify counselors by their thinking, feeling, and behaving. Usually these categories are interdependent and reciprocal; that is, sometimes we act based upon well-thought-out plans and sometimes we act based upon how we feel about a situation. At other times, though, the categories are not interdependent or reciprocal because we may act spontaneously without time to think consciously or feel about the situation. When attention is focused on the inner life of the counselor and client simultaneously, the relationship becomes more interdependent and reciprocal. The more interdependent and reciprocal the helping relationship becomes, the more positive and beneficial it becomes for the client.

Kanfer and Goldstein (1980) indicate that as the relationship develops, clients tend to become more open to their feelings, explore these feelings more deeply, and listen to self and others more accurately. The relationship can then serve as a powerful influence for positive change in the client. The power of a relationship like this applies to all helping fields. In medicine the patient will comply with the doctor's orders, in school students often work better for some teachers, and in work settings better work performance is often connected to positive working relationships between supervisor and worker. Such relationships are powerful because certain core elements and building blocks of the relationship are present. These four elements, *human relations core, social influence core, skills core and theory core,* are presented in the text that follows.

HUMAN RELATIONS CORE

There is little question that relationships are essential for effective helping to occur. In order for these relationships to be effective, however, it is essential that special conditions are present. The two researchers who have investigated these conditions and who have repeatedly found a core of conditions in positive working relationships are Rogers (1951) and Carkhuff (1969, 1984). These core conditions are: *empathy, respect* (positive regard), and *genuineness* (congruence). Empathy is the ability to understand others from their internal self or internal frames of reference. It is an accurate understanding of what the client feels and intends. Furthermore, empathy means that the counselor can accurately communicate this understanding to the client. Respect is a positive, nonpossessive, and nonjudgmental attitude toward the client. It is a positive acceptance of the client. Genuineness is the core of an authentic relationship. It is an attempt at transparency, at being who we are as persons as well as counselors.

Responding with Empathy

Research has suggested that empathy is the most powerful factor in bringing about positive change (Rogers, 1961; Carkhuff, 1969). Empathy, by definition, involves understanding another person by using that person's internal self (frame of reference) as the basis for understanding and communication. Brammer and Shostrom (1982) suggest that when one responds empathically to a client, one is trying to "think with, rather than for or about the client. It also is the capacity to respond to another's feelings and experiences as if they were your own" (p. 160). Therefore, understanding and communication are the two essential elements of empathy.

When being empathic, the counselor must not only understand the internal world of the client's thinking, feeling, and behaving, but must also communicate this understanding to the client. The counselor can't say, "I know how you feel" and expect to communicate any real meaning to the client. At the same time, the counselor does not have to "feel" what the client feels; rather the counselor has to conceptualize what the client is feeling.

Learning how to be empathic with clients involves the ability to express not only the meanings of which the client is aware, but also those meanings of which the client is only vaguely aware. This skill involves effort on the counselor's part to give up personal hunches and assumptions and be willing to listen actively to the client's perception of his or her own experience of the problem or need for help. Essentially the counselor blocks out personal beliefs about the client's problem and listens empathically in order to understand the beliefs and feelings of the client so that the client can hear the level of caring. This caring attitude encourages the client to develop a more caring attitude toward himself or herself that in turn allows the client to hear more fully his or her inner experiencing. As the client becomes more congruent with these experiences, the potential for growth increases. Such client growth is a result of the reciprocal nature of the relationship, which the counselor facilitates.

How does the counselor learn to be empathic? Several programs and guidelines for learning to be empathic are available. Possibly the most notable are those developed by Truax and Carkhuff (1967), Carkhuff and Berenson (1967), and Carkhuff (1969, 1984). These researchers found that empathy is the key element in an accurate and effective helping relationship. Their early research found that there are measurable levels of empathic response, and this knowledge has resulted in the development of a scale for measuring the level of empathy communicated by the counselor. The scale shown in Table 3-1 is set up by levels of empathic response, with one being the lowest level of response and five the highest. Various research findings have found consistently that at least a Level 3 response is necessary for the empathic helping response to occur.

Some guidelines for the formulation of empathic responses are helpful during counselor training. Carkhuff (1969) suggests the following:

1. The counselor is most effective in empathically understanding the client if he or she intensely concentrates upon the client's verbal and nonverbal expressions.
2. The counselor is initially most effective when he or she employs responses that are interchangeable with the client's responses.
3. The counselor will most effectively communicate empathic understanding when the language of his or her responses is most attuned to the language of the client.
4. The counselor is most empathically understanding when he or she responds in a feeling tone that is similar to the feeling tone of the client.
5. The most responsive counselor is the most empathically understanding counselor.
6. The counselor is most empathically communicating to the client when, after an interchangeable base of responses are established, he or she tentatively expands and clarifies the client's experiences at higher levels.

TABLE 3-1 EMPATHIC UNDERSTANDING IN INTERPERSONAL PROCESSES: A SCALE FOR MEASUREMENT

Level 1: The verbal and behavioral expressions of the first person either *do not attend to* or *detract significantly* from the verbal and behavioral expressions of the second person(s) in that they communicate significantly less of the second person's feelings than the second person has communicated himself.

Examples: The first person communicates no awareness of even the most obvious, expressed surface feelings of the second person. The first person may be bored or uninterested or simply operating from a preconceived frame of reference which totally excludes that of the other person(s).

In summary, the first person does everything but express that he is listening, understanding, or being sensitive to even the feelings of the other person in such a way as to detract significantly from the communications of the second person.

Level 2: While the first person responds to the expressed feelings of the second person(s), he does so in such a way that he subtracts *noticeable affect from the communications* of the second person.

Examples: The first person may communicate some awareness of obvious surface feelings of the second person, but his communications drain off a level of the affect and distort the level of meaning. The first person may communicate his own ideas of what may be going on, but these are not congruent with the expressions of the second person.

In summary, the first person tends to respond to other than what the second person is expressing or indicating.

Level 3: The expressions of the first person in response to the expressed feelings of the second person(s) are essentially *interchangeable* with those of the second person in that they express essentially the same affect and meaning.

Example: The first person responds with accurate understanding of the surface feelings of the second person, but may not respond to or may misinterpret the deeper feelings.

In summary, the first person is responding so as to neither subtract from nor add to the expressions of the second person, but he does not respond accurately to how that person really feels beneath the surface feelings. Level 3 constitutes the minimal level of facilitative interpersonal functioning.

Level 4: The responses of the first person add noticeably to the expressions of the second person(s) in such a way as to express feelings a level deeper than the second person was able to express himself.

Example: The facilitator communicates his understanding of the expressions of the second person at a level deeper than they were expressed, and thus enables the second person to experience and/or express feelings he was unable to express previously.

In summary, the facilitator's responses add deeper feeling and meaning to the expressions of the second person.

Level 5: The first person's responses add significantly to the feeling and meaning of the expressions of the second person(s) in such a way as to (1) accurately express feelings levels below what the person himself was able to express or (2) in the event of on-going deep self-exploration on the second person's part, to be fully with him in his deepest moments.

Examples: The facilitator responds with accuracy to all of the person's deeper as well as surface feelings. He is "together" with the second person or "tuned in" on his wave length. The facilitator and the other person might proceed together to explore previously unexplored areas of human existence.

In summary, the facilitator is responding with a full awareness of who the other person is and a comprehensive and accurate empathic understandings of his deepest feelings.

Source: From *Helping and Human Relations* (Vol. 2, pp. 315-317) by Robert R. Carkhuff, 1969, New York: Holt, Rinehart & Winston. Copyright 1969 by Robert R. Carkhuff. Reprinted by permission.

7. The counselor will most effectively communicate empathic understanding when he or she concentrates on the nonverbal expressions of the client.
8. The counselor will most effectively communicate empathic understanding when he or she is guided by the client's behavior in assessing the effectiveness of his or her own responses.

Ivey (1983) suggests that three types of empathy exist: *basic empathy, subtractive empathy,* and *additive empathy.* In basic empathy, the counselor responses are roughly interchangeable with those of the client. In subtractive empathy, the counselor's response usually takes something away from the client. In additive empathy, congruent ideas and feelings are added. These additions are basic to the client but have not previously reached his or her awareness. Ivey's examples of five levels of empathy in response to a client are shown in Table 3-2. (For a discussion of empathy from a multicultural perspective, see Chapter 6.)

TABLE 3-2 LEVELS OF EMPATHY

Client: I don't know what to do. I've gone over this problem again and again. My husband just doesn't seem to understand that I don't really care anymore. He just keeps trying, but it doesn't seem worth bothering with him anymore.

Level 1 Counselor *(subtractive):* That's not a very good way to talk. I think you ought to consider his feelings, too.

Level 2 Counselor *(slightly subtractive):* Seems like you've just about given up on him. You don't want to try anymore.

Level 3 Counselor *(basic empathy or interchangeable response):* You're discouraged and confused. You've worked over the issues with your husband, but he doesn't seem to understand. At the moment, you feel he's not worth bothering with. You don't really care.

Level 4 Counselor *(slightly additive):* You've gone over the problem with him again and again to the point you don't really care right now. You've tried hard. What does all this mean to you?

Level 5 Counselor *(additive):* I sense your hurt and confusion and that right now you really don't care anymore. Given what you've told me, your thoughts and feelings make a lot of sense to me. At the same time, you've had a reason for trying so hard. You've talked about some deep feelings of caring for him in the past. How do you put that together right now with what you are feeling?

Source: From *Intentional Interviewing and Counseling*, by A. Ivey. Copyright © 1983 by Wadsworth, Inc. Reprinted by permission of Brooks/Cole Publishing Company, Monterey, California 93940.

Responding with Respect

Respect is the ability to hold the person being helped in the highest regard and to value that person as someone with dignity and worth

(Rogers, 1957). When full respect and regard are given, the counselor places no conditions on the level of acceptance. The client is accepted because of his or her humanness and is given the freedom to manifest personal behavior or feelings without fear of judgement. These deeply held beliefs about helping are internal to the counselor and must be present in the counselor before unconditional respect can be communicated to and understood by the client.

Because the counselor's reality is different from the client's, a counselor does not always find it easy to accept others unconditionally. It is important to be aware of what level of respect the counselor is feeling and thinking. This awareness must then be communicated to the client. Rogers (1967) has found that most often our doubts or negative feelings about a client tend to reflect our own values and concerns more than a client's. For example, because you hold to a certain set of moral values, you may have difficulty accepting a client who does not share those values. To pretend acceptance interferes with the helping relationship even more than failure to accept differences.

As in the case of empathy training and assessment, a scale has been developed for the training and assessment of respect. The respect scale presented by Carkhuff (1969) also establishes Level 3 as a minimal response and is shown in Table 3-3.

Examples of counselor responses, from least to most facilitative, include (Carkhuff, 1969):

Client: The client questions his/her ability to handle a worsening school situation despite his/her diligent efforts.
1. Counselor: I suggest you study harder.
2. Counselor: You should leave school.
3. Counselor: You are confused about whether you continue school or leave.
4. Counselor: Even though your efforts in school have not worked so far, you're determined that if you can change directions, you will succeed.
5. Counselor: You are raising some basic questions about yourself in relation to you. You're not certain about your abilities, about where your life is headed, about who you are.

Responding with Genuineness

Genuineness, like empathy and respect, begins with the self. If counselors want to be genuine in their relationships, how do they think, feel, and behave?

THE HELPING RELATIONSHIP 103

TABLE 3-3 THE COMMUNICATION OF RESPECT IN INTERPERSONAL PROCESSES: A SCALE FOR MEASUREMENT

Level 1: The verbal and behavioral expressions of the first person communicate a clear lack of respect (or negative regard) for the second person(s).

Example: The first person communicates to the second person that the second person's feelings and experiences are not worthy of consideration or that the second person is not capable of acting constructively. The first person may become the sole focus of evaluation.

In summary, in many ways the first person communicates a total lack of respect for the feelings, experiences, and potentials of the second person.

Level 2: The first person responds to the second person in such a way as to communicate little respect for the feelings, experiences, and potentials of the second person.

Example: The first person may respond mechanically or passively or ignore many of the feelings of the second person.

In summary, in many ways the first person displays a lack of respect or concern for the second person's feelings, experiences, and potentials.

Level 3: The first person communicates a positive respect and concern for the second person's feelings, experiences, and potentials.

Example: The first person communicates respect and concern for the second person's ability to express himself and to deal constructively with his life situation.

In summary, in many ways the first person communicates that who the second person is and what he does matters to the first person. Level 3 constitutes the minimal level of facilitative interpersonal functioning.

Level 4: The facilitator clearly communicates a very deep respect and concern for the second person.

Example: The facilitator's response enables the second person to feel free to be himself and to experience being valued as an individual.

In summary, the facilitator communicates a very deep caring for the feelings, experiences, and potentials of the second person.

Level 5: The facilitator communicates the very deepest respect for the second person's worth as a person and his potentials as a free individual.

Example: The facilitator cares very deeply for the human potentials of the second person.

In summary, the facilitator is committed to the value of the other person as a human being.

Source: From *Helping and Human Relations* (Vol. II, pp. 319-320, by Robert R. Carkhuff, 1969, New York: Holt, Rinehart & Winston. Copyright 1969 by Robert R. Carkhuff. Reprinted by permission.

According to Egan (1977), genuine people do not role-play, nor do they change their values when they are with different people. Genuine people are comfortable with experiencing things, permitting this into their awareness, and expressing this to the client. Humans who are in need of help are more able to relate and disclose to someone who is real and who is perceived as genuine.

People who behave according to their values and perceptions are genuine and behave accordingly. These people behave according to an internally consistent theoretical or philosophical position. Counselors who desire to be totally visible to the client convey the impression of confidence. Therefore, counselors who are genuine can disclose themselves and still maintain the client's confidence.

As in empathy and respect training, a scale is provided to assess genuineness and to provide a guide for improving genuineness. The scale provided by Carkhuff (1969) is shown in Table 3-4. The client problem below shows examples of five levels of counselor response, from least to most facilitative:

Client: I'm so disappointed. I thought we could get along together and you could help me. We don't seem to be getting anywhere. You don't understand me. You don't know I'm here. I don't even think you care for me. You don't hear me when I talk. You seem to be somewhere else. Your responses are independent of anything I have to say. I don't know where to turn. I'm just so—doggone it—I don't know what I'm going to do, but I know you can't help me. There is just no hope.

Level 1 response: I have no reason to try and not to help you. I have every reason to want to help you.

Level 2 response: Only when we establish mutual understanding and trust and only then can we proceed to work on your problem effectively.

Level 3 response: It's disappointing and disillusioning to think you have made so little progress.

Level 4 response: I feel badly that you feel that way. I do want to help. I'm wondering, "Is it me? Is it you, both of us?" Can we work something out?

Level 5 response: I know I hear you saying you really have to know and now!—but—No! I haven't shared all. You'll have to convince me that I should. (Carkhuff, 1969, pp. 122, 186)

Based on the human relations core of empathy, respect, and genuineness, it is apparent that a central core of attitudes, beliefs, perceptions, and skills are needed to function as the best helper one is able to become. Although some people seem to be able to develop these attributes and skills through personal experience, most have found that special training and supervision are necessary.

SOCIAL INFLUENCE CORE

There are still other factors that are necessary to consider when engaging in helping relationships. The social influence core helps us to look at how we view ourselves as humans and how we believe others view us. Cormier and Cormier (1979) state that *self-image* is a quality that has significant influence on how we are able to function as helpers.

TABLE 3-4 FACILITATIVE GENUINENESS IN INTERPERSONAL PROCESSES: A SCALE FOR MEASUREMENT

Level 1: The first person's verbalizations are clearly unrelated to what he is feeling at the moment, or his only genuine responses are negative in regard to the second person(s) and appear to have a totally destructive effect upon the second person.

Example: The first person may be defensive in his interaction with the second person(s) and this defensiveness may be demonstrated in the content of his words or his voice quality. Where he is defensive, he does not employ his reaction as a basis for potentially valuable inquiry into the relationship.

In summary, there is evidence of a considerable discrepancy between the inner experiencing of the first person(s) and his current verbalizations. Where there is no discrepancy, the first person's reactions are employed solely in a destructive fashion.

Level 2: The first person's verbalizations are slightly unrelated to what he is feeling at the moment, or when his responses are genuine, they are negative in regard to the second person; the first person does not appear to know to employ his negative reactions constructively as a basis for inquiry into the relationship.

Example: The first person may respond to the second person(s) in a "professional" manner that has a rehearsed quality or a quality concerning the way a helper "should" respond in that situation.

In summary, the first person is usually responding according to his prescribed role rather than expressing what he personally feels or means. When he is genuine, his responses are negative, and he is unable to employ them as a basis for further inquiry.

Level 3: The first person provides no "negative" cues between what he says and what he feels, but he provides no positive cues to indicate a really genuine response to the second person(s).

Example: The first person may listen and follow the second person(s) but commits nothing more of himself.

In summary, the first person appears to make appropriate responses that do not seem insincere but do not reflect any real involvement either. Level 3 constitutes the minimal level of facilitative interpersonal functioning.

Level 4: The facilitator presents some positive cues indicating a genuine response (whether positive or negative) in a nondestructive manner to the second person(s).

Example: The facilitator's expressions are congruent with his feelings, although he may be somewhat hesitant about expressing them fully.

In summary, the facilitator responds with many of his own feelings, and there is no doubt as to whether he really means what he says. He is able to employ his responses, whatever their emotional content, as a basis for further inquiry into the relationship.

Level 5: The facilitator is freely and deeply himself in a nonexploitative relationship with the second person(s).

Example: The facilitator is completely spontaneous in his interaction and open to experiences of all types, both pleasant and hurtful. In the event of hurtful responses the facilitator's comments are employed constructively to open a further area of inquiry for both the facilitator and the second person.

In summary, the facilitator is clearly being himself and yet employing his own genuine responses constructively.

Source: From *Helping and Human Relations* (Vol 2, pp. 319-320) by Robert R. Carkhuff, 1969, New York: Holt, Rinehart & Winston. Copyright 1969 by Robert R. Carkhuff. Reprinted by permission.

They have identified three areas of self-image that can be problematic when misunderstood by oneself or miscommunicated to the clients. These three areas are *competence, power,* and *intimacy.* In this same domain of social influence, Dixon and Glover (1984) report that in a helping situation "the counselor seeks to enhance social power or ability to influence the client in order to contribute to client change" (p. 77). They have found in the counseling research literature that counselors' social power is influenced by the client's *receptiveness* of the helper's *expertness, attractiveness,* and *trustworthiness* and that these variables are reciprocally determined by the client and counselor. Following are brief descriptions of the sources that are reported to be part of the social influence core that helps people change.

Competence

The lack of competence is defined by Cormier and Cormier (1979) as feeling a lack of personal adequacy and is often associated with the fear of succeeding or failing. Counselors who feel inadequate often engage in negative self-statements such as "I'm not an effective helper" or "I'm no good." These feelings and cognitions are communicated to clients both directly by the client experiencing the lack of a meaningful relationship and indirectly by the counselor avoiding client issues that are perceived by the counselor to be too threatening.

Counselors who feel competent manifest this feeling by asking for feedback, accepting mistakes, or sharing that they are puzzled about what to do. Competent counselors are also more likely to set realistic expectations for the client and behave positively toward the client but at the same time hold the client responsible for incongruencies.

Power

Power is considered to be the ability to influence while authority is the ability to control. Power and control cannot be generalized as negative connotations in counseling, however. Counselors who rely primarily on listening and reflection of feelings and content with the client may feel powerless and fear the consequences of becoming more influential or taking greater helper risk. At other times, however, feelings of powerlessness may cause the counselor to become rigid or coercive and to want to convert the client overtly to a particular point of view.

Intimacy

Cormier and Cormier (1979) state that "generally, a counselor who has trouble with intimacy may fear rejection or be threatened by closeness and affection" (p. 14). Such fears tend to cause interpersonal distance in the helping relationship. The fear of being discovered as not being lovable and then being rejected may cause the counselor to behave in ways that prevent accurate communication such as confronting the client about a discrepancy between verbal and nonverbal behavior. Ultimately, only people who can be sincere and open with each other can enter into an intimate relationship. Close emotional relationships require genuine commitment to each other and although the experience can be demanding and even threatening, it can also be very rewarding.

Expertness

As you will see, there is some similarity between expertness and competence, but there is also a difference. Counseling expertness exists when the client believes that the counselor has the proper training, reputation, and behaviors to be helpful (Dixon & Glover, 1984). According to Kerr, Claiborn, and Dixon (1982) expertness is established during the interviews but can be established prior to the interview as well. During the interview the counselor's model of expertness can range from the basics of eye contact and general attending to being active and demonstrating effective use of extended knowledge and process skills. Before the interview expertness can be communicated by the physical setting such as a comfortable office with diplomas and certificates on the wall and proper physical appearance of the staff. Also important is the manner in which the counselor's title, status, and experience are communicated to the client. Following social psychology theory, all these factors have an impact on the client's ability to be influenced in a positive way.

Expertness is manifest in a variety of ways and is especially impactful at the early stages of counseling. A statement by Schmidt and Strong (cited in Cormier & Cormier, 1984) depicted how college students described an expert helper:

> The expert shakes the student's hand, aligning the student with himself, and greets him with his first name. He seems interested and relaxed. He has a neat appearance but is not stuffy. . . . He talks at the student's level and is not arrogant toward him. The expert assumes a comfortable but attentive sitting position. He focuses his attention on the student and carefully listens to him.

His voice is inflective and lively, he changes his facial expressions and uses hand gestures. He speaks fluently with confidence and sureness. The expert has prepared for the interview.... He asks direct and to-the-point questions. His questions are thought-provoking and follow an apparently logical progression. They seem spontaneous and conversational.... The expert moves quickly to the root of the problem.... He makes recommendations and suggests possible solutions. (p. 34)

Attractiveness

Interpersonal attractiveness is defined by Schmidt and Strong (1971) and Dixon and Glover (1984) as the client's positive thinking and feeling about the counselor. Attributes that influence attractiveness are related to the human relations core of empathy, respect, and genuineness. For example, counselor self-disclosure of feelings, attitudes, and experiences that are similar to those held by the client cause attractiveness to strengthen. Such perceived similarity, liking, and compatibility determine the client's attractiveness to the counselor and can influence the quality of the working relationship.

Trustworthiness

Even though trust is accorded to certain high-status professionals such as physicians, in counseling trustworthiness tends to occur more slowly. It is slower to develop primarily because it is based on the congruence that the client perceives in the counselor's verbal and nonverbal behavior and/or the counselor's demonstrated interest in helping as being greater than interest in economic or other personal gain. Violating confidentiality, engaging in irrelevant talk, not attending to client concerns, or cutting sessions short will reduce trust held by the client. Clients also view reliability and dependability as important trust-building counselor behaviors. Dixon and Glover (1984) report that the perceptions of trust across cultural groups such as Blacks, Whites, and Native Americans are similar and equally powerful for effecting change.

SKILLS CORE

Up to this point we have focused mostly on the helper as a person. Although the human qualities of the helper are of great importance, there are certain interviewing skills that are also essential for effective helping to take place. Perhaps the most accepted descriptors for defining and learning basic interviewing skills were developed by Allen Ivey. Ivey (1983) states that "microskills are communication skill units of the interview that will help you to develop a more intentional and rounded ability to interact with a client. They will provide specific alternatives for you to use with different types of clients" (p. 4). Ivey has also developed a hierarchy of successive steps for interviewing. The foundation of the hierarchy is based on *attending behavior* and then moves through *basic observing, listening,* and *questioning* skills; up to more *influential* and *confrontive* skills and finally to *skill integration,* which brings full understanding within different cultural situations or theoretical foundations. The skills presented here are those most commonly used and considered basic to all types of interviewing and helping roles.

Attending Behavior

Attending behavior in helping is just that, giving full attention to the client in a thinking, feeling, and behavioral way. Such attention communicates interest and respect, which increase the client's awareness of the counselor's caring and commitment to helping. Attention also reinforces clients to talk about themselves and to believe that the counselor is listening.

Attending behavior is easily observed and begins with general body posture. Sit comfortably facing the client squarely with direct eye contact. In this basic position a general message of openness, availability, and interest is communicated. Leaning forward and smiling while keeping eye contact are added ways to practice good attending behavior. Lastly, verbal attending, sometimes called *verbal tracking* or staying on the topic, and maintaining an appropriate vocal tone can add to the quality of attending.

Offering attention is more than an overt behavioral act. It is also being there with the person in a covert, psychological way. Egan (1975) and Cormier, Cormier, and Weisser (1984) suggest that the most important psychological factor is the counselor's freedom from internal distractions. Attending fully, that is applying the counselor's complete thinking, feeling, and behavior toward the client, has a facilitative dimension for the counselor as well as for the client. Research has found that during *task-facilitative* behavior the counselor's internal dialogue (the thinking and covert self-talk of the counselor) is about the client's conditions, and during *task-distractive* time the counselor's internal dialogue is about the counselor's needs, worries, or other distractions (Kurpius & Morran, 1985). This finding lends strong support for offering full attention because as the counselor becomes able to offer full thinking, feeling, and behavioral attention to the client, a solid connection is made between counselor and client that adds strength to the relationship and the potential for helping and being helped. Essentially, complete overt and covert attending forms the basic foundation of the helping relationship.

Inquiring

Inquiring is a joint venture between counselor and client. At the outset inquiring is counselor-induced with an *open-ended question* such as, "How can I be helpful?" This basic opening question begins the client's internal process of thinking and feeling about "How can I be helped?" "What is my real problem?" or "Can I trust this person to understand and accept me with my problem?" Later on the inquiry process deepens and takes on a more active exploratory analysis and synthesis process.

The counselor is instrumental in modeling and encouraging the client to inquire into feelings, beliefs, and behavior. "What is not going well?" and "What do I want to improve?" are two basic questions. Other questions are "How much change am I willing to ask of myself at this time?" and "What resources do I have as a person to make these changes?" Still other inquiring questions are "What do these feelings mean?" "Is my thinking clear?" "What behaviors should I modify?" or "Do I need to make an environmental change?"

The counselor behavior that produces client inquiry begins with asking open-ended questions, encouraging clients to reflect on themselves and to verbalize needs, hurts, confusion, or expectations. Open questions cause clients to attend to themselves and to talk more freely and openly.

There are also questions that can't be answered with a few words. Ivey (1983) states that open questions begin with what, how, why, or could. As an example, Ivey (1983) suggests a good opening question would be, "Could you tell me what brings you here today?" (p. 41).

Closed-type questions, on the other hand, lead clients to assume that the counselor is in charge. Less introspection occurs and brief, content-oriented responses result. Ivey (1983) suggests that "closed questions often begin with *is, are, do*. An example is 'Are you dining with your family?' " (p. 41).

Cormier, Cormier, and Weisser (1984) have found two additional types of questions that have proven useful in medical settings. These are *focused questioning* and *laundry list questioning.* Focused questions as defined by Cormier, Cormier and Weisser (1984) "are used when the patient is having difficulty responding to an open-ended question" (p. 131). Because focused questions often begin with "Have you," "Can you," or "Do you," such as "Can you describe your illness?" which might be answered with a "yes" or "no," there is a fine line between closed questions and focused questions. It is an important fine line, however, in cases where the traditional open-ended question is ineffective.

Cormier, Cormier, and Weisser (1984) report using laundry list questioning for the patient who has difficulty remembering or lacks knowledge or terminology to describe certain symptoms or illnesses. This approach, often used in the medical field or other technical fields, involves a list of items or questions to refine the information that was initially gained from an open question, the response to which is pursued by a focused question.

A series of points to remember for effective inquiry are stated by Evans, Hearn, Uhlemann, and Ivey (1984) as:

1. Ask a question that cannot be answered with "yes," "no," or a simple fact.
2. Ask a question that is on topic.
3. "What" questions are frequently fact-oriented.
4. "How" questions are frequently people-oriented.
5. "Could" and "can" questions provide greatest flexibility for response.
6. "Why" questions often provoke defensive feelings and are not recommended. (p. 41)

Reflection of Content, Paraphrase, and Summarization

In *reflection of content* it is important to *paraphrase* the cognitive aspects of a client's statement or to *summarize* the collective meaning of a series of statements. The purpose is to rephrase or summarize what the client has stated as a way to validate your accuracy, encourage continued discussion, or confirm greater cognitive understanding for the client (Cormier, Cormier, & Weisser, 1984). Sometimes it is also used to delay focusing on the affective side of the situation when doing so might be premature for the client. Evans, Hearn, Uhlemann, and Ivey (1984) warn that one should not "parrot" the client's message because doing so causes circular patterns to develop in the session. In post-interviews clients report discomfort, boredom, and sometimes anger toward interviewers who engage in parroting.

Reflection of Feeling

Whereas reflection of content is focused on cognition, *reflection of feeling* is an emotion statement. Reflection of feeling is a statement made by the counselor that describes and clarifies the client's present feelings. Sometimes clients are very aware of what they are thinking but are not as aware or do not understand the meaning of their feelings. Because the counselor hears and values feelings, reflecting client feelings can help clients to feel understood and accepted by the counselor which, in turn, leads to better client self-understanding.

Three steps to reflecting feelings are stated by Cormier, Cormier, and Weisser (1984) as: Learn to identify the feelings and the emotional tone of a client statement, watch for nonverbal cues to help clarify affective states, and use affective words that communicate the feeling of the client.

It should be noted that reflection of feeling is a powerful technique when used properly and that overuse can cause clients to introspect beyond their capability to understand and productively process the emotional experience. At other times, especially with beginning interviewers, there is a tendency to use reflection-of-feeling words without a true understanding of the client's feelings. An even more common error is repeatedly to use the question "How do you feel about that?" or restate a client statement using a lead such as "You feel that." These are cognitive statements, and seldom is the client able to identify a particular feeling and pursue that feeling. Feelings are reflected only when the statement is a reflection of the client's personal experience of that feeling.

Most feelings fall into three categories: *positive feelings, negative feelings,* or *ambivalent feelings.* These three feeling states are categorized by Cormier, Cormier, and Weisser (1984) as happiness, sadness, fear, uncertainty, and anger. They also have developed a collection of words for each of these five categories that will help the counselor to recognize and be able to reflect these feeling states to the client. These words are presented in Table 3-5.

Skills are the actual interviewing behaviors that the helper uses to communicate with the client. Although developing and refining these skills is important, it is the appropriate use of a given skill in a given situation that is the ultimate goal of learning how to be a better helper.

THE THEORY CORE

At this point we have established that in helping relationships helpers can increase effectiveness by learning more about self, human rela-

TABLE 3-5 LIST OF COMMONLY USED AFFECTIVE WORDS

Happiness	Sadness	Fear	Uncertainty	Anger
Happy	Discouraged	Scared	Puzzled	Upset
Pleased	Disappointed	Anxious	Confused	Frustrated
Satisfied	Hurt	Frightened	Unsure	Bothered
Glad	Despairing	Defensive	Uncertain	Annoyed
Optimistic	Depressed	Threatened	Skeptical	Irritated
Good	Disillusioned	Afraid	Doubtful	Resentful
Relaxed	Dismayed	Tense	Undecided	Mad
Content	Pessimistic	Nervous	Bewildered	Outraged
Cheerful	Miserable	Uptight	Mistrustful	Hassled
Thrilled	Unhappy	Uneasy	Insecure	Offended
Delighted	Hopeless	Worried	Bothered	Angry
Excited	Lonely	Panicked	Disoriented	Furious

Source: From *Interviewing Strategies for Helpers: A Guide to Assessment, Treatment and Evaluation* (p. 69) by L.S. Cormier and W. H. Cormier, 1979, Monterey, CA: Brooks/Cole. Copyright © 1979 by Wadsworth, Inc. Reprinted by permission.

tions, skills, and situations. One additional factor for increasing effectiveness is to understand how different theories can guide the helper to understand the client's problems more fully and accurately and to choose the intervention that is likely to be most effective. Learning to use theory as a guide to helping is not as demanding as one would think because even inexperienced helpers work from a frame of reference that is grounded with some assumptions and future outcomes. At the outset beginners try out different theories to determine what seems helpful. They learn that some theories follow techniques that are less personal and more analytic. As personal experience becomes more grounded in theory and research, counselors learn that different theories help the counselor view the client from more than one perspective; as a result they may learn ways to be more helpful with a greater range of client differences.

Since the time of Freud when it was found that one approach was not successful with all clients, many theories have been developed. In 1975 the National Institute of Mental Health recognized the existence of over 130 different approaches to therapeutic practice in which the helping relationship was found to be influential. These approaches can be viewed as different ways to integrate and synthesize the human relations, social influence, and skills cores already mentioned. Because of space limitations for dealing with 130 approaches, Corey's (1982) classification will be used as the model to organize these approaches within the context of the helping relationship. In addition, each of the various cores will be integrated into each theory to demonstrate how theory and practice are interconnected.

The Helping Relationship from the Psychoanalytic View

The development of a growing relationship with the client is basic to the psychoanalytic process (see Chapter 2). Rather than the relationship being considered a reciprocal process that creates an interdependence between the counselor, client, and situation, it is focused more on teaching the client meanings of past behaviors, thoughts, and feelings, so that client awareness increases and change occurs. Following the psychoanalytic approach, the counselor shares little personally in the relationship. The psychoanalytically oriented counselor attempts to understand the client—to be empathic—but uses the model of the id, ego, and superego personality structure rather than the client's own frame of reference to organize the process. Respect for the client is essential, although sharing this regard verbally would be unlikely. The behaviors that would express the counselor's genuineness would be seen in adopting consistently the expert role and in being nondefensive (understood in terms of the transference relationship). Being open and willing to share should be seen in the use of interpretations of the client's behaviors, thoughts, and feelings; very little of the psychoanalytically oriented counselor's personal feelings, thoughts, and behaviors would be shared.

Moving into the social influence components, the areas of competence and expertness become important. The counselor must be competent and be viewed by the client as an expert in interpreting the shared verbalizations. The training, reputation, and behaviors of the counselor all contribute to the client's view of the counselor as expert in the field. Because much of the process of psychoanalysis is new and different for the client, the counselor who uses this approach has the potential for using the power of the relationship to influence the client as changes are made.

Intimacy may not develop between the client and counselor, as the genuine commitment to each other may not be shared directly. The counselor is committed to helping teach the client the meaning of current behavior as related to the client's past, but the sharing of oneself by the counselor is not a foundational concept in psychoanalysis. The issues of attractiveness and trustworthiness are seen as components of the conflicts and projections that are uncovered via *free association, dream analysis,* and *interpretations.*

The skills of attending and inquiring are used often by the psychoanalytically oriented counselor to uncover resistances and conflicts. Reflection of content and feeling, summarizing, and paraphrasing would all be used less by the counselor in a psychoanalytic approach than would free association, dream analysis, hypnosis, transference analysis, interpretation, and analysis of the counselor's countertransference feelings for the client. (For a discussion of transference and countertransference in a multicultural context, see Chapter 6.) The psychoanalytically oriented counselor encourages the client to develop resistance and transference in order to enable the client to experience crises, work through them, and make changes before the relationship is terminated.

The Helping Relationship from an Existential-Humanistic View

The core of the existential-humanistic helping relationship (see Chapter 2) is the belief that persons are responsible for their own lives, that people are inherently good, that they have a natural tendency to move toward growth and authentic behavior, that anxiety can stimulate individuals toward that growth, that the here and now is important, and that people have freedom to choose. The counselor encourages the client to become fully aware of the present moment; empathy becomes crucial as the counselor endeavors to understand the client's internal self. The relationship is mutually interdependent as both the counselor and client seek to increase their awareness and both can be changed by the process. The respect that the counselor has for the client is manifested in regarding the client highly. The counselor will explore personal feelings and beliefs about the client and will share them openly. The relationship is a genuine exchange between the two people—full of spontaneous, nondefensive interactions that consistently show to the other person what the relationship is.

The counselor's competency and expertness would be evident as the relationship progresses, with the counselor setting realistic expectations for the client and yet expecting the client to take responsibility for incongruencies. Expertness is manifested as the counselor helps the client to integrate polarities and dichotomies held by the client. Focusing on the present allows the client to discover that hanging onto the past only justifies an unwillingness to take responsibility for oneself. The power in an existential-humanistic relationship stems from the willingness of the counselor to experience the present, the counselor's expertise in helping the client to work on unfinished business, and the counselor's observations of body messages and blocks to awareness that the client may have.

An intimate relationship will develop between these two people as they share the experience of encountering themselves and taking charge of making responsible decisions. Confrontations about discrepancies between verbal and nonverbal behaviors will be shared with the client. Trustworthiness will be modeled for the client as the counselor helps the client, remains congruent in his or her own verbal and nonverbal behavior, and maintains confidentiality. The client will perceive the counselor as attractive as the helper exhibits the three human relations core variables of empathy, respect, and genuineness.

The skills of reflecting, attending, summarizing, and inquiring are used extensively by the humanistically oriented counselor. The emphasis is on a shared journey rather than on the use of skills that influence the client or make use of the counselor's power. Many of the skills that humanistically oriented counselors use are borrowed from Gestalt and Transactional Analysis views. Again, those techniques that focus on awareness, freedom and responsibility, meaning, centeredness, and anxiety will be incorporated into a counselor's repertoire of skills.

The Helping Relationship from the Client-Centered View

This viewpoint stresses the importance of the counselor's looking at the client's subjective or phenomenological world. The counselor is seen as a facilitator in the process of helping clients to find their own direction. Emphasis is placed on the process of being, rather than on an end or finished product.

The root of effectiveness is the counselor's being and personal attitudes. These components are viewed as the instruments for change to occur in the client. The traits of accurate empathic understanding, unconditional positive regard or respect, congruence, and genuineness are foremost considerations. Clients' perceptions of their own human experiences are understood by the counselor via empathy. As the counselor models one half of a congruent relationship with the client, the client will experience increased faith in personal abilities, accept responsibility for change, and set attainable personal goals. Respect for the client is modeled by behaviors that de-emphasize any negative qualities in the client, stress the positive aspects, and evidence a trust that the client can make changes toward a personally defined state of being.

The social influence areas become prominent when the relationship and not techniques are stressed. Although the power to influence clients is not considered a major factor in the client-centered approach, counselors must be aware that their influence stems from their genuineness and realness. Many times counselors are mistakenly reluctant to intervene directly for fear that they are being too directive rather than client-centered. The attractiveness of the counselor for the client allows the counselor to emphasize self-disclosure to promote positive feelings, attitudes, and thoughts. A truly intimate counselor-client relationship is the process for change as well as part of the intended outcome. Commitments to each other precede intimate helping relationships. The competence and expertness of the counselor are important, but sometimes less important than the counselor's willingness just to "be" in the relationship. Little advice is given, and much dialogue is shared between the two. Trust levels are strengthened throughout the stages of growth as congruent counselor behaviors become the norm for the client to model.

The counselor uses all the skills described in the microskill approach. Reflection of content and reflection of feeling are commonly used, while nonverbal behavior and dynamics are used sparingly but effectively. Additional skills such as summary, paraphrase, attending, inquiring, direct and open-ended questions, clarifying, and silence are considered effective tools when used appropriately.

The Helping Relationship from the Gestalt View

The Gestaltist helping relationship is similar in some ways to the humanistic-existential approach. The principle of client awareness is foremost; it focuses on the what and how of behavior and experience in the here and now. The counselor helps the client to integrate a personal awareness of self and of the world and to fill in any gaps between the two arenas. The gaps are projected onto the helper who then skillfully frustrates the client into avoiding them. Very often the "I-thou" relationship is coined to summarize the concepts of the Gestalt viewpoint (Buber, cited in Greenberg, 1985, pp. 254-255).

The human relations core of empathy, respect, and genuineness is embedded in the Gestalt process of differentiating between reality and fantasy (Perls, 1970). The focus on the client's feelings, increased awareness of the moment, body messages, and blocks to awareness all allow the counselor to show a caring attitude and simultaneously to help the client to identify unfinished business. The Gestalt counselor displays value for the client as a human being through encouraging responsible control by the client for the client's own life. Only if the counselor is aware, integrated, and able to be open and spontaneous to all of the client's experiences, both positive and negative, can a genuine relationship develop.

The competence of the counselor is seen best in endeavors to promote maturity in the client and to remove the blocks that prevent the client from taking self-responsibility. There are many skills and tools that Gestaltists use; their use, however, must not become an excuse by the counselor for not self-disclosing. That is, competence should not be masked behind endless games and techniques. The Gestaltist attempts to influence the client to realize personal potential for dealing with whatever gaps are present in the client's own personality. The type of intimate relationship experienced by a Gestalt counselor and client would develop more slowly than within a client-centered relationship. Part of this slower process is due to the Gestaltist's more liberal use of direct confrontation. Because clients are allowed to set their own goals in counseling, they would need to perceive some basic similarities between their counselors and themselves in order to believe that they, too, can direct their own lives. Gestalt counselors would most likely depend upon attending to clients and allowing them to begin leading fuller, self-supportive lives in order to establish themselves as "experts." Trust in such relationships would stem from counselors' experience of themselves in the person's here and now, continued efforts to integrate the polarities identified in themselves, and being dependable. Sometimes Gestaltists are criticized for using too many techniques instead of focusing more on the relationship. Some of the common techniques used are *empty chair, exaggeration, reversal, rehearsal, staying with the feeling,* and *dream work* (Perls, 1970).

The Helping Relationship from the Transactional Analysis View

Change in the client can occur using the transactional analysis, or TA, approach when focused on client interactions, cognitions, and behaviors. The terminology is easily understood in terms of a structure known as *P-A-C, Parent-Adult-Child.* The counselor teaches the client how to evaluate present decisions in light of these *ego states* and contracts with the client to make positive changes, to decide and/or to redecide. There is an equality in TA between the counselor and the client as they proceed toward autonomy for the client. Awareness, spontaneity, and intimacy are incorporated into the autonomy goal for the client.

The human relations core elements are less emphasized in this didactic approach than in some others like client-centered therapy. Although empathy, respect, and genuineness are not totally overlooked, they are not the primary foci. Observable behaviors and *transactions* between people are studied, and attempts are made to rid the client of the troublesome aspects of the Parent or Child state.

The role of the expert for the TA counselor is seen at the beginning of the relationship as clients are taught about P-A-C. The counselor soon relinquishes this role, however, as the client learns more about transactions. TA counselors must constantly be aware of their own transactions with clients, noting any *contamination* and/or *game playing* and would competently analyze these with their clients. Trustworthiness develops as the counselor continues to interact with the client from the Adult ego state rather than operating from the Child and/or Parent state. The power that the counselor has in the relationship is shared with the client as the client learns to analyze competently and to make personal decisions. As the relationship progresses, the client sees evidence of the counselor being helpful, and the outcome is an autonomous individual who has learned to relate in a more authentic manner.

TA has borrowed some techniques from Gestalt therapy, but many are exclusively TA practices. The structural analysis encourages awareness of the P-A-C ego states and how they can become contaminated. Teaching occurs very frequently as does transactional analysis; the *complementary, crossed,* and *ulterior transactions* are identified (Berne, 1961). To heighten awareness or assist in making new decisions or in redeciding and attaining autonomy, the counselor might use the *empty chair, role-playing, family modeling, analysis of rituals, pastimes, games, rackets,* and *scripts* (Goulding & Goulding, 1978). Once again, due to the TA language and its didactic focus, the core skills of attending, reflecting, and inquiring are emphasized less in this approach than others.

The Helping Relationship from the Behavioral View

As Corey (1982) states, the relationship between the counselor and the client is not highlighted in behavioral counseling; however, following a behavioral view, it is not ignored as has been reported at times in the past. The emphasis is on observable and specifiable behaviors and precise goals set by the client. The agent of change is not so much the relationship, but the learning and practice of new behaviors to be used in the client's environment. The environment is given a greater focus than the client's internal locus of control. With the development of the person-situation interaction by Bandura (1978), however, greater emphasis is now being placed on the internal mediation of the client. Some of the mediational aspects cross into cognitive-behavioral views to be covered next.

The behaviorist neither focuses on perceptions of the client's world nor strives to empathize with the client as a primary goal. But the basic belief in the worth of the client as a human is foundational for the relationship to continue into the *identification* of behaviors, *prescrip-*

tion of behavioral techniques to change the behaviors, and *evaluation* of them. The genuine behaviorist would be respectful of the client but would not actively facilitate inquiry into the client's own experiences in the helping relationship.

Power would be emphasized more as the counselor specifies goals, observes behaviors, and suggests plans to change maladaptive behaviors. Attractiveness would not be a prime consideration because the client's positive feelings for the counselor would be of less importance than the logical sequence of learning new behaviors or unlearning old ones. The behaviorist would be viewed as an expert, competent in assigning techniques to deal with the client's problem behaviors. The relationship will probably not be described as intimate because a reciprocal relationship of sharing and being intimately together usually does not develop.

The behaviorist would make use of many skills such as *systematic desensitization, implosive therapy, assertiveness training, aversion therapy, extinction, operant conditioning, modeling,* and *token economies* (Corey, 1982). Perhaps in this area the behaviorist differs most in the use of these techniques over those of the skills core identified earlier in this chapter.

The Helping Relationship from a Cognitive-Behavioral View

The role of cognition as an important part of behavioral counseling is a rapidly developing point of view (Bandura, 1974, 1978; Mahoney, 1974; Meichenbaum, 1977). According to Meichenbaum and Cameron (1981) there is growing appreciation for the cognitive-behavioral approach, which demonstrates the reciprocal relationship between thinking, feeling, behaving, and environmental consequences that occur to clients in daily living.

Most of the early research on cognitive-behavioral counseling has been with children (Meichenbaum & Asarnow, 1979). However, there is a growing interest in applying the theory and interventions for adults in universities and business and industrial settings (Kurpius, Benjamin, & Morran, 1984; Kurpius & Morran, 1985; Silver, Kurpius, & Mahdavi, 1984). In either group, the relationship conditions are important and necessary, and the human, social, and skills core are interrelated to the theory.

Empathy, for example, is described by Stone (1980) as a complex process, which is usually conceptualized as including both cognitive and affective dimensions. Stone (1980), in reviewing the work of Wexler (1974), views respect and genuineness as "redundant" because there is little overt activity. Overall, Stone conceives these conditions as *information-processing functions,* which are outlined by Wexler (1974) as *attentional functions, organizing functions,* and *evocative functions.* In addition, there are levels of *empathic communicating,* which are stated as *subtractive, interchangeable,* and *additive.*

Empathic responding is easily understood as an attentional and organizational function because, according to Stone (1980), nonempathic responding to the client's need could detour the client from the problem. By using reflection of content and of feeling, the counselor helps the client attend and focus on the problem. The additive dimension tends to stress that proper counselor language, such as that specified in the human relations core and the skills core, can influence the analysis and synthesis process in which clients engage.

As these processes unfold and are enhanced by the counselor, client cognitive processing increases, which leads clients to become more aware of their needs, goals, and priorities. As a result, clients are better able to check out their perceptions and assumptions of reality for their situation. Overall, with special attention to information processing, clients can both accept and challenge their thinking, feeling, and behaving in relation to who they are and where they are going.

The social influence core is closely linked to cognitive-behavioral interventions. Clients who perceive the counselor as expert and competent will develop trust in the relationship. Also important is the client's belief in the power of the interventions. Kendall and Hollon (1979) have found that client change is directly related to the degree to which the client believes in and is willing to be influenced by the counselor.

When counseling from a cognitive-behavioral base, counselors are sometimes more active and suggestion-oriented, but the importance of the client's internal experience is the primary guiding force. Mahoney (1974) states that clients learn how to establish a rational philosophy of life, learn how to solve problems, and how to gain insight into their person, their environment, and their behavior. They also learn the reciprocal effect of this triadic processing.

The interventions used in cognitive-behavioral counseling follow the internal experiencing, problem-solving, and situation dimensions. Because the intended outcome of the counseling process follows a self-directed approach, most of the interventions tend toward insight-oriented counseling as can be noted in their titles. The interventions most commonly used are *cognitive restructuring, cognitive self-instruction, self-management, problem solving,* and *attribution.* Cognitive restructuring is best known and is similar to what Albert Ellis called the *ABC system* of his rational emotive approach. Ellis (1973) described A as the activating event, B as the beliefs people hold about the event, and C the consequence resulting for the individual. Cognitive techniques used by Ellis are *disputing* irrational beliefs, *engaging* in rational self-talk, and *replacing* irrational beliefs with rational beliefs. Following cognitive restructuring, clients are helped to develop appropriate behaviors to act out their beliefs. Dixon and Glover (1984) and Stone (1980) have each developed text material that provides greater depth in each of the interventions. Cognitive-behavioral theory is rapidly gaining acceptance in counseling, consultation, and training.

CONSULTATION AND THE HELPING RELATIONSHIP

Under almost all conditions and within almost all theories, the quality of the helping relationship is related to the quality of the helping process and subsequent outcomes. Although it is true that consultation differs from counseling on some dimensions, it does not differ greatly on the importance of building and maintaining a high-quality working relationship.

In an overview of consultation, Kurpius and Robinson (1978) state, "Initially a consultant must be a skilled relationship builder, earning the consultee's trust and confidence. The basic counseling skills of listening, attending, reflecting accurately, and probing objectively help to create this open consultant-consultee relationship" (p. 5).

Although the relationship principles of consultation are similar to counseling, the context, role, and functions are different for consulting. One difference is that most consultation occurs in work-related situations. Counselors, psychologists, and members of other professions who value helping people are becoming increasingly more active as consultants to individuals, groups, and total organizations. When consulting with individuals, there is considerable similarity to counseling individuals, as in team building. In system and organization consulting, respect, trust, competence, and other skills are just as important as in counseling.

As has already been confirmed for counseling, caring seems to be taking on increasing importance in the work setting. Peters and Waterman (1982) in their best-seller *In Search of Excellence* placed caring and respect for the individual employee at the top of their list of factors that describe the best-run companies in America. They also proposed still another type of caring, which they referred to as "closeness to the customer."

In his earlier work, Laswell (1976) addressed the future of society and stated that the concern for human dignity is becoming one of its highest goals. The criteria he established for defining dignity are *affection, well-being, respect, enlightenment, wealth, power, morality,* and *skills*. Two additional consultant characteristics that are growth-producing for humans, proposed by Kurpius and Christie (1978), are *collaboration* and *inquiry*. They stated that inquiring minds are synonymous with human growth and that collaboration and shared participation are developing in almost every facet of society.

Although the context, role, and functions for consultants are different, the basic characteristics of the helping relationship differ very little. Block (1981) encapsulates this similarity by suggesting that consultants should place a value on the affective and interpersonal side of the consultant-consultee relationship and urges consultants to be as authentic as they can be with consultees. He further states that these constructs must become part of the consultant's value and belief system if they are to become characteristic of the helping relationship.

The Human Relations Core for Consulting

When comparing the similarities and differences between counseling and consultation, two differences are usually discussed. As already mentioned, the locus of consultation tends to be in the work setting, whereas counseling tends to occur in clinical settings. A second major difference is that in counseling the focus is on the person, while in consultation the focus is more likely to be on issues that cause human problems. Obviously issues also are associated with people, but at the outset, consultants and consultees more commonly attend to situations, facts, and consequences that are causing human problems. For example, if a client comes to a counselor and states, "I am depressed," the counselor may inquire about the depression by saying, "Can you tell me more about your depression?" In consultation, given this same statement by a consultee, the consultant will more likely focus on the issue and say, "What is happening in your work that is causing you to feel the way you do?" If the consultee continues to talk about this depression and demonstrates a need for direct personal help, either the focus should shift to personal concerns or, after clarifying the nature of the problem, a referral should be suggested.

In consultation, especially when the definition and expectations for consultation have been agreed upon, the consultee is usually motivated to solve problems that are work-related and consequently will more commonly begin to describe a work situation that is not going well, where help would be appreciated. Thus, the consultee's response to the consultant's issue-focused question about the work situation might be, "I have been worried about our continued absenteeism problem. Nothing I have tried seems to be working." From this job-related problem statement, the consultant knows that the presenting issue is absenteeism and that the interventions tried so far have not been effective. Now the consultant might respond with, "Let's look at the interventions you have tried and see if we can figure out a way to reduce absenteeism." In the last example, the consultant's response is supportive and encouraging, but the attention is directed toward the work problem contributing to the depression.

As one can conclude from the brief definition of consultation, respect and genuineness are perhaps more important values and behaviors than is empathy. That is not to say that being empathic and understanding the consultee's internal frame of reference are not important, but it does suggest that in consultation, at least in the early stages, responding with high-level empathy as the primary focus is less appropriate for the consultant and suggests one way to distinguish consultation from counseling.

Social Influence Core for Consulting

The social influence phenomenon is the same in all helping relationships. People in need of help and those who are motivated to be helped are responsive to helpers who are competent, trustworthy, intimate, and attractive. Expertness and power are also sources of perceived helpfulness by consultees. As one can see, the integration of the human relations core, basic skills core, and social influence core forms a unique and impressive balance for consultants to take to their consultees.

Skills Core

The basic skills in counseling are also basic to consulting. As stated earlier, collaboration and inquiry are paramount. Attending, listening, questioning, clarifying, reflecting, and summarizing are the actual behaviors the consultant uses and personally models for the consultee. Using these basic skills will provide a communication link that will enhance a collaborative, problem-solving relationship with the consultee.

Higher-level skills that are needed by the consultant are more conceptual and global in nature. These are process skills, which require the consultant to integrate personal characteristics with human relations, social influence, and theory into one repertoire of helping. These different process skills help consultees to conceptualize problems and solutions in creative ways and are called upon at each stage of the consulting process, that is, at *entry, data gathering, problem definition, goal setting, intervention, evaluation,* and *termination.* Using higher-level process and conceptual skills requires considerably more training and fieldwork under direct supervision because, as is true in counseling, the greater the problem, the greater the skill level needed by the consultant.

Theory Core

In an overview of the field of consultation, Kurpius and Robinson (1978) stated that consultation can be viewed as atheoretical. More recently Gallessich (1985) and Kurpius (1985) have found that consultation is still functioning without a coherent, integrated theory. One might argue that counseling also lacks theory because most counseling theories have emerged from personality theories.

Consultation is similar in this regard. That is, most consultants rely on a variety of theoretically based concepts, constructs, principles, models, and techniques depending on the situation and the consultant's frame of reference. For example, a *content consultant* tends to transfer knowledge directly to the consultee or consultee system. In medical settings this may involve the cardiologist describing to a general practitioner the best treatment for a heart patient. In schools, a counselor functioning as a consultant may suggest certain classroom management principles, which may stem from behavioral theory, to a teacher. Organizational consultation situations usually are based on organization theory, systems theory, or social psychology theory.

Process consultation, which is increasing in usage, assumes that people have the basic knowledge to define and solve problems but lack confidence, a supportive climate, or process skills. When the consultant is engaged in process consultation, all of the above-mentioned theories are used as well as *communication theory, attribution theory, change theory,* and *motivation theory* to suggest just a few.

So, although consultation is not known to hold a single theory, the very nature of the purpose and process of consultation lends itself to become the user of many already-established theories. As one can note in the consultation literature, it is more common to find the use of models to depict the foundation upon which consultation rests than it is to find a single theory.

SUMMARY

When we think about the significant difference a positive helping relationship can make, one might assume that all relationships would be positive and helpful. Unfortunately, this is not the case. There is a positive side to this observation, however. We know what basic core elements will develop each of us to become more helpful. This basic core, as outlined in this chapter includes: (1) the personal characteristics of the helper (values, beliefs, assumptions), (2) the identity one has for offering basic human conditions (empathy, respect, genuineness), (3) the skills necessary to communicate effectively (attending, inquiring, reflecting), (4) the therapeutic power in social influence factors (trust, competence, intimacy), and (5) the assumption that theory and practice are interdependent and reciprocally determined, depending upon the helper, the client, and the situation. Counselors and consultants who practice from the core areas frame of reference can enhance the quality of helping to the benefit of both the helper and the person(s) being helped.

In closing, it seems appropriate to underscore the essence of the helping relationship by citing the extensive review of the helping relationship literature by Gelso and Carter (1985). In this review Gelso and Carter (1985) found that even though "the relationship usually emerges silently and imperceptibly" (p. 159), relationships are greatly influenced by the attributes, skills, and theories of the helper. And in addition, all approaches to counseling tend to agree that a sound, working relationship is essential if effective helping is to occur.

REFERENCES

Bandura, A. (1974). Behavior theory and the models of man. *American Psychologist, 29,* 859–869.

Bandura, A. (1978). The self system in reciprocal determinism. *American Psychologist, 33,* 344–358.

Berne, E. (1961). *Transactional analysis in psychotherapy.* New York: Grove Press.

Block, P. (1981). *Flawless consulting.* San Diego, CA: University Associates.

Brammer, L. M., & Shostrom, E. L. (1982). *Therapeutic psychology: Fundamentals of counseling and psychotherapy* (4th ed.). Englewood Cliffs, NJ: Prentice-Hall.

Carkhuff, R. R. (1969). *Helping and human relations,* Vol. 2. New York: Holt, Rinehart & Winston.

Carkhuff, R. R. (1984). *Helping and human relations,* Vol. 2. New York: Holt, Rinehart & Winston.

Carkhuff, R., & Berenson, B. (1967). *Beyond counseling and therapy* (2nd ed.). New York: Holt, Rinehart & Winston.

Corey, G. (1982). *Theory and practice of counseling and psychotherapy* (2nd ed.). Monterey, CA: Brooks/Cole.

Cormier, W. H., & Cormier, L. S. (1979). *Interviewing strategies for helpers: A guide to assessment, treatment, and evaluation.* Monterey, CA: Brooks/Cole.

Cormier, L. S., Cormier, W. H., & Weisser, R. J., Jr. (1984). *Interviewing and helping skills for health professionals.* Monterey, CA: Wadsworth.

Dixon, D. N., & Glover, J. A. (1984). *Counseling: A problem-solving approach.* New York: John Wiley.

Egan, G. (1975). *The skilled helper.* Monterey, CA: Brooks/Cole.

Egan, G. (1977). *You and me.* Monterey, CA: Brooks/Cole.

Ellis, A. (1973). Are cognitive behavior therapy and rational therapy synonymous? *Rational Living, 8,* 8–11.

Evans, D. R., Hearn, M. T., Uhlemann, M. R., & Ivey, A. E. (1984). *Essential interviewing: A programmed approach to effective communication* (2nd ed.). Monterey, CA: Brooks/Cole.

Gallessich, J. (1985). Toward a Meta-theory of consultation. *The Counseling Psychologist, 13* (3), 336–354.

Gelso, C. J., & Carter, J. A. (1985). The relationship in counseling and psychotherapy: Components, consequences, and theoretical antecedents. *The Counseling Psychologist, 13* (2), 155–244.

Goulding, R., & Goulding, M. (1978). *The power is in the patient: A TA/Gestalt approach to psychotherapy.* San Francisco: TA Press.

Greenberg, L. S. (1985). An integrative approach to the relationship in counseling and psychotherapy. *The Counseling Psychologist, 13* (2), 251–259.

Ivey, A. E. (1983). *Intentional interviewing and counseling.* Monterey, CA: Brooks/Cole.

Kanfer, F. H., & Goldstein, A. P. (Eds.). (1980). *Helping people change* (2nd ed.). New York: Pergamon.

Kendall, P., & Hollon, S. (1979). *Cognitive-behavioral interventions: Theory, research and procedures.* New York: Academic Press.

Kerr, B. A., Claiborn, C. D., & Dixon, D. N. (1982). Training counselors in persuasion. *Counselor Education and Supervision, 22,* 138–148.

Kurpius, D. J. (1985). Consultation interventions: Successes, failures and proposals. *The Counseling Psychologist, 13* (3), 368–389.

Kurpius, D. J., Benjamin, D., & Morran, D. K. (1985). The effects of teaching a cognitive strategy on counselor trainee internal dialogue and clinical hypothesis formulation. *Journal of Counseling Psychology, 32,* 263–271.

Kurpius, D. J., & Christie, S. G. (1978). A systematic and collaborative approach to problem solving. In D. J. Kurpius (Ed.), *Learning: Making learning environments more effective.* Muncie, IN: Accelerated Development.

Kurpius, D. J., & Morran, D. K. (1985, March). *A study of counselor internal dialogue and counselor performance.* Paper presented at the meeting of the American Educational Research Association, Chicago, IL.

Kurpius, D. J., & Robinson, S. E. (1978). An overview of consultation. *The Personnel and Guidance Journal, 56,* 305–384.

Laswell, H. D. (1976). The future of world politics and society. In D. L. Schraum (Ed.), *Communication and change.* Honolulu, HI: The University of Hawaii Press.

Mahoney, M. J. (1974). *Cognition and behavior modification.* Cambridge, MA: Ballinger.

Meichenbaum, D. H. (1977). *Cognitive-behavioral modification: An integrative approach.* New York: Plenum.

Meichenbaum, D., & Asarnow, J. (1979). Cognitive-behavioral modification and meta-cognitive development: Implications for the classroom. In P. C. Kendall & S. Hollon (Eds.), *Cognitive-behavioral interventions: Theory, research and practices* (pp. 11–36). New York: Academic Press.

Meichenbaum, D. H., & Cameron, R. (1981). Issues in cognitive assessment: An overview. In T. V. Merluzzi, C. R. Glass, & M. Genest

(Eds.), *Cognitive assessment* (pp. 3–15). New York: Guilford Press.

Perls, F. S. (1970). Four lectures. In C. J. Gelso & J. A. Carter, The relationship in counseling and psychotherapy. *The Counseling Psychologist, 13,* 155–244.

Peters, T. J., & Waterman, R. H. (1982). *In search of excellence.* New York: Harper & Row.

Rogers, C. R. (1951). *Client-centered therapy.* Boston: Houghton Mifflin.

Rogers, C. R. (1957). The necessary and sufficient conditions of therapeutic personality change. *Journal of Consulting Psychology, 21,* 95–103.

Rogers, C. R. (1961). *On becoming a person.* Boston: Houghton Mifflin.

Rogers, C. R. (1967). *Person to person: The problem of being human.* New York: Pocket Books.

Schmidt, L. D., & Strong, S. R. (1970). Expert and inexpert counselors. *Journal of Counseling Psychology, 17,* 115–118.

Schmidt, L. D., & Strong, S. R. (1971). Attractiveness and influence in counseling. *Journal of Counseling Psychology, 18,* 348–351.

Silver, S., Kurpius, D. J., & Mahdavi, E. (1984). *The effects of a cognitive-behavioral training program on manager trainee internal dialogue and conceptual hypothesis formulation.* Paper presented at the meeting of the American Educational Research Association, New Orleans, LA.

Stone, G. L. (1980). *A cognitive-behavioral approach to counseling psychology.* New York: Praeger.

Truax, C., & Carkhuff, R. (1967). *Toward effective counseling and psychotherapy.* Chicago: Aldine.

Wexler, D. A. (1974). A cognitive theory of experiencing, self-actualization, and therapeutic process. In D. Wexler & L. Rice (Eds.), *Innovations in client-centered therapy* (pp. 49–116). New York: John Wiley.

CHAPTER 4
GROUPS

John C. Dagley
George M. Gazda
M. Carole Pistole

Although traditional counseling has developed within a dyadic relationship, the group context is an important and growth-oriented part of modern approaches to personal change. The explosion in group counseling and therapy that occurred in the 1960s and 1970s has provided the counseling profession, as well as individuals interested in personal change, with a quality option to traditional dyadic interview therapy. Because of the position that group work has assumed within the profession, an understanding of counseling is not complete without an introduction to the concept of groups.

This chapter is an introduction to the fundamental concepts, principles, and theoretical models of group work, as well as some of the more common leadership techniques and strategies. Special issues and concerns of contemporary group work are highlighted as well as noteworthy directions in research and practice.

THE GROUP FIELD

Definitions and typologies of groups abound in the professional literature. Sociologists, psychologists, counselors, political scientists, psychiatrists, and others representing a variety of academic disciplines define and type groups on the basis of distinct, yet overlapping criteria. Simply stated, each discipline describes the group in the context of its own logic and focus. For the purposes of this chapter, "all aggregates which bear the name 'group' do not always possess the quality of 'groupness' " (Ellis, Werbel, & Fisher, 1978, p. 464). For example, the currently popular statistical grouping that the social and political arena calls "Yuppies" is an aggregrate that does not meet the special criteria of particular interest to the helping professions.

What then are the principal criteria for considering a collection of people a group? Knowles and Knowles's (1959) definition of a group requires the following qualities: (1) a definable membership, (2) a group consciousness or a collective perception of unity, (3) a sense of shared purpose, (4) interdependence in needs satisfaction, (5) communication and interaction, and (6) the ability to act in a unitary manner. For Luft (1984) some interaction must take place, some purpose must be shared, some differentiation of behavior must develop, and some sense of worth in membership must be present for a group to exist. Cartwright and Zander (1968) identified a similar but more comprehensive set of criteria for defining a group as a collection of interdependent people characterized by (1) frequent interaction, (2) identification by self and others as a member, (3) sharing of norms, (4) participation in interlocking roles, (5) identification with each other, (6) valuing of the group as rewarding, (7) interdependent goals, and (8) a collective perception and action as unity. A reasonable synthesis of these and other definitions of groups in the research literature is that *an aggregrate of people can be identified as a group when the group members see themselves and are seen by others as psychologically interdependent and interactive in pursuit of a shared goal.*

Types

The study of small group behavior is a study of comparisons and contrasts, because, in terms of specific principles and characteristics, every group is like every other group, like some other groups, and like no other group. There are so many types of group interventions in today's helping professions that one needs an organizational framework to begin to develop an understanding of the similarities and differences. Groups are commonly classified by such shared properties as *size, duration, function, participant qualities, settings, level of prevention,* and *nature of leadership.*

As one organizational system, Conyne (1985) has proposed a classification grid comprised of two major dimensions, *purpose* and *level.* He suggests that the purpose of group intervention is usually to *prevent,* to *correct,* or to *enhance* personal or task behavior. Furthermore, he proposes that each of these purposes may take slightly different forms in group work depending upon the specific level of intervention emphasized, such as individual, interpersonal, organizational, or community.

Figure 4-1 presents a comprehensive perspective of the variety of ways groups can be structured and implemented to achieve different purposes for a number of populations in many settings. A compatible but different typology is apparent in Figure 4-2. Gazda (1984) presents the overlapping, yet distinct nature of the most common groups and group processes encountered in the helping professions. The rubrics *guidance, counseling,* and *psychotherapy* offer a rich simplicity and distinct comprehensiveness in terminology that is about as clear as possible in the somewhat nebulous world of group work.

Gazda's classification scheme is similar in nature and scope to the current emphasis in community psychology and public health on the concept of *prevention—primary, secondary,* and *tertiary*. Primary preventions, like guidance groups, are designed for groups (more than two individuals) identified as high-risk populations relative to disease or life crisis. The intervention activities are aimed at preventing problems and at promoting the development of healthy behaviors. Examples are public education programs on drug or alcohol abuse. Secondary preventions have both preventive and remediative elements. Most often these preventions focus on reducing the duration, or chronicity, of a disorder or disturbance. These efforts may take the form of a direct intervention program such as a counseling group focused on grieving and death adjustment, an indirect program such as a skill development group, or a time-limited, direct and indirect program such as a crisis intervention racial encounter group. Tertiary preventions are remediative in nature as are psychotherapy groups. Compared to primary prevention, these treatment efforts are more individual in nature. Rehabilitation, reeducation, and restoration activities are designed to facilitate a full, effective return to health.

In sum, current schemes used to classify groups seem to be both overlapping and distinct. Whether one uses Conyne's (1985) emphasis on prevention, correction, and enhancement of personal or task behavior; Gazda's (1978) system of guidance, counseling, and psychotherapy; or the current terminology of primary, secondary, and tertiary, fine distinctions can be made between similar types of groups. A historical perspective of how the group field developed can help to make sense of the purpose and usefulness of these distinctions.

History

Historical antecedents of current professional work in groups can be traced to Gustav LeBon, a French social psychologist who in 1895 was concerned with the "group mind" of large numbers of people (Luft,

		Correction		Enhancement	
		Personal	Task	Personal	Task
Individual	Type	Personality Change	Rehabilitation	Personal Growth	Skill Development
	Eg.	Psychotherapy	Remedial Social Skills	Personal Development	Human Relations Skills Training
Interpersonal	Type	Interpersonal Problem Solving	Resocialization	Interpersonal Growth	Learning
	Eg.	Counseling	Social Control	T-groups	Systematic Group Discussion
Organization	Type	Employee Change	Organization Change	Management Development	Organization Development
	Eg.	Employee Assistance	Social Climate	Team Development	Quality Circles
Community-Population	Type	Secondary/Tertiary Prevention	Community Change	Health Promotion/Primary Prevention	Community Development
	Fg.	Mutual Help	Action	Life Transition	Futuring

Rows: Intervention Level Emphases
Columns: Intervention Purpose Emphases

FIGURE 4-1 CONYNE'S GROUP WORK GRID

Source: From *The Group Workers' Handbook: Varieties of Group Experience* by R. K. Conyne, 1985, Springfield, IL: Charles C Thomas. Copyright 1985 by Charles C Thomas. Reprinted by permission.

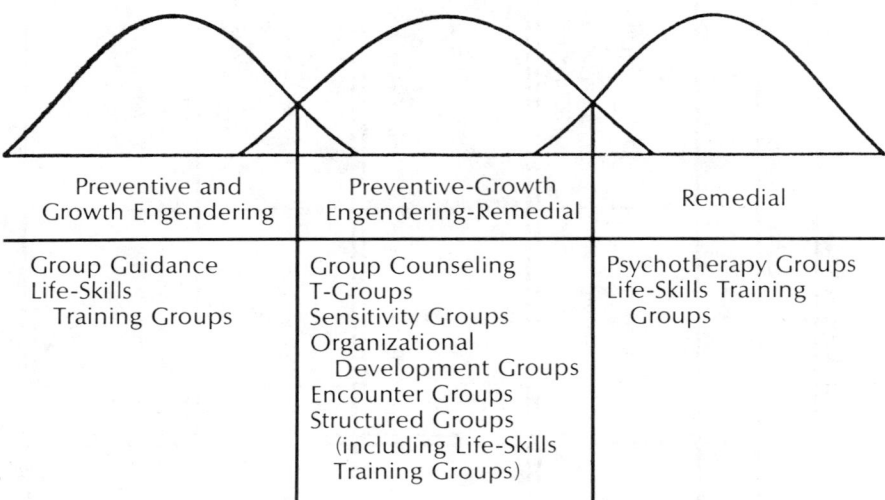

FIGURE 4-2 RELATIONSHIPS AMONG GROUP PROCESSES
Source: From *Group Counseling: A Developmental Approach* (3rd ed., p. 6) by G. M. Gazda, 1984, Boston: Allyn & Bacon. Copyright 1984 by Allyn & Bacon. Reprinted by permission.

1984; Rutan & Stone, 1984). From then until 1940 professional interest in groups exhibited a gradual but continual growth. This early growth of the group field is reflected in the increase in publications from one per year to about thirty per year (Zander, 1979) as well as by the development of small groups for personal change.

The evolution of modern group work developed from a subtle shift in the practice of prophylactic medicine by physicians such as J. A. Pratt, J. L. Moreno, and Alfred Adler (see Chapter 2). In the early part of this century, Pratt used the "class" method for assisting Boston's tubercular patients in discussing and learning about their common problems (Gazda, 1982; Rutan & Stone, 1984). About the same time, Moreno, working in Vienna with both children and adults, began to develop such action methods as psychodrama that provided an energy and vitality still evident in group work today. Adler's contribution, in the 1920s in Vienna, was in introducing group guidance methods with families.

Not until the 1930s were the parameters of small therapy groups developed by Slavson in New York as the forerunner of current small, intensive counseling and therapy groups. This development set the stage for Moreno to coin the term "group therapy" in 1931. Then in the early 1940s, two national associations for group psychotherapists emerged. J. L. Moreno founded the American Society of Group Psychotherapy and Psychodrama in 1941–42, and S. R. Slavson founded the American Group Psychotherapy Association in 1942. The same year Kurt Lewin, speaking in Washington, DC, predicted that group work would emerge as an important theoretical and practical field (Zander, 1979).

Following World War II the study of groups became a lively and creative research area particularly for social psychologists (Zander, 1979). Increased research activity was based on the belief that science could provide understanding to increase effective functioning of democratic organizations (Zander, 1979). From this research, which addressed topics such as increasing leader skill, improving members efforts, and assessing conditions under which organizational change is facilitated, emerged the human relations movement of the 1960s and the establishment of group dynamics within college curricula (Zander, 1979). Concurrently, emphasis on teaching about groups experientially through having members examine and discuss their own learning led to an emphasis on understanding self as the primary interest in group work (Zander, 1979).

The experiential emphasis and the influence of Lewin also had an impact on groups organized for personal change. From 1945 to 1970, the "clinical" field was split into two camps. There was the emotional component, represented by *T-groups* (for *Training*) and *laboratory* (or *sensitivity*) groups spawned by Lewin, and the intellectual component, represented by the analytic, therapeutic groups (see Gazda, 1982; Zimet, 1979). The merging of affect and intellect, with both being considered essential in the process of personal change, was a legacy of the encounter group movement (Zimet, 1979). As already noted in the discussion of typologies of groups, most recently a preventive approach to "mental health" seems evident in the field with professionals proposing the use of groups to facilitate mastery of skills associated with lifespan developmental issues (Gazda, 1984; Zimet, 1979).

In conclusion, theoretical and practical work in the group field since 1940 has produced an expanding field of professional interest. Today "the use of small face-to-face groups to produce changes in attitudes, behaviors, and feelings of individuals" (Hartman, 1979, p. 543) has become a part of American culture (Stockton & Morran, 1982).

Importance

S. H. Foulkes (1951) has suggested that the group is the essential psychological unit, with the individual being an abstraction. This thinking is consistent with Freud's (cited in Foulkes, 1951):

> We must conclude that the psychology of the group is the oldest human psychology; what we isolated as individual psychology, by neglecting all traces of the group, has only since come into prominence out of the old group psychology by a gradual process which may still, perhaps, be described as incomplete. (p. 324)

The implication is that, for each of us, the group exists inherently within our "psyche." A more convincing explanation of this concept requires a more complete background. Opportunities for small group interaction are ubiquitous in today's society. Anthropologists suggest that such has been the case for our species since early *Homo sapiens* hunted in small groups. From the time human infants come into the world as some of its most defenseless creatures, they encounter life as social beings. With the family of origin serving as the first small group, human beings learn to interact in a multitude of groups and settings. Early small group experiences, particularly those involving the family, have a significant impact on the psychological development of the child. The reciprocal influence of individual and small groups continues throughout life, one affecting the other through simple and complex interactions. There is little doubt that human beings spend far more time together in small groups than alone or in large groups. And even when alone, the effect of small groups is present in the societal and cultural forces transmitted, at least through the family of origin. To understand human behavior, then, one needs to understand human behavior in its social context. The study of groups *is* the study of human behavior in its social context. In groups it is possible to see social and interpersonal behavior in action.

In the context of everyday life, the study of small groups is relevant not only for graduate students in counseling and other helping professions but also for all other individuals interested in improving self-understanding and personal effectiveness. As we mature, each of us develops our own way of relating to others; however, we do not usually stop long enough to listen to ourselves and assess the effectiveness of our interpersonal style. Because so much of society is made up of small group activity—in schools, communities, workplaces, churches, families, professional and social associations—it is important to learn how to increase our effectiveness as group participants and leaders. A group can offer the opportunity to add substance to our awareness of interpersonal style. An example from a *growth group* experience can help to clarify this thought.

Mary Jo worked hard at being different from the other members of the group. Throughout the early stages of the group, she always seemed to do or to say the "right" things from wearing a high-fashion but conservative dress to conversing articulately. For her to analyze a group member's comments in an accurate though somewhat removed fashion was not at all unusual. But for several months the group members ignored Mary Jo—not conversationally but emotionally. This relationship continued until she was able to ask the group directly and emotionally what she was going to have to do to get somebody's attention. Subsequent interactions enabled her to understand the distancing factor of her "correct" actions and patterns. Although Mary Jo did not undergo complete metamorphosis, she did learn to loosen up enough to disclose more of a range of thoughts and feelings, thereby eliciting a warmer and more natural acceptance from others. Specifically, she learned to share a thought before it was perfectly congealed in her mind. Thus, she began to experience a little more comfort in spontaneity and freedom of expression.

This example brings us to a point where we can offer some of the specific values of a group counseling experience. Each enumerates a way in which groups are important to the counseling profession because each of these qualifies as a learning opportunity available in *group* as opposed to *individual* counseling.

1. A group offers each individual the opportunity to reality-test self-perceptions.
2. In a group interaction situation, distorted perceptions and false assumptions of self and others may become more apparent and lose their value.
3. Groups may provide a sense of psychological safety to support the elimination of self-defeating behaviors.
4. Groups approximate "in vivo" or real-life interaction situations, thus providing members with chances to try out new behaviors in a safe environment.
5. Responses of others can help an individual to appreciate the universality of some personal concerns.
6. Groups enable members to increase abilities to give and to solicit appropriate self-disclosures and feedback.
7. Interaction with others in a group can enhance one's empathy and social interest.
8. Groups of some duration offer individuals opportunities to

make systematic progress toward personal changes, receiving reinforcement for changes.
9. Groups have a unique way of helping members to develop a deeper understanding and acceptance of individual differences.
10. Consistent feedback from others in a group can enhance a person's accuracy of perception and communication.

This list helps convey how groups can provide learning opportunities that are not so readily available in a dyadic counseling context. Therefore, group experiences can be powerful, contributing to major life changes. We need to remember that the impact of this experience derives from the unique qualities intrinsic to groups.

More than any other single descriptor, the word "dynamic" seems to be an appropriate term to capture the vitality, force, and interactive influence so evident in small groups. More important, as the term dynamic implies, the forces that interact to influence individual behavior in groups are fluid and changing, not static.

KEY CONCEPTS

Very generally, group functioning may be viewed from the perspective of either *outcome* or *process*. From the perspective of outcome, the concern is whether the group *does* work. That is, outcomes are to be understood as products of the processes, the effects or results of group actions (Luft, 1984). In contrast, process is concerned with *how* the group functions. In counseling, processes are specific group leader actions or group activities. More important, these processes are related to *group dynamics*—a particularly important concept in group work.

Group Dynamics

The term "group dynamics" is used by professionals in more than one way. For some, "group dynamics is a field of inquiry dedicated to advancing knowledge about the nature of groups, the laws of their development, and their interrelations with individuals, other groups, and larger institutions" (Cartwright & Zander, 1968, p. 19). Others use "group work" in a similar manner, differing only in focus, with primary attention given to the study of the complex and interdependent forces of the small group for the express purpose of improving professional work in groups such as leadership and involvement. For instance, Knowles and Knowles (1959) refer to group dynamics as the complex forces that act on every group, whether known to members or not, throughout the group, influencing its behavior. Although a group has certain static characteristics such as size, it also has dynamic aspects. "It is always moving, doing something, changing, becoming, interacting, and reacting" (Knowles & Knowles, 1959, p. 12). The interactive effect of these internal and external forces on the group's direction and movement constitute its dynamics.

Several concepts are key to understanding group dynamics. Among these are *goals, structure, norms, roles, cohesiveness, stages of development,* and *leadership variables.* Each concept deserves a separate description, though in reality, the dynamic movement of a group is most influenced by the collective interaction of these forces.

Goals. A characteristic common to all groups is the presence of a shared goal or set of goals. Regardless of the exact nature of the goal, it is more likely to be achieved if it has arisen from the mutual consensus of group members. Goals differ in ways other than origin and nature. For example, the clearer and more distinct a group's goals are, the more likely the goals are to be achieved. The clarity of goals can also affect group cohesiveness (defined later); defined goals also serve as a source of attractiveness and/or exclusiveness. In spite of the apparent value of goal clarity in goal achievement, goal setting remains a major weakness in group work. After completing a comprehensive review of three decades of group research, Gazda and Larsen (1968) concluded that goals are often too general, too unrelated to group processes, and too inclusive. In actuality, goal setting is not the easy task it appears to be at first glance. Group goals are not individual goals nor are they a collective sum of individual goals. A group goal is something different.

Counseling groups often form on the basis of a preestablished goal, be it specific or general, task-related or problem-centered, social or skill development. Common group counseling goals are self-improvement, human growth, increase in group effectiveness, improved communication in the group, enhanced physical health, and so on. For these expressed goals to warrant consideration as the goals of the group, they must become the property of the group.

> What sets the group goal apart is that, in content and substance, it refers to the group as a unit—specifically, to a desirable state of the unit. The concept resides in the minds of individuals, as they think of themselves as a group or unit. (Napier & Gershenfeld, 1981, p. 194)

Structure. In the same sense that a person cannot "not" communicate, a group cannot "not" have structure. Popular parlance would have us believe that some groups are structured, while others are unstructured. Indeed, some groups do seem to have more structure than others, or perhaps more formal structure, but all groups have structure in that all develop characteristic rules and procedures, ways of interacting, rituals and traditions, roles, and communication systems.

Structure can be inferred from patterns and relationships. "The structure of a group refers to the arrangement of its parts and how those parts relate to one another and to the group as a whole" (Luft, 1984, p. 16). A group's structure is influenced by environmental factors but for the most part emerges from within. Structure is functional. It enables a group to pursue its purpose. If a group does not achieve a workable structure unique to its needs, however, it will more than likely stall. Effective structure changes with the evolution of the group (Luft, 1984) and with the psychological maturity of the group members (Hersey & Blanchard, 1983). The challenge is to develop idiosyncratic ways of effectively working together. Structures can fail to serve, but structures do exist for groups.

Leaders take part in the development of group structure, particularly in the early stages of a group. Structuring on the part of the leader is a directive technique used to define goals, to orient the group to expectations, and to communicate basic rules and procedures (Gazda, 1976; Muro & Dinkmeyer, 1977; Wilborn & Muro, 1979). Others use the term structure to refer to activities designed to facilitate early movement in groups, to resolve specific problems, or to facilitate skill development (Drum & Knott, 1977; Johnson & Johnson, 1975). Some group leaders consciously refrain from structuring a group and by so doing end up actually providing a very specific type of structure. Thus, what at first appears to be an unstructured situation is actually a deliberate move to structure expectations and procedures.

In relation to these last few points, some research indicates how structure is important as a condition for the process of therapy. After reviewing literature on structure, Bednar, Melnick, and Kaul (1974) concluded "that when the therapeutic goals are clear, desired client behaviors identified, and the therapeutic process explained, [in brief, under high structure conditions,] clients tended to engage in therapeutic work more quickly" (p. 33). Later research conducted by Rose and Bednar (1980) found that group members engaged in higher levels of group process and group cohesiveness when the group was provided structure by pretraining members with exercises using positive and negative interpersonal feedback. This is consistent with other research (Kivlighan, McGovern, & Corazzini, 1984), which demonstrated that the process and outcome of group therapy were enhanced when the content of training was matched with the group's developmental stage. Group members exhibited more appropriate expressions of anger and intimacy when training in effective communication of anger and intimacy (a structuring exercise) was provided during the phases of the group's development that were congruent with anger or intimacy. In sum, the research indicates that, at least during the early part of the group's development, structure is an important element to therapeutic progress.

Norms. A group's rules of behavior, whether spoken or silent, formal or informal, visible or invisible provide members with parameters of acceptable behavior. In group dynamics, these standard rules of conduct are referred to as norms. The normative system is one part of a group's structure. Norms serve many functions in our daily lives. The process of learning the codes of conduct operational in our society is called socialization. From birth we learn how to fit in, to belong, to become fully participating members of the human community. In the process, we improve our sense of comfort in contributing to and sharing with others in groups.

Norms serve important functions in professional helping groups. A norm can emerge within a group that is different from a norm outside the group, for example, that it is permissible to experience and express your feelings about self and others. Even in this instance, though, a group may specify conditions of appropriateness. Nevertheless, with this norm in operation, members are expected to self-disclose as well as respond to others' disclosures, thereby facilitating growth. Norms are more easily felt than consciously recognized.

Ground rules can be considered preliminary elements of a normative system. These are the conditions that are more or less predetermined by the leader or the environment. It is not unusual for group leaders to set such specific guidelines as "Smoking is not allowed," "Fighting is not permitted," or "Confidentiality is expected to be upheld by group members." Only when ground rules become a part of the group's standard operating procedures, in other words internalized by the members, do they become norms.

Once norms are fairly well established, there is a tendency for the group to exert pressure on its members to conform to the norms. "Under certain conditions members of a group may be more responsive to the norms of a group than they are to their own internal needs or the influence of the counselor" (Bonney, 1965, p. 971). Numerous research studies have documented the presence of this pressure, particularly in highly cohesive groups. Cartwright and Zander (1968) identify three functions of group pressures to uniformity—*group movement, group maintenance,* and *social reality-testing.* Group members are expected to behave in certain ways. Any deviation from the norms may incur positive or negative consequences, depending on the power and influence of the deviant and on the constructiveness or group-enhancement nature of the deviation. The role of the counselor is to remain alert to the presence of potential pressures to conformity and to help the group avoid blind responses to the pressures.

Roles. How do individuals go about the process of choosing roles in their various groups? Is there a pattern in role assumption for each individual? For example, does the person play the role of humorous tension reliever in the majority of his or her groups? What are the possible goals of someone who blocks or dominates the group? If one has successfully fulfilled the assignment of the role of mediator in the family of origin, how often does he or she assume the same role in other groups? What about role assignment? These and similar questions have been of interest to personality theorists and group researchers for some time. In the process of becoming, people develop choice patterns in adopting or accepting roles.

In general, a role refers to the expectations of self and others as to the behavior of a group member. Research suggests there are three basic kinds of group roles—*task, maintenance,* and *individual* (Benne & Sheats, 1948). Two of these, task and maintenance, are positive contributors to goal achievement, while the third set of roles, individual, is negative, particularly when the individual or self-orientation is at odds with the group goal.

According to Benne and Sheats (1948) and Bales (1951), the task roles include the *information provider,* the *opinion giver,* the *data analyzer,* the *opinion/information seeker,* the *clarifier,* the *summarizer,* the *initiator,* and the *elaborator.* Group maintenance roles, those involved with building and continuing interpersonal relationships, include the *encourager,* the *expediter,* the *processor,* the *observer,* the *compromiser,* the *conciliator,* the *follower,* and the *standard-setter.* Individual roles are negative contributors to group action. Such roles as *dominator, blocker, monopolist, critic, aggressor, recognition-seeker,* and *nonparticipant* are self-oriented rather than group-oriented. These narcissistic behaviors are typically defensive in nature and counterproductive to group goal achievement.

In contrast, task and maintenance role behaviors help the group form and maintain the kind of positive social-emotional atmosphere that allows for task achievement behavior to emerge. Both the task and maintenance roles are important for effective group functioning, especially when each predominates in an interdependent cyclical manner

(Bales, 1951). If a group stays in a maintenance-dominant mode for too long, however, it will flounder for lack of progress toward task achievement just as the group's concentrating solely on task roles will weaken the structure of the group because of the buildup of unreleased tension. Thus, there is a need for flexible role taking (Hansen, Warner, & Smith, 1980), with members capable of changing roles in relation to the task and relationship needs of the group.

As we have just seen, role behaviors can serve important functions in groups and enhance the group's ability to achieve its purpose. Roles are typically not represented in their purest forms, however; rather, members move into and out of particular roles with some degree of regularity. Sometimes the roles are clear and definite, while at other times roles are ambiguous or even conflicting. "Role conflict arises out of discrepancies between how one is expected to behave and one's natural inclinations" (Luft, 1984, p. 21).

Cohesiveness. Cohesiveness, a concept referred to previously, is a group's bonding, the collective sense of "we-ness" or unity. Cohesiveness is important to a group. The degree to which members wish to remain a part of the group has an impact on the group's ability to achieve shared goals. The more attracted to the group a member is, the more likely he or she will actively contribute to the group's pursuit of its goals.

Cohesiveness is a complex concept, intertwined to a degree, with the aforementioned pressure to conformity. "Cohesiveness is essential to the efficient functioning of a group, but this condition inevitably brings with it the danger of overconformity to group norms and the consequent stifling of creative productions" (Bonney, 1974, p. 453). Nevertheless, to accomplish its task(s), a group needs a strong sense of commonality of purpose. In relation to this, it is important to understand that cohesiveness is affected by factors and conditions outside the group as well as inside. For example, a group's collective identity as a unit is directly affected by its perceived image as a unit by others and its perceived attractiveness by others.

Development. The developmental growth of groups, and of individuals as well, moves along at such an uneven, unpredictable pace and in such an unobtrusive fashion that it is virtually unnoticeable to the neophyte except from a distance. To be seen and understood up close, developmental growth requires a seasoned perspective. "Every group with its unique cast of characters, all interacting complexly with one another, undergoes a highly individualized development" (Yalom, 1970, p. 231).

Though each group is unique in its development, effective small groups seem to move through identifiable, yet overlapping, stages from the time of conception, prior to the actual meeting of a group for the first time, through its termination. Patterns of development are recognizable in groups as they move toward maturity and effectiveness. Although several different labels have been given by researchers to specific stages within the developmental sequence, there seems to be a general consensus that a group can be conceptualized as experiencing two or three stages between its beginning and end stages. After comprehensively reviewing small group research studies reported over a twenty-year span, Tuckman and Jensen (1977) drew the conclusion that groups go through five developmental stages—*forming, storming, norming, performing,* and *adjourning.* Yalom (1970) identifies four phases—*orientation, conflict, cohesion,* and *termination.* Bonney (1974; 1976) describes the developmental stages of group maturation as *establishment* (with overlapping substages of exploration and socialization), *transition, experimentation, operational,* and *creative.*

Gazda (1976) has proposed an integrative model of group development, consisting of four rather definite stages which usually occur in a given group session as well as across sessions—*exploratory, transition, action,* and *termination.* The exploratory stage is characterized by the kind of uneasiness experienced by most people in new situations. In this formative stage, members engage and disengage quite tentatively, probing and exploring a new environ with new relationships rather self-consciously. The chief tasks are identifying operational goals and developing a base of trust and facilitative interaction. During the second stage, transition, the sense of trust broadens and deepens as interactions move beyond the superficial level. This stage truly serves a "transitional" purpose in that it represents a major way station for the group where confrontations may evolve into agreements and mutual commitments. At this point, the group, supported by a hard-earned spirit of cohesiveness, moves forward to confront its purpose. At this next stage, the action stage, the group accomplishes its productive, creative work. After this phase, the group moves toward and through issues and concerns of termination. Knowledge of the group development process, tempered by an appreciation of the idiosyncrasies of each group's development, can help group leaders facilitate effective movement.

Leadership. Leadership is a complex concept in group dynamics. The multidimensional nature of group leadership prohibits a simple definition in concrete terms. The variety of meanings commonly assigned to the term leadership can be understood in the context of a bipolar framework. "To some, leadership is a property of a group while to others it is a characteristic of an individual" (Cartwright & Zander, 1968, p. 362). Furthermore, to those who emphasize the group, leadership means the assignment or assumption of positions of influence within the group and/or the performance of leadership functions. For those who view leadership in terms of the individual, it means the possession of personal traits and/or styles of influencing others. At this point in the development of group leadership theory, it seems fair to draw a tentative conclusion that the term *leadership refers to the interactive influence of the leader's position, functions, traits, and style on group members, individually and collectively.*

Authority. Leadership is defined by some researchers in terms of positions of authority. A leader is the person assigned the position of leader. Authority rests in the position, not the person. The power to influence others rests with the person only because of his or her assumption of the position. Although this approach to understanding group leadership has some merit, it has generated less research attention than the others.

Functions. A number of studies have investigated the functional dimensions of group leadership. Primarily, attention has been given to identifying the key functions that serve to facilitate a group's goal achievement. Leadership is defined, then, in terms of group actions, not necessarily the leader's actions. The distributed-functions view of leadership emphasizes the importance of situational determinants of group leadership functions. In other words, leadership is not seen as a universal set of behaviors but as a number of particular behaviors appropriate in specific groups for specific purposes. Leadership is shared by the leader and the members. Research has failed to identify any set of functions universally determined to be the peculiar responsibility of the leader (Luft, 1984). The identified functional dimensions usually focus on task functions and group maintenance functions, reflective of group roles discussed earlier. Hersey and Blanchard (1983) have added a systematic conceptual framework to the functional-situationally determined approach to leadership. For them, leadership style relates to the maturity of the group members.

Personality. A large number of research studies over the years has attempted to determine personality traits related to group leadership effectiveness. The lists so generated have been seemingly endless. The correlations of leadership effectiveness and selected personality characteristics, such as flexibility, perceptiveness, intelligence, common sense, courage, and enthusiasm, appear to be positive but small. Personality variables account for little of the variance, even if research findings could be considered consistent, which is a questionable assumption at best. Generally speaking, the research findings have been contradictory and disappointing. "The search for special characteristics in the personality of the leader has failed to yield convincing results" (Luft, 1984, p. 118). Thus, there seems to be little clear evidence to support the "great man/woman" theory of leadership. Personal qualities or traits that distinguish leaders from nonleaders are not apparent at this time, though the lay public continues to cherish the simplistic notion of charismatic leadership.

Style. Lewin, Lippitt, and White (see White & Lippitt, 1968) carried out a series of early experiments designed to study the influence of leadership style on groups. These studies, classics in group dynamics research, compared *authoritarian, democratic,* and *laissez-faire* leadership styles. They produced evidence that leadership style does influence group atmosphere and behavior. Among other findings, their studies revealed that the democratic style of leadership is the most effective, generally speaking, but that different styles are effective under different conditions.

Other Concepts

Keeping in mind the dynamic forces that operate in a group, other concepts become relevant in group work. Although these will be presented only briefly, counselors should be aware that *group composition, therapeutic factors,* and *ethics* are meaningful issues within the context of group counseling.

Group composition. The composition of a group has a significant impact on its dynamics. Composition, the combined nature of members' intrapersonal and interpersonal characteristics, has a collective unity and interactive force of its own, not wholly predictable and often greater than a sum of its parts. The success of a group in achieving its goal(s) depends to a great degree on its composition.

The process of composing a group, though, is not a simple matter of selecting "ideal" members, nor of creating an "ideal" mix of members. There is no single ideal group member profile. Nevertheless, pregroup interviews can enable a leader to enhance opportunities for the emergence of group cohesion, for the effective use of modeling, and for the balancing of goal-related member characteristics (Gazda, 1978). In general, the homogeneity of members positively affects group cohesion and goal achievement, although heterogeneity is an important contributor to such group goals as consciousness-raising or conflict resolution. Effective group members come in all styles, types, shapes, and forms. If one characteristic is common to all effective members, it is the capacity to develop trust, the sine qua non of group work.

Therapeutic factors. Beginning with Corsini and Rosenberg's (1955) classification and enhanced by Yalom's (1975) taxonomy, professionals have been involved in delineating therapeutic factors that contribute to positive outcomes in group therapy. Yalom's (1975) comprehensive list includes eleven categories of *curative factors: instillation of hope, universality, imparting of information, altruism,* the *corrective recapitulation* of the primary family group, *development of socializing techniques, imitative behavior, interpersonal learning, group cohesiveness, catharsis,* and *existential factors* (pp. 3–4; see Yalom, 1975, for more detail). What is meaningful within the context of this chapter is that the reader be aware of therapeutic factors as an explanation of how therapeutic change occurs. Supposedly through the therapist's facilitation of the complex interdependent action of these factors, clients improve their functioning. Yalom (1975), in talking about therapeutic factors states:

> Their interplay can vary widely from group to group; factors which are minor or implicit in one group approach may be major or explicit in another. Furthermore, patients in the same group may be benefited by widely differing clusters of curative factors. (p. 4)

The purpose of clinical and research interest in these factors is to develop a set of systematic guidelines to enable the therapist to be more expert in facilitating productive change. After reviewing the theoretical, empirical, and clinical research on therapeutic factors (from 1955 to 1979), Bloch, Crouch, and Reibstein (1981) agreed with Yalom's (1975) statement: "There is little truly definitive research demonstrating the efficacy of any of the curative factors and even less research bearing on the question of the comparative value or the interrelation of these factors" (pp. 70–71). Although it would be useful to have evidence supporting and specifying the operation of these factors in group therapy, they currently have, at least, heuristic usefulness. Not only do they provide a way to talk about mechanisms of change, but also they can be used singly or in clusters to specify the treatment modality used in group therapy research. For instance, the group leader may focus on universality as the treatment technique (see, for example, Oppenheimer, 1984). Specifying a therapeutic factor as the focus of treatment enables researchers to communicate meaningfully about a somewhat standardized treatment technique. The differences between groups can then be more surely considered a result of the variable under study than because of a variable that is extraneous to the research project, such as treatment.

Ethics. As in other disciplines, ethics are the standards and agreed-on practices, consistent with broader ethical commitments (for example, political, moral, and religious) that reasonable and responsible practitioners and clients will generally support (Gazda, 1984; see Chapter 9 and Appendix B). Although ethics do not provide absolute rules, they do provide useful guidelines for behavior. These guidelines change, however, as the culture and scientific evidence dictate. Most generally, to be ethical, professionals need to "be aware of prevailing community standards and of the possible impact of conformity to or deviation from these standards on rendering their services effectively" (Corey, 1985, p. 32).

Currently, commonalities of beliefs are emerging in group work. The consensus of professionals (Gazda, 1984) suggests guidelines for the following areas: for the training of group leaders, for recruitment of group participants, for screening of group participants, for confidentiality, and for termination and followup. One factor involved in commonalities of emerging beliefs is the attention ethical considerations receive in the current literature. For instance, when examining encounter groups, Howes (1981) suggested that there is a need for concentrated effort at implementing ethical guidelines and ensuring adequate training of leaders. One of the reasons ethical guidelines and standards are so important in group work is that the group experience has its own particular and unique risks and limitations.

Indeed, the risks and limitations of group work are substantial. Counseling, whether with individuals or groups, offers opportunities for personal change, while change usually comes with an accompanying natural sense of uncertainty and a destabilizing discomfort. Although change may be seen as inevitable in life, it is not inevitably comfortable. So, one of the risks of participating in a group experience is that one's life may be upset, at least temporarily, as he or she sets aside old, familiar habits in favor of untried behaviors and thoughts. A new, healthier, and more positive concept of self-worth can be unsettling for the person who has spent a lifetime expecting and even eliciting the classic put-down.

Another risk of participating in a group experience is that one's resources for support outside the group can be relatively nonexistent. In fact, one's environment can even exert an influence in direct contrast or contradiction to the group's influence. For example, it is difficult for a young boy to learn how to express himself in a small group when he is forced to remain mute at home. Trying out new behaviors takes courage, particularly when the new behavior is not supported by "significant others." (See Chapter 6 for more discussion of this issue.)

Other risks in group work are inversely related to the skills of the leader and to the facilitative personal characteristics of group members. There seem to be no exact cause-and-effect relationships in group work; thus, much of what goes on in groups is somewhat unpredictable. Nevertheless, there can be some identifiable risks associated with group process. One such risk is a breach of confidentiality. Inappropriate use of members' self-disclosures, the "scapegoating" or ganging-up on a single group member, ineffectiveness or incompetency of group leaders, and the presence of an excessive pressure to conform to group norms are other easily recognized risks.

Unfortunately, groups are not panaceas. Sometimes they serve only cathartic goals, possibly contributing to life problems rather than to action or resolution. A group can also be experienced as an end in itself rather than as a laboratory. Moreover, without proper safeguards, such as an adequately trained leader—one who meets the profession's qualifications as stated in ethical policy—groups can be destructive. Finally, even though risks and limitations come with the territory, awareness of such challenges can facilitate proactive and positive responses of competent group leaders. In addition, as presented in the next section, awareness of the lack of precision in group work spurs professional responsiveness in other areas as well.

PERSISTENT QUESTIONS

The professional questions around these key concepts and central themes can be organized around broader issues at the level of meta-analysis. The field of groups is young as a science, and therefore fundamental questions are still being asked. Both researchers and practitioners are concerned with documenting the effectiveness of groups and with defining the conditions under which groups function productively. Underlying these questions is the even more important issue of methodology.

Methodology

The concern with having a rigorous methodology for studying groups is reflected in the historical development of small group research. Despite the interest of French social psychologist Gustav Le Bon in the "group mind" as early as 1895, the empirical study of groups was not established until 1945. By then Kurt Lewin had coined the term "group dynamics" and founded the Research Center for Group Dynamics (Luft, 1984). The research between 1895 and 1942 can be construed as providing evidence that groups can be studied appropriately in a "scientific" manner. This demonstration was necessary before the study of groups and group phenomena were considered legitimate scientific concepts (Forsyth, 1983).

Le Bon's study of crowd behavior, which led to the "group mind" concept, was followed by Triplett's 1897 project comparing "the performance of school children working alone and in noninteracting groups" (Forsyth, 1983, p. 31). Opposition to the study of groups developed in the scientific community in 1924, however, when Floyd Allport argued that group mind, norms, roles—in effect, group processes—were "unscientific" (Forsyth, 1983). According to Allport, groups could be understood in terms of individuals; his contention was that the group was not an appropriate object of psychological study. As research continued and different methodologies were applied to group phenomena, however, the scientific quality of group dimensions emerged. In particular, Sherif's (1936) work with social norms demonstrated that group variables could be experimentally created, varied, and studied in a laboratory (Forsyth, 1983).

Following Sherif's contribution, other research focused attention on group variables and their importance to society. From 1937 to 1940, as mentioned earlier, Lewin, Lippitt, and White studied leadership style. In 1943 Newcomb found that attitudes are influenced by group processes (Forsyth, 1983), and during this same year, William Foote Whyte in *Street Corner Society* described his observational study of a group in action. This effort showed that an understanding of communities required taking groups into account (Forsyth, 1983). Then, the relevance of the study of group phenomena was demonstrated with a set of studies beginning about 1925 that resulted in a conclusion termed the "Hawthorne Effect" that group members change their behavior as a consequence of observation. In effect, these key efforts established the group field as a scientific activity and as important to society.

Although the methodology for studying groups was available, the issue of methodology was not solved. Current group work reflects ever greater methodological precision (McGrath & Kravitz, 1982), although conceptual and methodological issues still confound research efforts. Groups consist of several individuals interacting in a particular setting. Therefore, the group is a very complex entity, and its study involves numerous factors, such as the behavior of different individuals, that cannot easily be controlled. This complexity, resulting in control difficulties, comprises a major methodological problem for research (Bednar & Kaul, 1978; see also Chapter 8). When variables cannot be controlled, researchers cannot be certain that the results of the investigation are indeed the result of the particular factors under study. Moreover, it is not evident that the results will continue to be valid when there is a change in some of the factors such as when the population of group members under study are depressed persons instead of university students.

In addition to concerns about control and generalizability, the group area is plagued with more direct conceptual problems (Bednar & Kaul, 1978). The concepts, propositions, and terms used to describe group functioning are ambiguous and not commonly agreed upon (Zander, 1979). Reiterated, the precision, accuracy, and crispness of vocabulary required of a science is simply not present in current terminology. Not only do different professionals use different terms to describe the same thing (Zander, 1979), but this lack of agreement in meaning contributes to the paucity of overarching models or theories that could be used to generate an empirically derived, unified body of knowledge (Bednar & Kaul, 1978). Relatedly, there is difficulty with defining variables in terms that are concrete enough to facilitate measurement (Hartman, 1979). For instance, just what is the meaning of outcome, especially in concrete, quantifiable language? As a consequence of the definitional and complexity problems, it is difficult to manipulate group factors. Without being able to control whether or not a factor operates in a group, researchers cannot provide evidence about what causes what within a group context. This is a serious impediment to building empirically based theories.

Another issue that plagues group research at the conceptual level is deciding whether to assess groups from the group or the individual level (Hartman, 1979; see also Chapter 7). Research can be concerned with the properties and outcome of the group itself or with the behavior of individuals in the group. The question is whether to measure outcome from the perspective of the individual's goal or as a dimension of a more global functioning level. Within the group context, both the individual and the group per se are important, but a group versus individual orientation to research may result in different empirical data and, therefore, in different conclusions about groups' operations. This dilemma results in differential interpretations about what is happening in a group and thereby complicates further the "knowledge" available to researchers and practitioners.

A last issue that may be considered methodological in nature is relevant to other fields but will be discussed within the context of groups, where it is also valid. There seems to be a gulf between the needs of the practitioner and the researcher. The clinician deals with the complexity of the group as a whole and is interested in knowing one big, unifying, overarching thing (Hartman, 1979). In contrast, the empirical scientist looks at groups systematically in quantifiable and replicable terms and builds knowledge from smaller and more defined facts. To establish the little facts, it is necessary to concretize and control variables, but doing so deletes what is important to the practitioner, the "richness, complexity, and perhaps the essence of the clinical enterprise" (Hartman, 1979, p. 458). The conflict that reflects different philosophical approaches to science, that is, the need for an overarching theory versus the building of theory from many smaller bits of knowledge creates a gulf or split between the practitioner and the researcher (Hartman, 1979).

Because there is a symbiotic relationship between research and practice (Bednar & Kaul, 1978, p. 769), it seems useful to reiterate more specifically the major issues in this research-practice split (Coche & Dies, 1981). For one, the practical usefulness of research is qualified for several reasons. Within research studies, the unit of analysis is small (for example, the individual) and so neglects larger, more salient features of the group (Coche & Dies, 1981). Relatedly, the research is scattered, so that the practitioner, who is busy applying knowledge, must read a large number of studies before contradictory findings become meaningful (Coche & Dies, 1981). In addition, although the clinician's situation is "in vivo," research is frequently of an analog, or laboratory, nature. Whether laboratory findings will generalize and be meaningful within the context of people's everyday lives is always questionable. Therefore, the research serves mostly a heuristic function, at least until or unless it is extended to and replicated in "real" groups. As research methodology improves and a more coherent data base accumulates, these and other problems endemic to the research-practice split will be resolved (see Chapter 8 for a move detailed discussion of these points).

Research serves two major purposes in group counseling. Through refining theory, the effectiveness of knowledge about the workings of groups is increased. That is, techniques or methodologies can be modified or discarded as appropriate for particular problems or particular populations (Coche & Dies, 1981; Hartman, 1979). Just as important, research yields objective, replicable data, the material that is used to provide consumers and public agencies, such as insurance agencies, with documentation of the legitimacy and efficacy of group treatments (Coche & Dies, 1981). Because of the interrelatedness of research and practice, the researcher and practitioner have a common interest in providing evidence on the outcome and process of groups' functioning.

Outcome and Process

As might be suspected from the previous discussion, *group outcome studies* reflect an unsatisfactory quality of research (Hartman, 1979).

Therefore, after reviewing the outcome literature, Hartman (1979) cautions that conclusions about outcome should be tentative. Because of deficiencies in the literature, it is difficult to evaluate the meaningfulness of positive and negative findings or to form a base of small studies on which future studies could build and thereby contribute to an accumulation of knowledge (Hartman, 1979). Nevertheless, Bednar and Kaul (1978) hazard some preliminary conclusions. After reviewing outcome research and noting the methodological problems, they suggest that "group treatments have been more effective than no treatments, than placebo or nonspecific treatments, or than other recognized psychological treatments, at least under some circumstances" (Bednar & Kaul, 1978, p. 792). Although not all the time or with all groups or with equally positive results, *in general,* group treatment works. However, there is not enough concise information to make statements about the differential effectiveness of group versus other forms of psychological treatment (Bednar & Kaul, 1978).

Although outcome studies address "Do groups work?", *group process studies* attempt to account for how groups achieve their outcome. Though there are problems, the process research has attained a higher level of quality than the outcome research (Hartman, 1979). Partially, this is because process studies are derived from the laboratory study of small groups. Traditionally, laboratory group work has examined groups both as "task performance systems" and as "systems for structuring social interaction" (McGrath & Kravitz, 1982, p. 200). Moreover, for several years group work has focused on issues such as "the power of the group to influence members, communication networks, aspects of leadership, coding the comments of discussants and interpersonal power" (Zander, 1979, p. 421). How these topics would provide a base from which to study the process in group counseling is easy to understand.

To reiterate, the purpose of process research is to specify the mechanisms of change (Hartman, 1979). After reviewing the literature, Bednar and Kaul (1978) offer the following tentative conclusion:

> It seems reasonably clear that the perceptions, expectations, and beliefs that a group member holds about the treatment can have an immediate influence on his or her experiences in the group. That these phenomena can affect early group development seems clearly demonstrated, although the long-term and outcome implications of these effects remain to be explicated. (p. 809)

Beyond this, neither Bednar and Kaul (1978) nor Hartman (1979) find any clear evidence supporting the conceptually proposed curative forces or mechanisms of change in the group context. In sum, groups do work, but why or how they work is uncertain.

POSITIONS

Although there are no empirically based theories about how groups work, the field is characterized by several different types of conceptual approaches. For the purpose of this chapter, the reference to differential group approaches is more relevant for the practitioner, whose task is to use theories, than it is for the researcher, whose task is to construct theories. In comparison with individual therapy, there is some complexity associated with the positions that characterize the group field.

Research and Practice

As suggested in the previous section, the profession's concern with both research and practice is reflected in the approach to training the group therapist. "The intensive group experience represents a unique medium for therapy, and consequently demands specialized skills and training procedures uniquely suited to the group context" (Dies, 1980b, p. 337). In addition to general therapeutic skills, such as the ability to empathize, potential group therapists need to develop an understanding of dynamics and other group parameters (Dies, 1980b).

Therefore, training emphasizes in vivo, hands-on clinical experience (Dies, 1980b; Schwartz, 1981). However, adequate training should include exposing students to research, both the research literature and the research instrumentation (Dies, 1980b). This not only increases the therapist's knowledge base but also provides the practitioner with the tools for introducing systematic evaluation into the practice of group psychotherapy (Dies, 1980a).

In addition, this focus on research sets the stage for communication and collaboration between the researcher and practitioner (Dies, 1980a). This, in turn, can lead to more productive and meaningful research and the construction of empirically based theories to be used in guiding effective group counseling. In this fashion, through appropriate training, the profession can encourage the integration of research and practice approaches to group work.

Theoretical Orientations

At another level, the positions that characterize the group field are similar to those of individual therapy. The professional's approach to treatment is influenced by his or her specific theoretical orientation: psychoanalytic, behavioral, humanistic/existential, developmental, or whatever (see Chapters 2 and 3). Just as in individual therapy, the group psychoanalyst will be interested in intrapsychic dynamics; the group behavioral therapist will deal with increasing the frequency of specifically defined behaviors; the group humanistic/existentialist counselor will be concerned with the group members' here-and-now, phenomenological experience; and the developmental group counselor will try to isolate skill deficits, such as interpersonal communication, and instruct the group in effective skills to remove the deficit. An example can help us convey the relevance of the counselor's theoretical orientation. According to group psychoanalyst S. H. Foulkes (1961), the patient's symptom is old: It is the internalized result "of painful, traumatic, undigested, and unintegrated childhood experiences and constellations" (p. 23). Therapy based on this belief would differ in form from therapy based on an existential perspective. While Foulkes would attend to issues located in childhood, an existentialist (see Yalom, 1980) would focus more on such issues as death, isolation, freedom, and meaninglessness. Just as in individual therapy, the professional's philosophical and theoretical beliefs characterize the content and methodology of the counseling.

Group-as-a-Whole Versus Individual

Within each of these broad philosophical and theoretical orientations, there is a second position that is uniquely the province of the group therapist. Recall the discussion of "group dynamics" in the key concepts section. There are group therapists "who focus on the group setting and the group process to define the major therapeutic action" (Goodman & Schwartz, 1981), that is, they work with the group as a whole. In contrast, there are other clinicians who focus on individual clients while attending only minimally to the other group members (Goodman & Schwartz, 1981). Essentially, this kind of practitioner does individual work in the group setting. The choice of the individual versus group-as-a-whole approach is independent of the counselor's theoretical orientation. For example, psychoanalyst Alexander Wolf treats individuals within the group setting (Kissen, 1981), but psychoanalyst S. H. Foulkes (1961) uses a group-as-a-whole approach. It seems important to note that even with the group approach, "this form of psychotherapy is, in the last resort, alone in the service of the individual human being and the freer development of his individuality" (Foulkes, 1961, p. 31).

In addition, there are times that the counselor who focuses on the group will use *horizontal* or *group-as-a-whole interventions* and other times when he or she will use *vertical* or *individual-within-the-group interventions* (Kissen, 1981). Regardless of whether the intervention is horizontal or vertical, the approach involves using the group interaction, that is the dynamic processes, as cues or signals for therapeutic intervention (Kissen, 1981).

In general, the group counselor has more "theoretical" decisions to make than the individual counselor. The professional must integrate research and practical training, settle on a philosophical and theoretical orientation, and express his or her skills in a group-as-a-whole or in an individual-in-the-group approach. In relation to the latter, the group process research and knowledge of group dynamics will be more important for the group-as-a-whole practitioner. In some respects, this is a more complicated approach requiring skill mastery of an extra knowledge base, one that integrates the individual philosophical orientation, for example, psychoanalytic, with knowledge of groups. Thus, the different types of approaches characterizing the field reflect the greater complexity associated with groups, as is consistent with the experience of both the practitioner and the researcher in their concern with pursuing professional issues.

CURRENT COUNSELING ISSUES

In discussing how the group field has dealt with the counseling profession's current concerns, remember that the group area is young as a science, so that conceptualization and theory are not yet clarified or integrated into well-defined, empirically based terminology. Therefore, current concerns are often dealt with in an unsystematic fashion. In general, the professional interest is reflected in the dissemination of information through journal publications. As is typical of the group field today, much of the literature appears to be a scattering of individual interests rather than a concentrated program of activity. Moreover, the publications reflect the practitioner-researcher split. Some literature includes descriptions of group workshops or treatment sessions addressing these current issues, while other literature reports empirical research. Although the field is not yet sophisticated enough to generate theory in all areas of current interest, the work being done and being shared is important and expansive. A little bit of as yet unsupported knowledge is more useful than no knowledge or no attempt to gain consensus and objective understanding.

In this section, a sense of how the profession responds to current counseling interests through a discussion of gender issues, lifespan human development, and preventive approaches to helping is provided to foster an understanding of how professionals gain, share, and learn from a little bit of knowledge. In addition, current group research studies have addressed other issues as well, for example: sexuality and the elderly (Capuzzi & Gossman, 1982), cross-cultural counseling (Blustein, 1982), stress reduction (Archer & Reisor, 1982; Daley, Bloom, Deffenbacher, & Stewart, 1983), suicide prevention (Hipple, 1982), and drug treatment (Page & Wills, 1983).

Gender Issues

The group field's involvement with gender issues is reflected in the source and topics of published articles. The majority of work concerned with gender issues focuses specifically on women, with the amount of attention to women indicated by a recent issue of *The Journal for Specialists in Group Work* (1981), which is devoted entirely to women's concerns. Clinicians in private practice and in university counseling centers have concentrated on topics such as how women can deal with repressed anger (Hotelling & Reese, 1983) and with sexuality (Kingdon & Bagoon, 1983; Snow, 1981). In addition, researchers have examined the usefulness of "feminist therapy," focusing on societal stereotyping of women, for working with chronically and profoundly disturbed women (Alyn & Becker, 1984), as well as the utility of feminist therapy in contrast to other, more traditional approaches such as group assertiveness training (Ellis & Nichols, 1979).

Other research compared the effectiveness of (1) group treatment versus no treatment for women adjusting to mastectomy (Clarke, Kramer, Lipiec, & Klein, 1982), (2) groups composed wholly of women versus mixed gender groups (Walker, 1981), and (3) cognitive versus behavioral approaches with depressed Spanish-speaking American (Puerto Rican) women (Comas-Diaz, 1981). These examples from the current literature illustrate the scattering of information produced by professionals pursuing topics individualistically rather than building on each other's efforts and/or a theoretical model. Although the literature is both outcome- *and* process-oriented, it is easy to understand how the practitioner would need to read a vast amount of it to form empirically based opinions or even to keep abreast of current thinking on gender issues.

Lifespan Development and Prevention

In contrast to gender issues and the group field in general, the way the field is dealing with lifespan development and preventive approaches to helping is much more systematic and combines both research and practice. Gazda's recently developed Life-Skills Training Model represents a more synthesized approach to group work. This model is a comprehensive paradigm designed to facilitate effective human functioning throughout the lifespan. It emphasizes health promotion through prevention as well as remediation; it rests on a developmental base; and it uses a *taxonomy of life skills* classified developmentally according to four generic life-skill areas—interpersonal communication/human relations, physical fitness/health maintenance, identity development/purpose in life, and problem solving/decision making. Within this model, the term life *skills* is used to indicate all of those skills and the knowledge prerequisite to development of the skills, in addition to the traditional academic 3-R skills, that are necessary for effective living. Furthermore, the term *life* skills is intended to connote influence from all phases of human development. In the model, the life-skills components are represented as "descriptors," which, through research, were categorized according to developmental level, and families, or "generic areas," of related skills. This model is innovative in emphasizing prevention, with prevention being principally an educative mode. In schools, a developmental curriculum in the generic life skills is intended to be incorporated as a regular feature of the learning program. Also, life-skill training programs conducted in community mental health centers could be employed as outreach for preventive mental health education. Both of these possibilities provide for lifelong learning of the skills required for promoting healthful personal functioning.

Recapitulating, this model reflects the counseling profession's current interest in both lifespan development and preventive mental health. In addition, it represents progress in the group field, because it integrates research and practice in its derivation and provides a framework that can guide both practitioners and researchers.

SIGNIFICANT CONTRIBUTIONS

Even without rigorous or sophisticated empirical concepts and terminology, the group field has made an important and meaningful contribution within the counseling profession. One of the most immediate ways that groups enrich the counseling profession is through enlarging the professional delivery system. In a group more people are served, and the expense is reduced for individuals as well as for institutions, such as mental health centers, university counseling centers, or schools. This results in greater efficiency without having to sacrifice the quality of service.

In addition, groups constitute an especially effective way to disseminate preventive mental health and provide the opportunity for personal growth. For years groups have been used effectively for teaching traditional academic skills. Extending group learning to include personal skills is building on a method known to be useful. Relatedly, because they approximate real-life interaction situations, groups provide a nonartificial context for learning new relationship skills such as assertiveness. Whether members are learning such skills for personal growth or for preventive mental health, the group enables them to increase their abilities and their confidence by trying new behavior, giving feedback, and soliciting self-disclosure. The feedback can provide members with reinforcement for minimal changes and thereby contribute to their efforts to internalize the new behavior for use outside the group situation. In addition, the consistent feedback available in a group experience can facilitate members' accuracy of perception and communication.

Relatedly, because therapy groups can be considered an experimental analog of real-life interaction, the group context provides material that is more difficult to obtain in individual therapy. More specifically, counselors can view the person's interaction in vivo rather than having to depend on the client's self-report, which may be biased. In addition, this interaction of several people in the here and now can constitute the material for therapy. Through the use of this material, groups offer clients the opportunity to test the reality of self-perceptions and to recognize self-defeating behaviors. When distorted perceptions and false assumptions become more apparent, the safe psychological environment functions in such a manner that these old, nonconstructive behaviors will lose their value. Thus, self-defeating behaviors can be eliminated and new behaviors learned to replace them. Equally important, the group can facilitate empathy and the social interest of its members by helping them to appreciate the universality of some issues as they simultaneously develop a deeper understanding and acceptance of individual differences.

Finally, because of the complexity of group work, there is a unique benefit to the professional's personal development. No two groups are the same, so that each experience with a group provides the professional with a learning experience. The personal enrichment to the group leader is related to the fact that, for example, it is easier to understand the behavior of alcoholics when working with several than when working with just one. In the group, the counselor can use the interaction and participation of peers to enhance professional understanding. This enriches and broadens one's professional experience and thereby contributes to greater expertise and efficacy of treatment. In turn, expertise and efficacy of treatment contribute to the continuation and the future of group counseling.

CHANGE IN THE FUTURE

To some extent, forecasting is in the nature of hypothesizing, but it is also important to recognize that the basis of some predictions exists currently. That is, the seeds are already beginning to see fruition; the future will be about expanding already-established trends.

The group field will mature as a science. According to Bednar and Kaul (1978), "foundations of potentially useful models are beginning to appear in the literature" (p. 810). This optimism is echoed by McGrath and Kravitz (1982), who concluded that their review of small group research found "more and better . . . research. . . . We are especially impressed with the increased sophistication about and interest in formal models" (p. 218).

One way for progress to take place in research on groups is for practitioners to become more actively involved. Practitioners have "real" groups available in which to replicate and extend laboratory research. In addition, a broader perspective with respect to doing research may enhance research efforts in the group field. For instance, traditional *quantitative* research designs will need to be supplemented with *qualitative* research procedures that permit a more intensive analysis of a single group and individuals within the group (see chapter 8). The use of triangulation in qualitative research, for instance cross-validation of behavioral outcomes from group treatment, may include self-reports, observer evaluation, and objective tests of performance. Qualitative research designs permit researchers to focus more directly on specific patients/clients with specific problems, treated by specific techniques, in specific settings. Both process and outcome could be studied simultaneously in many qualitative research designs.

Other design-related changes will involve planning for an ongoing program of study rather than for a series of isolated, one-shot studies (D. K. Morran, personal communication, March 9, 1983). Similarly, the use of a measurement battery in combination with an ongoing program of research will provide for the collection of increasingly relevant data. Finally, using meta-analysis will permit the results of several studies to be combined, so that less emphasis is placed on any single study. Overall, these innovations in group research will facilitate a more rigorous theoretical base for group counseling.

Another prediction for the future is that we will see more development in skills training models (Gazda, 1985). There has already been a progression in skills training models. In the past, they have been rather narrowly focused, for example, assertiveness training, problem solving, and the like. More recently, there is a trend toward comprehensive models: (1) the taxonomy of life skills developed by the Occupational and Career Analysis and Development section of the Employment and Immigration Department in Canada (Smith, 1982); (2) the structured learning therapy model of Goldstein, Sprafkin, and Gershaw (1976); and (3) Gazda's position of Life-Skills Training briefly described in Larson (1984) and more fully developed in Gazda, Childers, and Brooks (in press). In particular, it seems probable that counselors will see even more comprehensive taxonomies and models that are similar to these three. This will fill the lack that has existed in therapies of all kinds for a theory for mental health prevention. Unlike remedial-oriented therapies, the skills-training or educational approach is appropriate for prevention as well as remediation, particularly when the developmental framework is employed. With comprehensive models of life-skills training, the profession will be in a position to develop health maintenance organizations (HMOs) where both prevention and remediation in mental health can be provided. In addition, with these models, comprehensive training programs can be created for the educational system providing a means for building mental health into everyone's life. Thus, there could be less need for remediation and traditional interview-type, dyadic therapy. In turn, as a long-range effect, we may see the human service worker of the future as a "life-skills trainer" and not as a "therapist." In essence, it seems possible that as counselors invest in "giving psychology away," the group context will become the predominant mode for mental health professions in the future.

REFERENCES

Alyn, J. H., & Becker, L. A. (1984). Feminist therapy with chronically and profoundly disturbed women. *Journal of Counseling Psychology, 31,* 202–208.

Archer, J., Jr., & Reisor, J. S. (1982). A group approach to stress and anxiety management. *The Journal for Specialists in Group Work, 7,* 238–244.

Bales, R. F. (1951). *Interaction process analysis.* Cambridge, MA: Addison-Wesley.

Bednar, R. L., & Kaul, T. J. (1978). Experiential group research: Current perspectives. In S. L. Garfield & A. E. Bergin (Eds.), *Handbook of psychotherapy and behavior change: An empirical analysis* (2nd ed., pp. 769–815). New York: John Wiley.

Bednar, R. L., Melnick, J., & Kaul, T. J. (1974). Risk, responsibility, and structure: A conceptual framework for initiating group counseling and psychotherapy. *Journal of Counseling Psychology, 21,* 31–39.

Benne, K. D., & Sheats, P. (1948). Functional roles of group members. *Journal of Social Issues, 4,* 41–49.

Bloch, S., Crouch, E., & Reibstein, J. (1981). Therapeutic factors in group psychotherapy. *Archives of General Psychiatry, 38,* 519–526.

Blustein, D. L. (1982). Using informal groups in cross-cultural counseling. *The Journal for Specialists in Group Work, 7,* 260–265.

Bonney, W. C. (1965). Pressures toward conformity in group counseling. *Personnel and Guidance Journal, 43,* pp. 1970–1973.

Bonney, W. C. (1974). The maturation of groups. *Small Group Behavior, 5,* 445–461.

Bonney, W. C. (1976). Group counseling and developmental processes. In G. M. Gazda (Ed.), *Theories and methods of group counseling in the schools* (2nd ed., pp. 313–342). Springfield, IL: Charles C Thomas.

Capuzzi, D., & Gossman, L. (1982). Sexuality and the elderly: A group counseling model. *The Journal for Specialists in Group Work, 7,* 251–259.

Cartwright, D., & Zander, A. (1968). *Group dynamics: Research and theory* (3rd ed.). New York: Harper & Row.

Clarke, D. L., Kramer, E., Lipiec, K., & Klein, S. (1982). Group psychotherapy with mastectomy patients. *Psychotherapy: Theory, Research, and Practice, 19,* 331–334.

Coche, E., & Dies, R. R. (1981). Integrating research findings into the practice of group psychotherapy. *Psychotherapy: Theory, Research, and Practice, 18,* 410–416.

Comas-Diaz, L. (1981). Effects of cognitive and behavioral group treatment on the depressive symptomology of Puerto Rican women. *Journal of Consulting and Clinical Psychology, 49,* 627–632.

Conyne, R. K. (Ed.). (1985). *The group workers' handbook: Varieties of group experience.* Springfield, IL: Charles C Thomas.

Corey, G. (1985). *Theory and practice of group counseling* (2nd ed.). Monterey, CA: Brooks/Cole.

Corsini, R., & Rosenberg, B. (1955). Mechanisms of group psychotherapy: Processes and dynamics. *Journal of Abnormal Social Psychology, 51,* 406–411.

Daley, P. C., Bloom, L. J., Deffenbacher, J. L., & Stewart, R. (1983). Treatment effectiveness of anxiety management training in small and large group formats. *Journal of Counseling Psychology, 30,* 104–107.

Dies, R. R. (1980a). Current practice in the training of group therapists. *International Journal of Group Psychotherapy, 30,* 169–183.

Dies, R. R. (1980b). Group psychotherapy: Training and supervision. In A. K. Hess (Ed.), *Psychotherapy supervision* (pp. 337–366). New York: John Wiley.

Drum, D. J., & Knott, J. E. (1977). *Structured groups for facilitating development: Acquiring life skills, resolving life themes, and making life transitions.* New York: Human Sciences.

Ellis, D. G., Werbel, W. S., & Fisher, B. A. (1978). Toward a systematic organization of groups. *Small Group Behavior, 9,* 451–469.

Ellis, E. M., & Nichols, M. P. (1979). A comparative study of feminist and traditional group assertiveness training with women. *Psychotherapy: Theory, Research, and Practice, 16,* 467–474.

Forsyth, D. R. (1983). *An introduction to group dynamics.* Monterey, CA: Brooks/Cole.

Foulkes, S. H. (1951). Concerning leadership in group-analytic psychotherapy. *International Journal of Group Psychotherapy, 1,* 319–329.

Foulkes, S. H. (1961). Group processes and the individual in the therapeutic group. *British Journal of Medical Psychology, 34,* 23–31.

Gazda, G. M. (Ed.). (1976). *Theories and methods of group counseling in the schools* (2nd ed.). Springfield, IL: Charles C Thomas.

Gazda, G. M. (1978). *Group counseling: A developmental approach* (2nd ed.). Boston: Allyn and Bacon.

Gazda, G. M. (1982). Group psychotherapy and group counseling: Definition and heritage. In G. M. Gazda (Ed.), *Basic approaches to group psychotherapy and group counseling* (3rd ed., pp. 5–36). Springfield, IL: Charles C Thomas.

Gazda, G. M. (1984). *Group counseling: A developmental approach* (3rd ed.). Boston: Allyn and Bacon.

Gazda, G. M. (1985). Group counseling and therapy: A perspective on the future. *The Journal for Specialists in Group Work, 10,* 74–76.

Gazda, G. M., Childers, W. C., & Brooks, D. K., Jr. (In press). *Foundations of counseling and human services.* New York: McGraw-Hill.

Gazda, G. M., & Larsen, M. J. (1968). A comprehensive appraisal of group and multiple counseling. *Journal of Research and Development in Education, 1,* 57–132.

Goldstein, A. P., Sprafkin, R. P., & Gershaw, N. J. (1976). *Skill training for community living: Structured learning therapy.* New York: Pergamon.

Goodman, M., & Schwartz, B. D. (1981). Foreword: Theory and practice of group psychotherapy. *Psychotherapy: Theory, Research, and Practice, 18,* 409.

Hansen, J. C., Warner, R. W., & Smith, E. J. (1980). *Group counseling: Theory and process* (2nd ed.). Chicago: Rand McNally.

Hartman, J. J. (1979). Small group methods of personal change. *Annual Review of Psychology, 30,* 453–476.

Hersey, P., & Blanchard, K. H. (1983). An introduction to situational leadership. In W. R. Lassey & M. Sashkin (Eds.), *Leadership and social change* (3rd ed., pp. 142–159). San Diego, CA: University Associates.

Hipple, J. (1982). Group treatment of suicidal clients. *The Journal for Specialists in Group Work, 7,* 245–250.

Hotelling, K., & Reese, K. H. (1983). Women and anger: Relearning in a group context. *The Journal for Specialists in Group Work, 8,* 9–16.

Howes, R. J. (1981). Encounter groups: Comparisons and ethical considerations. *Psychotherapy: Theory, Research, and Practice, 18,* 229–237.

Johnson, D. W., & Johnson, F. P. (1975). *Joining together: Group theory and group skills.* Englewood Cliffs, NJ: Prentice-Hall.

Kingdon, M. A., & Bagoon, S. R. (1983). Sexuality awareness workshop for women. *The Journal for Specialists in Group Work, 8,* 17–23.

Kissen, M. (1981). Exploring general systems processes in group settings. *Psychotherapy: Theory, Research, and Practice, 18,* 424–430.

Kivlighan, D. M., Jr., McGovern, T. V., & Corazzini, J. C. (1984). Effects of content and timing of structuring interventions on group therapy process and outcome. *Journal of Counseling Psychology, 31,* 363–370.

Knowles, M., & Knowles, H. (1959). *Introduction to group dynamics.* New York: Association Press.

Larson, D. (Ed.) (1984). *Teaching psychological skills.* Monterey, CA: Brooks/Cole.

Luft, J. (1984). *Group processes: An introduction to group dynamics* (3rd ed.). Palo Alto, CA: Mayfield.

McGrath, J. E., & Kravitz, D. A. (1982). Group research. *Annual Review of Psychology, 33,* 195–230.

Muro, J. J., & Dinkmeyer, D. (1977). *Counseling children in the elementary and middle schools.* Dubuque, IA: Wm. C. Brown.

Napier, R. W., & Gershenfeld, M. K. (1981). *Groups: Theory and experience* (2nd ed.). Boston: Houghton Mifflin.

Oppenheimer, B. (1984). Short-term small group intervention for college freshmen. *Journal of Counseling Psychology, 31,* 45–53.

Page, R. C., & Wills, J. (1983). Marathon group counseling with i licit drug users: Analysis of content. *The Journal for Specialists in Group Work, 8,* 67–75.

Rose, G. S., & Bednar, R. L. (1980). Effects of positive and negative self-disclosure and feedback on early group development. *Journal of Counseling Psychology, 27,* 63–70.

Rutan, J. S., & Stone, W. N. (1984). *Psychodynamic group psychotherapy.* Lexington, MA: Collamore.

Schwartz, B. D. (1981). An eclectic group therapy course for graduate students in professional psychology. *Psychotherapy: Theory, Research, and Practice, 18,* 417–423.

Sherif, M. (1936). *The psychology of social norms.* New York: Harper.

Smith, P. (1982). *The development of a taxonomy of the life skills required to become a balanced self-determined person.* Ottawa, Canada: Employment and Immigration Counselor, Occupational and Career Analysis and Development Branch.

Snow, L. J. (1981). Female sexuality groups: Growth workshops for college women. *The Journal for Specialists in Group Work, 6,* 109–114.

Stockton, R., & Morran, D. K. (1982). Review and perspective of critical dimensions in therapeutic small group research. In G. M. Gazda (Ed.), *Basic approaches to group psychotherapy and group counseling* (3rd ed., pp. 37–85). Springfield, IL: Charles C Thomas.

Tuckman, B. W., & Jensen, M. A. C. (1977). Stages of small-group development revisited. *Group and Organizational Studies, 2,* 419–427.

Walker, L. J. S. (1981). Are women's groups different? *Psychotherapy: Theory, Research, and Practice, 18,* 240–245.

White, R., & Lippitt, R. (1968). Leader behavior and member reaction in three "social climates." In D. Cartwright & A. Zander (Eds.), *Group dynamics: Research and theory* (3rd ed., pp. 318–335). New York: Harper & Row.

Wilborn, B. L., & Muro, J. J. (1979). The impact of structuring technique on group functions. *The Journal for Specialists in Group Work, 4,* 193–200.

Yalom, I. D. (1970). *The theory and practice of group psychotherapy.* New York: Basic Books.

Yalom, I. D. (1975). *The theory and practice of group psychotherapy* (2nd ed.). New York: Basic Books.

Yalom, I. D. (1980). *Existential psychotherapy.* New York: Basic Books.

Zander, A. (1979). The psychology of group process. *Annual Review of Psychology, 30,* 417–451.

Zimet, C. N. (1979). Developmental task and crisis groups: The application of group psychotherapy to maturational processes. *Psychotherapy: Theory, Research, and Practice, 16,* 2–8.

CHAPTER 5
LIFE-STYLE AND CAREER DEVELOPMENT

Edwin L. Herr

Concerns about life-style and career development have been central emphases in counseling since the profession's beginnings in the United States in the late nineteenth and early twentieth centuries (see Chapter 1). While perhaps oversimplifying the matter, it is fair to contend that many, if not most, of the problems that youth and adults bring to counselors originate in their anxieties about or information deficits regarding career opportunities, decision making, work behavior, job search, and the transition to work.

Theories, concepts, and research about how individual career development unfolds and how it affects one's life-style clarify where and how counseling might be effective in enhancing or remediating career behaviors. Thus, in thinking about life-style and career development, it becomes important to distinguish among several different notions. For example, what meanings do we attach to life-style and career development? Or what do we mean by career guidance, career counseling, and other interventionist terms?

THE MEANING OF LIFE-STYLE AND CAREER DEVELOPMENT

In general, the term career development is used to describe a number of lifelong processes and the influences upon them that lead to one's work values, choice of occupation(s), creation of a career pattern, decision-making style, role integration, self- and career identity, educational literacy, patterns of work adjustment and related phenomena. How these patterns evolve as the individual pursues one set of values and interests rather than another, makes or avoids decisions, and compromises with or engages in risk-taking also fashions the life-style that characterizes one's life.

The current body of speculation and research we have come to call *career development* was described nearly twenty-five years ago as "a search for the psychological meaning of vocationally relevant acts (including the exploratory behavior of youth) and of work itself in the human experience" (Borow, 1961). This definition is still relevant to the continuing effort to understand how people formulate, prepare for, and live with the elements of career behavior, which are so frequently their central definitions of who they are and how they find meaning in their lives.

Though much more will be said in a subsequent section about the major theories of career development, it is useful here to extend the overview of some of the parameters of career development a bit further. For example, implicit in the quote from Borow cited above is the notion that career development is a process that continues throughout life. Although much of the early theoretical work in this area focused on adolescence, more recent theoretical work and research have focused on adulthood, creating comprehensive visions of how career behavior arises and how it changes at various points across the lifespan. Researchers are increasingly aware that career development is a dynamic, constantly changing set of behaviors that interact with events in the larger society, with family circumstances, and with all of the other social, physical, emotional influences which shape, stimulate, or arrest human development.

Theories of career development have addressed two broad categories of concern, which for our purposes here will be identified as *structural* and *developmental*. A structural approach tries to describe and measure individual differences in career development in order to use such information as predictors of success in various educational and occupational alternatives. A trait-and-factor approach is basically a structural approach. Most testing for individual differences rests upon structural assumptions: that different manifestations of career development, such as career maturity, level of aptitude, or types of interest held, can be analyzed in terms of their structure and measures of the inherent elements developed so that individual differences can be assessed and predicted. A developmental approach is not only concerned about understanding the structures that underlie different facets of career behavior, but more importantly, if and how such structures change over time and what factors influence such changes. (N.B. These terms are used differently than in Chapter 2, where structural is used as a particular developmental approach.)

As approaches to career development have proceeded both in structural and developmental terms, the interaction of life-style and career development has received increasing attention. Much of this attention has been devoted to definitions of the term career. For example, McDaniels (1978) has contended that career is not synonymous with one's job or occupation; it is a "life-style" concept that involves the interaction and the sequencing of work and leisure activities in which one engages throughout a lifetime. Hansen and Keierleber (1978) have argued that notions of career must include choices related to work, education, and family as interrelated phenomena affecting role integration. Gysbers and Moore (1981) proposed that the term *life career development* be used instead of career in order to emphasize the integration of roles, settings, and events in a person's life.

Super (1976) has defined career as:

> The course of events which constitutes a life; the sequence of occupations and other life roles which combine to express one's commitment to work in his or her total pattern of self development; the series of remunerated and nonremunerated positions occupied by a person from adolescence through retirement, of which occupations is only one; includes work-related roles such as those of student, employee and pensioner together with complementary avocational, familial, and civic roles. Careers exist only as people pursue them; they are person-centered. (p. 4)

Although many other definitions of career could be cited, these should be sufficient to make the point that life-style is a function of career development. The term career encompasses life-style and reflects the notion that it is not only occupations that are at issue in the term but "how persons integrate their work life with their other life roles: family, community, leisure" (Herr & Cramer, 1984, p. 14). Careers are unique to each person. They are not so much chosen directly as they are shaped and reshaped by what one does or does not choose, not in one instance but across time, by the compromises with available opportunities one makes, and by the complex interaction of psychological, sociological, educational, economic, and chance factors that affect every individual in unique ways.

A final, major point that needs to be reinforced here is that despite the existence of theories of behavior or the presence of career guidance and counseling, career and life-style development occurs in the life of every individual. It can be smooth, or jagged, or positive, or negative but proceed it will. Like sexual development or socialization in general, career development is a central component of human behavior whether or not organized systems of career guidance, counseling, or education exist to facilitate the process. Having said this, however, it is useful to make another point: Because career development is not a positive experience for all people, career guidance and counseling represent intervention strategies or sets of techniques designed to intervene in and improve career behavior both before it represents a problem to individuals and to remediate it where unrealistic choice, anxiety, ineffective work adjustment, or other life-style dilemmas have arisen. In this sense, the term career development does not describe an intervention process but rather the object or target of such intervention. Conceptual and research insights into patterns of career development and life-style comprise the theory of behavior—including the psychological, cultural, and economic influences upon it—which intervention strategies and techniques might modify in order to facilitate more positive and purposeful career development than would occur randomly.

CAREER GUIDANCE AND CAREER COUNSELING

Regardless of the reasons youths and adults initially come to counselors, it is a safe assumption that before their dilemmas, information deficits, or anxieties are fully brought to closure and new, constructive actions taken, *career guidance* or *career counseling* will be a major part of their interaction with a counselor. Career guidance and career counseling, however, are not terms with a single meaning. Rather they represent clusters of interventions or responses to different types of career development or life-style concerns. For example, career guidance can be defined as a set of multiple processes, techniques, and questions designed to assist an individual to understand and to act on self-knowledge and knowledge of opportunities in work, education, and leisure and to develop the decision-making skills by which to create and manage his or her own career development. This may include the development of attitudes, knowledge and skills concerned with decision making, information acquisition and processing, assertiveness training, anger management, communication and social skill development, job search, job interview, job adjustment skills, and placement into a chosen occupation, job relocation, stress management, and preretirement matters (Herr & Cramer, 1984). McDaniel (1978) has effectively summarized many of these perspectives in defining career guidance as an organized program to assist an individual to assimilate and integrate knowledge, experience, and appreciation related to: (1) self-understanding, (2) understanding the work society and those factors which affect its constant change, including worker attitude and discipline, (3) awareness of the part leisure may play in a person's life, (4) understanding of the necessity for the many factors to be considered in career planning, and (5) understanding the information and skills necessary to achieve self-fulfillment in work and leisure (p. 1).

McDaniel, like most other observers, believes that career counseling and career guidance are not interchangeable terms. He states the relationship very effectively when he says,

> Career counseling is much the same as other kinds of counseling except it focuses on the career development needs of the individual. It is one aspect of a career guidance program. There is a concentration of self-understanding, career information, career planning and career decision-making in a dynamic relationship. There is special attention to values and attitudes n the context of a fluid social-psychological-economic environment. Just as in all types of counseling (both individual and group) the personal relationship between the counselor and the counselee is critical. Other aspects of development such as intellectual, educational, physical, social, personal, emotional, psychological, are considered as appropriate when they relate to one's career. (McDaniel, 1978, p. 1)

However one defines career guidance and career counseling as representative of the techniques useful in facilitating career development, such definitions ultimately must be translated into a counselor's role with an individual, or a particular population, within a particular type of setting or institution. Although each counselor ultimately works out the specifics of such a role within the constraints and opportunities afforded by a particular context—private practice, a school, a community agency—the professional associations concerned with counselors or with the career guidance/career counseling aspects of the counselor's role have developed a number of position papers that provide assistance to counselors dealing with different populations and settings and trying to formulate an effective role.

Space does not permit a summary of all the position statements that are relevant to the content of this chapter, but it is useful to inventory some of the major professional association statements of the past fifteen years. They include:

- The joint American Vocational Association-National Vocational Guidance Association "Position Paper on Career Development," 1973.
- The American Personnel and Guidance Association position paper "Career Guidance: Role and Functions of Counseling and Guidance Practitioners in Career Education," 1975.
- The Association for Counselor Education and Supervision position paper, "Counselor Preparation for Career Development/Career Education," 1976.
- The American Personnel and Guidance Association "Study of the School Counselor in Career Education," 1980.

- The National Vocational Guidance Association position paper on "Vocational/Career Counseling Competencies," 1981.
- The American School Counselor Association statement on "The Role of the School Counselor in Career Guidance: Expectations and Responsibilities," 1984.

There are also other statements that provide excellent insights into how counselor functions in career guidance or career counseling might be conceived (see, for example, Mitchell, 1975; Phillips-Jones, Jones, & Drier, 1981). However, two dimensions emerge from these various statements. One is that it is possible to identify central or *modal types of role functions* that counselors tend to play in a particular setting with specific populations, and a second is that inherent in being able to engage effectively in career guidance or career counseling, a counselor needs to have a *set of competencies* that can be specified. An example of each of these two dimensions of counselor role and of counselor competency will suffice.

First, on the topic of counselor role and function, the most recent position statement cited above is that of the American School Counselor Association (1984), which indicates that the school counselor as a career guidance professional should concentrate on the delivery of a series of common, core experiences leading to career maturity through awareness, exploration, experience, and planning. The common core experiences, which the school counselor should provide for *all* students, include:

- Individual and group counseling to clarify work values and develop coping and planning skills.
- Formal and informal assessment of abilities, personality traits, and interests.
- Occupational/career information through community linkages such as field trips, speakers, shadowing experiences, internships.
- A career information center providing job-hunting skills, interviewing skills, educational and training opportunities, and financial aid possibilities.
- Training, goal setting, and decision making for the selection of tentative career paths based on the above.
- An opportunity for integration of academic and career planning leading to the selection of a high school curriculum as it relates to the appropriate career clusters.
- An opportunity for continuous evaluation and revision of the goal-setting process and action planning including an annual review of all students' plans of study.

Although the functions of the school counselor in career guidance have been found to be important in working with elementary, middle, and senior high school students, counselors working with adults in a career guidance role may engage in functions that differ from those of the school counselor. For example, one study (Griffith, 1980) of the career development services offered by 118 corporations to their employees included the following emphases in which counselors in industry would likely be engaged. They include:

- Support for external training
- Alcohol/drug counseling
- Retirement planning
- Support groups for minorities/women
- Job separation counseling
- Career exploration
- Career ladders
- Advancement strategies
- Personal financial planning
- Family/marital counseling

Neither the position statement on the role of the school counselor in career guidance by the American School Counselor Association nor the study of career development services offered in industry is exhaustive of the functions counselors are likely to perform in such settings. But they give a sense of the likely or the most frequent functions in which counselors will probably engage in that setting. As the list of position papers suggests, one is likely to find somewhat different functions being performed by counselors who work in the college setting, or with handicapped clients, or with economically disadvantaged populations.

However the counselor's functions are defined, there is ultimately the question of what competencies the counselor needs in order to perform such functions. In 1981 the National Vocational Guidance Association advocated that the counselor engaged in vocational or career counseling should demonstrate competencies in six areas. Selected examples of each of these areas are:

General Counseling—Knowledge of general counseling theories and techniques; ability to use counseling techniques in effectively assisting individuals with career choice and life/career development concerns; skills in building a productive relationship with the client; ability to assist the client to identify personal factors as well as contextual factors related to life/career decision making.

Information—Knowledge of education, training, employment trends, labor market, and career resources; basic concepts related to vocational/career counseling including career development, career pathing, and career patterns; career development and decision-making theories; strategies to store, retrieve, and disseminate vocational/career information.

Individual/Group Assessment—Knowledge of appraisal techniques and measures of aptitude, achievement, interest, values, and personality; strategies used in the evaluation of job performance, individual effectiveness, and program effectiveness; ability to interpret appraisal data to clients and other appropriate individuals or groups of people.

Management/Administration—Knowledge of program designs, needs assessment techniques and practices, and performance objectives used in organizing and setting goals for career development programs; knowledge of management concepts and leadership styles used in relation to career development programs; ability to prepare budgets and time lines and to design, compile, and report on evaluation of career development activities and programs.

Implementation—Knowledge of program adoption and planned change strategies and of personal and environmental barriers affecting the implementation of career development programs; ability to implement individual and group programs in career development for specified populations; ability to devise and implement a comprehensive career resource center and to implement pilot programs in a variety of career development areas.

Consultation—Ability to provide effective career consultation to influential individuals, the general public, and business and professional groups; ability to convey program goals and achievements to key personnel in positions of authority.

Such competency analyses as that of the National Vocational Guidance Association provide insight into the knowledge and skills that are required to be effective in both understanding and intervening in lifestyle and career development issues. In addition, such competency assessments provide structure for and insights into the appropriate content for the preservice and the inservice training of counselors. Finally, these competency assessments testify to the complexity, the multiple facets of career development, and professional responses to it.

CAREER DEVELOPMENT AND CHOICE THEORY: AN OVERVIEW

One of the clear trends in career guidance and counseling is the explosion of programs and practices in the field, the settings in which they are offered, and the range of populations now being served (Herr, 1981). Increasingly, these programs and practices are based upon the dramatic growth in research and theory in career development and choice that has occurred during the past thirty years (Gysbers, 1984a, 1984b).

The theory and speculation encompassed by the term career development (used interchangeably with the earlier term vocational development) includes a variety of emphases or approaches. In general, these approaches attempt to describe why career behavior is different among individuals, how it comes to be that way, and the importance of such behavior in people's lives. Because of the complexity and comprehensiveness of the questions that might be addressed under the broad rubric of career development, different approaches focus on different parts of career development or use conceptual lenses from different disciplines, such as psychology, sociology, economics, or anthropology.

The areas in which career development research and theory have been interested during the past three decades have become both broader and more specialized. Some theoretical approaches are most concerned with how an occupational choice is made at a particular point in time or the behavioral elements that comprise effective adjustment within a work setting. Some approaches emphasize exploratory behavior; others induction or transition behavior. Some theory and research is concerned with the structure of choice behavior or decision making, work behavior, or other forms of career maturity in a life stage, whereas other inquiries are principally concerned with how such structures change over time, and with the continuities and discontinuities in career patterns throughout life. Some approaches emphasize the mechanisms and stimuli that underlie individual action; other approaches address the individual-environmental transactions that emphasize the impact of economic events and social change on individual opportunities to choose. (See Chapter 2 for a discussion of the theoretical assumptions that underlie each of these approaches.)

Because of the large number of research studies and conceptual attempts to explain career behavior it is helpful to attempt to classify the major theories of career behavior or choice so that they can be contrasted or compared. Observers have developed different ways to classify such theories; there is no one right way to do so.

Classifications of Career Development and Choice Theory

Hilton (1962) classified the early theories of career development as models of *attribute matching, need reduction, economic man, social man,* and *complex information processing.* Crites (1969) divided the theories into those that are *psychological in origin* and those that are *nonpsychological.* Pitz and Harren (1980) have described the theories dealing specifically with career decision making as *normative* (or *prescriptive*) and *behavioral* (or *descriptive*). Super (1981) has contended, "The approaches and theories of the past 75 years fall into three main categories: those that *match people and occupations,* those that *describe development leading to matching,* and those that *focus on decision-making*" (p. 8). Holland and Gottfredson (1976) have described the two main approaches to understanding careers as the *developmental view* and the *differential view.*

Each of these classification structures has useful characteristics. However, for our purposes we will use a somewhat different structure in which theories are classified as (1) *trait-and-factor, actuarial,* or *matching,* (2) *decision,* (3) *situational* or *sociological,* (4) *psychological* or *personality,* and (5) *developmental* (Herr & Cramer, 1984).

Trait-and-Factor, Actuarial, or Matching Approaches

In 1909 Frank Parsons, the "Father of Vocational Guidance," enumerated in his classic book, *Choosing a Vocation,* his three-step process of vocational guidance (see Chapter 1). As he defined it, that process involved:

> First, a clear understanding of yourself, aptitudes, abilities, interests, resources, limitations, and other qualities. Second, a knowledge of the requirements and conditions of success, advantages and disadvantages, compensation, opportunities, and prospects in different lines of work. Third, true reasoning on the relations of these two sets of facts. (Parsons, 1909, p. 5)

What Parsons outlined, beyond a process of vocational guidance, was a trait-and-factor, actuarial, or matching approach to career behavior. Such an approach assumes that the individual can be described as having certain traits (such as interests, skills, aptitudes), that the different occupations or educational alternatives available to the individual require differing amounts and configurations of such traits, and that by matching individual traits and the requirements of different occupational or educational opportunities through a process of "true reasoning" (decision making), a choice would occur.

The trait-and-factor approach as conventionally understood is not focused on development but on identifying and describing the factors or traits which account for individual differences in learning or in job performance. The logic of the approach, which has origins in differential psychology and has both shaped and been shaped by the psychometric or testing movement in vocational guidance, is that individuals can be conceived of as being characterized by or possessing a constellation of traits which can be observed and measured (see Chapters 2 and 7). Such traits might include aptitudes, interests, values, psychomotor abilities, energy levels, temperaments, and related characteristics. The assumption is that these patterns of personal traits are more or less unique to each individual in ways similar to the assumption that different occupations or educational experiences can be described in terms of their unique requirements for different combinations or quantities of these individual traits.

In essence both the individual's pattern of traits and the requirements for different jobs, occupations, and learning situations can be profiled. When these profiles are compared or matched, it is then possible to identify what the individual can do, has the potential to do, and what the occupational or educational option requires the person to do if he or she is to experience success in that situation. It is also assumed that the individual, if he or she knows about his or her personal traits, can order these in some priority ranking and choose in accordance with them.

Trait-and-factor approaches to understanding and predicting career behavior have been the conceptual underpinnings of many vocational guidance and employment systems since the turn of the twentieth century. They have stimulated the development of tests and inventories to assess individual traits, the use of job analyses and occupational aptitude profiles to create classifications of occupational information, the formulation of predictive systems for assessing the weight or the importance of individual traits in the accomplishment of various occupational tasks, and the establishment of counseling models built upon the availability and use of such information. These are each important contributions to the history and progress of career guidance and career counseling.

The limitations of trait-and-factor, actuarial, or matching approaches in terms of theory development or practice take several forms. For one, trait-and-factor approaches focus on individual differences or differences in work and educational environments, but they do not attempt to explain how such differences came to be, how they developed. Furthermore, matching individuals and jobs or educational opportunities is frequently a static activity that tends to underestimate either the potential for change in the individual or in the environment or underplays the amount of individual difference a given environment can tolerate. Therefore, at its worst, a trait-and-factor approach can be overly deterministic unless the individual involved is an active participant in the choice process, helping to decide not only what is the best literal fit of individual characteristics and the requirements of different alternatives but rather how available choices accord with the particular person's assessments of what such a fit should be, given one's values, personal preferences, and willingness to make commitments at a particular point in time.

Regardless of the criticisms of a trait-and-factor approach, the information such an approach provides about individual differences and differences in the typical job or educational options available to them has been an important influence on thinking about career development and life-style matters. Actually, most of the remaining approaches to career development include trait-and-factor information, but its content and the emphases given to it vary markedly.

Decision Approaches

Approaches that fall within this category tend to be more concerned with the process of decision making than with individual traits or with occupational or educational requirements. Decision theory applied to choice-making styles or the processes of decision making tended to arise from economics and probability models in mathematics. A basic assumption in such a model is that one chooses an educational or occupational goal that will maximize one's gain and minimize one's chance of loss. To say this, however, is to enter a complicated arena that acknowledges that what each person values is likely to differ in degree and in kind. A particular occupational or educational choice might represent very different things to different people: greater prestige, security, social mobility, leisure time. Thus, the value that drives choice is not simply monetary gain but rather a range of other outcomes, which differ in importance to different persons.

Another notion fundamental to decision approaches is the assumption that at a point of choice, the individual has several possible alternatives. One may be to do nothing and avoid the choice options available. Beyond maintaining the status quo, however, it is likely that the individual has several other alternatives among which to choose. In each of these alternatives certain events are likely to occur, they have probabilities of occurrence and different value weightings to the individual, which can be estimated. If the outcomes of each possible event—

success, failure, monetary gain, enhanced happiness, admission to a prestigious job, geographical relocation, variety, security—are multiplied by its value to the person and its probability of happening, the person has a way of estimating the alternative that is likely to have the greater sum of value to him or her (Hills, 1964). Many techniques have been advocated to help with this estimation process (for example, Katz, 1963). Certainly, the rise of values clarification exercises and other such career guidance approaches is relevant to helping one clarify the ways by which to approach decision making and the individual values associated with it.

From a theoretical standpoint, however, decision theory approaches have emphasized other concepts that are useful in understanding career behavior. One is the importance of risk-taking style. People differ in their willingness to live with ambiguity and uncertainty of outcomes. Some would prefer the security of stable, even if lower, pay and the likelihood of a permanent position rather than the possibility of greater rewards cast within a context of variety and tenuousness. Thus, a number of studies of decision theory have examined the developmental influences, the personal histories, and the family and community belief systems that shape risk taking among people and its effects upon the choices they make.

Another important concept in decision-making theory is investment. One can be helped to conceptualize any choice alternative as requiring both tangible and intangible investments by the chooser, such as capital, prestige, time, tuition, union dues, deferred gratification, the risk or stigma of failure. Such investments can be identified and their values to the individual clarified.

Another concept relevant to decision theory is the importance of personal values in choice. Such an approach would suggest that it is not enough to have a close fit between individual traits and occupational or educational requirements, however important that may be to particular persons. Such a choice is seen as requiring an active assessment by the individual of the odds faced in any alternative. Such a deliberation places personal values at the heart of decision making. Implicit in such a requirement is the identification and the definition of one's values: what they are and what they are not, where they appear and where they do not appear (Katz, 1963).

Major views of decision making tend to combine values, preferences, risk-taking style, and self-concept in various combinations. For example, decision theory is frequently expressed in mathematical terms as *expectancy* x *value*. Many theorists use this type of formulation but weight its elements somewhat differently. Lawler (1973) suggests that all theorists using such a frame of reference maintain that the tendency to act in a particular fashion or to implement a particular choice depends on the "expectancy" that the act will be followed by a given consequence (or outcome) to the actor. Lawler then goes on to point out that when people make choices, they are really acting on two types of expectancies. The first has to do with the person's estimate that he or she will perform in the way a particular situation requires. The second expectancy has to do with the person's estimate that if the required performance is achieved, it will actually lead to the desired outcome: for example, money, security, and prestige.

A variation on expectancy x value formulations is that embodied in self-efficacy approaches (Bandura, 1977). Such an approach adds focus to the first expectancy outcome that Lawler identified: whether the individual really believes that he or she can successfully execute the behavior required to perform the desired outcomes. In such a view, the individual's belief about personal abilities and the relationship of previous accomplishments to the requirements of the current choice become elements that differ in magnitude, generality, and strength among persons and across choice situations.

An approach that attempts to apply social learning theory to career selection and in so doing helps to explain some of the factors giving rise to different individual patterns of expectancy x value or self-efficacy has been proposed (Krumboltz, 1979). Krumboltz suggests that the factors most influential in determining career selections are: (1) *genetic endowment* and *special abilities,* (2) *environmental conditions* and *events,* (3) *instrumental* and *associative learning experiences,* and (4) *task approach skills* (TASs). The interactions among these four types of influencers lead in each individual case to three categories of outcomes: (1) *self-observation generalizations* (SOGs)—overt or covert statements evaluating the individual's actual or vicarious performance in relation to learned standards, (2) *task approach skills*—which might include such skills as value clarifying, goal setting, alternative generalizing, information seeking, estimating, and planning, and (3) *actions*—entry behaviors such as applying for a specific job or training opportunity or changing a college major.

Perhaps of most direct importance to counselors is the influence that decision theory has had on formulating models of the steps important in the choice-making process. Such models have been helpful in creating a rationale as well as program themes for individual and group approaches to career guidance or career counseling and to the creation of computer-assisted guidance systems. In varying ways, these models reflect perspectives on expectancy x value considerations, self-efficacy issues, the importance of personal values and a knowledge of alternatives, and a problem-solving process that combines these various elements into a stimulus for systematic actions.

One classic model that emphasizes three elements of the decision-making process and describes the information requirements of each is that of Gelatt (1962). Gelatt's decision model proposes that information is the "fuel" of the decision maker and that the types of information required depend upon which of three essential systems is operating. The three systems are, first, a *predictive system,* which requires information about alternative actions, possible outcomes of actions, and probabilities of outcomes of actions; second, a *valuing* system, which requires information about the individual's relative preferences among probable outcomes; and, third, a *decision* system, which requires information about priorities or rules by which the individual wishes to act upon the information analyzed in the predictive and valuing systems.

Pitz and Harren (1980) suggest that any type of decision problem can be analyzed in terms of four sets of elements:

1. the set of *objectives* that the decision maker seeks to achieve;
2. the set of *choices,* or alternative courses of actions, among which the decision maker might choose;
3. a set of possible *outcomes* that is associated with each choice;
4. the *assessment* of each outcome with respect to how well it meets the decision maker's objectives. (pp. 321–322)

Bergland (1974) has suggested that the problem-solving steps in a decision-making process might include the following:

- defining the problem
- generating alternatives
- gathering information
- processing information
- making plans and selecting goals
- implementing and evaluating plans

Sociological Approaches

As we have reviewed them thus far, trait-and-factor approaches have shown that individuals differ in traits that are measurable and that have relationships to performance and satisfaction in different occupational and educational settings. The insights included under decision theory in the previous section combine to explain the influences of and the steps in the decision-making process itself as well as how persons integrate self-knowledge and knowledge of alternatives available to them into a plan of action, a choice. Situational or sociological approaches add a further dimension to our understanding of life-style and career development. Such an emphasis is concerned with the fact that individuals do not live in a vacuum; career development and life-styles are functions of the transactions that choosers have with their personal environments, including family, community, social class, and nation.

Situational or sociological approaches to career development accentuate the reality that one's environment both provides the kinds of choices from which any individual can choose and also shapes the likelihood that persons holding membership in different groups are likely to make certain choices and not others. A sociological or situational view of career development suggests that the narrowness or the breadth of the individual's cultural or social class boundaries has much to do with the choices a person is likely to consider, make, or implement. In this sense, the social structures of a family, a school, a community, a work setting, and a nation can be seen as both generators and filters of information ultimately communicated to an individual (Borow, 1966, 1984). Thus, the information and the encouragement that the poor receive as compared with that available to persons in middle and upper socioeconomic classes is likely to differ in kind and in degree. The sources of information, the role models of successful accomplishment in different educational or work choices, and the subtle forms of reinforcement to value some alternatives rather than others vary throughout the socioeconomic continuum. Similar differences in information and encouragement vary across racial groups, ethnic and religious groups, and between males and females.

Sociological and situational approaches to life-style and career development accentuate the reality that one simply cannot choose what one does not know about, does not know how to prepare for, or does not know how to obtain access to. Such differences in information and encouragement affect choice making, work adjustment, and life-style patterns.

To understand the functioning of any given individual's psychological characteristics—traits—it is important to consider the characteristics of the social grouping, the geographical setting, and the historical period in which the individual has been born and reared. It is the social context that influences the self-image. In the words of decision theory, the social context influences one's feelings of self-efficacy with regard to various types of performance, the ranking of the personal traits one is likely to use in work, the educational and occupational alternatives about which one is likely to know or which one is likely to consider appropriate, and the financial and psychological resources one is likely to have available.

Sociological or situational perspectives provide insight into the family and historical influences upon risk-taking behavior and the choice outcomes that different people value. If one's basic survival needs—such as food and shelter—have been met erratically, it is easy to understand why that person chooses jobs that offer stability and a secure, if modest, income. If one's family values have constantly reinforced a set of behavioral standards to be achieved in order to avoid being considered unworthy of the family's support, it is understandable that one's motivation will differ from another whose environment has reinforced other behavioral standards. If one's gender or one's race have been obstacles to access to certain opportunities, it takes an extraordinary amount of desire, persistence, and ability to gain access to such opportunities. Sociological or situational perspectives address the probability that while vocational and life-style preferences of people across social and economic class lines may be similar, their expectations of being able to achieve such preferences are likely to differ. The person raised in an environment that does not support planfulness and a commitment to long-range goals, that does not value deferred gratification as a price one pays to achieve better skills or to save for a better future, or that does not provide knowledge of how to cope effectively with the environment is going to experience different aspirations and career development of a different character from an individual who experiences none of these environmental characteristics.

Sociological and situational perspectives have a long and important history in their probing of the effects of social class on occupations chosen and on other characteristics of the acquisition of work identity and career mobility (Blau, Bustad, Jessor, Parnes, & Wilcock, 1956; Hoggart, 1957; Hollingshead, 1949; Lipsett, 1962). Indeed, recent sociological perspectives have raised questions about whether the emphases in many current career development theories on the primacy of individual action and value preferences is valid. Roberts (1977), taking a sociological perspective, raises the implicit question as to whether people choose or are chosen; the latter conditions are a function of their socioeconomic status, class boundaries against certain opportunities, levels of aspiration, and related phenomena.

The probable answer to Roberts's question is that some people choose their occupational and life-style roles, and others do not. Increasingly, research studies are reinforcing the view that the kind and quality of exploratory experiences, understanding of work opportunities, decision making, and related elements of career behavior are experienced differently by groups that differ on socioeconomic, gender, and racial terms (Herr & Enderlein, 1976; Herr, Weitz, Good, & McCloskey, 1982). The work of Lo Cascio (1967), Gribbons and Lohnes (1968), and Herr and Cramer (1984) has shown that career development is not a smooth, linear progression to upward mobility. Rather, there are different patterns of continuity and discontinuity, of delay, and of impairment associated with economic advantagement, gender, and differences in educational and intellectual level. These again are sociological or situational phenomena.

Personality Approaches

Sociological or situational approaches to career development and life-style are, in a sense, macro approaches. They describe the social mechanisms within which individual action is possible and by which it is circumscribed. Personality approaches might be considered micro approaches, attempts to identify individual as opposed to group mechanisms that shape career behavior.

Personality approaches, as compared to the other four categories of career development theory discussed in this chapter, emphasize needs and drives intrinsic to individual personality, which choices of work are intended to satisfy. For example, they contrast with the trait-and-factor approach, which emphasizes observable and measurable behavior (rather than inferred states as in the personality approaches) to explain the motivations of people to choose and to behave as they do.

The advocates of intrinsic motivation come from a variety of conceptual origins (see Chapter 2). Certainly, those who favor Freudian psychoanalytic approaches to the explanation of work choice and adjustment would favor need or drive states as stimuli to select one form of work rather than another (Bordin, Nachman, & Segal, 1963; Brill, 1948).

But there are other theorists—such as neo-psychoanalytic, self-theorists—who also embrace a need-drive explanation for much career behavior. The general assumption among such approaches is that because of differences in personality structure, individuals develop specific needs and seek satisfaction of these needs through occupational choices and selection of work settings. The further assumption is that different occupational or educational areas are populated by people of different needs with different personality types. In the personality approach, one of the major features is a self-classification, which may be either conscious or unconscious, by which persons seek out environments that are likely to gratify their particular need profile.

Roe (1956), for example, is a theorist whose personality approach to career development bridged psychoanalytic and self-theory approaches. Her approach had three major aspects. First, she adopted the theory of *prepotent needs,* formulated by Maslow (1954), to vocational behavior. Oversimplifying the matter, the assumption is that persons tend to select work that will meet the needs that they feel are most urgent or are not routinely gratified from such sources as psychological, safety, belongingness and love, self-esteem, information, beauty, and self actualization (see Chapter 2). A second dimension of Roe's work is an emphasis on the effect of *child-rearing practices upon adult orientations* to people and things. Her basic premise was that child-rearing environments that were overprotecting, democratic, or rejecting shaped differently the kinds of interactions people have with other people—toward or away from them—and with things. In turn, these interactions were seen to be manifested in adult interest patterns related to choice of occupational families. The third aspect of her work was to delineate a two-dimensional classification of *occupational groups by field and level.* The eight fields in which all occupations were grouped included Service, Business Contact, Organization, Technology, Outdoor, Science, General Culture, and Arts and Entertainment. These fields were classified by the degree to which they gratified needs involving people and things. The second dimension, that of level, included six different levels of responsibility, training, or education including professional and managerial I and II; semiprofessional, small business; skilled; semiskilled; and unskilled. The assumption of Roe's theory was that *the occupational level attained is a function of genetic endowment as reflected in intelligence, attained education, and capability for responsibility; the field chosen is a function of one's level of interest in people or things.*

Holland's (1966, 1973) approach is currently the preeminent and most empirically based personality approach. It gives major and explicit attention to individual behavioral predisposition and personality type. A basic assumption of the Holland approach is that as a result of the interaction between heredity and environment, the individual develops a hierarchy of preferred methods for dealing with social and environmental tasks; these preferences are reflected in one's *modal personal orientation.* This modal personal orientation, or behavioral style, is classified into one of six personality categories—*artistic, conventional, enterprising, investigative, realistic,* and *social.* According to the theory, these are not pure types, but most persons can be classified in some distribution across three of them, such as Realistic-Enterprising-Investigative (RIE). One will then seek occupations or educational settings that satisfy and are compatible with the hierarchy of preferences the individual possesses.

The other part of the Holland equation is classification of the environment in ways comparable to classification of personality. The assumption is that because people seek out and gravitate to settings where they perceive that others share their values and interests with regard to work activity, leisure time, and so on, specific occupations or educational units tend to attract persons of similar personality types. As a result, different occupations or curricula are populated to a larger degree than other occupations with persons of a particular personality configuration. In this sense, it is possible to classify *occupations and other environments* into the same six types as personality: artistic, conventional, enterprising, investigative, realistic, and social. Changing career patterns, occupational or educational maladjustments, and other choice or adjustment difficulties could be explained by Holland's theory by suggesting that people who have certain patterns of preferences, their behavioral styles, achieve in some occupational or educational settings and not in others. Therefore, the role of career counseling and guidance is to match as congruently as possible the personality style and the characteristics of the work or educational setting. If this fails, persons will either need to take on the characteristics and role requirements of the occupations they have chosen or leave those fields to continue seeking a role that *is* congruent with their particular values, needs, and work habits.

Holland, like Roe, also identifies level hierarchies within occupational environments. According to him, the level of occupational responsibility or skill to which one gravitates depends upon the person's intelligence and self-knowledge. Self-knowledge refers to the amount of accurate self-information the individual possesses; self-knowledge is different from self-evaluation, which refers to the worth the person attributes to him or herself.

Holland's theory (1973, pp. 2–10) can be summarized by its emphases that *individual behavior is a function of the interaction between one's personality and one's environment, and that choice behavior is an expression of personality.* Thus, persons inhabiting specific environments, whether occupational or educational, have similar modal personal orientations, and their responses to problems, work values, and interpersonal situations are likely to be similar. Therefore, the choice problem is to locate and gain access to those environments that permit people to express their personality styles. As persons explore occupational or educational possibilities, they rely on stereotypes about themselves and about their choice opportunities to guide this search. If their preferences are clear and their information about self-characteristics or occupation is accurate, they will likely make effective choices. If their understanding of their personality type or appropriate occupational choices is unclear, they are likely to be indecisive and vacillate among possible choices.

Developmental Theories

In their own fashion, each of the preceding perspectives focuses on some aspect of the implied assumption that persons are better suited for some occupation or job families than for others. The personality and trait-and-factor approaches attempt to identify the bases on which such individual differences in occupational fit might be identified. The decision approaches speak more directly to how people choose whatever they choose. The sociological approaches stress the importance of the social structure in determining what kinds of information and encouragement people of different socioeconomic, gender, or racial backgrounds are likely to receive, how this affects their likely awareness and consideration of alternatives, and how such social factors influence continuity and discontinuity in individual career development. The developmental approaches tend to include many of the concepts advanced in each of the first four perspectives but do so with particular emphasis on the unfolding of career development across the lifespan.

The developmental approaches have expanded the vision of researchers and theorists from occupational choice as an *act* to occupational choice as a *process.* Such a view reinforces the perspective that choice is not confined to a certain period of life but has its roots in the early life of the child and reoccurs throughout one's lifespan, changing its premises in response to institutional, social, and economic pressures.

Ginzberg and his colleagues (Ginzberg, Ginsburg, Axelrod, & Herma, 1951) were among the first theorists to give voice to career development and life-style patterns as longitudinal processes. They asserted that "occupational choice is a developmental process; it is not a single decision but a series of decisions made over a period of years. Each step in the process has a meaningful relation to those which precede and follow it" (p. 185).

Using a developmental process as their organizing premise, Ginzberg et al. identified a series of life stages in which preadolescents and adolescents face certain factors that ultimately relate to occupational choice. These stages were labeled *fantasy, tentative,* and *realistic,* and each of these was in turn divided into substages. For example, the tentative period was divided into *interest, capacity, value,* and *transition* substages, which emerge sequentially. Each of these factors tends to emerge in turn and to serve to filter further the alternatives one will consider. The tentative period is followed by the realistic stage, which is broken into *exploration* and *crystallization* substages. A major point that emerged from these perspectives in the original Ginzberg et al. work was that as children, adolescents, and adults cope with the tasks, self-insights, and information about the alternatives available to them in these different life periods, there is a constant compromising between wishes and possibilities. This synthesizing and compromising process in turn defines, filters, narrows, and makes more specific and realistic the range of choices that a particular individual is likely to consider. He and his colleagues originally viewed the process of filtering out alternatives as generally irreversible and as occurring predominantly during adolescence.

In a restatement of his theory in 1972, Ginzberg modified his original premise in several ways. First, he no longer emphasizes that choice making ends in adolescence or young adulthood; he now sees decision making as a process that continues throughout adulthood. Second, he has tempered his early view that the developmental processes of choice are irreversible. His recent work suggests that the individual may return to alternatives earlier reflected as personal circumstances change to accommodate such possibilities. Finally, he has replaced the earlier notion of *compromise* as a major aspect of choice with the concept of *optimization.* While subtle in their differences, optimization really suggests more individual power to try constantly to improve the occupational fit between people's changing selves and circumstances.

Perhaps the developmental approach that has received the most attention and been the most encompassing in its influence upon research and theory in career development and life-style matters is that of Super and his colleagues. Although the work of Super became visible at approximately the same time as that of Ginzberg and his colleagues, Super's influence has been more wide-ranging and sustained than that of Ginzberg. Many of the insights and refinements have evolved from a longitudinal study of the vocational behavior of a group of ninth grade boys, which began in the early 1950s and followed these persons into adulthood. Known as the Career Pattern Study, this longitudinal research of the same individuals from early adolescence into their late thirties became the crucible in which many of the ideas of Super and his colleagues have been tested.

Super's (1957, 1969, 1977) approach is in many respects multidisciplinary. In formulating his theoretical constructs, Super has integrated insights from differential, developmental, social, and phenomenological psychology with those from trait-and-factor, sociological, and personality approaches into an organized whole.

Perhaps the best known aspect of Super's theory is his life-stage structure, which incorporates developmental tasks in five periods across the lifespan. These life stages include *growth* (from birth to approximately fourteen years of age), *exploration* (ages fourteen to twenty-five), *establishment* (ages twenty-five to forty-five), *maintenance* (ages forty-five to sixty), and *decline* (age sixty and beyond). Each of these stages is divided into substages, which identify developmental tasks that individuals must confront and master if their career development is to proceed effectively. For example, during the exploratory stage the developmental tasks of major importance are *crystallizing* a vocational preference, *specifying* it, and *implementing* it; in the establishment stage, the years of early adulthood, the important developmental tasks are *stabilizing* in the chosen vocation, *consolidating* one's status, and subsequently *advancing* in the occupations. Each of these tasks and those in other life stages are broken down further into the behaviors and attitudes that comprise them.

Associated with a life-style/developmental-task structure that spans one's life are several other important concepts. One is vocational maturity, now typically labeled *career maturity*. This concept conveys the notion that there are certain behaviors that describe individuals' mastery of the developmental tasks associated with each life stage. Thus, one can think of career maturity as both a structural and a developmental concept because the elements of career maturity can be identified and assessed for particular life stages and they also change in different life stages.

Such notions of the structure of career maturity as well as its forms are reflected in the major assessments of it, for example, the adolescent and adult forms of the Career Maturity Inventory (Crites, 1973), the Super et al. (1971) secondary school and college forms of the Career Development Inventory, and the more recent Adult Career Concerns Inventory. These assessment instruments are used to appraise the individual's career development in comparison with others in his or her life stage and with respect to specific elements of career maturity at that life stage. For example, the Career Development Inventory, either the school or university form, developed by Super, Thompson, Lindeman, Jordaan, and Myers (1979) has eight scales. They include career planning; career exploration; decision making; world of work information; knowledge of preferred occupational group; career development attitudes; knowledge and skills of career development; career orientation total. The

Career Maturity Inventory, developed by Crites, has separate Attitude and Competency scales. The clusters within the Attitude scale include involvement in the choice process, orientation toward work, independence in decision making, preference for choice factors, and conceptions of the choice process. The scales or clusters embodied in each of these assessment instruments are mentioned to illustrate what are conceived to be examples of career maturity in different forms of these career development instruments.

Assessments of career development and of the concept of career maturity are important in Super's theory because they accent the importance of identifying and acting upon instances where career development has gone awry or is not as mature as it might be. The fundamental assumption of this perspective is that if a person experiences a lack of information or a deficit in reality-testing at a particular life stage, he or she is not likely to cope with certain later developmental tasks, and thus career development may be impaired. Such people may flounder in one developmental spot, or they may prematurely close off their consideration of training opportunities or occupational choices because of a lack of self-knowledge, planning, or an array of other possibilities. According to the theory, such circumstances do not reflect the quality of career development that persons are capable of achieving.

With respect to the characteristics of career (vocational) maturity, Super (1977) now postulates that the same five factors are as important in mid-career as in adolescence. They include *planfulness or time perspective, exploration, information, decision making,* and *reality orientation.* The important point is that although the sets of factors are important in career maturity at either of these time periods, the tasks, the topics to be explored, and the kinds of information needed by forty-year-old adults differ from those of adolescents. Such a view reaffirms the notion that individual career maturity is an important goal in each life stage but that its behavioral elements are likely to change across time, and such changes need to be reflected in career development assessment instruments.

Another key construct in Super's theory and research is the importance of the *development and implementation of the self-concept.* The theory assumes, in fact, that the individual chooses an occupation that will allow him or her to function in a way that is consistent with one's self-concept. The self-concept in effect represents a shaper of and a trigger for individual behavior. Thus, career guidance and counseling must attend to the individual's need for in-depth and accurate information about occupational alternatives, but at least as importantly, the individual needs to be assisted to avoid unrealistic estimates of ability and vague understandings of personal values and preferences.

One final aspect of Super's theory will be mentioned here although much more deserves to be said. This aspect of his recent formulations speaks quite directly to the matter of life-style issues in career development. Super (1980, 1981) has suggested in his formulation of a Life-Career Rainbow that most people play nine major roles in their life. In approximate chronological order they include: (1) *child* (son or daughter), (2) *student,* (3) *leisurite,* (4) *citizen,* (5) *worker* (including unemployed worker and nonworker as ways of playing the role), (6) *spouse,* (7) *homemaker,* (8) *parent,* and (9) *pensioner.* These roles are played in four principal theaters of life: (1) the *home,* (2) the *community,* (3) the *school* (including college and university), and (4) the *workplace.* The constellation of roles and their interactions constitute one's career.

Super suggests that the fact that people play several roles at the same time and in several theaters indicates that occupation, family, community, and leisure roles affect each other. He states, "Success in one facilitates success in others, and difficulties in one role are likely to lead to difficulties in another" (1980, p. 287). Further, "The simultaneous combination of life roles constitutes the *life style;* their sequential combination structures the *life space* and constitutes the *life cycle.* The total structure is the *career pattern*" (1980, p. 288).

Other Developmental Theorists

There are other theorists who deserve more attention than space permits here. One of these is Tiedeman, who with other colleagues, has advanced some important ideas influencing the way career behavior has been viewed by other researchers and by practitioners. For example, Tiedeman and O'Hara (1963) described the intersection of the *anticipation* of an occupational choice and the actual *induction* into the occupation chosen. Many other theorists have been concerned primarily about the exploration or anticipation of choice but not what happens when one tries to implement what has been chosen. According to Tiedeman and O'Hara the stages of the occupational induction process include the stages of *social induction, reformation,* and *integration.* In such a perspective it is assumed that the individual at the point of occupational induction has a set of ideas about what it will be like to work in that occupation. Such ideas have been developed during the anticipation process, which includes stages of *anticipation, exploration, crystallization, choice,* and *clarification.* The test of the effectiveness of such anticipation lies with whether one's ideas about the occupations chosen are congruent with the reality of the occupation when the person is inducted into it. In any induction process, there is some give-and-take between the individual and the environment (these are the stages of reformation and integration) in which the individual modifies his or her self-concept to take on the role requirements of the job expectations encountered and the job bends to some degree to the individual's style. If the demands of the job for reformulating one's self-concept are within individual tolerances for such reformulation, induction is likely to be successful. If, on the other hand, the demands by the job for accommodation by the individual go beyond personal limits of tolerance or adaptation, the individual is likely to leave the environment and to begin the processes of exploration and anticipation again.

Tiedeman and O'Hara also emphasize that career (vocational) development is a continuing process of differentiating ego identity. In this aspect of their formulation, they use Erikson's (1963) model of psychosocial crises at seven developmental stages (see Chapter 2) as an explanation for differences in career development. Throughout their theoretical perspectives, they stress the intimate interaction of the self-concept and the career concept as they develop over time through many small decisions.

In his more recent work, Tiedeman with others (Dudley & Tiedeman, 1977; Peatling & Tiedeman, 1977; Tiedeman & Miller-Tiedeman, 1977) have been increasingly concerned with emphasizing the power of the individual to create a career and in advancing notions of autonomy, competence, and agency as major ingredients of such processes. In so doing, Tiedeman and his colleagues are increasingly emphasizing the holistic nature of the human career and the need to see career and the process of career development as one.

One of the major and fairly recent phenomena in developmental approaches to career development and life-style issues is a move from generic theories of career development to theories that look more directly at certain populations. For example, the work of Knefelkamp and Slepitza (1976) blends developmental and cognitive approaches to focus on the career development of college students. In addition, a large number of theorists have begun to look at the career development of specific adult populations (Gould, 1978; Levinson, 1977; Lowenthal, Thurnher, Chiroboga, & Associates, 1976).

Many of the perspectives on career development for adults emphasize the important effects that various types of transitions have on career development. Schlossberg (1978), a leading adult theorist, has summarized the work of a number of other adult theorists into five propositions that are relevant to career development and life-style issues.

1. Behavior in adulthood is determined by social rather than by biological clocks.
2. Behavior is at times a function of life stage, at others of age.
3. Sex differences are greater than either age or stage differences.
4. Adults continually experience transitions requiring adaptation and reassessment of the self.
5. The recurrent themes of adulthood are identity, intimacy, and generativity.

Watts (1980) contends that there are at least three models for looking at the needs of adults for career guidance. One addresses *developmental stages* in the life cycle as they are related to various periods of chronological age. In such a perspective the role of career guidance would be to help persons adapt to the requirements of the developmental tasks characteristic of each stage. A second model focuses upon *roles*. It views aging as a process of learning new roles and relinquishing old ones. The career guidance response here would involve periodic stock-taking about roles and about the interactions and transitions between them. The third model focuses on *life events* that involve significant transitions. Here the career guidance role is concerned with "coping with crises and realizing the growth potential that may be innate within such crises" (p. 20).

In sum, this section has tried to illustrate the multiple factors that shape the processes and create the content of career behavior and the resulting life-style patterns by which different people are characterized. As Jepsen (1984) has observed, "Theoretical ideas serve an indispensable function in career guidance practice, especially in the fundamental tasks of problem identification and intervention design. Formal career development theories provide perspective for framing practical problems" (pp. 153–154). The previous sections have tried to help the counselor think in such terms. The remainder of the chapter will look more directly at some of the approaches to affecting life-style and career development through the use of information, career exploration, and career decision-making processes.

OCCUPATIONAL AND EDUCATIONAL INFORMATION

Explicit in some and implicit in other theories of career development is the importance of accurate and relevant information. Gelatt (1962), cited previously, called information "the fuel of the decision-maker." Given the complexity of the occupational and educational systems from which people choose, it is not possible to acquire directly all of the information that one needs to inform one's choice making. Rather, one must turn to sometimes abstract, sometimes vicarious, as well as concrete and personal methods of acquiring information about occupational and educational opportunities and their differences.

Before turning to the sources of information about one's alternatives, however, it is essential to affirm that such information only has meaning insofar as the data acquired are evaluated within a framework of what individuals know about themselves. Without accurate self-knowledge about one's aptitudes, interests, values, and attitudes toward learning and work, the individual has no real basis for evaluating the importance of the information available or its relevance to the decisions that need to be made.

As suggested elsewhere (Herr & Cramer, 1984), the process of career development requires that information continually reinforce planfulness; the interaction of educational or training alternatives, occupational alternatives, and self-characteristics is mandatory if effective career decision making is to occur. Occupational and educational information is meaningful only as it contributes to such interaction. Information of any kind is essentially neutral unless it fits into a relevant, current system of individual choice making.

In an information-rich society such as the United States the sources of occupational and educational information take many forms: printed matter, audiovisual media, individual and group interviews with resource persons from educational or occupational settings, simulations and gaming techniques, role-playing, field trips, formal curricula designed to convey information systematically about occupations and educational opportunities, direct experience (parttime work, work study, cooperative education, industrial shadowing), computer-assisted career guidance and information retrieval systems, and career resource centers.

Within each of these classifications of source material are many examples of occupational and educational information that are used differently with different populations. For example, in 1981 a national survey of career information systems in secondary schools was conducted by the Educational Testing Service and funded by the National Institute of Education. School and student questionnaires from 3,412 secondary schools and 4,883 students indicated that a wide range of information offerings is available to students. No school has all of the resources available, and some schools have very little occupational and educational information. Approximately 25 percent of the schools have some type of computer system; only 18 percent use simulations. The top ten resources and the nationwide percentage of schools that used them are shown in Table 5-1.

TABLE 5-1 CAREER INFORMATION RESOURCES FOR HIGH SCHOOL STUDENTS

Resource	Percentage of Schools Using Them
Occupational Outlook Handbook	92
Conference with counselors	83
Dictionary of Occupational Titles	83
Career days, speakers, etc.	75
Occupational handbooks for the military	75
Vocational school directories	74
Externally produced AV materials	71
College directories arranged by occupation	70
Occupational information units in subject matter courses	62
Job site tours	59

Source: From *Survey of Career Information Systems in Secondary Schools: Final Report of Study* (p. 243) by W. Chapman & M. R. Katz, 1981, Princeton, NJ: Educational Testing Service. Copyright 1981 by Educational Testing Service. Reprinted by permission.

The information from the student questionnaires suggests that the informational resources students use most, although not exclusively, are not those provided by the school. Parents or relatives, friends, and employed workers ranked 1, 2, and 3 as persons with whom students had talked about occupations. Counselors and teachers lagged far behind. Parents or relatives and someone in the proposed line of work were named as frequently as were formal publications.

While several other points about the availability and the use of information were apparent from this national survey, perhaps the one that is most important is that students generally do not lack career resources. Rather, they lack a meaningful, personal context in which to put the information. This finding reinforces Katz's observation of more than twenty years ago that students "often don't know what information they need, don't have what information they want, or can't use what information they have" (Katz, 1963, p. 25). Career guidance approaches in schools must be designed to help students determine what questions to ask, what information will answer their questions, and where to find the information they need; and help them structure the information and interpret it and arrive at a strategy for making decisions based on information (Chapman & Katz, 1981, p. 252). As will be discussed in the next section, youths and adults need to be educated to some paradigm of decision making in which information of different types has a visible role and is integrated into awareness, exploration, and action elements of such a paradigm (Herr & Cramer, 1984).

Another view of sources of occupational and education information comes from analyses of resources used by adults in seeking employment. One such study (Herr, Weitz, Good, McCloskey, & Long, 1981) found that 956 adults from different educational and socioeconomic backgrounds cited the sources in Table 5-2 as their prime sources of information about occupational choices and employment opportunities.

TABLE 5-2   SOURCES OF CAREER INFORMATION FOR ADULTS

Source	Rank
Newspaper ads	1
U.S. Employment Service	2
Postsecondary institution	3
Career development and placement agency	4
Private employment agency	5
Professional publications	6
CETA (Comprehensive Employment and Training Act)	7
Professional organizations	8
H.S. counselor or teacher	9
Labor unions	10
Veterans Administration	11
Bureau of Vocational Rehabilitation	12

Source: From *Research on the Effects of Secondary School Curricular and Personal Characteristics Upon Post-Secondary Educational and Occupational Patterns: Final Report for National Institute of Education* (p. 136) by E. L. Herr, A. Weitz, R. Good, G. McCloskey, & T. E. Long, 1981, University Park, PA: Vocational Development Study. Copyright 1981 by Vocational Development Study. Reprinted by permission.

These adults, like those studied in other investigations (Campbell & Cellini, 1981), frequently suffered from a lack of information or more important, methods of using information effectively in the decision making in which they engage.

Whether in schools or in agencies, a major problem for counselors is the management of occupational and educational information. If the career guidance program uses one of the existing computer-assisted career guidance systems (such as DISCOVER, SIGI, GIS, or Choices), management and updating of such information is largely a function of what software one leases or purchases. However, where counselors manage printed, audiovisual, or similar material themselves, they need systems by which to classify, file, and retrieve the information. Weinstein (1982), in reviewing the data from the Educational Testing Service national study of career information resources in secondary schools, indicated that the top-ranked methods for filing career information materials were (1) alphabetically by occupational title, (2) by Dictionary of Occupational Titles code number, (3) by type or level of education or training, (4) by interest field, (5) by Dewey decimal system, and (6) by type of industry of employer. Whichever system one uses, it seems clear that information is only valuable if it is current, if it is relevant to the questions an individual is exploring, and if the individual can put the information into some system of exploration and decision making.

CAREER DEVELOPMENT EXPLORATION TECHNIQUES

Although information may be the fuel for decision making, it cannot stand alone in facilitating career development. Indeed, after an extensive review of research literature, Holland, Magoon, and Spokane (1981) suggested that we now have a rough understanding of how career interventions work. An ideal intervention or a series of related interventions would include (1) occupational information organized by a comprehensible method and easily accessible to a client, (2) assessment materials and devices that clarify a client's self-picture and vocational potentials, (3) individual or group activities that require the rehearsal of career plans or problems, (4) counselors, groups, or peers that provide support, and (5) a comprehensible cognitive structure for organizing information about oneself and occupational alternatives. In the previous section, we discussed (1); in this section and the next we will discuss (2) through (5).

Program Planning

One of the clear outcomes of the evolution of career development theory over the past thirty years has been the use of insights into how career behavior unfolds and the elements that comprise it as organizing themes for programs designed to provide career development exploration. While there are many such examples of the translation of theory into program planning structures, one excellent example is that of the Minnesota Career Development Curriculum Project (Tennyson, Hansen, Klaurens, & Antholz, 1975). This project has extracted from career development theories a series of Career Management Tasks that need to be completed by children, adolescents, and young adults. By way of illustration the Career Management Tasks important to students in grades 7 to 9 and persons beyond high school include:

Grades 7–9
1. Clarification of self-concept
2. Assumption of responsibility for career planning
3. Formulation of tentative career goals
4. Acquiring knowledge of occupations, work settings, life-styles
5. Acquiring knowledge of educational and vocational resources
6. Developing awareness of the decision-making process
7. Acquiring a sense of independence

Post–High School
1. Developing interpersonal skills essential to work
2. Developing information-processing skills about self and the world of work
3. Reintegration of the self
4. Acquiring a sense of community
5. Commitment to a concept, career
6. Acquiring the determination to participate in change

Although tasks for the elementary school children or for students in grades 10 to 12 are not included here, the examples given illustrate the type of planning and organizing structure that the Minnesota model represents. The full model then adds content and activities that relate to each of the themes noted. In such a structure, career guidance activities can be directed at specific behavioral goals to be achieved. Counselor accountability can be more readily achieved, and resource needs can be more clearly articulated.

Examples of Career Development Programs

Because of space limitations here, examples of career development programs in operation will be limited in number. However, those chosen will illustrate current practices with elementary school, middle school, senior high school children and youth, college students, and adults. In most of these programs opportunities for exploration of personal characteristics, and of occupational and educational information are combined with training in decision making. The program examples have been chosen to reflect the range of individual and group techniques that can be used in facilitating career awareness, exploration, and decision making.

Elementary School. Schmidt (1976), working with a team of elementary teachers and counselors in the Colorado Springs School District, designed a career guidance program built around two components: *self-concept* and *career awareness*. The first was concerned with increasing the self-concept of elementary children, and the second was built on the first to help students explore careers. The self-concept component was divided into four basic areas: *strength building* in which students were taught how to identify strength in others, *values identification* by which students could be helped to clarify their own value systems, *goal setting* in which students established min goals important to larger aspirations and monitored their progress in achieving them (decision making), and *life management* in which they discussed obstacles to their self-made goals and developed strategies for overcoming them. Component 2, career awareness, involved the use of several types of commercial resources. One, Career Kits for Kids, was used in grades K to 2 and allowed students to role-play different types of workers and wear hats and uniforms that fit each particular role. Real workers in the selected areas were invited to provide actual work process examples for the children and show them the tools used in the occupations. In addition, the children made up puppet shows and songs about different forms of work. The second commercial resource used in this component was a series of six filmstrip units (Career Discoveries, by Guidance Associates) that dealt with broad career areas such as "people who influence others or people who make things." The emphases here were on the types of persons in different jobs, their life-styles, and the strengths or values and goals they brought to their jobs. Again, guest speakers were used, and students compared their personal profiles developed in the self-concept component to those appropriate to different work options.

In a second example, Nelson (1979) has described the CREST program, which through three storybooks for children and related materials and activities, translates the concepts of choice awareness in a way that is intended to be understandable and engrossing for children. It helps them see the many ways in which they are in charge of themselves and the many alternatives they have as they choose. Research on the project indicated that children in the experimental condition were able to produce more choices, and those choices were judged to be more positive, than were those of children in the control condition. Teacher responses were also found to be quite positive about the value of the CREST program.

Middle School. Winter and Schmidt (1974) have reported on the use of a *cluster approach* to integrate career education into the eighth grade language arts curriculum. They developed seven modules including: *introduction to careers, self-awareness, decision making, occupational* *clusters, economic awareness, investigating an occupational cluster,* and *planning for the future.*

The first module had students define the word career, identify typical career patterns for men and women, and identify reasons for working. A filmstrip, "Why Work at All?" was shown to stimulate student discussion on reasons for working.

In the self-awareness module, students were expected to identify their strengths and weaknesses as related to their abilities and interests and to match these with at least two potential careers. The relationships between school subjects and possible jobs were also examined. Workbooks, personal checklists, interpretations of results of the Ohio Vocational Interest Survey, and the writing of personal character sketches were activities used to support this module.

The major content of the decision-making module was the curriculum on decision making, entitled Deciding, developed by the College Entrance Examination Board in 1972. The occupational clusters module was presented through "Popeye" comic books published by King Features Syndicate, which use cartoon characters to present information about jobs in each cluster. Students also constructed people pyramids showing how people from different clusters work together to produce different products.

The economic awareness module focused on how economics affects each student's life. Such concepts as economic systems, supply and demand, inflation, depression, and elements of production were discussed.

A variety of approaches was used in the module on investigating an occupational cluster. The Widening Occupational Roles Kit (WORK), Job Family booklets, and Job Experience Kits (all from Science Research Associates) were used as major resources for students in identifying a specific preferred cluster or area within a cluster to study. In addition, students wrote to at least one firm that offered jobs in the preferred cluster asking for information about the job and the firm. Students also took field trips to pertinent sites and had resource speakers from different occupations come to class to discuss their jobs.

In the planning module, students compiled lists of skills they would need to meet the requirements of jobs in the occupational cluster most related to their interests and aptitudes. Students also planned a tentative high school program of studies that would provide the necessary skills. During this module, the relevance of flexibility and tentativeness in planning as well as employment trends and the rapidity of change were considered.

Johnson and Myrick (1972) have described the use of a simulation technique for middle school students called MOLD (Making Of Life Decisions). In this simulation each student follows six basic steps:

1. Completes a personal profile sheet describing abilities and interests.
2. Becomes involved with small group procedures that assist him or her in self-appraisal.
3. Explores career fields and makes a tentative career choice based on his or her abilities and interests.
4. Plans on paper the next year of his or her life, making decisions about education, job, home life, and leisure activities. The student chooses from alternatives actually available in the community, not fictional or hypothetical possibilities.
5. Receives feedback on these decisions, such as grades earned in each course and whether or not he or she got a job applied for. This feedback is derived from probability tables, which take into account such variables as ability, study time, and chance.
6. Uses the results and plans the following year. In this way, contingency plans and consequences of immediate decisions can be accounted for.

This simulation is used with a filmstrip on career and educational planning, a review of materials in the guidance center, and small-group discussion of reasons for personal choices, where personal strengths are identified and reinforced.

Senior High School. A career development class was implemented and evaluated by Mackin and Hansen (1981) for use with eleventh and twelfth grade students at an inner-city high school in Minneapolis. Provided over eleven weeks, the Career Development program was based on developmental tasks for high school students drawn from the Career Development Curriculum developed by Tennyson, Hansen, Klaurens, and Antholz (1975). The goals of the curriculum are (1) to increase *self-awareness,* (2) to increase *career awareness,* and (3) to increase *decision-making and planning* skills. Self-Awareness consists of four units—self-concept, interests, abilities, and values and needs. Activities include student completion of a self-esteem measure, an adjective list, an occupational family tree, the Strong Campbell Interest Inventory, Holland's Self-Directed Search, standard achievement and aptitude assessments, selected readings, values auctions, and a paper dealing with self and society.

Career Awareness includes two units: Career Development and The Future. Activities include constructed personal lifelines, life-career rainbows, guest speakers, field trips, and occupational fantasy trips. Guest speakers include persons who would provide role models counteracting prevailing stereotypes of sex-types or racially typed roles.

Decision Making and Planning is devoted primarily to "teaching decision-making skills and helping students identify goals and plans for the attainment of these goals." Emphasis is on learning a process of decision making. Activities used include selected exercises from Decisions and Outcomes (Gelatt, Varenhorst, Carey, & Miller, 1973), analysis of decision-making styles, a force-field analysis of student plans, and a career plans paper.

An example designed to create a team effort to support career planning for academically disadvantaged students in East Lyme High School, Connecticut, has been described by Matthay and Linder (1982). The team included two special educators, two counselors, and two cooperative work experience coordinators. A group of fifty-one tenth grade students were included because of lack of decision-making skills, lack of motivation toward finishing high school, and low academic test scores (significantly below grade level and below state and local norms in standardized reading and math tests).

Participants in the program's career awareness classes met for forty-five minutes every day for one semester, participated in weekly individual counseling with the school counselors, and received tutoring from the special educators as needed. The classes consisted of action activities; individual assessments of interests, aptitudes, and exercises; values clarification discussions and activities; maintenance of journals; career decision-making exercises; audiovisual presentations; speakers; field trips; interviews with workers; assigned readings; and individual and group counseling.

College. At Cornell University, female students take a course entitled Career Environment and Individual Development (Babcock & Kaufman, 1976). This course meets for seven weeks, once a week for two hours, and is credit-bearing. The primary focus is the relationship between careers and individual behavior. To accomplish this end, values clarification exercises are employed, and students are taught decision-making methods, theories of occupational choice, job satisfaction factors, sources of occupational information, work-power projections, and techniques of career planning. Large- and small-group discussions are frequent, and videotapes are used. Assignments include reading, an interview with a worker in a chosen occupation, "shadowing" a person at work, keeping a decision-making diary, and writing a final paper on personal career plans. Students who took the course were matched with comparable samples who had received individual counseling and with a no-counseling control group. The course was more effective than individual counseling and no counseling in facilitating the career development of women as measured by Super's Career Development Inventory and by Graff and MacLean's Counseling Assessment Form.

In the General College at the University of Minnesota, a Career Planning Seminar meets for one hour each week for eleven weeks, and students are awarded two credits. The seminar is built around the use of the Programmed Guide to Career Decision-Making, a package of fifteen career exploration units (Magoon, 1969). Fundamentally, this program involves five steps: (1) *identifying the problem* (How do I go about the process of learning more about myself and the world of work so that I can make sound occupational and educational plans?), (2) *gathering appropriate information* (including self-clarification and understanding of the world of work), (3) *exploring alternatives* and *selecting a tentative choice* (synthesizing information and selecting two tentative occupations), (4) *implementing a choice* (developing an action plan), and (5) *evaluating the decision periodically* (Wollman, Johnson, & Bottoms, 1975).

Adults. A program at Livermore Laboratory in California serves the 7,000-plus work force by means of three major components: a career assessment center, individual career counseling, and several career assessment workshops. The workshops are conducted during working hours for about seven weeks. They are limited to eighteen participants per session, and require approximately forty hours of participant time. Workshops progress from overviews of career planning to assessment of values and interests, to decision-making concerns, to an achievement motivation program. Evaluations based on participant self-reports have been generally positive (Knowdell, 1982).

At the University of California's Santa Barbara campus a career development program serves staff employees (largely women) in groups of twelve (Eng & Gottdanker, 1979). The program consists of a self-assessment (such as the Self-Directed Search (SDS) or the Personal Orientation Inventory (POI)) and subsequent exercises focusing on skills analysis, personal work and environmental goals, self-imposed barriers, assertion and self-expression skills development, job interviews, and role-playing of interpersonal conflict situations. The aims of the program include increases in awareness of career options, understanding of how to achieve new goals, and self-confidence. Self-reports of participants suggested substantial changes in both attitudes and actual career shifts.

This brief review of career development and decision-making programs for different populations shows that there are many useful techniques for facilitating self, educational, and occupational planning and choice. Counselors can be creative in the use of resources and experiences that permit persons to project themselves into the alternatives from which they can choose and to evaluate their likely relationship to personal abilities, interests, and values. It is, however, important that counselors have a solid grounding in theories of career and life-style development. Without a conceptual frame of reference to which to relate program goals and the likelihood that the techniques used will be relevant, the counselor may engage in activities and techniques that miss full contact with the knowledge, attitudes, and skills people need to anticipate and implement effective career behavior.

PERSISTENT QUESTIONS

Weaving through the descriptions of theory, research, and practice that now characterize the area of life-style and career development are many unanswered questions. Because of the intimate relationship between changes in the social, political, and economic events that affect the career development of individuals and of groups, it is likely that theoretical and research questions will be emerging constantly; similarly, new conceptual perspectives on career behavior will likely continue to spawn new techniques and other intervention strategies.

Although it is not possible to be exhaustive about the major research questions and concerns in the field, some of the most prominent are:

1. Do existing theories of career and life-style development provide effective explanations of the career behavior of all population groups? The simplistic answer is probably not. Most of the theories identified in this chapter were built on research done with men, not women. Frequently, the samples used were more likely to be from the middle socioeconomic classes than from the poorest or most wealthy. Most of the research and theory of prime influence in the field describes the career behavior of Whites rather than that of minority group members whether Black, Hispanic, Asian, or Native American. These imbalances in theory are slowly being rectified. Indeed, it is possible that much of the existing theory, which has been based on White

males, does generalize to describe the experience of many females and minority persons. Research findings on such questions to date are mixed. (See Chapter 6 for a more detailed discussion of these issues.)
2. What are the comparative effects of different interventions on career behavior? Clearly the number of techniques, materials, and equipment available for use in career guidance and career counseling have grown dramatically in the past several decades. However, this growth in availability has not been accompanied by sufficient evaluation of the quality or the differential effects of such treatments, processes, or materials. As a result, it is very difficult to know whether one form of treatment, individual or group, is superior to another in achieving certain kinds of desired outcomes such as clarity of self-concept, problem-solving ability, use of information sources, or work adjustment. As Healy (1982, pp. 586–588) has suggested, many career counseling treatments are not specified in enough detail to allow researchers to compare them within or across studies.
3. How should career guidance and counseling approaches be differentiated with regard to the choices to be made: jobs, occupation, careers? Frequently, these terms are used interchangeably, but they represent different levels of choice complexity.
4. How can career development theory be combined more effectively with the methodology and content of lifespan psychology than has been true? Some lifespan psychologists (Vondracek & Lerner, 1982) contend that existing theories of career development are too unidimensional and do not adequately deal with the interaction between developmental, contextual, and relational systems.
5. To what degree are existing theories of career development and our methods of intervening in such development culture-bound? Do American models of career behavior generalize to the experiences of persons in other nations? Are the intervention strategies useful with certain population groups, such as Whites, also useful with other population groups such as Blacks? If not, how do cultural factors influence the career development and the intervention appropriate to different subpopulations?
6. What are the cost-benefit effects of career guidance in relation to individual productivity or social costs? Increasingly, government policy makers are imposing accountability measures and cost-benefit questions upon counseling of any form in any setting.

How, then, can the effects of career guidance be translated into the language of economics and of cost-benefit formulas?

CONTRIBUTIONS OF CAREER DEVELOPMENT TO THE PROFESSION OF COUNSELING

In the United States, concerns about career behavior, particularly widespread job dissatisfaction, distribution of immigrants across the burgeoning occupational structure, the social effects of the Industrial Revolution, and the need to develop vocational guidance as a method to respond to these phenomena were the "seed bed" from which counseling emerged at the beginning of the twentieth century (see Chapter 1). The National Vocational Guidance Association, the first major organization of counselors in the United States founded in 1913, was already forty years old when it amalgamated with three other organizations in 1952 to form the American Personnel and Guidance Association, now the American Association for Counseling and Development. A careful look at the background of many of the presidents of the American Personnel and Guidance Association as well as those who served in the Presidency of Division 17 (Counseling Psychology) of the American Psychological Association reveals earlier leadership in the National Vocational Guidance Association.

Thus, it is fair to suggest that many of the techniques, assessment strategies, theoretical perspectives, and leaders of counseling today were first honed in the crucible of career and life-style development problems. Through the decades of the twentieth century, the importance of vocational guidance, career guidance, or career development have ebbed and flowed as new views of mental health or needs for psychotherapeutic intervention captured the moment. However, invariably as economic downturns dominated the news or military conflicts requiring large-scale mobilization of persons and the classification of their skills and learning potential into military specialization were needed, calls for more career guidance and greater attention to individual career behavior have sounded through the nation.

Since World War II there has been a growing tendency to recognize that career counseling and psychotherapy are not clearly separate processes. Rather, they are being seen as complementary in their response to human needs for self-insight and acceptance and for finding ways to be productive in life. Crites (1981) has articulated these relationships clearly. It is also true that research has grown in recent years that shows that work is central to self-identity and that when people are unemployed, they are at increasing risk for stress-related physical disease, chemical dependency, child and spouse abuse, and mental illness

(Liam & Rayman, 1980). In these ways, as career development theory has broadened its views of career behavior and the negative effects associated with impaired career development, counseling has been influenced to become more holistic in its view of human behavior. As suggested elsewhere in this chapter, it is very difficult to divide people into their educational needs, their vocational needs, their personal needs, and their social and interpersonal needs and assign these different sets of concerns to different counselors. People act as wholes, as interacting subsystems of needs that spill from one set of motivations or concerns to another. Individual behavior is dynamic, and as it changes across time, developmental approaches to career development have been very helpful in providing insight into this complex and changing behavior.

CHANGE IN THE FUTURE

Because life-style and career development issues are likely to remain central concerns of theorists, researchers, and counselors far into the foreseeable future, it is inevitable that changes will occur both in the understanding of behavior and in the interventions used to facilitate it. As various parts of this chapter have suggested, theory in the future will likely be addressed more fully to the career development of women, and racial and ethnic minorities, as well as those with special problems (such as indecisiveness). It is likely that theoretical perspectives will increasingly use the lenses provided by sociology, economics, and political science as well as those of psychology to probe career behavior. More attention will be devoted to differentiating general principles of career development from those of particular concern to specific subpopulations, such as the poor, the educationally disadvantaged, and the disabled. It is in these types of populations that stereotypes, prejudices, and social barriers limit individual action and impose psychological or literal boundaries upon choice and mobility.

The future will also bring new forms of technology and new intervention techniques to assist counselors and clients to deal with issues related to career development and life-style. Microcomputers and related technology (such as laser disks and video disks) will serve as prostheses for desolved clients as well as "mind multipliers." They will provide increasingly comprehensive information about work, education, and role integration. They will provide more sensitive simulations of decision-making problems and new forms of assessment.

Technology will be more fully integrated in the future with other techniques of guided imagery, individual and group counseling, life-skill development, leisure counseling, anger management, assertiveness training, and self-efficacy development. Such approaches will be systematically brought to bear on the multidimensional problems that most people experience as they anticipate and cope with shaping a career. Research will address the comparative effects of such interventions and the cost-benefit ratios they represent.

Almost inexorably, programs of career guidance and counseling will become more comprehensive in the future. They will increasingly have programmed and preplanned elements. They will be articulated over extended periods of time—kindergarten to grade 12, the four years of college, the total length of one's stay in a rehabilitation or correctional facility, throughout one's career in a corporate setting. They will address populations across the lifespan at many different stages of career development—initial exploration, transition from school to work, mid-career crises, occupational dislocation, and preretirement. Such comprehensive programs will occur in many settings: schools, colleges, community agencies, and workplaces.

Each of the trends expressed here has been summarized and extended in the third decennial volume published in 1984 by the National Vocational Guidance Association to analyze the current state of the art in career development and career guidance. Gysbers (1984b), the volume's editor, indicates that as one looks to the past and to the future in career development theory and practice, four predominant trends are apparent. They in summary form provide an appropriate ending for this chapter and a guide to changes in the future.

1. The meanings given to career and career development continue to evolve from simply new words for *vocation* (occupation) and vocational development (occupational development) to words that describe the human career in terms of life roles, life settings and life events that develop over the lifespan.
2. Substantial changes have taken place and will continue to occur in the economic, occupational, industrial, and social environments and structures in which the human career develops and interacts and in which career guidance and counseling takes place.
3. The number, diversity, and quality of career development programs, tools, and techniques continue to increase almost in geometric progression.
4. The populations served by career development programming and the settings where career development programs and services take place have increased greatly and will continue to do so. (Gysbers, 1984b, p. 619)

REFERENCES

Babcock, R. J., & Kaufman, M. A. (1976). Effectiveness of a career course. *Vocational Guidance Quarterly, 24,* 261–266.

Bandura, A. (1977). Self-efficacy: Toward a unifying theory of behavioral change. *Psychological Review, 84,* 191–215.

Bergland, B. W. (1974). Career planning: The use of sequential evaluated experience. In E. L. Herr (Ed.), *Vocational guidance and human development.* Boston: Houghton Mifflin.

Blau, P. M., Gustad, J. W., Jessor, R., Parnes, H. S., & Wilcock, R. C. (1956). Occupational choice: A conceptual framework. *Industrial Labor Relations, 9,* 531–543.

Bordin, E. S., Nachman, B., & Segal, F. J. (1963). An articulated framework for vocational development. *Journal of Counseling Psychology, 10,* 107–116.

Borow, H. (1961). Vocational development research: Some problems of logical and experimental form. *Personnel and Guidance Journal, 40,* 21–25.

Borow, H. (1966). The development of motives and roles. In L. W. Hoffman & M. L. Hoffman (Eds.), *Review of child development research,* Vol. 2. New York: Russell Sage Foundation.

Borow, H. (1984). Occupational socialization: Acquiring a sense of work. In N. C. Gysbers (Ed.), *Designing careers* (Chap. 6). San Francisco: Jossey-Bass.

Brill, A. A. (1948). *Psychoanalytic psychiatry.* London: John Lehman.

Campbell, R. E., & Cellini, J. V. (1981). A diagnostic taxonomy of adult career problems. *Journal of Vocational Behavior, 19,* 175–180.

Chapman, W., & Katz, M. R. (1981). Survey of career information systems in secondary schools: Final report of study. Princeton, NJ: Educational Testing Service.

Crites, J. O. (1969). *Vocational psychology.* New York: McGraw-Hill.

Crites, J. O. (1973). *Career maturity inventory.* Monterey, CA: California Test Bureau/McGraw-Hill.

Crites, J. O. (1978). *Theory and research handbook for the career maturity inventory.* Monterey, CA: California Test Bureau/McGraw-Hill.

Crites, J. O. (1981). *Career counseling: Models, methods, and materials.* New York: McGraw-Hill.

Dudley, G. A., & Tiedeman, D. V. (1977). *Career development, exploration, and commitment.* Muncie, IN: Accelerated Development.

Eng, J. E., & Gottdanker, J. S. (1979). Positive changes from a career development program. *Training and Development Journal, 33* (1), 3–7.

Erikson, E. H. (1963). *Childhood and society* (2nd ed.). New York: W. W. Norton.

Gelatt, H. B. (1962). Decision-making: A conceptual frame of reference for counseling. *Journal of Counseling Psychology, 9,* 240–245.

Gelatt, H. B., Varenhorst, B., Carey, R., & Miller, G. P. (1973). *Decisions and outcomes.* New York: College Entrance Examination Board.

Ginzberg, E. (1972). Restatement of the theory of occupational choice. *Vocational Guidance Quarterly, 20,* 169–176.

Ginzberg, E., Ginsburg, S. W., Axelrod, S., & Herma, J. R. (1951). *Occupational choice: An approach to a general theory.* New York: Columbia University Press.

Gould, R. (1978). *Transformations: Growth and change in adult life.* New York: Simon & Schuster.

Gribbons, W. D., & Lohnes, P. R. (1968). *Emerging careers.* New York: Teachers College Press, Columbia University.

Griffith, A. R. (1980). A survey of career development in corporations. *Personnel and Guidance Journal, 58,* 537–543.

Gysbers, N. C. (1984a). Major trends in career development theory and practice. *Vocational Guidance Quarterly, 33,* 15–25.

Gysbers, N. C. (1984b). Major trends in career development theory and practice. In N. C. Gysbers (Ed.), *Designing careers* (Chap. 23). San Francisco: Jossey-Bass.

Gysbers, N. C., & Moore, E. J. (1981). *Improving guidance programs.* Englewood Cliffs, NJ: Prentice-Hall.

Hansen, L. S., & Keierleber, D. L. (1978). Born free: A collaborative consultation model for career development and sex-role stereotyping. *Personnel and Guidance Journal, 56,* 395–399.

Healy, C. C. (1982). *Career development: Counseling through the life stages.* Boston: Allyn & Bacon.

Herr, E. L. (1981). Comprehensive career guidance: A look to the future. *Vocational Guidance Quarterly, 30,* 367–376.

Herr, E. L., & Cramer, S. H. (1984). *Career guidance and counseling through the life span: Systematic approach.* Boston: Little, Brown.

Herr, E. L., & Enderlein, T. (1976). Vocational maturity: The effects of school, grade, curriculum and sex. *Journal of Vocational Behavior, 8,* 227–238.

Herr, E. L., Weitz, A., Good, R., & McCloskey, G. (1982). A secondary school curriculum and career behavior in young adults. *Journal of Vocational Behavior, 21,* 243–253.

Herr, E. L., Weitz, A., Good, R., McCloskey, G., & Long, T. E. (1981). *Research on the effects of secondary school curricular and personal characteristics upon post-secondary educational and occupational patterns.* Final Report for National Institute of Education. University Park, PA: Vocational Development Study.

Hills, J. R. (1964). Decision theory and college choice. *Personnel and Guidance Journal, 43,* 17–22.

Hilton, T. J. (1962). Career decision-making. *Journal of Counseling Psychology, 9,* 291–298.

Hoggart, R. (1957). *The uses of literacy.* London: Chatto & Windus.

Holland, J. L. (1966). *The psychology of vocational choice.* Waltham, MA: Blaisdell.

Holland, J. L. (1973) *Making vocational choices: A theory of careers.* Englewood Cliffs, NJ: Prentice-Hall.

Holland, J. L., & Gottfredson, G. (1976). Using a typology of persons and environments to explain career: Some extensions and clarifications. *The Counseling Psychologist, 6,* 20–29.

Holland, J. L., Magoon, T. M., & Spokane, A. R. (1981). Counseling psychology: Career interventions, research, and theory. *Annual Review of Psychology, 32,* 279–300.

Hollingshead, A. B. (1949). *Elmtown's youth.* New York: John Wiley.

Jepsen, D. A. (1984). Relationship between career development theory and practice. In N. C. Gysbers (Ed.), *Designing careers* (Chap. 5). San Francisco: Jossey-Bass.

Johnson, R. H., & Myrick, R. D. (1972). MOLD: A new approach to career decision making. *Vocational Guidance Quarterly, 21,* 48–53.

Katz, M. (1963). *Decisions and values: A rationale for secondary school guidance.* New York: College Entrance Examination Board.

Knefelkamp, L., & Slepitza, R. (1976). A cognitive development model of career development—an adaptation of the Perry scheme. *The Counseling Psychologist, 6,* 53–58.

Knowdell, R. L. (1982). Comprehensive career programs in the workplace. *Vocational Guidance Quarterly, 30,* 323–326.

Krumboltz, J. D. (1979). A social learning theory of career decision making. In A. M. Mitchell, G. G. Jame, & J. D. Krumboltz (Eds.), *Social learning and career decision making* (pp. 19–49). Cranston, RI: Carrole Press.

Lawler, E. E. (1973). *Motivation in work organizations.* Monterey, CA: Brooks/Cole.

Levinson, D. J. (1977). The mid-life transition: A period in adult psychosocial development. *Psychiatry, 40,* 99–112.

Liam, P., & Rayman, P. (1980). Health and social costs of unemployment. *American Psychologist, 37,* 1116–1123.

Lipsett, L. (1962). Social factors in vocational development. *Personnel and Guidance Journal, 40,* 432–437.

Lo Cascio, R. (1967). Continuity and discontinuity in vocational development theory. *Personnel and Guidance Journal, 46,* 32–36.

Lowenthal, M. F., Thurnher, M., Chiroboga, D., & Associates. (1976). *Four stages of life.* San Francisco: Jossey-Bass.

Mackin, R. K., & Hansen, L. S. (1981). A theory-based career development course: A plant in the garden. *The School Counselor, 28,* 325–334.

Magoon, T. M. (1969). Developing skills for solving educational and vocational problems. In J. D. Krumboltz & C. E. Thorensen (Eds.), *Behavioral counseling: Cases and techniques.* New York: Holt, Rinehart & Winston.

Maslow, A. H. (1954). *Motivation and personality.* New York: Harper & Row.

Matthay, E. R., & Linder, R. (1982). A team effort in planning for the academically disadvantaged. *The School Counselor, 29,* 226–231.

McDaniel, C. (1978). The practice of career guidance and counseling. *INFORM, 7* (1), 1–2, 7–8.

Mitchell, A. M. (1975). Emerging career guidance competencies. *Personnel and Guidance Journal, 53,* 700–705.

National Vocational Guidance Association. (1981, September). *Vocational/Career Counseling Competencies Approved by the Board of Directors.* Falls Church, VA: Author.

Nelson, R. C. (1979). The CREST program: Helping children with their choices. *Elementary School Guidance and Counseling, 14,* 286–298.

Parsons, F. (1909). *Choosing a vocation.* Boston: Houghton Mifflin.

Peatling, J. H., & Tiedeman, D. V. (1977). *Career development: Designing self.* Muncie, IN: Accelerated Development.

Phillips-Jones, L., Jones, B., & Drier, H. (1981). *Developing training competencies for career guidance personnel.* Falls Church, VA: National Vocational Guidance Association.

Pitz, G. F., & Harren, V. A. (1980). An analysis of career decision-making from the point of view of information-processing and decision theory. *Journal of Vocational Behavior, 16,* 320–346.

Roberts, L. (1977). *From school to work: A study of the youth employment service.* Newton Abbott, England: David & Charles.

Roe, A. (1956). *The psychology of occupations.* New York: John Wiley.

Schlossberg, N. K. (1976). The case for counseling adults. *The Counseling Psychologist 6,* 33–36.

Schlossberg, N. K. (1978). Five propositions about adult development. *Journal of College Student Personnel, 19,* 418–423.

Schmidt, J. A. (1976). Self-concepts and career exploration. *Elementary School Guidance and Counseling, 11,* 145–153.

Super, D. E. (1957). *The psychology of careers.* New York: Harper & Row.

Super, D. E. (1969). Vocational development theory: Persons, positions, processes. *The Counseling Psychologist, 1,* 2–9.

Super, D. E. (1976). *Career education and the meaning of work* (Monographs of Career Education). Washington, DC: Office of Career Education, U.S. Office of Education.

Super, D. E. (1977). Vocational maturity in mid-career. *Vocational Guidance Quarterly, 25,* 294–302.

Super, D. E. (1980). A life-span, life-space approach to career development. *Journal of Vocational Behavior, 16,* 282–298.

Super, D. E. (1981). Approaches to occupational choice and career development. In A. G. Watts, D. E. Super, & J. M. Kidd (Eds.), *Career development in Britain.* Cambridge, England: Hobsons Press.

Super, D. E., Bohn, M. J., Forrest, D. J., Jordaan, J. P., Lindeman, R. H., & Thompson, A. A. (1971). *Career development inventory.* New York: Teachers College, Columbia University.

Super, D. E., Thompson, A. S., Lindeman, R. E., Jordaan, J. P., & Myers, R. A. (1979). *Career development inventory.* Palo Alto, CA: Consulting Psychologists Press.

Tennyson, W. W., Hansen, L. S., Klaurens, M. K., & Antholz, M. B. (1975). *Educating for career development.* St. Paul, MN: Minnesota Department of Education (Revised 1980, National Vocational Guidance Association).

Tiedeman, D. V., & O'Hara, R. P. (1963). *Career development: Choice and adjustment.* New York: College Entrance Examination Board.

Tiedeman, D. V., & Miller-Tiedeman, A. (1977). An "I" power primer: Part one: Structure and its involvement of intuition. *Focus on Guidance, 9* (7), 1–16.

Vondracek, F. W., & Lerner, R. M. (1982). Vocational role development in adolescence. In B. Wolman (Ed.), *Handbook of developmental psychology* (Chap. 33). Englewood Cliffs, NJ: Prentice-Hall.

Watts, A. G. (1980). Educational and careers guidance services for adults: A rationale and conceptual framework. *British Journal of Guidance and Counselling, 8* (1), 11–22.

Weinstein, E. (1982, April). Student access to career information resources. *NVGA Newsletter, 21* (4), 4–5.

Winter, J., & Schmidt, J. S. (1974). A replicable career program for junior high. *Vocational Guidance Quarterly, 23,* 177–180.

Wollman, M., Johnson, D. A., & Bottoms, J. E. (1975). Meeting career needs in two-year institutions. *Personnel and Guidance Journal, 53,* 676–679.

CHAPTER 6
SOCIAL AND CULTURAL FOUNDATIONS

Clemmont E. Vontress

Culture and social class present significant considerations for counselors. Current professional literature is filled with articles about counseling racial and linguistic minorities. Today, American counselors, psychologists, and psychiatrists are employed in many foreign countries. They, too, report insights about counseling culturally different people. American college and university enrollments are enlarged by the presence of increased numbers of foreign students. The problems they experience in adjusting to the American educational system constitute new challenges for counselors on college campuses.

Counselors have traditionally demonstrated an awareness of social and cultural influences on their clients. As Aubrey points out in Chapter 1, Frank Parsons (1909), the "Father of Guidance," recognized the impact of sociocultural forces on adolescents around the turn of the century. Such recognition was also evident in the work-related educational and guidance programs for deprived youth enabled by the New Deal legislation under the Franklin D. Roosevelt administration in the 1930s. During the 1960s, many of the Kennedy-Johnson anti-poverty programs such as the Job Corps and the Neighborhood Youth Corps included counseling as an important component. In the same period, the National Defense Education Act enabled counselors-in-training and those already on the job to enroll in courses, workshops, and degree programs to enhance their counseling skills with disadvantaged clients.

Although counselors have generally considered the cultural and social backgrounds of their clients to be important, it is only recently—during the last twelve or so years — that this consideration has developed into a recognized subspecialty of the profession. This new interest area is known as *cross-cultural, intercultural,* or *multicultural counseling.* In this chapter, cross-cultural counseling refers to counseling in which the counselors and client(s) are manifestly different due to socialization acquired in distinct cultural, subcultural, racio-cultural, or socioeconomic environments. *Culturally different* refers to an individual or group whose culture is different from that of the counselor or observer.

CULTURE

The central theme of cross-cultural counseling is *culture;* therefore, an understanding of its nature is crucial to helping clients from various cultures and socioeconomic groups within cultures. For anthropologists, culture connotes a way of life of a people (Hall, 1966): the sum total of their beliefs about and procedures for coping with their environment. The way people live is visible and invisible, conscious and unconscious (Bronowski, 1971). They believe and behave in certain ways because that is the way "it has always been." They were born into it. They are unable to define completely their culture to others or even to themselves.

Although most clients are not interested in culture per se, counselors are obliged to be students of it as a human necessity. Most people are products of five concentric and intersecting cultures: (1) *universal,* (2) *ecological,* (3) *national,* (4) *regional,* and (5) *racio-ethnic* (see Figure 6-1). The cultures are neither entirely separate nor equal. The most external one, the universal, which is biologically determined, influences all others. No matter what the conditions are under which people live, they still must adjust to the fact that they are human beings. For example, Blacks in the United States are first of all culturally alike because they are members of the human species; as such, they share the behaviors of all members of the human group. Second, they are forced to adjust to the same climatic conditions as are all other Americans. Third, as members of the national culture, they take on behavior, attitudes, and values of Americans in general. Fourth, they are influenced by the regional culture. Thus, Elwin, a Black native Mississippian, is apt to betray his roots by his accent. Fifth, because of their African ancestry, White Americans react to them as if they were inferior, a fact that leaves psychological scars on all members of the group as Karon (1975) points out.

Universal Culture

Although humans live all over the world, they are biologically alike (Montagu, 1974). The biological sameness contributes to a general

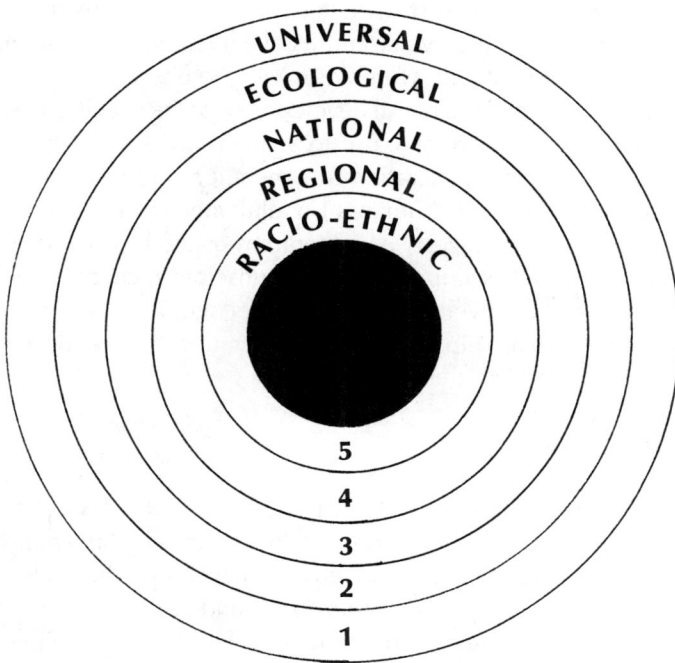

FIGURE 6-1 CULTURAL INFLUENCES ON THE INDIVIDUAL (CENTER DOT)

universal culture. People are dimorphic (male and female), a fact that permits limited variations in patterns of heterosexual loving and mating behavior. From the sexual union of male and female come infants. Universally, a common set of behaviors exists for protecting and ensuring the survival of newborn children. Basic to child care is the parent's instinct to hold and nurture the newborn. Human speech apparatus permits members of the species to communicate with one another. The organism's requirements for food, water, sleep, and shelter dictate a host of other behaviors, which vary little from culture to culture (Greenwood & Stini, 1977). The structure of the human body, its requirements for survival, its life cycle, and its eventual demise dictate a universal system for maintaining symbiosis with the physical environment. During the course of the social development of the species, people learn to play a variety of roles basic to survival. These are internalized and transmitted from generation to generation (Storr, 1973). In satisfying their survival needs, humans also fulfill themselves psychologically, as Maslow (1954) suggests in his hierarchy of needs conceptualization (see Chapter 2). It is important that counselors recognize themselves as products of a universal culture. This recognition enables them to identify with and to help clients from disparate cultural and socioeconomic backgrounds more effectively.

Ecological Culture

If culture is defined as the way of life of a people, then it follows that where a group is situated on earth determines in large measure how its members relate to the natural environment and to themselves. People in the Arctic develop tools, procedures, and clothes required for survival that are quite different from those developed by their fellow humans in Saudi Arabia. Where humans live also influences language significantly. Language derives from the need to name objects, processes, phenomena, feelings, attitudes, values, relationships, and the like (Cohen, 1956). For example, Eskimos have a rich vocabulary to define various kinds of snow. On the other hand, people in Mali in West Africa have none, because snow is not a climatic phenomenon in that part of the world.

Ecological conditions also influence what food people eat and clothes they wear as Lidz (1976) points out. In general, they learn to eat and enjoy food indigenous to the immediate locale. A people's usual body covering is also influenced by geographic conditions. For example, men and women alike in the Arabian desert countries wear light-weight and light-colored dresslike costumes with ample headgear. An American exposed to the blistering heat and sandstorms of Kuwait understands quickly the practicality of the Kuwaiti mode of dress. The loose, gownlike attire does not stick to the skin and cause burning as do pants and shirts, and the head covering allows for quick protection of the face from the sand, which is often hurled through the air with deadly velocity during unexpected and intense wind currents.

National Culture

To conceptualize a national culture is reasonable for various reasons. First, most (though not all) countries have a *single official language*, essential to doing business in basic institutions, such as schools, banks, governmental offices, and the like. The common language serves as a unifying cultural force, even though other languages may be spoken in ethnic communities. Second, each country has a *central government* that establishes, regulates, and administers institutions, agencies, laws, and procedures essential to the welfare of people residing in its confines. These, too, are significant cultural components. Even international sojourners are obliged to submit to the behavioral requirements of the host society. Third, each country has a *world view* (C. Kluckhohn, 1962). It is perpetuated via schools, which socialize a comfortable conformity (Flam, 1970); the media, which disseminate common information; and the government, which regulates, protects, serves, and informs bureaucratically. Although there may be several national subcultural groups, they cannot escape the influence of the overarching national culture (Gassel, 1970). For example, American society is often characterized as racist. In fact, the Report of the U.S. National Advisory Commission on Civil Disorders (1968), which was established by Lyndon B. Johnson, President of the United States, after the assassination of Martin Luther King, Jr., and the ensuing rioting indicates that there are two societies in the United States, one Black and one White. If racism is endemic to the society, then Blacks themselves are racists (anti-Black) against themselves. Americans, Black and White, cannot escape their visible and invisible and conscious and unconscious culture, because they are products of it.

Regional Culture

Culturally, humans evolved from a nomadic to a stationary existence. Groups that used to roam from one part of the environment to another in search of food finally settled in select areas, thereby creating cultures specific to regions (Farb, 1978). Regional cultures remain, in spite of the drawing of national lines of demarcation. For example, in Ivory Coast, a former French colony in West Africa, the various ethnic groups are usually identified with a specific region of the nation. Illustrative are the Agni and the Baoule who occupy different parts of the rain forest and raise coffee, cocoa, and yams as main crops; and the Lagunaires, who reside on the coast, which is famous for its tall coconut trees. Regional differences are in fact cultural differences, because as Horney (1937) points out, human social life is a response to the practical problems of earthly existence.

Regional cultures are also evident in the United States. Historically, the climate of the South permitted the cultivation of crops and a way of life that differed significantly from that of other parts of the country. Jordan (1968) indicates that the rich and fertile soil of the South contributed to the institutionalization of slavery in America. Faris (1976) supports this contention and adds that racial prejudice and discrimination in general cannot be divorced from regional and geographical conditions. Whether servant or master, people who live in a given region for whatever reason usually adapt out of necessity to that locale. That is, they develop a culture peculiar to the region. In large measure, the Civil War in the United States was a war over regional or cultural differences (Shoben, 1961).

Racio-Ethnic Culture

Although *race* and *ethnicity* are often used as if they were the same, there are distinct differences between the concepts. As Baker (1974) points out, race is a subspecies perception, in the sense that people look different because of external variations in hair texture, skin color, body size, lip features, and the like. Certain members of the species react to the physiological features as if they were specific differences. Often strange-looking people are considered *ipso facto* inferior to the dominant norm-defining group. Therefore, any number of things may happen when visibly different groups come together.

For example, the large group may absorb the minority group until the differences are merged and are no longer noticed or considered significant. Central and South American countries reflect this phenomenon. The people there are a mixture of European, indigenous Indian, and African ancestry. Racism, U.S.-style, is almost unknown. On the other hand, the most powerful racial group may "inferioritize" the smaller or weaker racial element. Usually, it does so by denying the minority group equal opportunity in the society. Over a period of time, the minority group comes to feel that indeed it is inferior to the majority group. South Africa and the United States are examples of this phenomenon. In such cases, each race develops a race-related culture; that is, each develops a *modus operandi* for dealing with the other. They become culturally different for that reason alone.

On the other hand, ethnicity is not as culturally differentiating as race. If *ethnic* is defined as "of or pertaining to group learning," then it is clear that any group of people can learn to behave differently from any other group for whatever reason. The reason may be emotionally charged, as is the case in the United States and South Africa, or it may be fairly innocuous as in the case of American European ethnics who choose to perpetuate their language and culture in North America. For example, some Americans choose to proclaim their Irish heritage on festive occasions. At other times, they are just "plain Americans." Compare this with the situation of Black Americans, who are "stuck" with their racial identity. They cannot take it off and put it on at will. Their racial difference is clearly visible. The dominant racio-cultural group responds negatively to this difference. As ostracized Americans, their cultural difference is forced upon them (U.S. National Advisory Commission on Civil Disorders, 1968).

SOCIAL CLASS

To know the culture of a people is to know a great deal about them. Every culture has a structure of expectancies (R. Kluckhohn, 1962). These unconscious and conscious and implicit and explicit expectations are translated into behavior and are transmitted from one generation to another. People "just know" what is proper situational and occasional behavior. In many ways the same description holds true for social class. It, too, is a complex of expected behavior generally adhered to by a continuously interacting social group (Farb, 1978). However, social class ought to be perceived as a subcultural variation. Although it has been defined in various ways by different writers, one thing seems to hold fairly constant in the definition: differential levels of material possession or economic advantage (Harris, 1979). In general, people with economic advantage (money, property, and other transferable assets) are more able to manipulate their environment than those with no such advantage. Their assets allow them to build and buy things, to go places, and to influence others on their behalf. Moreover, it allows them to "refine" their existence. They can pay increased attention to their higher-order needs as defined by Maslow (1954).

Social class influences human behavior significantly. It determines what people value, the extent to which they are given to introspection, their language, *Weltanschauung,* and their interpersonal relationship style. Value connotes the importance of a thing, condition, or situation to a person. It also suggests priority. People without a place to sleep are apt to place great value on finding one, before doing anything else, especially in cold weather. Introspection is also related to level of existence. Individuals who have taken care of the essentials for survival have time to reflect on themselves, to look within, and to consider the quality of their existence. People who must devote primary attention to basic survival needs have little time for or inclination to look within themselves. Language allows a group of people to negotiate their common environment. They name objects, processes, feelings, values, and the like, which are necessary for survival. The more objects, procedures, affective relationships, and values they experience in their environment, the more words they need to communicate their observations, actions, and sensations, and the more complex becomes their written and oral expression. This phenomenon helps to explain social class differences in language usage (Vontress, 1982).

Another manifestation of social class is *Weltanschauung* or "world view." In the United States, the more assets (real or negotiable) people have, the more they feel capable of controlling their existence. Such self-perception usually translates into an outlook on life that differs significantly from those who feel that they have little control over what happens to them. In discussing this point, Laurin-Frenette (1978) declares that one of the big differences between poor people and rich people is that the former feel externally controlled.

Social class also has an impact on interpersonal style. For example, people who experience "hard times" may be more group-oriented and mutually supportive than those who are wealthy (Hofferth, 1984). Members of the monied class may be individualistically inclined, because they feel that they and their money do not need anybody. How economic advantage influences interpersonal behavior differs, however, from one culture to another. In some cases, the basic values of society may be more important and enduring than worldly goods. For example, in Hispanic cultures, the ideas of *personalismo, dignidad, respeto,* and *camaraderio* are general interpersonal values that appear to overarch social class differences (Anthony, 1964).

In the United States, social class differences are confounded by attitudes toward race. As Villemez (1980) and Hirschman and Wong (1984) indicate, White social class ranking and its Black counterpart should not be considered the same. Social class suggests differential levels of opportunity, respect, and influence in society. Blacks, no matter how high their class may be as measured by wealth, are unable to exert the same degree of control over their existence as are Whites with comparable wealth, simply because they are Black. Race reduces to a large extent what their money can buy (Villemez, 1980). Although they may be segmented into upper, middle, and lower class, the intra-group differences are not as great as they are among Whites, mainly because of the singular effect of race. Race and the reactions of Whites to it are simultaneously a culturally isolating and unifying phenomenon. By being isolated by Whites, Afro-Americans are culturally unified. A significant cause of the unification is the hostility they feel toward racism and its far-reaching and restraining effect on their existence. In this sense, there is a common Black culture, which transcends social class. Because race has oppressed all Blacks, social class behavioral variations are not as distinctive as they are among Whites.

IMPORTANCE OF CULTURE AND CLASS

In counseling, cultural and social class status are important, because nearly every aspect of the enterprise is influenced in some way by them. Counselors and clients are products of their respective cultures. The behavior, thoughts, and values of clients must be viewed from a cultural perspective (Lidz, 1976). The theories and procedures used by counselors are also culturally inspired. Specifically, cultural and social factors influence (1) normative behaviors, (2) notions about the characteristics of an appropriate help-giver, (3) diagnoses across cultures, and (4) intervention strategies.

Normative Behavior

As soon as they are born, humans are taken over by parents and significant others who set about to socialize them into the ways of the group. Throughout their lives, they are rewarded for behavior sanctioned by their peers and punished for failure to adhere to the numerous implicit and explicit social expectations that make up the conscious and unconscious culture. Each culture develops a set of norms pertaining to almost every phase of human existence. Some of them are enforced by law; others are innocuous situational rules of social decorum. In general, the norms are established in the interest of the group, so that its members can interact predictably. Unpredictable behavior is generally discouraged. Individuals who manifest norm-violating and unpredictable behavior are generally reprimanded or punished by authority of the group. Knowledge of normal social expectations in the native cultures of clients helps counselors to determine possible sources of adjustment difficulties in host cultures and in new social environments. For example, basic to the adjustment of international sojourners to the American culture is that they learn the social amenities of the society. In a like manner, upwardly mobile lower-class people occasionally commit social *faux pas* in their climb to middle-class status.

Notions of Appropriate Help-Givers

Cultures also differ in terms of who is an appropriate consultant for advice and counsel about decisions and problems in life. In general, natives of traditional cultures consult the eldest member of their extended family or a respected citizen of the immediate community. In this country, it is the cultural rule to go to "perfect strangers" (counselors, psychologists, social workers, and psychiatrists) for assistance with problems in living. It is an accepted practice for "troubled" individuals to pay somebody to help them regain a normal perspective on, or position in, society. This custom is usually perceived as strange and even demeaning to people socialized in personalistic societies in which people are deemed far more important than bureaucratic protocol. To a large extent, preference for help-givers is culturally determined (Foulks, 1980). Individuals with problems usually do what is generally done in their culture and social class when people experience difficulties and indecisions in life.

Diagnosis Across Cultures

Psychotherapeutic diagnosis is also done within a cultural context. In the United States, individuals grow up not merely in the American culture but in racial, ethnic, and social class subcultures as well (Farb, 1978). This means that the effective cross-cultural counselor must be something of a psychological anthropologist (Canino & Canino, 1980). For example, in diagnosing adolescents from first-generation Black middle-class Southern families, counselors must be able to determine the influence of lower-class child-rearing practices on children; the degree to which the Southern environment has shaped their values, attitudes, and behavior; and the extent to which their conduct may be bizarre in the Black community generally, in the Black middle-class community in particular, and in the mainstream society. Clients may be well adjusted in one and maladjusted in another. In fact, many "strange" Blacks and Whites escape rejection in their own racio-ethnic community by seeking refuge in the other. That is to suggest that a Black may be bizarre in his or her own culture but not in the White counterpart, and vice versa. Each cultural group demands more rigid social conformity from their "own kind" than it does from outsiders.

Intervention Strategies

Culture also dictates appropriate treatment modalities (Foulks, 1980). In one society, it may be customary to seek out a respected person in the community who lectures, scolds, or threatens the individual into conformity. In another, the accepted practice may be to consult benign, professionally trained strangers who listen passively to clients with the expectation that they will solve their own problems. In general, clients from traditional societies expect authoritative helping from individuals they seek out for counsel and advice. They are disappointed with authority figures who force them to solve their own problems. On the other hand, American middle- and upper-class clients seem to demand counselors who respect their ability to think through their own difficulties in living. The desire to "do it myself" is undoubtedly related to the premium placed on rugged individualism in American society. Adolescents are socialized to "get out on their own" and to be independent. Therefore, they learn early in life not to defer unnecessarily to parents or other authority figures when they are faced with problems to solve or decisions to make.

CENTRAL THEMES

Over the years, several concepts and themes continue to surface in the cross-cultural counseling literature. Because the ideas generally relate to the counseling process itself, they are discussed here under four headings: (1) *the relationship,* (2) *diagnosis,* (3) *recommendations* and *predictions,* and (4) *intervention barriers.*

The Relationship

Counseling is a dynamic process. The psychological environment in which it occurs changes constantly and imperceptibly. It is influenced by the clients —their social, racial, and ethnic background; their expectations and experience with helping professionals; by the counselors —their race, sex, age, professional training, and personality; by the nature of the clients' problems; and by numerous other variables. In spite of the fluid nature of the relationship, an attempt is made to examine various aspects of the interaction as they relate to assisting culturally different clients.

Psychotherapeutic Surrender. Effective counseling depends on a sound therapeutic alliance (Zetzel, 1956). Establishing a productive alliance is probably the most difficult aspect of cross-cultural counseling. Clients are expected to do something they are not accustomed to doing: surrendering themselves psychologically to culturally different counselors. Five concepts common to the counseling literature suggest the dimensions of the problems. The first is *rapport,* an idea which connotes an overtly congenial contact such that participants communicate with spontaneity and openness. Although immediate affability between strangers is often considered a positive value in middle- and upper-class American culture, it is likely to be perceived otherwise by members of the American lower class in general, by individuals from minority groups, and international sojourners. In particular, people from Third World countries often perceive interpersonal distance as an indication of power and ability to help (McClelland, 1975). In the Black ghetto, a glad-handed White counselor is apt to be suspect, because socialization of lower-class Blacks has taught them that Whites of that ilk are generally "up to no good."

A second contributor to psychotherapeutic surrender is *trust.* According to Thass-Theinemann (1968), individuals trust most those like themselves, people of the same cultural origin or "roots." For example, inhabitants of the Appalachian backwoods are polite to most folks, but they do not trust anyone who is not "from 'round here" (Coles, 1971). In fact, Hampden-Turner (1971) suggests that lower-class people are suspicious of "big people," because they recognize that they are "out of class" with them. They know that "well-heeled," middle-class and upper-class people can afford loss and have a great capacity for survival. Therefore, they feel that if "push comes to shove," they are always going to be the losers in relationships with them. The same attitude prevails among international sojourners who relate to Americans, because they know they are in "strange territory."

Careful *listening* also enhances psychotherapeutic surrender. In counseling, lower-class clients seem devoid of good listening skills. This phenomenon can be understood by recognizing that language is reciprocally seductive. Each speaker takes turns in trying to seduce the other to his or her way of seeing things, and by so doing, each runs the risk of submitting to the point of view, values, or behavior of the other. Because counselors are smugglers of middle-class values, which are often alien to lower-class clients, the safest and most polite thing to do is to "tune them out." In fact, the tuning-out can often be seen in the faces of middle-class Whites who interact with Black counterparts. They expect Blacks to pay rapt attention to them, but refuse to risk being persuaded in turn. This observation suggests that people feel most comfortable being persuaded by their "own kind." Indeed, being a good audience contributes to psychotherapeutic surrender.

The fourth, though negative factor in psychotherapeutic surrender, is *resistance.* Clients unable to play the spontaneous verbal role to which counselors are accustomed are likely to be labeled uncooperative or resistant to the goals of counseling. They are perceived as saboteurs of the helping enterprise because of their reluctance to introspect in affective language. Although the inclination may be intentional, in large measure it is a reflection of social experience and expectation. It is also closely related to trust and transference. Distrustful clients and those exhibiting negative transference are apt to be perceived as resistant to counseling.

The fifth factor related to psychotherapeutic surrender is *self-disclosure*. Reluctance to self-disclose is especially problematic among American minorities and international sojourners who are less than fluent in English. In general, people who are under constant physical and psychological assault, whether real or imagined, are inclined to insulate themselves psychologically from their fellows. The insulation is general rather than selective. For example, Blacks, especially men, find it difficult to reveal their inner selves not only to people whom they perceive to be sources of problems in life (Whites in general), but also to family members (Jourard, 1964). There are other clients who are unable to self-disclose because their ability to speak English is not sufficient to express introspective ideas. Even those fluent in English may still be unable to communicate the essence of themselves fully to the counselor. Because language is a part of culture, there is a difference in knowing a person in a foreign language and in knowing that same person in his or her native language. They reveal willy-nilly the totality of themselves in the adopted language to members of the host culture.

Empathy. Empathy is a significant aspect of the counseling relationship. (See Chapter 3). The concept came into the psychological literature as a translation of the German *Einfuhlung* (Stotland, Mathews, Sherman, Hansson, & Richardson, 1978), which suggests a single feeling shared by two people. Szalita (1981) indicates that it is an objective and insightful awareness of the feelings, emotions, and behavior of another person. Katz (1965) points out that when individuals experience empathy, they feel as if they are experiencing the feelings of others as their own. They perceive as another, although the perceiving is cognitive and distant (Stewart, 1956). The empathizing person is aware of the process and guards against losing objectivity. Carl Rogers (1962) advises counselors to sense the subjective worlds of their clients as if they were their own, but never to forget the "as if" quality.

Although there are varying conceptions of empathy, almost all schools of counseling stress the importance of counselors' being able to understand to some degree what their clients communicate and feel. Ochanine (1938) and Katz (1963) discuss empathy as a cultural phenomenon. People empathize best with those with whom they have shared experiences. The duration and depth of the experiences determine the degree of empathy (Scheler, 1954). The more similar counselors are to their clients in terms of race, ethnic heritage, language, values, and the like, the more they are able to empathize with them.

Visualizing the feelings of others is basic to counseling. It is especially important in counseling clients from social and cultural groups in which cooperation and interdependence are valued over individualism and competition (Barshay, 1964). For example, for the Japanese, empathy *(omoiyari)* ranks high among the virtues considered indispensable for one to be really human, morally mature, and deserving of respect. In fact, Lebra (1976) is inclined to call the Japanese culture an "omoiyari culture." Omoiyari refers to the ability and willingness to feel what others are feeling, to experience vicariously the pleasure and pain that they are undergoing, and to help them satisfy their wishes. Similar or parallel sentiments are endemic to many other non-Western cultures. They are also pervasive among various subcultural groups in the United States.

Structuring. A very complex society has developed in the United States. The family, once the setting in which problems in living were solved, has relinquished progressively one role after another to outsiders. In school, children consult their counselors about a variety of concerns. In the family, members go to counselors to improve dynamics at home. On the job, personnel specialists, drug counselors, and equal employment opportunity officers help employees to make decisions about securing work; about maintaining status, equality, and opportunity; and about retirement. In general, middle- and upper-class Americans consult counselors as "perfect strangers" when they are faced with difficulty in living. In so doing, they are generally ready to reveal their most private thoughts and experiences.

Going outside the family for help is culturally foreign, however, to many clients. Therefore, defining the counseling situation is prerequisite to a productive outcome. Clients from cultures and subcultures in which the family remains the context for solving problems in living need to learn the roles of the counseling alliance. They need instruction in their role and that of the counselor. Neglecting to attend to role-teaching may lead to client embarrassment and counselor failure. For example, it is important that an international Chinese college student understand why she needs to reveal personal content about herself to an American whom she has never met. Likewise, it may seem improper for an adolescent boy born and reared in Appalachian Kentucky to "talk private talk" with "that pretty young lady counselor." The greater the social and cultural gap between the counselor and the client, the more important structuring becomes.

Transference. Transference is psychological transposing. Clients respond individually to counselors as if they were other people. The phenomenon is an unconscious association triggered by the counseling situation. Earlier relationships leave the client with psychic traces, which reassemble in encounters closely approximating them. The stimulus charge emanating from the counselor is sufficiently strong to cause automatic retrieval of the remnants of the previous situations. Psychologically, the client reenacts scenes already played. In this sense, transference is a distortion of reality. Instead of conducting themselves as new situations demand, clients use old lines for new parts in new scenes.

Transference may be categorized into three types: (1) *positive,* (2) *negative,* and (3) *ambivalent.* According to Greenson (1964), positive transference is shorthand for love reactions of any kind. They include fondness, trust, amorousness, liking, concern, devotion, admiration, yearning, tenderness, and respect. He indicates that the nonsexual, nonromantic, and mild forms of love contribute to an effective therapeutic alliance. In fact, Scheflen (1965) argues that an effective counseling relationship embodies some of the same features as courtship. On the other hand, negative transference is used to designate feelings suggesting various forms of hate (Singer, 1970). These include anger, hostility, mistrust, bitterness, envy, dislike, contempt, and annoyance. Ambivalent transference is based on the recognition that counselors are authority figures and are therefore reacted to as are authority figures in general, with ambivalence (Greenson, 1964).

Whether, why, in what direction, and to what extent culturally different clients transfer emotions derived from previous interpersonal relations to counseling situations depends on several factors. Perhaps the most important one is the culture or subculture in which they have been socialized. Individuals born and reared in one socioeconomic class have little quality contact with people socialized in other social classes. For example, members of the lower class know members of the middle and upper classes primarily as subordinates of one kind or another: students, welfare clients, employees, and the like. They and the "big people" are worlds apart socioculturally. Their feelings toward their "betters" are difficult for them to describe and tend to crop up at the most unexpected times. One of these is when they go to see counselors and social workers. It seems understandable if they transfer negative and ambivalent feelings onto people who unconsciously remind them of other "high and mighty," many of whom treat them as if they were "nobody."

Regardless of social class, members of non-White national minority groups are often treated as "nobody" by members of the majority group. Although the conditions under which Blacks, Native Americans, Hispanics, and other non-Whites live have improved considerably during the last twenty years, the majority of them are still demanding equal social and economic treatment by the majority racial group. Therefore, in counseling relationships, minority group clients approach majority group counselors with varying degrees of distrust, fear, envy, and other feelings that can be characterized as negative transference. In general, such feelings are moderated to the extent that clients and their immediate cultural peers experience equal treatment in the society at large. That is to suggest that negative transference is not as problematic among middle-class Black clients as it is among their lower-class counterparts. Negative transference is also directed toward counselors of their own group to the degree that the counselors appear to identify with the dominant racial group.

Upon entry into this country, international sojourners bring their respective cultures, but more importantly, they bring attitudes and feelings about the host society, its government, culture, and people. Their perceptions of the United States derive from numerous sources in their own countries: American-made television shows, newspapers, radio, contact with Americans abroad, books, and magazines. These perceptions, accurate or distorted, have an impact on their relationships with counselors whom they may consult for whatever reason. That the clients are culturally and linguistically different makes it difficult to sort out the sources of the complex emotions they may transfer onto American counselors (Ruesch, 1961).

Countertransference. Countertransference is transference in reverse (see Chapter 3). Counselors react to their clients as though they were other people whom they have experienced (Greenson, 1964). The reactions may be conscious or unconscious in the sense that culture is visible and invisible, conscious and unconscious. As products of it, people as infants and children are shaped by the amorphous surrounding of humans and their artifacts, procedures, and values. When they reach adulthood, they become aware of some components of culture. However, most of it remains in the mind and out of sight. They automatically respond predictively to people, situations, and artifacts, because "that's the way it has always been." Therefore, in cross-cultural counseling, transference may be perceived as the total emotional response of counselors to racially, ethnically, and nationally different clients because their cultural conditioning predisposes them to do so. If Whites as a group have always perceived Blacks to be inferior to them, then it is apt to be difficult for them as counselors to discard this cultural baggage each time they see Black clients. American counselors are a part of American culture; therefore, they manifest both its strengths and weaknesses (Burton, 1967).

In general, the countertransference potential in counselors lies dormant. However, several things may trigger it, the most important of which is transference in the client. According to Racker (1968), every transference situation provokes a countertransference situation. For example, if an adolescent from Spanish Harlem addresses an Anglo counselor in hostile racial terms, the counselor may repress or emotionally block overt reaction. However, the automatic, unconscious, and negative countertransference cannot be suppressed. Unresolved conflicts in counselors are another powerful source of countertransference (Yulis & Kiesler, 1968). For example, White female counselors who are wrestling with instinctual impulses may be quick to perceive the potential for sexual violence in their Black adult male clients, because they unconsciously sense such clients to be representatives of their own libidinal instincts, which they seek to repress (Flescher, 1953). It is easy to understand how such intrapsychic conflicts translate into negative countertransference.

Although it is usually described in benevolent terms, counseling is in fact a power relationship. McClelland (1975) points out that helping behavior implicitly involves a power goal, even though those who display it may consciously deny that influencing others in any way motivates them. The need to be superior to others is a frequent source of countertransference in helping clients whom counselors perceive to be racially, culturally, nationally, or socioeconomically inferior to them. In counseling Blacks, Whites often become "Great White Fathers." They insist on taking charge of the clients and in protecting them from "the system," if they put themselves in their hands. Clients who reject their missionary overtures may be cast aside as undeserving of real assistance.

Language. Language is the most important component of culture because it enables members of a group to cooperate in the interest of survival. With it, individuals are able to let others know what they think, feel, know, and value. In using symbols that their cultural peers understand, they share their existence with them. The sharing is holistic in that people communicate with their entire bodies, not just with speech. Individuals feel a language when speaking. The feeling is evidenced by the fact that bilingual and multilingual people usually shift to an entirely different set of gestures when they switch from one language to another. Language is conscious and unconscious. Gestures are essentially unconscious. By themselves or as accompaniments to words, they are indispensable in communicating feelings. In cross-cultural counseling, verbal and nonverbal language peculiarities may constitute real problems for counselors.

The *verbal difficulties* may be classified into three areas: (1) *class and regional peculiarities,* (2) *connotative impediments,* and (3) *clients' inability to speak English.* Cohen (1956) points out that people who are separated for whatever reason progressively acquire ways of communicating that are unique to the isolated group. The separation may be caused by geography (for example, the speech peculiarities of New Englanders compared to rural Georgians) or it may be socioeconomic (for example, lower-class versus middle-class speech patterns). Consider how many middle-class people would be able to understand the poor Appalachian father who says to his son, "Amma gonna take a scantlin' to you bo' " ("I am going to paddle your body!"). With such language, the counselor's understanding is impeded for two reasons. The speaker uses unfamiliar words, and they are edited and clipped in such a way that their comprehension by the uninitiated audience is impossible. When communicating with such clients, counselors often find themselves asking speakers to repeat themselves. Once they finally understand, they reiterate in loud standard English what the client has said. To this, it is not unusual for flabbergasted clients to ask, "What's wrong with the way I said it?"

Even counselors accustomed to the speech of their lower-class clients may be handicapped in communicating with them for another reason. According to Steiner (1975), people in one socioeconomic class do not speak to those in another social class in the same way they communicate with their cultural peers. The more alike socioculturally, the deeper is their psychic intercourse; that is, the more deeply they understand each other, the more psychologically gratifying is the communication.

The second communication problem area in cross-cultural counseling is connotative. Although members of a culture may share the same official dictionary, they do not share identical experiences whereby words acquire the personal connotations that individuals unconsciously convey in their conversations, that is, meanings associated with words derive from environmental experiences. People without privy to such experiences will not be moved by words depicting the experiences in the same way as people who are. For example, poor Black clients from the urban ghettos often say to White counselors that the counselors just "can't understand." They mean that Whites cannot identify with their experiences because they have not "been there," have not lived what the Blacks have known firsthand.

Cross-cultural counselors also encounter connotative language impediments in communicating with clients from other English-speaking countries. For example, a college student from Nigeria may communicate in perfect English. However, there are several English concepts that are somewhat meaningless to him. *Ice, sleet, snow, hail,* and *defogger* are just words to him unless he has experienced weather conditions in which he has personally internalized the symbols.

In like manner lower-class people are generally not accustomed to introspective analysis and expression of their feelings. Therefore, words such as *agonize, mortify, mystify, horrify, depression, elation, electrified, edgy,* and *hilarious* do not evoke significant experiential imagery and emotion in the unconsciousness of the audience for meaningful response. The reason for the lack of reaction is not so much that the individual does not understand the cognitive meaning of the word as it is that the individual's socialization fails to imprint these sensations in the person's recognition. People feel and identify sensations that are useful to their existence. Lower-class existence in this country requires that people attend to first things first, a phenomenon implicit in Maslow's (1954) concept of hierarchy of needs.

The third type of verbal problem that monolingual, English-speaking cross-cultural counselors encounter is total inability to communicate with clients who speak little or no English. Progressively the United States is becoming a country of many languages. For example, on the West Coast, throughout Florida, in major Eastern cities, and on reservations, countless Americans live out their entire lives unable to speak English. International visitors, diplomats, students, and business people and their families from almost every country in the world add to the number of non-English speakers, many of whom need counseling from time to time. Agencies and institutions that serve them have two options: to seek bilingual and multilingual employees or to use interpreters.

When interpreters are necessary, counselors should select them carefully and establish guidelines for their most effective use. In selecting them, it is important that they be persons whom clients can respect as they respect counselors. Counselors who are visiting the homes of clients who do not speak English, therefore, should not use the clients' children, neighbors, or friends as interpreters. Although they may be fluent in English, children are undesirable because acting as interpreters puts them in a coequal or superordinate relationship with their parents (Canino & Canino, 1980). Moreover, they are unable to understand and appreciate adult concerns, especially those pertaining to sex and family-related matters. Using neighbors and friends as interpreters is a violation of client confidentiality. In school and community settings, it is also undesirable to use custodians or service employees, who may be sources of embarrassment and uneasiness for middle-class clients unaccustomed to social class mingling.

Ideally, interpreters should be persons whom clients perceive as counseling staff (MacKinnon & Michels, 1971). To be able to capture the essence of both languages, they need to be completely bilingual and bicultural, so that they can make easy distinctions between the sense of the communication and the verbal meaning of it (Mounin, 1976). Some languages are rich in allegories, proverbs, and idiomatic expressions, especially as used by lower-class speakers (Steiner, 1975). So little is said and so much is meant that the translator is confronted with intractable problems. People in the same language group are usually quite culturally diverse. Generally, they represent many national, regional, racial, ethnic, and economic cultures. When two or more of these cultures are mixed, the interpreter's attempt to make a correct interpretation is confounded.

Nonverbal language probably contributes more to human communication than its verbal counterpart. In counseling, it is especially important, because introspective psychology places inordinate stock in its revelations. Basic counseling techniques such as reflection of feelings and interpretation rest on the assumption that in conversation much more is transmitted than speakers imagine or intend. It is transmitted unconsciously by people with their entire bodies as they interact with others. To understand this rich body of unspoken language, counselors must take into consideration the cultural heritages of speakers (Fast, 1970). Wachtel (1967) and Scheflen (1965) are among those who call attention to the difficulty of understanding the meaning of gestures, postures, inflections, and affective expressions in the communications of people from other cultures. *Paralanguage,* like language, is a product of culture.

Some cultures and subcultures rely more heavily on nonverbal communication than others. For example, in Japan there are a number of interesting features of nonverbal communication. According to Argyle (1975), there is more nonverbal language, and it has a greater degree of subtlety than elsewhere. He attributes this to the result of Zen teaching, which emphasizes the value of silence and perception without speech, the cultural homogeneity of the Japanese and their code of prescribed decorum, and to the fact that most social behavior takes place inside small, closely knit groups in which people know each other very well. In conversation, a lot is left unsaid, and long silences are commonplace. The cultural ideal is to talk as little as possible.

In addition to being taciturn, the Japanese are also reluctant to look directly into the eyes of people with whom they interact (Argyle, 1975). They avoid especially looking for long periods at the faces of their superiors. The avoidance of eye-to-eye contact with others is probably a reflection of their respect for the privacy of the souls of their fellows, because eyes are considered windows of the soul. This cultural phenomenon is an important consideration in counseling, a profession whose members have been taught to place great emphasis on the face in diagnosing veracity and character. In fact, for mainstream Americans, diagnosing Asians and Asian-Americans in general is problematic, because they have been socialized to internalize their individual feelings (Ruesch & Kees, 1972).

Many Appalachians and Native Americans are as reserved in verbal behavior as people of Asian heritage. For example, in the backwoods of Kentucky, folks who "come a-visiting" may spend the whole day sitting, walking, or whittling together and talk only occasionally, as if there is no need to verbalize to each other what they know, feel, or want. At the end of their stay, the visitors announce well in advance of departure the intent to leave. Then after a rather long period (perhaps thirty or forty minutes), they leave. Although little is said, much is communicated during such meetings. Counselors interacting with clients from such cultural backgrounds are apt to feel inadequate, because they have been taught to place a great deal of stock in client-counselor verbalism.

Personalism. Personalism is a concept that sheds much light on the cross-cultural counseling relationship. It conveys the idea that human beings are a part of nature; as such, they have no recourse but to adjust to its demands (Angeles, 1981). People must adapt to their natural environment and all of its geographical differences. This fact a one means that they, though alike biologically, must adjust to the most immediate natural environment. That is to say that those in Russia are necessarily different culturally from their fellows in Kuwait. The natural environments differ, forcing each national group to cope differently in order to survive. The disparate coping procedures result in different cultures, in the sense that culture is the way people organize themselves to conform to the requirements of nature.

According to this line of reasoning, people who live close to a harsh nature are culturally different from those who live under conditions of a beautiful, peaceful, and abundant geographical setting. For example, natives in northern countries of the world are apt to be more persistent, stubborn, determined, and impersonal than their counterparts in the carefree tropics. The more difficult the conditions of existence, the more humans must depend on each other to survive. A significant number of people throughout the world live under severe environmental conditions that demand respect for and cooperation with others. Blacks in the ghettos of the United States must "hang together" in order to overcome the hurdles of White racism. People in the Middle East must cooperate to survive the harshness of the desert.

That would suggest that people from the lower class in the United States and sojourners from Third World countries generally are apt to be more person-oriented than Americans in general. They care about people as individuals and want to know about their existence. A cultural incongruency results when they encounter people who are independent, competitive, and uncaring about the individual person. Illustrative of the cultural incompatibility is the Hispanic matronly client who asks her astonished young Anglo female counselor, "Are you married?" before the interview starts. To her, the counselor as a person is more important than the counselor as a professional helper. Therefore, inquiry into her personal life is appropriate. Personalism is also evidenced by the adolescent from the Black ghetto who wants to "check out" the counselor before "spilling my guts to the dude." He wants to know whether the counselor is "for real," at least as he knows reality. The client's concern for and inquiry about the counselor as a human being may be disarming to counselors who have been taught to distance themselves socially from their clients. Social remoteness is embodied in empathy as emphasized by American counselor educators who instruct counselors-in-training not to become too involved with their clients, to identify with their difficulties but to maintain at all times a requisite professional distance.

In general, the most effective cross-cultural counselors are those who recognize, respect, and relate to their clients as persons first and as clients second. Those who relate to them in a bureaucratic, ritualistic, superficial, and "professional" manner may be suspect because they are perceived to be indifferent to them as individuals. They are considered impersonal and therefore undeserving of "the time of day."

Diagnosis

In counseling, *diagnosis* is the process of defining the client's condition, its etiology, and manifestations (Gough, 1971). In short, it calls for counselors to make judgments about their clients. In doing so, they must perceive relationships between past and present activities, expressive behavior and inner traits and states, and between cause and effect (Taft, 1955). Indeed, the requirements are a tall order, even when clients and counselors are cultural and social peers. They often constitute insurmountable barriers to the formation of tenable diagnoses of culturally different clients. The main difficulty is the "strangeness" of clients they are expected to "analyze." It is no secret that people understand best those whom they know and least those whom they do not (From, 1971). In spite of the professional education that counselors receive, this observation still generally applies to them.

Clients from other countries, from the lower class generally, and from racial minority groups are especially difficult for counselors from the dominant cultural group to diagnose. In order to diagnose international clients, they need some knowledge of the distinctive qualities of the cultures from which they come. In particular, counselors need to know how and why individuals are rewarded or punished for their behavior in order to ascertain why clients feel or behave as they do in various situations at home and abroad. For example, to understand the situational and general behavior of Japanese and Americans of Japanese descent, familiarity with their word "bun" is useful. It is generally translated into English as portion, share, part, or fraction. To the Japanese, the concept also reflects the image of the society as an organic whole. As parts of the whole, individuals are beneficiaries of a psychologically buoyant support system; on the other hand, they are apt to experience great shame and despair when they feel that they have failed to contribute their share to the total welfare of the family, community, or other social collectivities to which they belong (Lebra, 1976).

Each distinct socioeconomic group in the United States constitutes a unique culture. Kadushin (1966) and Sennett and Cobb (1973) are among the social scientists who describe the distinguishing characteristics of members of different status groups. In general, there are psychic barriers that separate the upper, middle, and lower classes one from the other, making it difficult for counselors to understand and empathize with clients from social classes other than their own. According to Gross (1978), counselors are inclined to diagnose middle- and upper-class people as being more "normal" than individuals from the lower class.

Race also interferes with diagnosis in two ways. First, counselors who for whatever reason fail to understand and empathize with the social history of their clients are at a decided disadvantage in attempting to understand them, because people are natural extensions of their past. For example, an awareness of the conditions under which Blacks live in this country is requisite to diagnosing their maladies. In this connection, Kardiner and Ovesey (1962) insist that it is wrong to label Black clients paranoid without first assessing their environment and general experiences with racism. Second, race may hamper diagnosis because of the counselor's reaction to it. Counselors who consciously or unconsciously respond negatively to their clients because of their racial identity are unable to make fair judgments about them (Blake, 1973). Gross, Herbert, Knatterud, and Donner (1969) have shown that psychotherapeutic diagnoses generally become less accurate as the raciocultural distance between diagnosticians and their clients increases.

Recommendations and Prediction

Usually, after diagnosing the client's situation, the counselor decides what ought to be done, why, by whom, and to what extent. In psychotherapeutic professions, these decisions are generally referred to as *recommendations.* The counselor also predicts the probable outcome of the recommended intervention. This step is called *prognosis.* Although the two procedures are often discussed as separate aspects of helping, they are, in fact, inseparable because the helper does not or should not consider implementing a therapeutic idea without considering its consequences.

Because human existence takes place within a cultural context, all adjustment or lack of it is tied to the conditions of life in which individuals find themselves and the unique qualities that they possess for coping with them. Therefore, in cross-cultural counseling the most effective recommendations and predictions are those that are based on (1) *accurate assessments* of clients' temporary or permanent cultural settings, and (2) an *analysis of their abilities* to function individually as required in such settings. For example, in counseling Black high school honor students faced with the choice of attending either predominantly White or historically Black colleges, counselors need not only information about the receptivity to Black students of the college environments in question but also an assessment of each student's ability to succeed academically in impersonal, indifferent, and often hostile social situations. Not all clients from the same social, racial, ethnic, or cultural backgrounds are alike. It is important that counselors keep this fact in mind as they make recommendations for and predictions about their clients.

Intervention Barriers

Although intervention is often conceived to be separate from the counseling relationship and diagnosis, it cannot be divorced from them.

According to most counseling theorists, intervention or the very act of making a difference in the life of the client cannot be achieved without a positive relationship between the client and the counselor and a tenable diagnosis (Vontress, 1985).

In cross-cultural counseling, there are several intervention barriers that may be classified as external and internal. Because the locus of control of most minority group members is external, their lives are circumscribed by negative attitudes and treatment by members of the dominant cultural group that act as *external intervention barriers.* Although personnel counselors may help Black clients obtain good positions in prestigious firms, they have little or no control over the prejudice and discrimination the new workers encounter in the workplace. *Internal intervention barriers* are those that result from resistance imposed by clients themselves or by significant others. For example, Asian-American families are closeknit and most likely to be extended: grandparents, aunts, and uncles are very important parts of the immediate family. Therefore, it is a good thing for counselors to ask clients whether it would be helpful to consult others about the problem at hand (Greeley, 1974). On the other hand, minority group clients from highly individualistic families usually make their own decisions about important matters such as education, marriage, and employment, even during adolescence. In the Black ghettos, parents lose control over their children at an early age, compared to their middle- and upper-class counterparts. Intervention and intervention approval are in the hands of the individual client and no one else.

PERSISTENT QUESTIONS

During the last forty years, numerous questions have been raised concerning the counseling and testing of the culturally different. Two of these— *client preference for counselors* and *test bias*—have endured as issues. Although considerable research (Harrison, 1975) has shown that clients generally prefer counselors of their own racio-cultural background, the matter continues to stimulate much discussion and investigation. There are at least two reasons for the lingering concern. First, dominant-group counselors withdraw from the notion that they are ineffectual with minority group clients just because of race. Second, although the research generally shows preference based on race, there is usually a glimmer of hope left for counselors who feel that the research fails to reflect their successful experiences with minority group clients. The hope is made possible by researchers who fail to control for such variables as sex, socioeconomic status, age, degree of assimilation or adjustment to discrimination, type of presenting problem, and other differentiating client characteristics. On the other hand, it is important to compare the research on client preferences for counselors of various racial and cultural backgrounds with the sociological literature, which indicates with confidence that people feel most comfortable around cultural peers (Pelto & Pelto, 1979) and self-disclose more readily to them than they do to cultural outsiders (Chelune & Associates, 1979).

Test bias also continues to attract significant attention in the counseling profession (see Chapters 7 and 8). Abroad, American-trained counselors and psychologists working with native clienteles often find themselves in a dilemma. Do they take time and money to develop psychometric instruments standardized on the foreign group, or do they translate American-made tests into the language of their clients and use them with little or no cultural revision? The latter course of action is the easiest thing to do. In this country, debate over the appropriateness of using tests standardized on the general population to test members of racial and linguistic minority groups goes on (see Cole, 1981; Olmedo, 1981; Schmidt & Hunter, 1974).

Although seldom verbalized, at issue is the priority of minority group cultures. Those who think that one test is acceptable for everybody apparently believe that Americans are Americans: people who want "a piece of the action" must be like everybody else, culturally speaking. On the other hand, minority group people generally question this position, especially those who experience discrimination, which makes impossible their attempts to be just like everybody else, even if they wanted to. For whatever reason, the majority of minority group clients are culturally different. Whether they are disadvantaged in taking tests standardized on the general population depends on the degree to which they are sufficiently bicultural and bilingual to compete effectively with members of the dominant culture.

DIFFERENT VIEWS

Although cross-cultural counseling as a subspecialty in the profession is relatively new, two significant polemic themes have already developed in the field. These center around the *emic-etic* distinction and the *autoplastic-alloplastic* dilemma (Draguns, 1981). *Emic* is an anthropological concept that relates to the word emigration. It suggests the uniqueness that a specific racial or ethnic group takes to, or develops in, a new country or environment in which it is a minority. The emic view holds that the best vantage point for understanding and helping members of such groups is from their perspective—a culture-specific focus. Exponents of the *etic* view take a global view of humanity. Humans are more alike than they are different. Therefore, counselors are advised to acknowledge the sameness of humanity and focus on similarities instead of cultural differences (Vontress, 1979).

The emic-etic distinction has significant implications for counselors in at least three areas: (1) *the counseling relationship,* (2) *diagnosis,* and (3) *counseling methodology.* Counselors espousing the culture-specific view concern themselves with approaches uniquely designed to relate to, and communicate with, minority group clients. For example, they may study "Black English" or racio-cultural behaviors in an attempt to enhance their rapport with members of the Black community. On the other hand, counselors of the etic persuasion are inclined to approach their minority group clients as they would other clients. They assume that human beings are universally alike and therefore consider it neither appropriate nor beneficial to modify their behavior to accommodate racial, ethnic, or cultural differences.

In diagnosis, the emic-etic distinction is most obvious in terms of defining mental health. Counselors espousing the etic view assume that there is a single, universal definition of mental health, which transcends culture (Pedersen, 1981). In this connection, Page (1971) provides five basic "culture-free" criteria for evaluating the degree of normality-abnormality in cultures around the world. They are *defective psychological functioning, defective social functioning, loss of self-control, society's evaluation,* and the *personal distress factor.* On the other hand, authorities adhering to the emic position maintain that mental health is relative. In this purest form, cultural relativity considers all behavior to be relative to its particular cultural context (Offer & Sabshim, 1974). What is crazy in one society may be sane in another.

The divergent views also have implications for counseling methodology. Counselors adhering to the emic view are inclined to adjust to some extent their techniques to the cultural expectations of their clients. For example, they would not be inclined to use obligatorily a client-centered approach with Middle Eastern clients who are accustomed to authoritarian helpers. However, counselors who believe that people are universally alike are apt to use without modification their usual theories and methodologies, no matter who their clients are.

The autoplastic-alloplastic dilemma is generally implicit in counseling. It refers to the relationship of individuals to their surroundings. According to Draguns (1981), in coping with the environment, all humans respond either *autoplastically,* by changing themselves to accommodate external circumstances, or *alloplastically,* by imposing changes upon the world at large. In counseling, this question is always difficult. In cross-cultural counseling the dilemma becomes more problematic. For example, should minority group clients, when confronted with a racially unjust situation, adjust to it by altering their perception of the condition or should they fight to change the cause of the situation? The latter alternative may not be feasible if the cause of the difficulty is White racism. Most social scientists agree that racial attitudes are endemic to the American culture. On the other hand, minority group clients should be encouraged to take advantage of laws and institutional administrative procedures designed to protect their constitutional rights.

International sojourners are also faced with the dilemma. How many of their values and behaviors must they modify or compromise in order to adjust or otherwise negotiate the foreign environment? In general, collegians from abroad choose to negotiate the host environment, that is, they adapt to it, just enough to achieve their educational goals. Trying to adjust to the new culture by changing it to a more comfortable fit is usually not possible. That is not to say that cross-cultural counselors should not be change agents in their attempts to improve conditions that have a negative impact on culturally different clients. It is imperative, however, to recognize what is immediately changeable and what is not. Counselors who attack "the system" in blind frustration on behalf of their clients run the risk of endangering their own mental health.

COPING WITH CULTURAL DIFFERENCES

Members of the counseling profession continue to show an awareness of the influence of culture and social class on intervention. The awareness is reflected in several actions taken over the last twenty years. During the 1960s and 1970s local, state, and federal governmental agencies instituted programs and workshops designed to help counselors, personnel workers, and supervisors to be more sensitive to the special needs of minority group employees. In the private sector some of the activities have been picked up by employee assistance specialists.

As a result of the civil rights movement during the last four decades and the general sensitivity of the counseling profession to the problems of minorities and the disadvantaged generally, culture-related preservice and inservice training of counselors has become a priority in many quarters. Courses on topics such as counseling the disadvantaged, counseling minorities, and cross-cultural counseling appear in college and university catalogues. In many states such courses are required for certification as a school counselor. Since 1965 there has been a spate of articles and books on counseling racial and ethnic minorities. For nearly thirty years counselors, psychologists, social workers, and helping professionals generally have addressed the problems of counseling minorities at their local, state, and national conventions. In 1972 the Association for Non-White Concerns in Personnel and Guidance (now the Association for Multicultural Counseling and Development) was established as a division of the American Personnel and Guidance Association (now the American Association for Counseling and Development), to ensure "appropriate recognition of non-White concerns" (McFadden & Lipscomb, 1985).

Recognition of the importance of culture in counseling is also evidenced by the existence of the American Association for Counseling and Development's International Relations Committee. Its convention programs, *Internationally Speaking* newsletter, and network activities are important sources of information about counseling in other countries.

In settings where counselors work, culture, race, ethnicity, and social class have received considerable attention. In the 1960s paraprofessional and peer counselors from minority groups throughout the country were working in public schools, colleges, universities, governmental agencies, and other settings where culturally different clients are served.

SIGNIFICANT CONTRIBUTIONS

Cross-cultural counseling has expanded the profession. In earlier days, counseling was often conceived as a face-to-face verbal interaction between two people from fairly similar backgrounds. The 1954 Supreme Court decision outlawing public school segregation, the civil rights movement, and the discontinuation of legal segregation of the races in this country created culturally and racially diverse clienteles for counselors. Whites started counseling Blacks, and Blacks, Whites. A humanistic venture was set in motion. Counselors gained a whole new cultural perspective. Exposure to multiracial clienteles caused them to see people as people. As a result, they have become more astute observers and analyzers of human behavior. The whole counseling profession has grown as a result of this increased level of understanding of humanity.

The cultural expansion of the profession has also caused counselors to become more flexible in their approaches to counseling. Confronted with the perplexities of cultural differences, they have been forced to relax a variety of previously held views and practices. For example, when they discovered that Black ghetto clients generally are "not into talking about feelings," they were forced to resort to more active and cognitively oriented counseling styles. Out of this situation have come many "closet" eclectic counselors. Over the last ten or fifteen years, writers interested in cross-cultural counseling have discussed many variations in counseling that are made necessary by the cultural differences of clients.

THE FUTURE

Based on the interest shown in cross-cultural counseling during the last three decades, it is tenable to predict continued professional growth in the years ahead. First, there is apt to be an increase in the number of colleges and universities offering courses pertaining to counseling the culturally different, as more and more counselor educators become knowledgeable and interested in the field. Second, a few counselor-training institutions are apt to institute advanced degree programs in cross-cultural counseling, not only to help counselors work more effectively with minority group and foreign-born clients in this country, but also to help graduate students from abroad learn counseling approaches that are feasible to export to their cultures. Third, because cross-cultural counseling is an interdisciplinary field, it seems reasonable to expect that the whole profession will eventually come to realize the advantage of counselors' being broadly trained in the life sciences. Finally, theory builders are expected to become active in an effort to conceptualize counseling theories that transcend culture (Vontress, 1985).

SUMMARY

In this chapter, social and cultural foundations of counseling have been discussed as "cross-cultural counseling," the subspecialty of the profession that considers how culture, social class differences, race, and ethnicity influence counseling. Culture is the most important concept in the subspecialty; therefore, an understanding of it is basic to appreciating how it influences intervention with the culturally different. Culture and related concepts permeate the discussion of the counseling process and the various issues and questions associated with it. Several of these have been discussed in brief.

Cross-cultural counseling is the newest and most exciting subspecialty in the profession. It is necessarily global in scope. As such, it is challenging to counselors who must become increasingly sensitive to cultural differences. At the same time, the increased sensitivity to people as people is apt to make their work more rewarding, because contacts with people from other cultural and social backgrounds can be significant sources of personal insight and growth.

REFERENCES

Angeles, P. A. (1981). *Dictionary of philosophy.* New York: Barnes & Noble.

Anthony, L. (1964). Respeto, relajo, and interpersonal relations in Puerto Rico. *Anthropological Quarterly, 37,* 53–67.

Argyle, M. (1975). *Bodily communication.* New York: International Press.

Baker, J. R. (1974). *Race.* New York: Oxford University Press.

Barshay, H. (1964). *Empathy: Touchstone of self-fulfillment.* New York: Exposition Press.

Blake, W. (1973). The influence of race on diagnosis. *Smith College Studies in Social Work, 43,* 184–192.

Bronowski, J. (1971). *The identity of man* (rev. ed.). Garden City, NY: The American Museum of National History, Natural History Press.

Burton, A. (1967). *Modern humanistic psychotherapy.* San Francisco: Jossey-Bass.

Canino, I. A., & Canino, G. (1980). Impact of stress on the Puerto Rican family: Treatment considerations. *American Journal of Orthopsychiatry, 50,* 535–541.

Chelune, G. J., & Associates (1979). *Self-disclosure: Origins, patterns, and implications of openness in interpersonal relations.* San Francisco: Jossey-Bass.

Cohen, M. (1956). *Pour une sociologie de langage* [A tentative sociology of language]. Paris: Éditions Albin Michel.

Cole, N. S. (1981). Bias in testing. *American Psychologist, 36,* 1067–1077.

Coles, R. (1971). *Children of crisis:* Vol. 2. *Migrants, sharecroppers, mountaineers:* Boston: Little, Brown.

Draguns, J. G. (1981). Counseling across cultures: Common themes and distinct approaches. In P. B. Pedersen, J. G. Draguns, W. J. Lonner, & J. E. Trimble (Eds.), *Counseling across cultures* (rev. & expanded ed., pp. 3–21). Honolulu: University Press of Hawaii.

Farb, P. (1978). *Humankind.* Boston: Houghton Mifflin.

Fast, J. (1970). *Body language.* New York: M. Evans.

Faris, E. (1976). *The nature of human nature and other essays on social psychology.* Chicago: University of Chicago Press.

Flam, L. (1970). *La philosophie au tournant de notre temps* [The philosophy of our time]. Paris: Presses Universitaires de France.

Flescher, J. (1953). On different types of countertransference. *International Journal of Psychotherapy, 3,* 357–372.

Foulks, E. F. (1980) The concept of culture in psychiatric residency education. *The American Journal of Psychiatry, 137,* 811–816.

From, F. (1971). *Perception of other people.* New York: Columbia University Press.

Gassel, I. (1970). Les groupes humains et leur finalité [Human groups and their finality]. In P. H. Chombart de Lauwe (Ed.), *Aspirations et transformations sociales* [Social striving and change] (pp. 41–56). Paris: Éditions Anthropos.

Gough, H. (1971). Some reflections on the meaning of psychodiagnosis. *American Psychologist, 26,* 160–167.

Greeley, A. M. (1974). *Ethnicity in the United States: A preliminary reconnaissance.* New York: John Wiley.

Greenson, R. R. (1964). *The technique and practice of psychoanalysis* (Vol. 1). New York: International Universities Press.

Greenwood, D. J., & Stini, W. A. (1977). *Nature, culture, and human history.* New York: Harper & Row.

Gross, H. S., Herbert, M. R., Knatterud, G. L., & Donner, L. (1969). The effect of race and sex on variation of diagnosis and disposition in a psychiatric emergency room. *Journal of Nervous and Mental Disease, 148,* 638–642.

Gross, M. L. (1978). *The psychological society.* New York: Random House.

Hall, E. T. (1966). *The silent language.* Greenwich, CN: Fawcett.

Hampden-Turner, C. (1971). *Radical man: The process of psychosocial development.* Garden City, NY: Anchor Books-Doubleday.

Harris, M. (1979). *Cultural materialism: The struggle for a science of culture.* New York: Random House.

Harrison, D. K. (1975). Race as a counselor-client variable in counseling and psychotherapy: A review of the research. *The Counseling Psychologist, 5,* 124–133.

Hirschman, C., & Wong, M. G. (1984). Socioeconomic gains of Asian Americans, Blacks, and Hispanics. *American Journal of Sociology, 90,* 584–607.

Hofferth, S. L. (1984) Kin networks, race, and family structure. *Journal of Marriage and the Family, 46,* 791–806.

Horney, K. (1937). *The neurotic personality of our time.* New York: W. W. Norton.

Jordan, W. D. (1968). *White over Black: American attitudes toward the Negro 1550–1812.* Baltimore, MD: Penguin Books.

Jourard, S. M. (1964). *The transparent self.* Princeton, NJ: D. Van Nostrand.

Kadushin, C. (1966). Social class and the experience of ill health. In R. Bendix & S. M. Lipset (Eds.), *Class, status, and power: Social stratification in comparative perspective* (2nd ed., pp. 406–412). New York: Free Press.

Kardiner, A., & Ovesey, L. (1962). *The mark of oppression.* Cleveland, OH: World Publishing.

Karon, B. P. (1975). *Black scars: A rigorous investigation of the effects of discrimination.* New York: Springer.

Katz, R. L. (1963). *Empathy.* New York: Free Press.

Kluckhohn, C. (1962). *Culture and behavior.* New York: Free Press.

Kluckhohn, R. (Ed.). (1962). *Collected essays of Clyde Kluckhohn: Culture and behavior.* New York: Free Press.

Laurin-Frenette, N. (1978). *Classes et pouvoir: Les théories fonctionnalistes* [Classes and power: Basic theories]. Montréal: Les Presses de L'université de Montréal.

Lebra, T. S. (1976). *Japanese patterns of behavior.* Honolulu: University Press of Hawaii.

Lidz, T. (1976). *The person: His and her development throughout the life cycle* (rev. ed.). New York: Basic Books.

MacKinnon, R. A., & Michels, R. (1971). *The psychiatric interview in clinical practice.* Philadelphia: W. B. Saunders.

Maslow, A. H. (1954). *Motivation and personality.* New York: Harper.

McClelland, D. C. (1975). *Power: The inner experience.* New York: Irvington.

McFadden, J., & Lipscomb, W. D. (1985). History of the Association for Non-White Concerns in Personnel and Guidance. *Journal of Counseling and Development, 63,* 444–447.

Montagu, A. (1974). *Man's most dangerous myth: The fallacy of race* (5th ed.). New York: Oxford University Press.

Mounin, G. (1976). *Les problèmes théoriques de la traduction* [Theoretical problems of translation]. Paris: Gallimard.

Ochanine, D. (1938). *La sympathie et ses trois aspects: Harmonie, contrainte, délivrance* [The three aspects of sympathy: Harmony, compulsion, relief]. Paris: Librairie Le Rodstein.

Offer, D., & Sabshim, M. (1974). *Normality: Theoretical and clinical concepts of mental health* (rev. ed.). New York: Basic Books.

Olmedo, E. L. (1981). Testing linguistic minorities. *American Psychologist, 36,* 1078–1085.

Page, J. D. (1971). *Psychopathology: The science of understanding deviance.* Chicago: Aldine-Atherton.

Parsons, F. (1909). *Choosing a vocation.* Boston: Houghton Mifflin.

Pedersen, P. B. (1981). The cultural inclusiveness of counseling. In P. B. Pedersen, J. G. Draguns, W. J. Lonner, & J. E. Trimble (Eds.). *Counseling across cultures* (rev. & expanded ed., pp. 22–58). Honolulu: University Press of Hawaii.

Pelto, G. H., & Pelto, P. J. (1979). *The cultural dimension of the human adventure.* New York: Macmillan.

Racker, H. (1968). *Transference and countertransference.* New York: International Universities Press.

Rogers, C. R. (1962). The interpersonal relationship: The core of guidance. *Harvard Educational Review, 32,* 416–429.

Ruesch, J. (1961). *Therapeutic communication.* New York: W. W. Norton.

Ruesch, J., & Kees, W. (1972). *Nonverbal communication.* Berkeley: University of California Press.

Scheflen, A. E. (1965). Quasi-courtship behavior in psychotherapy. *Psychiatry, 28,* 245–257.

Scheler, M. (1954). *The nature of sympathy* (P. Heath, Trans.). New Haven, CT: Yale University Press.

Schmidt, F. L., & Hunter, J. E. (1974). Racial and ethnic bias in psychological tests: Divergent implications of two definitions of test bias. *American Psychologist, 29,* 1–8.

Sennett, R., & Cobb, J. (1973). *The hidden injuries of class.* New York: Vintage.

Shoben, E. J. (1961). Two cultures of the civil war. *Teachers College Record, 62,* 562–563.

Singer, E. (1970). *Key concepts of psychotherapy* (2nd ed.). New York: Basic Books.

Steiner, G. (1975). *After Babel: Aspects of language and translation.* New York: Oxford University Press.

Stewart, D. A. (1956). *Preface to empathy.* New York: Philosophical Library.

Storr, A. (1973). *C. G. Jung.* New York: Viking Modern Masters.

Stotland, E., Mathews, K. E., Jr., Sherman, S. E., Hansson, R. O., & Richardson, B. Z. (1978). *Empathy, fantasy, and helping.* Beverly Hills, CA: Sage Publications.

Szalita, A. B. (1981). The use and misuse of empathy in psychoanalysis and psychotherapy. *The Psychoanalytic Review, 68,* 3–21.

Taft, R. (1955). The ability to judge people. *Psychological Bulletin, 52,* 1–23.

Thass-Theinemann, T. (1968). *Symbolic behavior.* New York: Washington Square Press.

U.S. National Advisory Commission on Civil Disorders (1968). *Report.* Washington, DC: Government Printing Office.

Villemez, W. J. (1980). Race, class, and neighborhood: Differences in residential return on individual resources. *Social Forces, 59,* 414–430.

Vontress, C. E. (1979). Cross-cultural counseling: An existential approach. *Personnel and Guidance Journal, 58,* 117–122.

Vontress, C. E. (1982). Social class influences on counseling. *Counseling and Human Development, 14,* 1–12.

Vontress, C. E. (1985). Theories of counseling: A comparative analysis. In R. J. Samuda & A. Wolfgang (Eds.), *Intercultural counseling and assessment: Global perspectives* (pp. 19–31). Toronto: C. J. Hogrefe.

Wachtel, P. L. (1967). An approach to the study of body language in psychotherapy. *Psychotherapy, 4,* 97–100.

Yulis, S., & Kiesler, D. J. (1968). Countertransference response as a function of therapist anxiety and content of patient talk. *Journal of Consulting and Clinical Psychology, 32,* 413–419.

Zetzel, E. R. (1956). Current concepts of transference. *International Journal of Psycho-Analysis, 37,* 369–376.

CHAPTER 7
APPRAISAL OF THE INDIVIDUAL

Lawrence Litwack

Counselors form helping relationships with a wide range of individuals, including clients, significant others, colleagues, and peers to assist individuals and groups who seek help in moving toward a variety of personal goals. Regardless of the setting in which they work, the use of appraisal techniques may facilitate and enrich the assistance that counselors provide.

The focus of this chapter is on the development of a framework for assessing the individual, including principles and procedures of individual and group testing, methods of data collection and interpretation, and the study of individual differences. The chapter rests on two foundations. First is the necessity to understand the individual and the groups of which the individual is a member. Without such understanding, counselors can only move in a trial-and-error fashion, randomly exploring problem-solving approaches with clients while trying to build and maintain bridges of communication.

Second, and equally important, is the necessity for counselors to know and understand the system within which individuals and groups function. This may be a nuclear family system and/or a sociocultural system. Ignoring these systems means ignoring powerful factors that affect people's lives and will influence the effectiveness of any appraisal and counseling techniques.

RATIONALE FOR APPRAISAL

Appraisal, as used here, is defined as:

The process of assessing or estimating the depth or breadth of various attributes of a person. Such assessment of human behavior may include formal measures such as standardized psychological tests, as well as informal measures such as observations, interviews, rating scales and checklists, and similar less structured techniques. Appraisal is never an end in itself; it is always designed as a means to an end, ideally mutually agreed to in advance by the counselor and the client.

There are many reasons for individual or group appraisal as an important part of professional practice. The major reasons include:

1. *Placement.* In a variety of situations, counselors are asked to make professional recommendations regarding the best placement for an individual within a system. Examples may include appropriate placement of new employees, placement of transfer students in schools and colleges, and placement of individuals in special training programs or special classes (see Chapter 5).
2. *Admissions.* Particularly when the ratio of applicants to spaces available is great, counselors are asked to assist directly or indirectly in screening and decision making. Appraisal results frequently are used as major determinants in the process. Perhaps the best example can be found in the admissions criteria used by colleges and professional schools.
3. *Diagnosis.* Through the use of differential diagnoses counselors can identify specific strengths and weaknesses of individuals and groups that may assist in educational planning, teaching strategies, and remediation efforts.
4. *Counseling.* Using carefully selected appraisal techniques helps counselors achieve a deeper understanding of individuals and groups. Such understanding enables counselors to plan more intelligently with clients to facilitate the latter's movement toward desired objectives.
5. *Educational Planning.* Educational institutions benefit from group appraisal techniques that identify group strengths and weaknesses. Such data facilitate the development of remedial and advanced placement programs, as well as curricular planning and development.
6. *Licensure/Certification.* Counselors need to know about and assist individuals in planning and preparing for appropriate licensure/certification examinations necessary to practice a profession. Examples include the National Board for Certified Counselors (NBCC) exam for counselors, the National Council Licensure Examination (NCLEX) for nurses, and licensure examinations for psychologists and social workers (see Chapter 9).
7. *Self-understanding.* A major reason for using appraisal techniques is to facilitate client self-understanding and personal

development. Just as appraisal techniques will facilitate the understanding of an individual reached by others, they may also increase self-understanding and self-acceptance of an individual.
   8. *Time-saving.* In many instances, perhaps a major advantage of appraisal techniques is that they may save time for both the counselor and client in obtaining useful information prerequisite to decision making and movement. Through the range of appraisal techniques, it is possible to obtain data over a much wider range in a much shorter time. This allows for rapid movement toward the integration of the data into the counseling process.

THE APPRAISAL PROCESS

Depending upon the setting, the type of appraisal, and the reasons for appraisal, others besides counselors may be involved in the appraisal process. Generally speaking, counselors are prepared through their graduate programs to administer and interpret most methods of appraisal, both formal and informal. This is true regardless of the counseling specialty or setting in which a counselor operates. The data gathered by counselors frequently provide keys to increased understanding and decision making.

Psychologists, who frequently join counselors as part of a mental health team, are generally more fully prepared to administer and interpret some of the more clinically oriented assessment procedures, such as projective tests (to be discussed later in this chapter). They are also usually able to handle the same range of appraisal techniques as counselors, depending upon their academic preparation. Those psychologists who have been prepared in traditional psychology programs are typically not as well prepared to use those assessment procedures that are particularly appropriate for career counseling or academic planning.

Administrators, particularly those in school settings, often are heavily involved in making critical decisions about the use of group testing programs designed to compare the overall performance of their students with that of students from other settings. Administrators also do much of the interpretation of group test results in various constituencies outside the school.

Teachers and psychometrists are frequently asked to do some of the actual test administration under the direction of a counselor or psychologist. Teachers also represent major consumers of test results of both individuals and groups as they seek better ways of understanding individual differences in their teaching methods and materials. This raises an important question about how best to make test results available to individuals and significant others.

The appraisal process itself usually occurs as a result of one of several situations. One instance occurs as part of ongoing institutional group programs or standard groups of tests required by some agencies for all new clients. Appraisal is sometimes the result of a decision by others, such as courts, administrators, parents, or counselors. An example would be the diagnostic assessment packages required by some public agencies for the provision of services such as rehabilitation, job training, and so forth. Finally, appraisal may be based upon either the request of an individual or a mutual decision reached between a counselor and client.

On the local level, appraisal may occur on either an individual or group basis. There are national testing programs, however, that are always given on a group basis. Examples would be licensure exams such as the NBCC and NCLEX, mentioned earlier, and admissions tests such as the American College Test (ACT), Scholastic Aptitude Test (SAT), and Graduate Record Examination (GRE). National testing programs are usually administered on predetermined dates at predesignated sites under carefully controlled testing conditions. Local programs may be scheduled almost on a need basis depending on time and the availability of appropriate testing materials.

Appraisal is a complex process, dependent upon the skills of the examiner, the needs of the agency or institution, the needs of the individual as perceived by others, and the needs of the individual as self-perceived. All elements need to be considered if the appraisal process is to produce meaningful data that are useful to all concerned. Rather than a mysterious or haphazard series of isolated testing episodes, sound professional practices depend upon an orderly and integrated appraisal plan that is carefully woven into the fabric of counseling. With this in mind, an overview of the major kinds of *formal* and *informal appraisal procedures* is in order.

Methods of Formal Appraisal

A variety of formal and informal assessment techniques forms important parts of a counselor's repertoire. In making professional judgments about the specific formal assessment measures to select, there are certain test characteristics that help to distinguish among the instruments available. Counselors need to understand these distinctions so that they can make appropriate decisions in individual counseling situations.

Group versus Individual. A group test is one that may be administered to one or a number of individuals at the same time by one examiner. Individual tests may only be administered to one person at a time on a one-to-one basis. Examples of group tests would include most achievement and interest tests, while examples of individual tests would include certain intelligence tests, selected projective tests, and most performance tests. Each of these different types will be discussed later.

Power versus Speed. A power test is one in which there is either no time limit or a generous one, which would allow almost all examinees ample time to finish; a speed test is carefully timed and places the emphasis on the speed and accuracy of the respondent. Examples of power tests include some aptitude tests, while examples of speed tests include those assessing typing speed and accuracy. Many tests are classified as neither because, as with many achievement and scholastic aptitude tests, the time limits imposed usually allow many to complete the test within the time allowed.

Spiral versus Cyclical. Spiral tests are those in which test items get progressively more difficult; cyclical tests are those which have a number of sections, each of which is spiral in nature, which have the examinee repeatedly go through a cycle of easy to more difficult questions.

Vertical versus Horizontal. Vertical tests are those that have a number of forms for different age or grade levels; horizontal tests or test batteries measure abilities in a number of areas at the same time. Examples of vertical tests include most achievement tests and some scholastic aptitude tests; examples of horizontal tests include general aptitude tests. Many tests are neither, that is, they measure one element at one point in time; examples include most personality tests. Some tests of each type may also have *parallel forms,* that is, other forms of a particular test proven to be equal that can be used in particular situations for research purposes or to evaluate the effectiveness of a program.

Special versus General. Most commonly used in reference to aptitude tests, special refers to those tests that measure a single aptitude such as art, music, mechanical comprehension, or spatial relations; general refers to aptitude batteries that measure aptitudes in a number of areas at once.

Structured versus Unstructured. Structured or *standardized* tests sample performance under prescribed conditions, are scored by the test administrator or by a computer according to prescribed procedures, and usually limit respondents to choosing the correct answer from a limited number of choices provided. Unstructured tests provide clear or ambiguous stimuli to which respondents react in a free or open response pattern. Most group tests are standardized or structured; many projective and situational tests are deliberately unstructured.

Paper-and-Pencil, Oral, Performance. Paper-and-pencil tests include most standardized tests given in schools and colleges. Oral tests of necessity are generally individual tests even if given in a classroom or group setting. They provide both respondent answers and respondent test behaviors as material for analysis. Performance tests are generally individual, and include procedures such as tests of manual dexterity, as well as situational or problem-solving tasks that require respondents to work through and demonstrate their ability to solve a problem or complete an assigned task.

In reviewing the above distinctions, keep in mind that many tests fall into multiple categories, while some tests will only be found under a few headings. Keep these differentiations in mind in reviewing the various types of formal methods of appraisal.

TEST SELECTION AND USAGE IN COUNSELING

In making decisions about selecting and using any testing instruments, counselors need to be very clear in advance about the desired outcomes. A number of possible reasons for testing, in general, were given earlier. The decision whether or not to use specific instruments depends, however, not only upon the general purposes of a testing program, but also upon the specific purposes for selecting this type of instrument. There are several factors to keep in mind in making choices among a range of tests.

The first issue is that of the validity and reliability of the specific test being considered. *Validity* refers to the degree to which the test actually measures what it claims to measure. For example, tests designed to predict later performance, such as an aptitude test, need to have high predictive validity, if in fact they are to do what they are supposed to do. *Reliability* refers to the consistency of scores or position obtained by the same persons. For example, if there is no reasonable relationship between an individual's score or placement today and the score or placement demonstrated one month later, then the usefulness of results is in serious question if used other than as a picture of a person at one point in time. A reliable test may not be valid, but a valid test is necessarily reliable. Thus, counselors need to understand these concepts and review the data on any test being considered before making a final decision about adopting or administering a particular instrument.

A second major issue relates to the *norms* of a particular test, that is, the normal or average performance by others who took the test as part of the initial experimental group. Ordinarily, counselors would compare an individual's performance with the norm group to provide meaning. If a norm group was only composed of suburban Whites, however, then test results would be highly suspect for a Hispanic urban client. It is important to select a test with appropriate norms or to develop local norms.

A third issue revolves around questions of *test access* and *qualifications* for test administrators. Some tests require advanced academic preparation to administer and interpret, while others may be administered and interpreted by knowledgeable classroom teachers. For example, tests of school achievement are routinely given by teachers, while certain tests of personality are typically only the province of those with advanced preparation. There are also certain tests that may be very useful in individual cases, but that are restricted as part of national testing programs. Examples include the School and College Ability Test (Form C), the Graduate Record Examination, the Miller Analogies Test, the SAT, and the ACT. Such tests typically are restricted access tests.

The final issue deals with *ease of administration and scoring.* Factors to consider include the cost of materials, the time required to administer, the method of scoring (hand versus computer), and the readability of test materials. Each is a factor that may allow or negate the use of a specific measure. For example, if a client needs results from a particular assessment process immediately, then a test that must be computer-scored by a national service, which usually takes a week to ten days, would not be particularly useful.

Obviously, if all these factors are to be taken into consideration, then counselors need to be knowledgeable about individual tests, as well as thoroughly familiar with additional sources of information when necessary. Once these factors have been considered, there are still certain precautions in the use of the test that need to be taken. These include the following:

1. Be thoroughly familiar with all materials related to the test, including the manual, test booklet, answer sheets, and scoring materials.

2. Be careful about generalizing from single scores.

3. The past does not always predict the future; assess individuals as they are today.
4. Don't let test data justify counselor bias or inaction.
5. Don't get fixed ideas from the test data and then try to impose your own solution upon the individual.
6. Interpret results in ways most understandable and useful to the client or group.
7. Help individuals understand that test data reflect only one facet of an individual's abilities and experience.

There are several key points that serve to sum up the discussion of principles and methods of formal appraisal. First, the actual process of measurement is secondary to that of defining objectives; the specific counseling goals must first be determined. Second, many educational and psychological measurement techniques and instruments are only tools. Finally, and related to a later section, formal tests and measurements must be supplemented by informal observation, anecdotal descriptions, and other nontesting techniques to obtain a comprehensive picture of the individual that will be of most use in the counseling process.

STANDARDIZED TESTS

Most of the tests given in the United States today are standardized paper-and-pencil instruments that can be given to individuals and to groups of whatever size desired whenever the need arises. Such instruments fall into one of five broad groups, each of which will be discussed briefly. These tests include measures of *achievement, aptitude, intelligence, interest,* and *personality.* Because you will in all likelihood receive specialized academic preparation in these areas at some point in your academic program, the purpose here is to define each type, provide some examples of each, provide sources of information about tests and testing, and explore several of the key issues involved in selecting and using tests. A number of tests will be mentioned in this discussion. Information about the publishers of these instruments can be found in Appendix I.

Achievement

Achievement tests are designed to measure the degree to which an individual or a group has acquired certain information or mastered designated skills. Although such tests are regularly developed by teachers or supervisors, there is also a wide variety of standardized achievement tests currently in use. Some of the purposes of achievement testing are:

1. To check the attainment of minimum performance standards.
2. To select candidates for a job or applicants for admission.
3. To classify students for ability grouping.
4. To waive students out of specific courses.
5. For diagnosis and remediation.

There are several different types of standardized achievement tests currently in wide use. The first type is designed to measure achievement in *single subject* areas, such as reading, arithmetic, foreign language, and so on. Such tests are usually administered at the completion of a course to compare student performance to the performance of previous students or to the performance of comparable groups in other settings. In using such a test and in interpreting test results, it is important to be certain that the objectives of the test match those of the course.

A second major type is the achievement *test battery* which is designed as a horizontal test to measure achievement in a number of specific areas during one testing period. The third major type includes *diagnostic* tests designed to identify individual strengths and weaknesses.

A number of examples of achievement tests are currently in use. In education, the most common type used are comprehensive achievement tests such as the Metropolitan, California, Iowa Tests of Educational Development, and Sequential Tests of Educational Progress (STEP). Such test batteries, which are usually both vertical and horizontal, are frequently given annually on a schoolwide basis.

Another example of achievement tests can be found in the standardized tests used for decision making or licensure/certification. Examples include the College Entrance Examination Board (CEEB) Achievement Tests, Graduate Record Examination (GRE) Advanced Tests, National Teacher Examination, the National Board for Certified Counselors (NBCC) examination, National Mental Health Counselor Certification (NMHCC) examination, and the licensure examinations required of psychologists and social workers.

Aptitude

Aptitude tests are designed to predict an individual's ability to learn in a specific area and/or to make predictions about future behaviors. Similar to achievement tests, aptitude tests are generally available in general batteries or as measurements of special or single-area aptitudes. Aptitude tests are typically used in advance to predict later performance, while achievement tests are typically given afterwards to assess the results of learning.

Aptitude tests are used for several purposes. One is to facilitate decision making for admission or educational placement, particularly when there are more applicants than available positions. Another widespread use of such tests is for diagnostic purposes to assist in course and curricular planning. There are a number of examples of aptitude tests currently in widespread use, including measures of general, academic, and special aptitudes.

Several good examples of *general* or *multiple aptitude* test batteries are the Differential Aptitude Test (DAT), designed for use on the secondary level to assess a number of areas at once, and the General Aptitude Test Battery (GATB) developed by the United States Employment Service for use with high school students and a general adult population to assess both paper-and-pencil and manual dexterity aptitudes.

Typical examples of *scholastic* or *academic aptitude* tests include the School and College Ability Test (SCAT), the Scholastic Aptitude Test (SAT), the Graduate Record Examination (GRE), and the Miller Analogies Test (MAT). Examples of *special* or *single-area aptitude* tests include aptitude tests used for admission to professional schools such as the Law School Aptitude Test (LSAT), the Medical College Aptitude Test (MCAT), and the Graduate Management Aptitude Test (GMAT).

Other special aptitude tests measure potential in areas such as music (Seashore Measures of Musical Talent), art (Design Judgment Test), clerical (Minnesota Clerical Test), mechanical comprehension (Bennett Mechanical Comprehension Tests), and spatial relations (Minnesota Paper Form Board). Most aptitude tests at times may resemble achievement tests, in part because they obviously are affected by prior learning. A good example of a test that seems to serve both an academic aptitude and single-area achievement function would be the American College Test (ACT) used for college admissions purposes. The mathematics, science, and social studies sections are clearly influenced by prior academic learning. The English score is more marginal in that it relies on specific English courses.

Intelligence

Intelligence tests are designed to measure an individual's aptitude for academic work or other situations requiring the application of reasoning and verbal ability. Generally, they offer some indication of an individual's ability to function in the world on a daily basis. Intelligence tests are characterized as individual or group and verbal or nonverbal performance.

Individual intelligence tests are given by professionals who have had advanced preparation, such as psychologists, psychometricians, or counselors with post-master's course work. Such tests are usually given for diagnostic purposes to individuals experiencing academic difficulty, for decision making with children applying for early admission to school, or to individuals being evaluated for placement in special education or gifted classes, and for ability grouping within classes.

A major advantage of individual tests is that the examiner may observe the behavior and methods of problem solving that the examinee uses. Major disadvantages are that such tests require a more highly trained examiner and are more time-consuming. The best examples of individual tests are the Stanford-Binet (an individual intelligence test widely used in schools), the Wechsler intelligence test series (most commonly used in clinical or diagnostic situations), and nonverbal tests that rely on pictures as stimuli such as the Peabody Picture Vocabulary Test and the Columbia Mental Maturity Test.

Group intelligence tests are used primarily in schools as part of annual schoolwide testing programs. They have an advantage of economy of time over individual tests. Examples of group tests using a spiral format include the Otis-Lennon Mental Ability Tests and the Henmon-Nelson Tests of Mental Ability. Examples of group tests using a cyclical format include the Cognitive Abilities Tests and the California Tests of Mental Maturity. Group intelligence tests are primarily verbal in nature; they thus correlate well with academic aptitude tests.

Nonverbal or performance intelligence tests are designed for individuals with language deficiencies, with certain disabilities, and/or to lessen the impact of cultural influences on test results. Examples include the performance section of the Wechsler, the Leiter International Performance Scale, and Tests of General Ability (TOGA).

Although most intelligence tests use a mean or average score of 100, any intelligence test score is relative, depending on the test used, the norms and standard deviation, and the validity of the test administration. Test results tend to be more unreliable in preschool years because of the wide variation in children's learning experience. Consequently, these tests serve only as an indication of the lower limits of the actual ability level; in other words, the individual is at least at the level indicated by the achieved score. The actual level may be significantly higher if factors contributing to a lowered score could be identified and alleviated.

Interest

Interest *tests, checklists,* or *inventories* are designed to appraise a person's preferences or interests for a variety of activities and topics. Such instruments are generally untimed. Although sometimes given to individuals in pre- or early adolescence, they have their greatest use with older adolescents and adults. Because of the instability of interests below that level, extreme care should be taken in using and interpreting interest test results administered to students younger than tenth grade.

There are several problems with interest inventories that do not seem to apply to test groups discussed earlier. One lies in the ease with which clients can avoid giving honest or truthful responses on an interest inventory. Thus, such inventories are of marginal usefulness if it is advantageous to the examinee to present responses in a certain way or if there is no motivation to respond to test items as honestly as possible (such as frequently occurs in schoolwide mandatory testing programs, or in screening programs in business and industry to determine employment, promotion, or retention of individuals).

A second problem is the tendency of some individuals to respond in socially desirable ways or to agree when in doubt. A test format in which respondents are forced to make a choice (yes/no, either/or) help to alleviate this problem somewhat. A third problem lies in the emphasis many inventories place on a variety of professional roles; that is, they are not designed for individuals planning to enter skilled or semiskilled occupations.

Several leading interest inventories currently provide the majority of interest assessments in this country. The first is the Strong-Campbell Interest Inventory. It uses major groupings according to the Holland plan, which classifies occupations into six types—Realistic, Investigative, Artistic, Social, Enterprising, and Conventional (see Chapter 5). In addition, responses are scored by interest and occupational areas.

The second major test group includes the Kuder General Interest Survey (Form E), designed for use in junior and senior high schools, and the Kuder Occupational Interest Survey, or the Occupational Interest Survey (OIS, Form DD) for use with college students and adults. The OIS is particularly useful with college freshmen and sophomores because of the inclusion of both occupational and college major scales.

A third test that has demonstrated its usefulness is the Minnesota Vocational Interest Inventory, which assesses interests in general areas as well as a variety of skilled and semiskilled occupations. There are a number of other assessment instruments used in the measurement of interests, but these are the most commonly used.

Counselors should use any interest inventory with a clear understanding of its strengths and limitations. The use of such inventories will save time and should provide a variety of alternatives for individuals to explore in moving toward career and occupational choices. They will not provide any guarantee of success in a particular field, however, an important distinction that must be made clear to clients.

Personality

Personality tests or inventories are designed to assess the qualities, traits, and behaviors that characterize a person's individuality. They include both paper-and-pencil inventories as well as individually administered unstructured tests. Such inventories have several very specific limitations and problems. First, they are highly vulnerable to faking, as well as eliciting socially desirable responses. The reliability and validity of such tests are also not particularly high. It is difficult in interpreting results to know whether respondents answered the way they honestly see themselves, the way they would like to be, or the way they think others see them.

Perhaps the best way of using such inventories is with the following limitations in mind. If we can safely assume that the individual completed the inventory as honestly as possible and that nothing of an emotionally upsetting nature had occurred just prior to the administration of the inventory, then the results would seem to present a picture of the individual as self-reported at the time the inventory was completed.

There are many examples of personality inventories currently in wide use. These include instruments such as the California Test of Personality (CTP), the Omnibus Personality Inventory (OPI), the Edwards Personal Preference Schedule (EPPS), and the Myers-Briggs Type Indicator (MBTI). Other inventories that are more complex and usually require advanced training to use include the California Psychological Inventory (CPI), the Minnesota Counseling Inventory (MCI), and probably the most widespread personality inventory used today, the Minnesota Multiphasic Personality Inventory (MMPI).

Projective tests are relatively unstructured or ambiguous stimuli. Most projective measures do not meet normal standards of validity and reliability, are vulnerable to many of the same limitations as personality inventories, and require much more training to administer and interpret. A major problem occurs in the potentially subjective scoring of such instruments by individuals trained in different interpretative methods.

There are a variety of such instruments currently used in clinical situations. These include word association and sentence completion tests, which may be administered in a paper-and-pencil group format, drawings such as the Machover Draw-A-Person Test, inkblots such as the Rorschach, and pictures such as the Thematic Apperception Test (TAT), the Children's Apperception Test (CAT), and the Blacky Pictures.

Projective tests need to be used very carefully because of the possibility of misinterpretation of responses and misuse of results. At best, they may suggest some areas of useful exploration in a counseling relationship. However, the importance of specialized training in the administration, scoring, and use of such instruments cannot be overemphasized.

SOURCES OF DATA ON TESTING

With the great range of commercially published tests currently available, it is not always easy for counselors to maintain an awareness of new developments in testing, as well as to remain current in the information necessary to make intelligent choices on test selection and usage. A range of resources is available that will help, each providing unique types of information.

Foremost among these resources are two publications edited by Oscar K. Buros. The first is the series of *Mental Measurements Yearbooks.* The most recent is the eighth, published in 1978. The yearbooks provide a wealth of information about all standardized tests published up to the time of publication. Each test description is accompanied by at least one critical review by a knowledgeable professional. Although some of the descriptive data, such as prices, rapidly become dated, the information and reviews help provide insight into a particular test that may be unavailable elsewhere.

The companion book to the yearbooks is *Tests in Print III* originally edited by Buros; the latest edition has been edited by James V. Mitchell (1983). This volume provides a good deal of supplementary information about published tests and lists the cross-reference to the yearbooks in which reviews of each test may be found. It is a useful reference source for quickly identifying tests available in a particular area and the yearbooks in which information about them may be found.

Another source of data is *textbooks* in measurement and evaluation. These are useful in covering the complete range of testing and assessment principles and practices. They do not give as much specific information about individual tests because they must be selective through necessity, and they usually cannot be relied upon for very current materials due to the time involved in book preparation and publishing. They are, however, a major source of information about statistical principles, testing procedures, and other general information that can be used as a yardstick against which to measure any individual test or assessment procedure. Three leading examples are Thorndike and Hagen (1977), Anastasi (1982), and Cronbach (1984).

A fourth source of data is *journals* that are devoted primarily to testing or have sections about new test information. Such journals provide much more current information and reviews of new tests than those sources mentioned previously. These journals include *Educational and Psychological Measurement, Measurement and Evaluation in Guidance, Journal of Counseling and Development, Journal of School Psychology,* and *Journal of Counseling Psychology.*

Another source of data comes from *test publishers.* This is the best source for the most current information on new tests and on test ordering information such as cost, scoring charges, and so on. However, it is not a good source for reviews or critical information, because the publishers tend to praise their tests rather than criticize them. Counselors are encouraged to get on the mailing list of test publishers to receive information on new materials routinely (see Appendix I).

A final source of data is the *testing materials* themselves, especially the test manual or supplementary technical reports. This would be the primary source for statistical data about tests norms, validity, reliability, scoring procedures, and similar information. Most test publishers will make specimen sets of a particular test available for review at a nominal cost. Such review is important prior to making a decision about which tests to have available or to use.

Generally, no single source of test information can be relied on to the exclusion of other sources. Counselors need to be aware of and use all available sources in order to obtain the comprehensive range of information necessary to make the most appropriate professional choices for individual and group appraisal.

INFORMAL METHODS OF APPRAISAL

To this point, our focus has been primarily on formal, standardized methods of appraisal. There are informal processes, however, that may provide counselors with valuable information about individuals with whom they come into contact and may facilitate self-understanding by clients. The use of such processes depends somewhat on the counselor's setting. For example, a school counselor may have direct access to informal data that would be unavailable to a counselor in private practice. These informal approaches constitute an invaluable part of the counselor's professional repertoire and are worth discussing briefly.

Systematic and informal observations enable the counselor to view individual behavior in both natural and controlled settings. Such an approach provides a picture of actual behavior, can be applied in natural settings, and is particularly useful with young children and others with whom verbal communication may be difficult. The disadvantages lie in the difficulty of placing the observer in the natural setting, controlling counselor subjectivity and bias, and trying to determine the significance of isolated items of behavior. By training observers to look for specific aspects of behavior, it is possible to focus observations in a way to lessen the judgmental influences. (See Chapter 8 for a more thorough discussion of these problems in research).

A logical outgrowth of observation is the need for a way to communicate what has been observed. One useful method is writing *anecdotal notes.* Anecdotal records provide an actual description of an actual event, describe the setting sufficiently to give meaning, clearly separate interpretation from description, and describe events that relate to an individual's personal development or social interaction. Problems lie in the bias of the observer, inaccuracy of reporting, tendency to make generalizations from samples, and difficulty in interpreting behavior. Inservice or continuing education and practice will help sharpen the focus of such anecdotal notes.

A second useful way of recording data based on observations is through the use of *rating scales* and *checklists.* The former provides a description of the characteristics to be evaluated, along with some means by which the observer may indicate the quality, frequency, or importance of each item. The latter focuses more on the existence or absence of a particular characteristic or behavior. Such instruments can be improved by selecting for evaluation a limited number of significant behaviors that are defined clearly and concretely, by creating conditions in which such behaviors may be observed, by selecting qualified observers, and by providing ample time for observation before rating. In some settings, counselors may team with teachers or other group leaders who interact with the individuals being observed on a regular basis. Together, it is possible not only to gather valid and reliable data, but also to attach meaningful interpretations to such data.

Appraisals of an individual based upon *self-reports* are also possible. One such method that has proven useful is the *autobiography,* giving individuals a method of presenting information about various aspects of their lives and giving some indication of self-concept. The *diary* focuses on more immediate life events. Individuals may complete such assignments on their own as a homework assignment and bring them in to discuss with the counselor. A great deal can be learned from autobiographies or diaries about the attitudes, self-image, and significant life events of a client.

A way of focusing on an individual's status within a group is through the use of *sociometric approaches.* Through the use of a *sociogram,* it is possible to produce a graphic display of a group's structure, which will reveal at a glance the existence of subgroups, as well as clearly identifying the leaders and isolates within the group. The latter information is particularly important in focusing on withdrawn or rejected individuals who might otherwise be overlooked. Such approaches will work only with relatively closed groups such as a counseling or therapy group, classroom, club, and the like (see Chapter 4). Probably the most effective use of sociometric approaches lies with elementary school children and the elderly who are relatively open with their likes and dislikes, although for different reasons. Care needs to be taken, however, not to stigmatize individuals by misusing the results of sociometric methods.

Another source of appraisal data is through the use of *records.* Some counselors prefer not to review records before working with a client. However, such an attitude is rather like the physician who refuses to look at previously gathered medical data because of the fear of prejudging the patient. This view assumes, of course, that the records on file meet the criteria of validity and reliability. Whether one thinks of cumulative records, permanent records, or reports from other helping professionals, records can greatly facilitate the appraisal process by providing a comprehensive view of the individual from information gained from a variety of sources.

Depending on the type of records available to a counselor, they may serve several purposes.

1. Provide a long-term view of physical, social, and psychological growth and development.
2. Suggest possible correlates of present difficulties.
3. Help to identify talent and reveal potentialities.
4. Help to establish educational and vocational goals.
5. Help in career counseling and job placement.
6. Assist in conferences with significant others, for example, spouses, parents, teachers, administrators, courts, fellow employees, employers, and so forth.
7. Provide specific information to facilitate decision making.

Generally, records designed to meet these objectives include five different classifications of data. First, there are *demographic* data, which require the least amount of interpretation and are verified most easily. Such data help describe an individual's history and current situation. Second, there are *descriptive* data, which include evaluative statements based on interpretations of individual behavior, case conferences, and judgments by significant others. Third, there are *communication* data, which include various communications about an individual between and among professionals. Finally, there are *test* data, which reveal specific performance on previous appraisal instruments used with an individual, usually accompanied by *interpretative* data. All such data are useful adjuncts to the counseling process, but all must be taken as information for counseling purposes rather than as definitive descriptors or predictors of behavior or achievement.

Another way of gaining information that may be used as part of the counseling process is through *structured* or *open-ended interviews*. Such interactions differ from the typical counseling session in several significant ways.

1. They usually are counselor- or interviewer-controlled.
2. Purposes of the interview are usually predetermined by the interviewer.
3. They are designed to gather data to be used as part of an appraisal process to facilitate decision making, such as placement decisions, counselor assignment, and so on.

Perhaps one of the best examples of such an interview is the *intake* interview required by many agencies as an initial appraisal device to determine the needs and best assignment for applicants for service.

One other method of data collection that is frequently used by counselors is *conferences,* which may be between the counselor and significant others, such as parents, professional colleagues, teachers, court officials, or others. Another common plan uses *case conferences,* which involve a team of professionals, all of whom have contacts in different ways with an individual. An example may be an agency conference for a school-aged child involving a counselor, psychologist, nurse, social worker, specialist (speech and hearing, reading, and so on), consultant, and others. Such conferences are designed for communication, appraisal, and planning purposes to facilitate the development of a coordinated problem-solving approach with an individual, involving many or all of those in the conference.

Informal methods of appraisal are obviously not as structured as are standardized tests. However, tests alone present only a small sample of behavior of the individual. By using a comprehensive plan involving both formal and informal measures, counselors come to understand more fully individuals and their environments, both past and present. Such information facilitates the growth of self-understanding by the client, as well as mutual understanding between clients and counselors. The more data available, the better the appraisal process, and the better the process, the more counselors will be able to facilitate client growth and development, problem-solving abilities, and decision making as primary counseling goals.

CURRENT ISSUES IN APPRAISAL

There are a series of issues or questions relating to the entire area of appraisal of which all counselors need to be aware. Perhaps more importantly, counselors need to think through their position on each and develop a sound rationale for each approach they decide to take. These areas are briefly presented here.

Criterion- versus Normative-Referenced Assessment

Criterion-referenced assessment compares group or individual performance with a predetermined set of criteria believed to be important and/or essential. *Normative-referenced* assessment compares individuals with each other and/or with others who took the same test previously. Most current standardized tests, and most teacher-made tests, are normative-based, that is, what you know is less important than how much you know compared with the norm group. An example of a criterion-referenced test is the assessment of handwriting, which compares student performance with a set of samples that serve as the criteria.

This area has key implications for counselors selecting tests. As a result of some recent court challenges, tests selected for use in a particular employment situation need to be directly related to the job for which individuals are applying. For example, a test of spatial relations or clerical speed and accuracy could not be used as part of a selection process for candidates for fire department training unless there was direct evidence indicating that the areas being measured were job-essential. Thus, this area becomes crucial for counselors involved directly in employee counseling and selection, or indirectly as consultants helping others set up testing programs.

Test Bias

Increasingly in recent years, questions have been raised about the presence of cultural, ethnic, and/or gender bias in tests. Such questions generally have arisen as a result of the lack of representation of certain groups in the norm group and the systematic exclusion of certain group members because they failed to score as well as others on particular tests. A discussion has continued in the helping professions and in the courts about the existence of test bias.

For example, Thomas S. Gunnings, a professor of psychology at Michigan State University, believes that cultural bias in educational and intelligence tests is a major problem. Gunnings has stated, "Tests per se do not include questions based on minority lifestyles and background issues. They do not measure the intelligence of the minority population. They are culturally biased" (cited in Harold, 1984, p. 12). Thomas Oakland differs somewhat with Gunnings. He states, "The major problem is not with tests. The major problem is how we use the results of those tests" (cited in Harold, 1984, p. 12).

The courts also disagree on the issue of test bias. One case that served as a landmark was *Larry P. et al.* v. *Wilson Riles et al.,* heard in U.S. District Court for Northern California in 1979. In that case, Judge Robert F. Peckman ruled that intelligence tests are culturally biased and that the intelligence tests used in California to place Black children in educable mentally retarded classes violated federal law and the California and the U.S. Constitutions. He banned IQ tests for that use until the state could show that such tests were valid. This ruling was upheld by the 9th Circuit Court of Appeals (Cordes, 1984a).

The impact of *Larry P.* has been somewhat offset by an Illinois case, *Parents in Action on Special Education (PASE)* v. *Joseph P. Hannon et al.* In that case, Judge John F. Grady ruled that intelligence tests are not culturally biased and that they are appropriate assessment tools when they are one of a number of other factors used in making placement decisions.

Questions of cultural bias in testing are not new and are not limited to racial minorities. In one instance, the appropriateness of using English-language intelligence tests for Hispanic children in California was questioned after an inordinate number of Hispanic children were classified as retarded. Rulings resulting from this case stated that children must be tested in their native language.

In another example, Giyou Hatano, a cognitive and developmental psychologist at Dokkyo University in Japan, stated,

> Japanese clinical psychologists and psychiatrists are the most outspoken critics of intelligence testing, he said, calling it "a justification of unfair social stratification." Shinohara [Mutsuharu Shinohara, a clinical psychologist at Wako University] has argued that intelligence tests are "a camouflage for unfair discrimination against the handicapped." (Hathaway, 1984)

Clearly, the key point for counselors is that serious questions have been raised about built-in test bias that discriminates against certain groups. The more individuals and groups are well represented in the norm groups of the tests, the less likely the problem will exist. In the final analysis, however, there are major limitations in using any test as a primary decision maker. No test was ever published with that stated purpose. (See Chapter 6 for a detailed discussion of culture bias in counseling.)

Use of Test Results

Another criticism of many tests is that they categorize, classify, track, limit, stereotype, label—the list of negative terms goes on indefinitely. A further complaint is that such identification may follow an individual forever as part of a file or permanent record. The cry is heard that test results are used to restrict some individuals from particular opportunities because of failure to attain a particular score.

In many respects, such criticisms are similar to complaints made about the use of diagnostic categories, that they are used to label an individual with something that is potentially harmful. The main point here is that standardized test results, numbers, and diagnostic categories are in and of themselves meaningless until someone places a value judgment on them. Put another way, no number ever made a decision; people make decisions.

Allowing test scores to justify action or inaction in place of professional judgment and without using all available data is a gross misuse of appraisal instruments and raises serious ethical questions about those who use tests in ways other than those for which the tests were specifically designed. This relates to the next issue.

Test Users

Because a major element affecting the use of appraisal instruments rests with the test administrator, it obviously makes sense to look at the qualifications of those giving tests. Such concerns have been reflected by participants at a meeting of representatives from the American Psychological Association (APA), the American Educational Research Association (AERA), and the National Council on Measurement in Education (NCME) during the summer of 1984. A major agenda item at that meeting was how best to ensure that those who administer, score, and interpret tests are qualified.

John H. Jackson, coordinator of the department of psychological services for the Milwaukee public schools and a member of the steering committee for this meeting, said that there is no current mechanism to handle questions about the qualifications of test users. He suggests four critical elements that should determine whether an individual is qualified to use a particular test. These are the *test chosen, testing conditions,* the *purpose of the test,* and the *specific testing background the test requires.* Jackson cited a 1977 study, however, that shows the indiscriminate distribution of sensitive tests that were supposed to be restricted, and complained that there is an apparent absence of official standards for these four factors, especially the two dealing with purpose and testing conditions (Cordes, 1984b).

In the final analysis, perhaps the only real protection at the moment comes from the ethical standards of the American Association for Counseling and Development (AACD) and the American Psychological Association (APA) regarding test usage. The complete AACD ethical standards may be found in Appendix A. Principle 8 of the Ethical Principles of Psychologists developed by APA deals with assessment and states:

> Principle 8. Assessment Techniques. In the development, publication, and utilization of psychological assessment techniques, psychologists make every effort to promote the welfare and best interests of the client. They guard against the misuse of assessment results. They respect the client's right to know the results, the interpretations made and the bases for their conclusions and recommendations. Psychologists make every effort to maintain the security of tests and other assessment techniques within limits of legal mandates. They strive to assure the appropriate use of assessment techniques by others.
> a. In using assessment techniques, psychologists respect the right of clients to have a full explanation of the nature and purpose of the techniques in language that the client can understand, unless an explicit exception to this right has been agreed upon in advance. When the explanations are to be provided by others, the psychologist establishes procedures for insuring the adequacy of these explanations.
> b. Psychologists responsible for the development and standardization of psychological tests and other assessment techniques utilize established scientific procedures and observe the relevant APA standards.
> c. In reporting assessment results, psychologists indicate any reservations that exist regarding validity or reliability because of the circumstances of the assessment or the inappropriateness of the norms for the person tested. Psychologists strive to insure that the results of assessments and their interpretations are not misused by others.
> d. Psychologists recognize that assessment results may become obsolete. They make every effort to avoid and prevent the misuse of obsolete measures.
> e. Psychologists offering scoring and interpretation services are able to produce appropriate evidence for the validity of the programs and pro-

cedures used in arriving at interpretations. The public offering of an automated interpretation service is considered as a professional-to-professional consultation. The psychologist makes every effort to avoid misuse of assessment reports.

f. Psychologists do not encourage or promote the use of psychological assessment techniques by inappropriately trained or otherwise unqualified persons through teaching, sponsorship, or supervision.

Perhaps the most comprehensive statement made about test users was the policy statement of the American Personnel and Guidance Association (now AACD) entitled "Responsibilities of Users of Standardized Tests" (see Appendix D). The statement contains sections on decision rules, qualifications of test users, test selection, test administration, test scoring, test interpretation, and communicating test results. It is essential that counselors know, understand, and follow the principles outlined.

Access to Test Results

Another question that needs to be raised is that of access to test results. It would seem logical that all clients receive the results of tests they have taken. The question remains, however, about how such results are to be interpreted and who may have access to test data. In the process of answering each question, counselors will need to be thoroughly familiar with appraisal instruments they use, as well as being very clear about the legal and ethical limitations on the release of data.

Test results may be communicated in narrative form, raw scores, percentiles, stanines, IQs, percentile bands, grade levels, age levels, standard scores—in short, in a number of different ways, all of which are correct. Thus, counselors will need to make choices about which method to use, as well as how to record scores. Such decisions need to be based on what will best communicate the meaning of the test results and how the results are to be used.

In recording test data, the same care needs to be taken as with other counseling material in terms of confidentiality. If certain appraisal procedures are given on a group basis and the results kept as part of a permanent record, then care needs to be taken in how to record scores, depending upon who has access to the records and their level of understanding about the meaning of test results.

As an extension of this, counselors need to do more to educate the public about what tests are and what they can and cannot do. For a variety of reasons, tests have been viewed with a certain mystique in the eyes of the public. The image has been fostered that tests are infallible, that test results can predict or guarantee success in something, or that they allow counselors and psychologists to read your mind. Unfortunately, at times counselors have contributed to the air of mystery by their unwillingness or inability to discuss the purpose and use of tests in terms the public can understand.

Appraising the Unmeasurable

An area that presents difficulties to educators, counselors, psychologists, and administrators is the measurement of attitudes. Coupled with this are the attempts to measure areas such as motivation and creativity. There are several difficulties in these areas. First, there is no generally accepted consensus on what such attitudinal or behavioral terms mean. Second, the assessment of attitudes is necessarily external, that is, either based on the perceptions of others, or upon self-report inventories that are vulnerable to the provision of socially acceptable answers.

Valid and reliable instruments exist to appraise many areas described previously and can be developed to report observed behavior. At present levels of sophistication, however, how to assess attitudes and somewhat ambiguous behavioral characteristics validly and reliably remains unknown. Although there are experimental instruments in several of these areas currently available, counselors need to exercise great care in attempting to measure something that is so relatively amorphous, especially when the results of such appraisals are so vulnerable to misuse and misinterpretation.

Are Tests Necessary?

Considering all that has been presented, a question legitimately can be raised about the necessity to use tests at all. Some would argue that skilled counselors can make sound judgments about individuals without using tests, based on analyses of available data and interactions with the client. Others would argue that counselors need all the data they can gather to be able to provide the most comprehensive counseling assistance for an individual.

Neither argument is particularly sound. Not to use available instruments means not to use informational and diagnostic tools that may facilitate the counseling process when used in ways that are ethically and professionally sound. Using tests indiscriminately essentially implies a shotgun approach that attempts to get as much data as possible in an effort to see what emerges that might be important. Such an approach is wasteful and reflects poor professional practice.

In summary, all helping professionals use the tools that are the most helpful for specific purposes. To reiterate a point made earlier, tests in and of themselves are neither good nor bad; used properly they become valuable adjuncts to the counseling process, facilitating counselor and client understanding and enhancing the ability of both to move toward the achievement of mutually agreed upon counseling goals.

THE FUTURE

To this point, the focus has been placed upon the current status of appraisal practices. Counselors need to be aware of current trends in appraisal, however, that may significantly change some of the ways in which appraisal is done. Each of these trends is worth mentioning briefly.

The movement that is having a great impact on the appraisal process is the use of computers in testing and assessment. *Computer-assisted testing* describes the process of enabling individuals to take an existing test via computer rather than in the traditional paper-and-pencil format. The advantages of the approach include flexibility of scheduling, ability to obtain a test result quickly, and flexibility in reporting when different formats are needed for different audiences (Wood, 1984).

Computer-based test interpretations range from indicating the groups associated with certain test scores to providing information and recommendations for counseling approaches and treatments. Advantages include pleasing clients who prefer the anonymity of computer testing, replacing the process of personal testing with an impartial and accurate machine, and a major saving in time and cost.

As Turkington (1984) points out, however,

> The most pressing worry of practitioners is the accuracy of computerized test interpretation . . . used by those with little training or awareness of test interpretation validity, computerized testing can actually do more harm than good. . . . Because test scores and interpretations come from a computer, they give a false impression of infallibility. . . . Because the tests are so easy to use . . . many who are untrained will use them incorrectly for decisions involving employment, educational placement, occupational counseling, mental health diagnosis or brain deficit assessments. (p. 7)

With these concerns in mind, counselors will need to know about both the possibilities and pitfalls of computers in testing so that they will be able to make intelligent decisions about how to use computer testing in ways that enhance their advantages and minimize their disadvantages.

A second trend that is beginning to surface is *less reliance on tests*. Bates College in Maine, for example, has dropped the requirement of college admissions test scores for admission consideration. Other educational institutions and programs are also questioning the necessity for test scores when an applicant presents sufficient other relevant data. A counter trend is a *greater reliance on tests* as ensurers of quality. For example, many states are exploring the concept of mandatory competency-based testing as a prerequisite for high school graduation in hopes of decreasing the serious educational deficits of many current graduates seen by employers and colleges. It is unclear at this point which trend will have the greatest influence.

A third force places greater attention on *preparation of test users* and *standards of ethical appraisal practices.* Both AACD and APA have groups devoting energies to a review of testing and appraisal principles and practices with a view toward enhancing professional practice and safeguarding the public.

The final trend is the continuing search for *new methods of measurement* in hitherto limited areas, such as maturation, motivation, creativity, attitude, and the like. Researchers and test publishers are working cooperatively to develop new methods and instruments that will improve the validity and reliability of previously available methods.

In summary, the appraisal process is a fluid one. It is important for counselors to be thoroughly familiar with current practices and to know and respect their limits. It is equally important to remember that appraisal is only one part of the ever-changing counseling process. Used properly, appraisal is a valuable tool; used improperly, it can be highly destructive. Counselors are urged to stay abreast of current developments and trends.

REFERENCES

Aiken, L. R. (1976). *Psychological testing and assessment* (2nd ed.). Boston: Allyn & Bacon.

American Personnel and Guidance Association. (1978, October 5). Responsibilities of users of standardized tests. *Guidepost, 21* (5), pp. 5–8.

American Psychological Association. (1974). *Standards for educational and psychological tests.* Washington, DC: Author.

Anastasi, A. (1982). *Psychological testing* (5th ed.). New York: Macmillan.

Buros, O. K. (Ed.). (1978). *The eighth mental measurements yearbook.* Highland Park, IL: Gryphon.

Cordes, C. (1984a, April). Will Larry P. face the supreme test? *APA Monitor, 15* (4), 126–127.

Cordes, C. (1984b, September). Publishers, users discuss quality, use of tests. *APA Monitor, 15* (9), pp. 14, 15, 16.

Cronbach, L. (1984). *Essentials of psychological testing* (4th ed.). New York: Harper & Row.

Harold, M. (1984, September). Bias hampers tests, schooling. *Guidepost, 27* (4), pp. 1, 12.

Hathaway, B. (1984, September). Japanese questions value of IQ tests. *APA Monitor, 15* (9), pp. 10, 11.

Mitchell, J. V. (Ed.). (1983). *Tests in print III.* Lincoln, NE: University of Nebraska Press.

Thorndike, R. H., & Hagan, E. P. (1977). *Measurement and evaluation in psychology and education* (4th ed.). New York: John Wiley.

Turkington, C. (1984, January). The growing use, and abuse, of computer testing. *APA Monitor, 15* (1), pp. 7, 26.

Wood, S. (1984). Computer use in testing and assessment. *Journal of Counseling and Development, 63,* 177–179.

CHAPTER 8
RESEARCH AND EVALUATION

Leo Goldman

Each of the preceding chapters has provided an overview of some aspect of the work of the counselor. Ideally, these descriptions of what counselors *should do* also describe what most practitioners *are doing*.

If there is one area of the counselor's world that is full of "shoulds," it is the area of research and evaluation. In their graduate courses, in journals, and at conventions, counselors are prodded not only to keep up with the research in the field, but also to be researchers, at least to the extent of evaluating their own work in some formal or systematic manner. In reality, however, the overwhelming majority of counseling practitioners neither keep up with the published research nor conduct any kind of formal research on their own. The gap between "should" and "is" will be a focus of this chapter in the hope that the ideas individual counselors develop about research will be ones that they will be able to carry out in their daily work.

THE CLAIMED CONTRIBUTIONS OF RESEARCH

Perhaps the most pervasive reason given for research in counseling is that we are a science-based profession and that practitioners must, at the very least, be consumers of research so that their professional activities are based on the best knowledge available. Journal editors sometimes return a manuscript describing a program or practice—even a very innovative one—with a comment that the idea seems promising but that publication must await research evidence of its value. Similarly, counselors in various settings are asked by academicians whether they evaluate their work systematically in order to have evidence that their time is well spent.

Advocates of research and evaluation believe that the practice of counseling becomes professionalized when its research foundations become more substantial. The process is seen as an interaction among theory, research, and practice (Harmon, 1978). According to this reasoning, a good theoretical formulation leads to specific hypotheses that can be tested in research, with the results being fed back to the theory and used to confirm it or to suggest modification. Practitioners are expected to approach their daily work within a theoretical framework and to test the theory by observing its consequences in practice. Further, the practitioner has the opportunity to generate researchable questions by examining the process and outcomes of work with clients. Researchers believe that these procedures allow both theory and practice to develop toward higher levels of soundness. Examples of the specific kinds of research that fit this framework are studies of the psychosocial characteristics of clients and others to whom counselors relate; changing conditions in family, school, work, and society in general; developmental patterns of individuals through the entire life cycle with reference to work, leisure, personal relationships, and other areas of living; interactions during counseling sessions; the outcomes of specified counselor behaviors; and a variety of other issues.

Such research efforts certainly seem worthy of their "should" status. A number of journals in counseling and related fields do publish reports of the kinds of studies listed above. Why, then, don't practicing counselors keep up with and use this vast amount of research? Why do so few practitioners do any kind of research or systematic evaluation themselves? Why does the gap between the ideal and the real continue to widen?

THE OTHER SIDE OF THE COIN

I went through the process of changing from a "should" person to a skeptic about the purported value of all this research activity (see Goldman, 1978). The conclusion for me at present is that research as it has been practiced has failed for the most part to make its claimed contributions. Furthermore, the response of many traditional researchers—that the value is not in any one study but rather in the accumulation over a period of years—has not been substantiated by the results of all the years of accumulated research.

It is not research as a concept that has failed, but research as it has been done. Somehow, research in the counseling field (and indeed in many other areas of psychology and education) has come to be defined in very limited ways. Some have challenged these ways in recent years (Goldman, 1976, 1977, 1978; Levine, 1974; Philosophy, 1984; Raush, 1974; Sprinthall, 1975, 1981), and broader conceptions of research seem to be seeping into the journals. For the most part, however, the published research continues to be characterized by major limitations that seem to be inherent in the traditional ways of studying counseling.

TRADITIONAL TYPES OF RESEARCH

Harmon (1978) points out that research methods can be divided generally into *inductive* and *deductive* approaches.

> Some types of research begin at the practical real world level and influence theory. Other types of research begin at the theoretical level and ultimately influence practice. The first type of research is essentially descriptive or survey research designed to answer the question "What have we here?" in an inductive fashion. . . . The second type of research is designed to aid us in spelling out relationships between the elements of a theory. It is designed to answer questions like "If we did this, what would happen?" This is a deductive approach to research. (pp. 47–48)

As Harmon explains, descriptive, correlational, causal comparative, and historical research efforts are basically inductive, while experimental research is deductive. Perhaps the most widely used of the major traditional research methods are the *correlational approach,* the *experiment,* and the *survey.* Each of these methods will be discussed very briefly in this section. More detailed explanations can be found in such research textbooks as Best (1981) and Borg and Gall (1983).

Correlational Approach

The correlational approach is based essentially on the *correlation coefficient* and seeks to ascertain whether two different qualities of characteristics called *variables* (things that vary from person to person or within one person at different times or from situation to situation) "go together." Usually the theoretical formulation is that one causes or influences the other or that they are measuring the same thing. In a simple design, a test is given to a group on two different occasions; if it is reliable, the two sets of scores should correlate with each other to a high degree.

As an example of a more complex research design, one might study the correlation between ego strength and effective coping on a stressful job. This seems reasonable enough, until one begins to examine carefully the measure of ego strength—usually a paper-and-pencil set of responses by each individual to multiple-choice or open-ended questions on a sheet of paper (see Chapter 7). At that point, the critical observer wonders how adequate such scratches can be as an indicator of a complex and intangible quality of a human being. Then the observer might well go on to wonder how one measures successful coping on a stressful job (such as counseling)—successful in whose eyes? for example, and successful in what sense? Is the counselor who blows up occasionally and stomps into the director's office demanding changes more or less successful than the person who suppresses such feelings and works as well as he or she can within the situation as it exists? On an even more complex level, what is the dynamic interaction between the individual counselor of a given level of ego strength and environmental situations? When such and such happens externally, how does the counselor react? What environmental responses does that elicit, and what does the counselor do next? And so on, and so on. And while all this interaction is going on, what feelings and thoughts are going on inside the counselor? Then one returns to the correlation coefficient—a number—and asks how that number can possibly represent the reality of what has been going on. In fact, these correlations, even when *statistically significant,* are usually so small as to be of little or no significance in theory or application. There are methods that get a lot closer to that reality that are described later in this chapter.

The Experiment

The experiment is held up by many researchers to be the "holiest of holies," the ultimate method for ascertaining the effect of one action or behavior on another. In its simplest description, the *experimental method* involves doing something to one group and then doing something else, or nothing, to another group and then concluding that, because the groups were comparable at the outset, Intervention A was more effective than B or than no intervention at all. (The group receiving no intervention is called the *control group.*) The approach is simple enough but so full of problems that one rarely reaches a clear-cut conclusion. Were the experimental and control groups comparable enough on every dimension that could conceivably affect the experimental outcomes? One would have to do an in-depth study of each subject to answer that question, and this is practically never done. Suppose one group does better than the others. What exactly made the difference? Was it the method used, the materials, the skill or personality of the person doing the intervention? Ideally, one would examine each of these possibilities in depth, but to do that edges into quite different research approaches, approaches that seek qualitative rather than quantitative data.

Survey Approaches

The survey is probably the simplest of the traditional approaches and usually involves distribution of a questionnaire of some sort to members of the group one is studying or to people regarded as a representative sample of a population in which one is interested. Even this simple approach often leaves more questions unanswered than answered. Unless one has a captive audience, such as an intact class, there is the problem of obtaining an adequate percentage of responses. Often a survey report will be based on questionnaire returns of 30 percent or 50 percent, with the comment that this is typical for that kind of sample and, therefore, may be regarded as adequate. There is really nothing one can say in conclusion from such a study, however, except that the 30 percent or 50 percent who responded believed so-and-so or reported such-and-such facts. Without any basis for judging the *representativeness* of those who chose to respond—and there is usually no adequate basis for assuming that the views of the respondents are identical to those of the nonrespondents—the results allow no generalizations. Anything less than a minimum of 75 percent yields very little from which the researcher can generalize with any confidence. Further, even with a substantial *response rate,* one has no basis for judging what each scratch on the paper represents. What did the individual understand the question to mean? What did he or she mean to convey by marking "almost always" or "sometimes"? An interview is far more valuable in this regard. In fact, one interview is often worth more than a thousand questionnaires.

Limitations of Traditional Research Methods

From an examination of traditional research methods such as those discussed above, the following emerge as major limitations on the value of those methods as sources of either theoretical or applied insights.

An Emphasis on the Measurable. The assumption prevalent among contemporary researchers seems to be that if something can't be measured with precision, it can't be studied. The fact is that counselors, unlike physicists and chemists, deal mostly with human characteristics and behavior that cannot be measured with any degree of precision.

What can be isolated and measured with some precision often is too trivial to be worth studying.

A Focus on Isolatable Parts of the Human Psyche and Behavior. Focusing on such items as a single response to a counselor's lead or a single personality characteristic lessens understanding rather than enhancing it. Again, the practitioner's reality is that one needs to observe the whole in order to understand properly any single part. Indeed, this attitude is also held by many theorists.

Failure to Consider the Interactive Nature of Interactions. For example, to understand how different people behave in a given kind of situation, it isn't enough to measure one (or several) traits of those people and to correlate the trait(s) with people's behaviors in a given kind of situation. Rather, one must examine the actual interaction of an individual: the situation offers a stimulus, the person reacts to the total situation as he or she interprets the situation, and then the environment responds in a certain way, which leads this particular person to react in a certain way, and on it goes in an extremely complex manner. The traditional research methods do not begin to deal with the complexity of such an interaction.

Heavy Reliance on Paper-and-pencil Instruments. There appears to be an assumption that it is "objective" to have someone express attitudes, values, and feelings by answering multiple-choice questions on a piece of paper. The only objective aspect is the scoring, which certainly is a convenience. Other than that, these "instruments" usually are much less useful than a well-conducted interview, where one can at least try to ascertain what the individual understands the questions to mean and what the individual's response means. Of course, much depends on the competence of the interviewer in asking good follow-up questions and in not influencing the individual's responses. But any kind of research requires competence on the part of the investigator, whether in designing an instrument or in searching the literature or in tabulating and interpreting the data.

Reliance on Increasingly Complex Statistical Methods. The single number that may emerge from a computer often tells nothing about the data themselves. The traditionalist lets the single number answer the question; one gets much more from seeing or hearing the raw data and their tabulations.

Excessive Reverence for the Controlled Experiment. This has led to an emphasis on laboratory and analogue studies that may indeed control some factors but in so doing set up a situation so far from the real thing as to make generalization all but impossible.

For the most part, research has built upon a model drawn from the physical sciences, a model that simply cannot deal with the incredible complexity and the intangible nature of the phenomena with which we deal in counseling. The end result is that the accumulated body of research in counseling and related journals has almost nothing to say to practitioners, or to theorists for that matter.

How do counselors decide how to do their work? Lacking a body of research that offers any real understanding or guidelines, counselors are left to rely on theories of counseling that make sense to them and on methods and techniques that seem to work. True, there have been studies galore to test the claims made for the theories and methods, but rarely do those studies provide any help. They almost always end up with a shrug of the shoulder, with suggestions that future research use more sensitive instruments, or control uncontrolled variables, or measure characteristics of the client or the counselor that this study didn't and so forth and so forth and so forth.

In fact, there are some research methods that may offer more hope, but before going on to those, we need to give brief attention once more to the question of why counselors do so little evaluation of their work. Two of the obvious reasons need no more than brief mention: heavy work loads and a lack of reward for doing systematic evaluation. But one additional reason is that the models of evaluation presented are so imposing as to be discouraging to most counselors. Even those who have completed a doctorate rarely do any kind of research on their jobs, whether basic, applied, or evaluative. Again, one important reason is the forbidding models that have been presented. The question that may well be raised is whether there are methods of evaluation that can realistically be undertaken by practitioners. The answer to this question is yes, and the remainder of this chapter will focus on a number of realistic and promising approaches.

SUGGESTIONS REGARDING BASIC AND APPLIED RESEARCH

An individual interested in research needs to be aware of the differences among *basic research, applied research,* and *evaluation.* Basic research is usually undertaken without any particular thought of possible applications and certainly with no specific applied outcome as the purpose. The research is intended to add to the understanding of the fundamental principles and processes of human development and human behavior. It normally begins with a theoretical framework and derives hypotheses, by deductive reasoning, that are to be tested in the study. Applied research begins with a specific problem or need derived from an area of practice. The study may or may not build from a theoretical formulation, although it almost always builds upon previous research when it is done well. The outcome is intended to provide practitioners with increased understanding, methods, or materials. Evaluation is designed specifically to ascertain the validity or effectiveness of a program, a procedure, materials, or other applied activity. It may not have the goal of generalizing results; that is, the purpose may be limited to answering the question: Was this particular intervention effective in certain defined ways?

In general, counseling practitioners are more likely to be involved in evaluation than in basic research. Some counselors, especially those at the doctoral level, may do basic or applied research on the job or on their own time. In those instances, they are likely to be most successful if they focus on the following promising research approaches (Goldman, 1976, 1977, 1978):

1. Study individual rather than group data.
2. Study the entire individual rather than parts, or at least study a part in relation to the whole.
3. Study people in real-life settings rather than in a laboratory.
4. Use observation and interview methods rather than questionnaires wherever possible.
5. Use the case study in a systematic way as a method of research.
6. Use the $N = 1$, or intensive experimental design (Anton, 1978), which allows for intensive analysis of individual case data.
7. Study topics of current importance and timely concern even if the methods must be rough-and-ready.

The research-oriented practitioner should shift from a concept of science and research as dealing with mathematical precision toward a concept that we are dealing with phenomena that are intangible, often difficult to define precisely, and constantly changing. Although we should seek as much objectivity and rigor as possible, we should also recognize that the greatest contributions to our understanding of counseling and clients have come from people who have used their intelligence, their sensitivity, and their imaginations, and that little has resulted from all the years of study that followed the sterile path of traditional, narrow research methods.

Although very few practitioners can realistically be expected to be research producers, it is feasible to expect that practitioners will cooperate with researchers by making data and clients available. It seems entirely reasonable for practitioners to seek assurance that the research will be done competently, with appropriate protection for the privacy and feelings of the clients, and that the study, as designed, offers some hope of making a contribution at least to the field of counseling, if not to the cooperating counselors.

RESEARCH AND EVALUATION BY THE COUNSELOR

There is often a fine line between applied research and evaluation. If counseling research is defined very broadly, it includes all activities of a formal or systematic nature that are intended to enhance our understanding of the people with whom we work and to assess the work of counselors in all its varieties. Certainly, this kind of definition can readily encompass evaluation and applied research, and even basic research into phenomena that undergird the content and process of counseling. For the remainder of this chapter, the focus is on the kinds of research that could be conducted by counselors in private practice and in schools, colleges, agencies, and institutions of various kinds. The presentation here is selective rather than comprehensive and emphasizes the kinds of research and evaluation that counselors can do, and indeed should do, in order to continue to grow professionally and to improve the quality of their work in order to serve the needs of their clientele better. For a more detailed discussion of evaluation principles and methods, the reader is referred to Burck (1978) and Oetting (1982).

Needs Assessment

The populations served by counselors may include families, communities, and organizational staff members as well as clients served directly through individual or group counseling. There are many ways to ascertain the needs of these populations. Needs assessment methods can, for convenience, be examined in terms of three general categories: *observation, interview,* and *questionnaire.*

Observation. Observation methods are useful mainly to counselors on the staffs of institutions or organizations such as schools, colleges, prisons, hospitals, or business firms. A newly hired counselor in such a setting would be well advised to take some time to get acquainted with the total organization and especially to observe firsthand the places where clients and prospective clients spend their time during the day. This includes such places as classrooms, extracurricular activities, student unions, residence halls, work sites, and various offices other than the counselor's. What helps to make such observation a form of research is to plan observation targets in advance, to make notes after the observations, and to develop on a continual basis explicit hypotheses about the institution.

Observation is especially important if one assumes the broad conception of counselor role as described by Morrill, Oetting, and Hurst (1974). Their "cube" model depicts four types of targets of counselor intervention: (1) *the individual,* (2) *primary groups* such as families or gangs, (3) *associational groups* such as classes or clubs, and (4) *the institution* or *community as a whole.* The model indicates that some needs are better met at target levels other than the individual; often a change at the family level, in a class, or within the entire institution can help many individuals at once by changing their environment. This entire way of viewing a counselor's total role is also emphasized in the literature of community counseling (Lewis & Lewis, 1983). Assessment in community counseling seeks to establish all the sources of a problem, whether within the individual or within some part of the individual's environment.

One systematic approach to observation is that of the *participant observer* (Balaban, 1978). In this approach, the observer participates to some extent in the situations being observed and may take part in discussions and even actions, but keeps detailed records of what occurred and of the observer's own introspections during and after the events. This leads to the development of insights and hypotheses that can then be followed up. One of the early examples of the participant observer, although it was not intended at the outset to be participatory in nature, was included in the classic Western Electric Hawthorne studies (Roethlisberger & Dickson, 1939), from which the term "Hawthorne effect" is derived. Observers interested in the effects of different lighting and other conditions on productivity at the Hawthorne plant found that almost any environmental change resulted in increased production rates. Eventually, researchers learned—by listening to and participating in worker conversations—that a small society had formed in each work site and that the workers' morale and attitudes toward their jobs had improved because they believed that the company cared about them and that these observers in particular were interested in them as people.

Interviews. A rich source for understanding attitudes, wants, and needs is the interview conducted with either an individual or a small group. In this kind of interview, the interviewer must communicate a real, nondefensive interest and a commitment to be of service. One can avoid taking sides in an interview by presenting one's position as follows: "I'd like to know how you view some things; this is a time that I will mostly listen. If I don't argue with you, it doesn't necessarily mean that I agree with everything you say. At a later time I'd like to tell you what programs we may institute to meet your needs better."

Counselors differ as to whether they find individual or group interviews more useful. One note of caution is to recognize that a one-to-one interview is not really a conversation between equals when one person is a professional staff member and the other is a student, patient, prisoner, or whatever. At least having several of "them" and one of "us" evens things out a bit.

Usually it is best to conduct a *structured* interview, which requires having a detailed outline of the areas to be covered and the specific facts, feelings, and attitudes to be explored. Most often one begins each topical area of questioning with a general question (for example, "What do you do when you are having problems with the courses you're taking?") and then has a list of follow-up questions to ask if appropriate (for example, "Do you ever go to a counselor for help?"). Such an interview schedule requires some time for initial preparation and then tryouts or a pilot study to be certain that the plan "works." It is also wise to try to summarize, through tabulation or other methods, the responses obtained from the pilot interviews in order to be certain that the responses from a number of individuals or groups can be compiled in some way that will be useful. In more formal research studies it is customary to set up a coding system for interpreting and classifying each response and also to verify the reliability of the system by having two or more judges apply it to the data from several interviews and then compare their codings.

Questionnaire. The questionnaire is probably the most frequently used method for assessing needs. Although it must be constructed very carefully so that the questions are clear, a questionnaire can be administered to large numbers of people in a relatively short time and can be tabulated quickly. Unfortunately, the results of this relatively easy procedure are not always of much help. There simply is no way to know what each person understood each question or item to mean, whether each person understood an item in the same way, what each person meant the response to mean, and with what attitude each person filled out the questionnaire. With all these unknowns, one is often hard put to derive any useful data from questionnaire studies. Most often they confirm what we already know or what we believe the respondents are likely to say. In any case, it is important to obtain as close as possible to a 100 percent response from the total population or from a carefully selected representative sample of that population.

The bias being expressed here is clearly for the greater depth and follow-up possibilities of the observation or interview method. One should consider whether one would learn more of real value from, say, twenty or fifty interviews or from hundreds of paper-and-pencil questionnaires. Whichever needs assessment methods are used, their value will be enhanced greatly to the extent that:

1. As many groups as possible are involved in planning the study and in making some commitment to act on the basis of the results. (Representative groups include, for example, administrators, teachers, social workers, nurses, and those to be studied and eventually served differently as a result of the study.)
2. Representatives of these same groups are actively involved in interpreting the results of the study, discussing their implications, and planning actions to be taken.

Action Research or Formative Evaluation

Action research as used here refers to a point of view, an emphasis, and an attitude, rather than a specific set of methods. Although it dates back to the pioneering work of Kurt Lewin as early as the 1930s (Marrow, 1969), action research has not had a major impact on formal textbooks or research courses. In practice, however, action research may well be used fairly widely, sometimes even by people who are not aware that what they are doing is action research. The critical requirement is reflected in Lewin's oft-quoted dictum "No research without action; no action without research."

Nuttall and Ivey (1978) describe four types of action research: *diagnostic, participant, empirical,* and *experimental.* Diagnostic research involves recognizing the emergence of a problem, diagnosing its causes, formulating possible methods of resolving the problem, and finally making recommendations for possible remediation. Participant action research adds an important component: the active involvement of the people who will be carrying out the recommended actions.

> The steps to follow in the participant action research model are as follows: (1) observing the emergence of a problem, (2) involving all important parties relevant to the causes and remediation of the problem, (3) brainstorming all the possible causes of the difficulty with participating members, (4) defining

the problem and determining whether further data are needed before intervening, (5) designing an interview or questionnaire to obtain further data, (6) training community participants to administer the instrument, (7) analyzing the data, (8) making final recommendations, and (9) involving the participants and others in carrying out the recommendations. (Nuttall & Ivey, 1978, p. 83)

Empirical action research involves performing a specific type of intervention, keeping a record of the counselor's activities and the client's reactions, and assessing the overall effects on clients. Experimental action research, the fourth type, goes beyond the empirical approach by attempting to come as close as possible to classical experimental designs while remaining focused on the field, rather than the laboratory, and on using the research to solve practical problems.

Action research seems to be very similar to *formative evaluation* (Scriven, 1967), which contrasts with *summative evaluation.* The former is intended to influence the progress of the project by giving feedback and offering suggestions for improvement continuously, whereas the latter is intended to provide information at the end of a project as to its outcomes or effects. Summative evaluation most typically includes the administration of questionnaires, tests, or other measures at the end of a project (posttest) and often also at the beginning (pretest) so that change may be attributed to the project. Of course, such change can only be attributed to the specific intervention if one or more control groups receive an alternative form of service or a placebo.

Formative evaluation may or may not use the more formal methods of data collection such as questionnaires, tests, structured interviews, grades in courses, or changes in observed behavior. An example of a formative evaluation in which I have been involved illustrates a very informal, nonquantified approach that may be feasible in many counseling settings. The project involves handicapped high school students (learning disabled and emotionally disturbed) who are enrolled in a five-month program of basic and vocational skills instruction to be followed by a summer internship on a job. My role is that of an external process (or formative) evaluator. I sit in on planning meetings, and because I am neither involved in the day-to-day activities nor responsible for the project's outcomes, I am sometimes able to see something in a different perspective and can make helpful suggestions.

For example, at a very early planning meeting, even before the students had arrived, I noted that there was no concrete plan for continuing staff meetings. I raised the question and was immediately reinforced by a staff member who otherwise might have hesitated to push the point. Similarly, in an individual conference with a newly hired staff member and in subsequent observation of that person in conversation with other staff I recognized (or at least hypothesized) that she tended to work in isolation rather than in active teamwork. I gently suggested that she should be included in a couple of meetings that day, meetings she had not planned to attend and in which the other staff had not thought of including her. The suggestion was acted on.

As an outsider, I raise questions and make suggestions, but my role is clearly different from all the project staff. The decisions made should be theirs; what I can offer them is a trained and experienced set of eyes and ears that are particularly attuned to the process by which things get accomplished. Also, in this case, I bring familiarity with some of the kinds of content that this project includes—career development, counseling, and instruction of handicapped students.

I expect to visit the project for at least a half day every other week. In addition to attendance at some of the regular staff meetings I will sit in on classes, tutoring sessions, and group counseling sessions and will informally interview students, their parents, and staff as opportunities present themselves. Conceivably, I might administer some more formal data-collection devices such as a brief questionnaire or a structured interview if that seems necessary or desirable in order to tap attitudes, opinions, or people's perceptions of the program. Because the project also has a summative evaluator who will be collecting more formative and quantifiable data, I will probably concentrate on the less formal, qualitative data.

An objection might be raised to calling this any kind of research or even evaluation on the grounds of subjectivity. But research is a search, and there are many ways to search, some of them (perhaps all of them?) dependent on the intelligence, sensitivity, and understanding of the searcher. Certainly, there is a place in research and evaluation for the best judgment of a qualified mind. We rely on qualified minds to do many other things; research without that kind of subjective, and preferably creative, element is not likely to offer much.

Ethnographic Research Approaches

Counselors interested in solving local problems may find interesting ideas in the area of *ethnographic research* (Dobbert, 1982; Goetz & LeCompte, 1984). Drawn from anthropology, this approach has been used in educational research for some years but rarely appears in counseling journals. Unfortunately, descriptions of the methods used often seem vague and fuzzy. This may well be a function of the nature of the basic approach, which is holistic rather than reductionistic, largely inductive rather than deductive, and subjective in the sense that the researcher as a person is regarded as a major research instrument.

Although ethnographic research sometimes uses the questionnaire, it much more often relies heavily on observation and interviews. Essentially it is the approach of the cultural anthropologist, who seeks to understand a society or culture in a broad sense, including such characteristics as its social structure, beliefs, values, and differential roles.

That any one study will any longer attempt to examine all aspects of a culture, even a small, primitive one, is extremely unlikely. Typically, however, there is an effort to seek patterns of relationships and behaviors. This approach contrasts with the traditional methods of research in counseling, and in psychology in general, which usually seek to isolate one or a very few narrow elements and to study them, sometimes in relation to one or more other elements, but rarely as dynamic patterns.

For example, in a traditional study of client expectations of counseling, the researcher would try to relate those expectations to the outcomes of counseling by administering a questionnaire to clients to assess their expectations and later collecting some sort of ratings by counselor and/or client and/or a third person as to changes in client feelings, knowledge, or behavior. The results would be expressed in some sort of correlational method that would say that clients with certain attitudes tend to have certain types of outcomes. Typically, the correlations are quite low, too low to be of any real value to a counselor. Furthermore, the correlations shed no light on the dynamics of the interaction.

By contrast, an ethnographic approach would emphasize the dynamics of the counselor-client interchange. The researcher might start by listening to tapes of interviews or by interviewing clients and counselors, first with general and then with specific questions. From this wealth of data, the researcher would try to tease out relationships and patterns. Depending on the skill of the researcher, the outcome would include insights as to the ways in which client expectations interact with the counselor as a person, the methods used, the setting in which counseling takes place, and things happening in the client's life during the process.

This is not to suggest that ethnographic methods are entirely inductive or subjective. As in any good research, the researcher tries to find appropriate theory that will help to guide the search and to make sense of the findings. Likewise, the researcher tries to be aware of any personal bias that might affect perceptions of a situation or interpretations of observations or other data. However, the researcher does not try to eliminate himself or herself as a factor in the study, as is the tradition in research based on physical science models, but recognizes instead that anyone administering a questionnaire, conducting an interview, or merely observing is almost certainly influencing the respondents in some way. It is important to try to understand the nature of that influence and to take that understanding into account when interpreting the data.

In fact, this point of view raises questions as to whether one should do this kind of research in one's own setting. For this reason, it is often preferable to bring in an outsider, who at least may be free of preconceptions about the situation and about whom people at the site have no specific preconceptions. An outsider has the task of gaining acceptance as a trusted person, however, and that may take considerable time.

N = 1 or Intensive Designs

An approach that overlaps more formal research and evaluation has been called $N = 1$ or *intensive experimental design* (Anton, 1978). Used most often in behaviorally oriented counseling, the method usually focuses on changes in behavior over time. In a typical design, one first obtains measures on the occurrence of the behavior under study (anxious feelings, acting-out behavior in a class or other setting, relating to people). This is the *baseline measure.* Next comes some kind of intervention, which might be an external intervention such as counseling, a specific kind of response by a counselor or teacher to the client's undesirable or desirable behavior, or an internal intervention by the client, such as trying to respond in a new way to an anxious feeling in oneself or to criticism by someone else. A record is kept, either by the client or an observer, of interventions and of whatever client behavior is being studied.

An "AB" design compares a series of baseline observations (A) with a series of treatment observations (B). In the more commonly used design, ABAB, there is a return to the baseline condition (a cessation of the intervention) and then a reintroduction of the intervention.

> If the counselor can demonstrate that the observed change occurs only when the treatment is "on" (B) and that the phenomenon under investigation "returns to baseline" when the treatment is "off" (A and A'), then a functional relationship has been established. Although it is still possible that extraneous factors may have produced the observed changes, the counselor makes such explanations less plausible by showing that the changes covary with the pressure or absence of the specific treatment. (Anton, 1978, p. 135)

There are many variations of this design. In order to ascertain whether the situation or setting in which the intervention occurs is an important factor, one can vary the situation. For example, teachers in different classes or group leaders in different groups in a residential setting would try the intervention and then keep records. One can also try more than one type of intervention (ABCABC) to compare the effects of the several interventions.

This approach is used most often in behaviorally oriented counseling (see Chapter 2) because of the emphasis on specific, recordable behaviors in that type of counseling. Some counselors have argued that this type of process is manipulative. As long as the client is aware of what is being tried and wants it to be done, however, this type of intervention is no more manipulative than any other. In fact, this kind of approach may well be less manipulative than others because the goals and procedures are made quite concrete and explicit at the outset.

Follow-Up Studies

It is always something of a shock to learn that a school, college, addiction program, counseling center, rehabilitation agency, or placement office knows nothing about what later happens to the people it serves except what is learned by chance when a former student or client drops by or writes. The reason given is almost always lack of time. However, the time needed to do a simple *follow-up study* is only a very small percentage of total staff time, so one must wonder whether time itself is truly the factor. Is it perhaps that a commitment to do a follow-up study also implies a commitment to change programs in some way if the results call for change?

In any case, there are evaluation questions that can best be answered by asking them of former clients, students, residents, inmates, and so forth. Such questions are:

- How many of our graduates obtained jobs of the kinds for which our programs prepared them?
- To what extent are our former patients staying free of addictive drugs (or alcohol, or cigarettes)?
- What has happened in the lives of the couples (or families) we counseled at a time of crises in their lives?
- What have been the college experiences of our high school graduates who went on to college?
- How much have people changed in their assertiveness (or decisiveness, or social skills) after attending our workshops?

Of course, these represent only a small sample of the areas in which counselors work. And, of course, these are general questions. In a follow-up study, one would usually spell out more specific questions under the general ones.

The methods of a follow-up study include some of the techniques described earlier in this chapter—the questionnaire, interview, and so forth. Some of the specific steps in planning and conducting a follow-up study are the following:

1. What are the most important questions we want answered? On the one hand we want to keep the questionnaire or interview (by phone or face-to-face) as short as possible in order to obtain a maximum response. On the other hand, we may be able to provide answers for more than one office or department of the organization. The person who will carry the major responsibility for the study would in the long run benefit from spending a little additional time at the outset checking with colleagues in order to be sure to include everything that can feasibly be included in the survey.

2. Perhaps even more important is to gain some commitment from people to pay attention to the results and to be willing to work for change in programs, staffing, and so forth, if that is what is called for by the survey results. This process has important implications for the questions to be asked of the respondents. There is, after all, not much point in asking people questions that will evaluate the organization in some way if there is no intention of changing the things being evaluated.

3. Almost always some kind of pilot study is valuable. If it is to be a questionnaire study, a questionnaire might be given or sent to a small sample to complete. Then either on the questionnaire itself, or by a telephone call, those sampled are asked to evaluate the questionnaire, for example: Are the questions clear? Was there something we didn't ask that you would have wanted to tell us? Then revision is made, and if there is any doubt, a second tryout is conducted. If the study is to be done by interview—telephone or face-to-face—then the evaluation of the interview schedule follows immediately upon the completion of the interview.

4. To repeat an earlier bias: one interview is usually worth many questionnaires. One reason has already been stated—the opportunity to clarify questions when needed and to ask follow-up questions when the responses are not full enough. A second reason is *sampling*. With a mailed questionnaire, one can never be certain of the differences between those who chose to respond and those who didn't. With a telephone interview, one has the opportunity to persuade the individual to participate, and the response rate is likely to be much higher than with a mailed questionnaire. Of course, one can use the telephone to try

to persuade people to return their questionnaires, but one is still dependent on the person following through.

Naturally, one has to settle for a much smaller number in the sample when using interviews. If the information being sought demands that one hear from as many of the people as possible in the category being followed up, then it probably is preferable to use a questionnaire and to use mail and phone follow-ups to the first mailing in order to maximize the response rate. If possible, the offer of some kind of token or actual payment should help increase the response rate. It is often valuable to do telephone or in-person interviews with a small sample of the questionnaire respondents, in order to obtain the greater depth and insights that interviews make possible, and to use these insights in interpreting the questionnaire results.

Longitudinal Studies

Sanborn (1978) described in detail methods by which counselors in practically any setting can do continuous collection of data over a lengthy period of time. Such *longitudinal studies* collect data that help the counselor to understand better and to evaluate each individual's development and progress. In addition, these methods can generate a rich body of data for studying the development of a select group of people in that institution and compare them with people going through the institution in other eras.

Actually, most counselors keep some kind of records of contacts with clients; what is needed now is to do this more systematically. One important principle is that the data collection be based on a planned program, beginning with agreement among all concerned as to the information that should be collected and ways it will be used. This provides guidelines for the counselor and anyone else who will be contributing to the accumulation. For example, instead of a few lines summarizing whatever the counselor happens to remember from a given interview, there will be a form—as simple and brief as possible—that provides space for the information and interpretations that have been decided are important to note about all interviews. Then, over a period of time—months or perhaps years in the case of an institution such as a school, college, or prison—it is possible to see changes and try to relate those changes to events within the institution or elsewhere.

When other data are systematically added to interview records—reports from teachers, psychologists, outside agencies, follow-up data—one not only has some basis for evaluating the work of the counselor and the institution as a whole, but also the basis for an ongoing assessment of needs and of changes both in the individuals and in their environment.

In fact, such data may well serve as the basis for applied or even more basic research into the development of people of that age group in that kind of setting. In order to accomplish this goal, however, the practicing counselor might well want to collaborate with a specialist in research; the collaboration, to be of maximum value, should begin at the point of planning the kinds of data to be collected.

Case Study

There has been a recent revival of interest in the *case study* as a method of research. Researchers such as Hill, Carter, and O'Farrell (1983) are interested in developing rigorous, quantifiable methods for using the case study. This quest may or may not turn out to be fruitful. Our purpose here is to consider the case study as a qualitative method for understanding an individual better and thereby improving understanding of people in general. It also offers a fringe benefit in the way of bringing the staff together for continuing professional education.

The regular use of case studies in a counseling office can make several kinds of contribution: increased understanding of the individual being studied, improved communication and collaboration among the staff, and continuing professional growth of the staff. One well-tested method is to agree on a weekly (or biweekly) *case conference* at each of which one or more individuals will be the object of study. The steps might be as follows:

1. Agree on the individual to be reviewed at a designated future meeting, and discuss the person briefly in order to spell out specific questions that need answering.

2. Each staff member (counselor, psychologist, teacher, social worker, physician, house parent) has a special area to study before the designated meeting, and all are to fill out a form that asks basic questions about the target individual.

3. At the appointed time, the group systematically compares notes and, with one acting as coordinator, teases out a consensus as to the individual's functioning, needs, and capabilities. Based on this discussion, a plan is made for interventions to be made by specific staff members, including counseling, environmental change, parent involvement, and so on. Often one staff member is designated as the key person to coordinate the several interventions and to be the primary contact with the target individual.

4. The staff does a brief follow-up review of the individual at a later staff meeting to see whether the planned interventions have had their intended effect and to change the strategy if necessary.

Under pressure of a busy office or institution, and especially in one where there are frequent crises, it is tempting to cancel case conferences as a luxury that can't be afforded. However, the case studies are not only valuable for the individuals being studied (more important sometimes than the crisis intervention), but perhaps equally important, they contribute toward an atmosphere of continuing professional growth and colleagueship and thus help to improve staff morale and stave off burnout.

ETHICAL AND LEGAL ISSUES IN RESEARCH

There has been a growing body of literature on the ethical and legal issues in research (see Bersoff, 1978). The topic is far too broad and complex to receive here anything more than commentary on a few selected points. The legal area is particularly complicated, and one is well advised to seek legal counsel if in any doubt.

The younger, the weaker, and the more troubled the client, the more vulnerable he or she is to invasions of privacy without true *informed consent*. It is the responsibility of the mature adult asking the questions—the researcher—to ensure that all clients, particularly the more vulnerable, are treated with the same respect they themselves would appreciate. In practice, this means not asking questions that the individual, if mature enough, would probably regard as too private, such as questions about financial status, sexual activities, fantasies, and family conflicts.

In the case of an adult (and the legal age of responsibility is itself a very complicated matter these days), it is merely a matter of informing the prospective giver of information fully of what is to be sought and receiving permission in writing to participate. In the case of a nonadult or an adult who is not fully competent by reason of mental deficiency or disorder, consent should also be sought of a parent, guardian, or other person legally and logically in a position to give that consent. (For a consideration of additional aspects of ethical issues in counseling, see Chapter 9.)

THE FUTURE

This chapter has presented a point of view rather than a neutral summary of traditional thoughts about research. There is some evidence that the kinds of research favored here are being thought about and written about increasingly, especially by young researchers, and that journals are becoming more open to these kinds of studies. With the use of these methods, counselors in any setting can understand their clients better, improve the effectiveness of their programs, and contribute to their own professional growth.

REFERENCES

Anton, J. L. (1978). Studying individual change. In L. Goldman (Ed.), *Research methods for counselors* (pp. 117–153). New York: John Wiley.

Balaban, R. M. (1978). Participant observation: Rediscovering a research method. In L. Goldman (Ed.), *Research methods for counselors* (pp. 155–175). New York: John Wiley.

Bersoff, D. N. (1978). Legal and ethical concerns in research. In L. Goldman (Ed.), *Research methods for counselors* (pp. 363–400). New York: John Wiley.

Best, J. W. (1981). *Research in education.* Englewood Cliffs, NJ: Prentice-Hall.

Borg, W. R., & Gall, M. D. (1983). *Educational research: An introduction* (4th ed.). New York: Longman.

Burck, H. D. (1978). Evaluating programs: Models and strategies. In L. Goldman (Ed.), *Research methods for counselors* (pp. 177–201). New York: John Wiley.

Dobbert, M. L. (1982). *Ethnographic research: Theory and application for modern schools and societies.* New York: Praeger.

Goetz, J. P., & LeCompte, M. D. (1984). *Ethnography and qualitative design in educational research.* Orlando, FL: Academic Press.

Goldman, L. (1976). A revolution in counseling research. *Journal of Counseling Psychology, 23,* 543–552.

Goldman, L. (1977). Toward more meaningful research. *Personnel and Guidance Journal, 55,* 363–368.

Goldman, L. (Ed.). (1978). *Research methods for counselors.* New York: John Wiley.

Harmon, L. W. (1978). The counselor as consumer of research. In L. Goldman (Ed.), *Research methods for counselors* (pp. 29–78). New York: John Wiley.

Hill, C. E., Carter, J. A., & O'Farrell, M. K. (1983). A case study of the process and outcome of time-limited counseling. *Journal of*

Counseling Psychology, 30, 4–18. (Article is followed by invited comments by G. S. Howard, M. J. Lambert, and a reply to them by Hill, Carter, & O'Farrell.)

Levine, M. (1974). Scientific method and the adversary model. *American Psychologist, 29,* 661–677.

Lewis, J. A., & Lewis, M. D. (1983). *Community counseling: A human services approach* (2nd ed.). New York: John Wiley.

Marrow, A. J. (1969). *The practical theorist: The life and work of Kurt Lewin.* New York: Basic Books.

Morrill, W. H., Oetting, E. R., & Hurst, J. C. (1974). Dimensions of counselor functioning. *Personnel and Guidance Journal, 52,* 354–359.

Nuttall, E. V., & Ivey, A. E. (1978). Research for action: The tradition and its implementation. In L. Goldman (Ed.), *Research methods for counselors* (pp. 79–116). New York: John Wiley.

Oetting, E. R. (1982). Program evaluation, scientific inquiry, and counseling psychology. *The Counseling Psychologist, 10,* 61–70.

Philosophy of science and counseling research. (1984). [Special section]. *Journal of Counseling Psychology, 31,* 415–476.

Pine, G. J. (1981). Collaborative action research in school counseling: The integration of research and practice. *Personnel and Guidance Journal, 59,* 495–501.

Raush, H. L. (1974). Research, practice, and accountability. *American Psychologist, 29,* 678–681.

Roethlisberger, F. J., & Dickson, W. J. (1939). *Management and the worker.* Cambridge, MA: Harvard University Press.

Sanborn, M. P. (1978). Longitudinal research: Studies in a developmental framework. In L. Goldman (Ed.), *Research methods for counselors* (pp. 203–234). New York: John Wiley.

Scriven, M. (1967). *The methodology of evaluation: Perspectives on curriculum evaluation.* Chicago: Rand McNally.

Sprinthall, N. A. (1975). Fantasy and reality in research: How to move beyond the unproductive paradox. *Counselor Education and Supervision, 14,* 310–322.

Sprinthall, N. A. (1981). A new model for research in the service of guidance and counseling. *Personnel and Guidance Journal, 59,* 487–493.

CHAPTER 9
PROFESSIONAL ORIENTATION

Joe P. Wittmer
Larry C. Loesch

A *profession* is typically defined as a vocational activity having (1) an underlying body of theoretical and research knowledge, (2) an identifiable set of effective skills and activities, and (3) a publicly professed, voluntarily self-imposed set of behavioral guidelines. For some professions, such as law, medicine, or engineering, long histories and social impacts have enabled the general public to apply these criteria readily, and thus they are easily recognized as "true" professions. But what of counseling. Is it a true profession?

Within the realm of the social sciences, the vocational activity known as counseling has a relatively short history. In fact, the roots of counseling are rarely traced before the beginning of the current century (see Chapter 1). The recency of its emergence, however, does not preclude counseling from being a profession.

Throughout its evolution, counseling has drawn heavily from a variety of professional fields, which in turn reflect a vast array of sciences. In many instances, counseling has been able to avoid "reinventing the wheel" because it has borrowed selectively the best of what other fields have to offer. Therefore, much of the theoretical and research knowledge base for counseling is actually a synthesis of the best information from other fields such as psychology, sociology, anthropology, biology, and speech. The counseling knowledge base is not, however, entirely borrowed. There have been and continue to be a considerable number of excellent theoreticians and researchers who clearly identify themselves as counselors. The cumulative result is a substantial theoretical and research base for the field of counseling.

Similarly, the field of counseling has drawn from other related fields, developed internally, and synthesized a set of identifiable skills and behavioral guidelines for providing services in an ethical manner. Moreover, the field has merged these skills and guidelines effectively with its theoretical and research knowledge base.

Therefore, counseling appears to fulfill the requisite criteria and may be recognized as a legitimate profession. However, counseling is still an *emerging* profession with full recognition as a true profession yet to be achieved. Nonetheless, rapid progress is being made primarily as a result of an evolving and increasing professional orientation among counselors.

THE SIGNIFICANCE OF PROFESSIONALISM

Professional orientation describes the attitude adopted by counselors toward their counseling and related professional activities. This attitude includes voluntarily adhering to, supporting, and contributing to the achievement and improvement of the goals, objectives, and behaviors deemed appropriate by the members of the counseling profession. Counselor conduct that reflects professional orientation is known as *professionalism.*

Professionalism among counselors and others who affect the provision of those services (such as counselor educators and counselor supervisors) is important for several reasons. First, professionalism serves to protect the public welfare. Ivey (1982) implied the importance of professionalism in this regard when he stated:

> It is clear that counseling can help *or* harm individuals and the uncontrolled provision of services can actually hurt the public through incompetence or charlatanry. . . . The prime responsibility of the government and the [counseling] profession is to represent and protect the public, the people whom both serve. (pp. 131–132)

How does the counseling profession fulfill its responsibility to protect the welfare of its service recipients? Primarily it does so through adherence to high standards of professionalism. More specifically, because all major aspects of counseling professionalism are intended and designed to allow for the provision of effective services while at the same time protecting service recipients from harm, counselors who exhibit high standards of professionalism will necessarily not be harmful.

Professionalism is also important as a means of improving the counseling profession. Professions, particularly emerging professions, must continue to improve to be effective in their responses to the needs of people in a changing society. Self-improvement is, therefore, a major responsibility for the counseling profession. Counselor professionalism also necessitates that counselors make contributions to the improvement of the profession. Such contributions are made not only through compliance with accepted standards of behavior, but also through other activities such as the publication of theory and research, public relations, consultation, education, professional self-development, and comprehensive involvement in the activities of professional organizations.

In general, there are no legal, social, moral, or biological mandates that people who could potentially benefit from counseling must actually partake of counseling services; participation in counseling is most often voluntary. Accordingly, for the counseling profession to manifest its potential benefits to society most effectively, it must be viewed favorably. Professionalism implies, therefore, that counselors must do all they can to improve the reputation of the counseling profession. Finally, professionalism is important for counselors because it emphasizes continuing self-improvement and development, which in turn enables counselors to provide the best possible service and to maximize their competence.

In sum, professionalism enhances both the reality and perception of professional competence. In a complex society, where legal and other challenges to competence are commonplace, counselors need to present effective professional postures that are accountable and defensible. Professionalism is the primary means by which counselors can achieve such postures.

In addition to individual manifestations, counselor professionalism is evident in much larger contexts. Large-scale efforts to achieve professionalism are typically the major emphases of professional organizations. For example, the American Association for Counseling and Development (AACD) currently emphasizes, through the allocation of substantial resources, three professional activities: (1) *accreditation,* (2) *certification,* and (3) *licensure.*

Accreditation

Pennell, Proffitt, and Hatch (1971) defined *accreditation* as a process in which "an association or agency grants public recognition to a school, institute, college, university, or specialized program of study having met certain established qualifications or standards" (p. 3). In the counseling profession, accreditation is a professional credential applicable to programs, not individual counselors.

Accreditation is important because of the presumption that graduates of accredited programs are better prepared to provide professional counseling services and better able therefore to serve the public welfare. This presumption, however, is not universally accepted in the profession. For example, Ivey (1982) stated:

> The traditional route toward consumer protection has been the careful delineation of educational and training standards so that one is adequately prepared to deliver services. Unfortunately, *education does not equal competence.* (p. 132)

Ivey's position is one with which it is difficult to disagree. Many people who are *educated* are incompetent in their professional activities. The obverse of Ivey's statement, however, does not follow; counseling competence *does* necessitate *some* type of prior education or training. If not, then counseling cannot be differentiated from mere conversation, and there would be no field of counseling. Although education does not guarantee competence, competent professionals must have had effective training. This latter rationale underlies the professional emphasis on accreditation.

The major factors involved in comparing the various types of accreditation in the counseling profession are: (1) What is the basis of the accreditation? (2) Who awards it? (3) What process is used to evaluate programs? and (4) What is accredited? A brief description of the evolution of the Council for the Accreditation of Counseling and Related Educational Programs (CACREP) illustrates these factors.

In the late 1950s, the Association for Counselor Education and Supervision (ACES), a division of AACD, initiated the development of standards that would, at least in theory, apply to all graduate-level programs that prepare counselors. In 1963 ACES endorsed these standards and committed itself to continuing to work on them and related standards. In 1967 the American School Counselor Association (ASCA), another division of AACD, issued guidelines for the preparation of secondary school counselors. Similar guidelines for the preparation of elementary school counselors and for student personnel workers were developed the following year. ACES's Commission on Standards and Accreditation was created in 1971 to review the existing preparation standards of various professions and to begin movement toward a formal process for accrediting programs. These efforts resulted in ACES's 1979 adoption of the *Standards for Preparation of Counselors and Other Personnel Services Specialists.*

ACES's efforts in regard to standards for preparation did not stop there, however. In 1977 it adopted the *ACES Guidelines for Doctoral Preparation in Counselor Education.* In 1979, with minor revisions, the entry-level and advanced standards were changed, respectively, to the

Standards for Entry Preparation (Master's and Specialists) of Counselors and Other Personnel-Services Specialists and the *Standards for Advanced Preparation (Doctoral) in Counselor Education.*

The impetus provided by ACES for preparation standards and accreditation spurred interest throughout AACD's membership. As a result other divisions of AACD began to collaborate with ACES on new efforts. In the late 1970s, preparation standards and accreditation were indeed professional matters pertinent to all counseling professionals. Thus, in 1980, AACD's Board of Directors resolved to adopt the existing preparation standards, to encompass further work on the development of professional preparation standards, and to move toward the establishment of an entity to implement an accreditation process for counselor preparation programs. These actions were refined and formalized by AACD's Board of Directors in 1981, the year AACD approved the establishment of the Council for the Accreditation of Counciling and Related Educational Programs (CACREP) (Wittmer, 1985b).

The first official CACREP meeting was held in September 1981. It should be noted, however, that ACES already had begun to accredit counselor education programs several years previously. In fact, ACES had accredited eight preparation programs and honored the accreditations assigned by the California Association for Counselor Education and Supervision (CACES) for several preparation programs in California before the first CACREP meeting was held. This noteworthy situation emphasizes the lineal relationship that extends from ACES through AACD to CACREP. Thus, CACREP did not create a "new" accreditation process in 1981, but rather refined and broadened substantially the accreditation process begun by ACES and CACES some fifteen years earlier.

Today, CACREP is an organizational affiliate of AACD. It is a legally separate, not-for-profit corporation technically distinct from AACD but retaining nontechnical linkages to AACD. For example, because CACREP is not self-sufficient financially, it receives some AACD financial assistance. Furthermore, it includes members who represent various divisions of AACD. In 1985 CACREP included a representative from each of the following divisions of AACD: Association for Counselor Education and Supervision (ACES), American Mental Health Counselors Association (AMHCA), American College Personnel Association (ACPA), National Career Development Association (NCDA), American Rehabilitation Counseling Association (ARCA), Association for Specialists in Group Work (ASGW), Association for Multicultural Counseling and Development (AMCD), and the Association for Measurement and Evaluation in Counseling and Development (AMECD). CACREP membership is also open to representatives from other divisions of

AACD. In addition, one CACREP member is AACD's representative; therefore, AACD is actually a CACREP member. Finally, there is an additional lay member, appointed by CACREP, to represent the public. Each representative serves a three-year term.

The governance of CACREP is facilitated through the leadership of a chairperson and a three-person Executive Committee, all of whom are elected from among CACREP members. It also has an executive director, who coordinates ongoing operations. The executive director is not, however, a voting member of CACREP. CACREP meets twice annually (fall and spring) to establish policies and functions and to make decisions on preparation programs that have completed the application process.

CACREP accreditation is program-specific. That is, it accredits specific preparation programs rather than entire departments that house counselor education programs. Currently, CACREP accredits four types of counselor preparation programs: (1) *school counseling,* (2) *student personnel services in higher education,* and (3) *counseling in community and other agency settings* for professional preparation at the entry level, and (4) *counselor education* for professional preparation at the doctoral level. Although the more than 450 counselor education programs in the United States use many different program titles, the CACREP accreditation awarded is given only under one of its four areas.

The bases for accreditation by CACREP are the generic preparation standards appropriate for the level and particular program for which accreditation is sought. It should be noted, however, that some specialty standards have been added to the original entry-level and doctoral standards. For example, ACPA requested that the specialty standards for programs in student personnel services in higher education encompass three possible (inter)program emphases: (1) *counseling,* (2) *developmental,* and (3) *administrative.* ACPA provided additional program standards to cover these emphases, which were subsequently adopted by CACREP. Similarly, CACREP has adopted additional specialty standards from AMHCA for counseling in community and other agency settings and from ASCA for the accreditation of school counseling programs.

After an application from a college or university counselor preparation department for accreditation of a program is approved by CACREP, there are three major phases to CACREP's accreditation process. In the first, the department applying completes a *self-study* in accord with CACREP's accreditation manual to determine if it fulfills each of the applicable standards. In addition, the department's self-study provides information on such things as program objectives, curricula, faculty and student characteristics, available program resources, feedback from program graduates, and evidence of program effectiveness. Upon completion, the department's self-study is forwarded to CACREP's executive director for initial review.

If the department's self-study is evaluated favorably, the second phase is implemented. This phase involves *site visitation* to the college or university campus by a three-member team, which is selected in collaboration with the department applying and CACREP's executive director. The chairperson of the site visitation team must have served previously on a site visitation team, and all team members must have successfully completed CACREP's training program for site visitation team members.

The site visitation team validates the department's self-study. That is, it does not independently evaluate the program for which accreditation is sought, but rather attempts to determine the accuracy of the information in the department's self-study. The site visitation team interviews faculty, students, and administrators affiliated with the program and reviews records and other available information pertinent to the program. Upon completion, the team submits a report to CACREP's executive director, using a predetermined format.

The final phase of CACREP's accreditation process involves an *evaluation* of both the self-study and the report from the site visitation team by the entire CACREP staff (excluding any member representative who served on the site visitation team for a program being evaluated). CACREP may render one of three decisions about a program's accreditation application: (1) *denial,* (2) *provisional approval,* or (3) *full approval.* Full approval is for a period of seven years. Provisional approval is for a period of two years, after which another decision is rendered (based on the documentation of any changes made during the provisional approval period).

In addition to CACREP, there are several other agencies that accredit specific counselor preparation programs. For example, programs preparing rehabilitation counselors can be accredited by the Council on Rehabilitation Education (CORE). Although rehabilitation counselor preparation programs are sometimes housed in counselor education departments and there are some similarities between their procedures and requirements, their accreditation processes are functionally separate at present. However, CORE and CACREP have been exploring possible points of collaboration in accreditation processes.

Counseling psychology preparation programs are sometimes housed with counselor education programs, and they can be accredited by the American Psychological Association (APA). Similarly, marriage and/or family counselor preparation programs can be accredited by the American Association for Marriage and Family Therapists (AAMFT). Because both of these types of preparation programs are relatively different from those accredited by CACREP, neither APA nor AAMFT are presently working on collaborative accreditation efforts with CACREP.

The National Council for Accreditation of Teacher Education (NCATE) accredits a variety of (teacher and other) preparation programs within colleges of education. Because school counselor preparation programs exist within colleges of education, they can be accredited by NCATE. Therefore, school counselor preparation programs can be accredited by *both* CACREP and NCATE. CACREP and NCATE are currently exploring the nature of their relationship because of the potential for dual accreditation of school counselor preparation programs.

Finally, counselor preparation programs housed in academic departments in state colleges or universities can be accredited by each state's Department of Education (DOE). These accreditations are usually linked to other state-controlled processes such as certification of school counselors.

Each of these accreditation processes has unique characteristics that allow it to be distinguished from the others. There are, however, at least six commonalities or accepted practices that typify accreditation processes.

1. Accreditation Is Voluntary. Graduation from an accredited program is not a *license* to do counseling, and conversely, graduation from a nonaccredited program is not a prohibition. Because of the assumption that accredited programs have higher standards, however, employers may require, and typically give preference to, graduates of accredited counselor preparation programs.

2. Accreditation Is Based on Standards. If no standards are applied, accreditation is nothing more than a listing. Generally, the more sophisticated the standards, the greater the prestige of the accreditation.

3. Accreditation Costs Money. Accrediting agencies charge for their accreditation processes, except in state DOE accreditations where both the process and the program are supported by state monies.

4. Accreditation Necessitates Self-evaluation. Persons affiliated with a program for which accreditation is sought must conduct some type of formal review and analysis of the program. There is, however, considerable diversity among program self-evaluation procedures.

5. Accreditation Has a Geographic Limit. DOE accreditations are *state-line bounded* while others are typically national or international in scope. In general, the accreditation processes enjoying greatest prestige are national in scope.

6. Accreditation Is Not Reciprocal. *Accreditation reciprocity* means that one accrediting agency accepts the accreditation of another agency as equivalent to and as a substitute for its own. Although some state DOEs have accreditation reciprocity agreements, there are no reciprocity agreements among organizations that accredit counselor preparation programs nationally.

Graduation from accredited counselor preparation programs is one way counselors can demonstrate a high degree of professionalism. Individuals typically have little control over accreditation as a credential, however, except in decisions about which graduate school and which preparation program to attend. Certification is another credential counselors can use to demonstrate professionalism, but unlike accreditation, it is one they can control individually.

Certification

Shimberg (1981) defined *certification* as "the process by which a governmental or nongovernmental agency grants recognition to an individual who has met certain predetermined qualifications set by a credentialing agency" (p. 1138). This means that a credentialing agency granting counselor certification *attests* or *affirms* that an individual can do counseling (presumably effectively) when the individual has fulfilled the standards of the agency. The designation *certified counselor* is thus an individual credential indicating that a person is able to counsel people.

Certification is sometimes referred to as a *title control* process because it only controls who may use the title *certified;* it does not control who may engage in counseling (Loesch, 1984). Nonetheless, it is an important credential, as Shimberg (1981) effectively noted:

> The purpose of certification is to enable the public in general and employers in particular to identify those practitioners who have met a standard that is usually set well above the minimum level. . . . Although noncertified individuals may legally practice their occupations, they may find job opportunities restricted as employers give preference to those who have met the certification standards. (p. 1139)

Thus, certified counselors enjoy professional prestige beyond that for noncertified counselors. Although Shimberg's comment only applies this differential to employment situations, it applies to other situations as well. For example, there is ample evidence that if clients hold favorable *initial* impressions of counselors, *potential* counseling effectiveness is increased. Therefore, the better the counselors' credentials, the greater the likelihood for effective counseling (Loesch, 1984).

Processes providing professional certifications for counselors have the shortest history of any professional counseling credentialing activity. Counselor certification evolved only after considerable professional effort had been invested in accreditation and licensure activities (to be discussed later in this chapter). The reason for this situation is unknown, but it may be that the need for certification became evident only when the limitations of accreditation and licensure were recognized. Accreditation processes are typically national in scope but focus on preparation programs. Licensure processes focus on individuals but are state-line bounded. A third professional credentialing activity, counselor certification, focuses on individuals *and* is national in scope.

The factors that may be used to compare different counselor certification procedures are similar to those for accreditation: What is the basis for certification? What process is used? Who awards it? To whom is it awarded? The evolution of the National Board for Certified Counselors (NBCC) counselor certification process serves to illustrate the nature of counselor certification.

In the late 1970s professional credentialing emerged as a primary focus of AACD. Plans for what was eventually to become CACREP were being finalized, counselor licensure laws had been passed in several states, and specialized counselor certification processes had been implemented by the National Academy for Certified Clinical Mental Health Counselors (NACCMHC) and the Commission on Rehabilitation Counselor Certification (CRCC). In this context, AACD charged its Registry Committee to (1) assess and determine the feasibility and desirability of an AACD (then APGA) register of professional counselors, and (2) research and analyze current existing registers of professionals. Concurrently, AACD asked an AMECD (then AMEG) consultant to evaluate examinations being used for counselor certification purposes (Loesch & Vacc, 1985).

AACD's Registry Committee responded by surveying AACD's membership in regard to perspectives on registry and by collecting information on existing professional credentialing processes, with particular emphasis on those used by the NACCMHC and CRCC. The result was a recommendation in 1981 to AACD's Board of Directors to proceed as rapidly as possible with the development of a registry/certification process. Consequently, in late 1981 AACD's Task Force on

Registry was convened to initiate the process that eventually lead to NBCC. It also accepted AMECD's conclusion that examinations currently being used for counselor certification were not suitable for its intentions.

The first NBCC meeting took place in April 1982. The group included a chairperson; one representative each from the NACCMHC, CRCC, and a state having a counselor licensure law; two AACD representatives; and a lay person representing the public. The NBCC initiated plans for incorporation, developed a Code of Ethics, defined eligibility criteria for certification, adopted a budget, and developed a time schedule for implementation. It also approved the appointment of a consultant to oversee the development of an examination specifically applicable to its process. NBCC then also clarified its purposes and goals by changing "registry" to "counselor certification" in its various documents.

NBCC is now a corporate affiliate of AACD. Similar to CACREP, it is a not-for-profit, legally separate corporation with nontechnical linkage to AACD. It has an executive director who coordinates its daily operations. NBCC is still constituted as initially composed except that it does not have AACD representatives. However, NBCC and AACD have a close working relationship. For example, NBCC and AACD collaborate on the development and use of the counselor certification examination.

NBCC counselor certification is *generic;* counselors receiving NBCC certification have fulfilled minimum, basic requirements applicable to *all* professional counselors. Thus, NBCC certification does not imply that a counselor can do any particular type of (specialized) counseling, but rather that the counselor can do fundamental counseling activities theoretically applicable to a wide variety of clients and settings. NBCC certification may be viewed as the foundation tier in a system where other, more specialized certifications are the upper tiers.

Certification within NBCC's process necessitates that candidates fulfill two separate but related types of requirements. The first involves *prior academic and experiential activities.* NBCC's minimum academic requirement is a master's degree in counseling or a closely related professional field. Within this minimum academic degree requirement, however, there are also specific requirements for particular educational (usually course) experiences. These specific requirements reflect the *core curriculum* areas of AACD/CACREP's entry-level standards for preparation, plus *supervised training such as practica or internships.* The minimum experiential requirement is three years of work as a counselor. Letters of reference attesting to the nature of the work experience and its quality are required. The work experience requirement is reduced, however, for graduates from CACREP-accredited programs because supervised training experiences in CACREP-accredited programs are typically greater than those in programs not accredited by CACREP.

The second requirement is *successful completion of NBCC's Counselor Certification Examination.* The examination assesses *cognitive* knowledge of counseling information and counseling skills; it is not a competency-based examination (Loesch & Vacc, 1985). The topics covered in the examination are the eight core curriculum areas from the AACD/CACREP entry-level standards of preparation: (1) *human growth and development,* (2) *social and cultural foundations,* (3) *the helping relationship,* (4) *groups,* (5) *life-style and career development,* (6) *appraisal of the individual,* (7) *research and evaluation,* and (8) *professional orientation.* (The chapters for this book were selected to conform directly to these specific content areas.) Scores on the examination are reported for each of the areas, but the minimum criterion score for certification eligibility is from the examination total score.

By the beginning of 1986, NBCC had certified approximately 15,000 professional counselors who were awarded the designation of *National Certified Counselor* (NCC), for an initial period for certification of five years. In order to continue to be certified beyond the initial period without reapplying, NCCs must complete a minimum of 100 contact hours of approved (inservice) professional development activities such as courses, workshops, or convention programs prior to the end of the five-year certification period in addition to paying appropriate fees.

In addition to NBCC, there are a few other agencies that provide certification intended for and appropriate to professional counselors. For example, NACCMHC grew from the efforts of some AMHCA members to provide a professional credential for mental health counselors working primarily in community agencies or private practice. The designation provided is *Certified Clinical Mental Health Counselor* (CCMHC). NACCMHC's certification process closely approximates NBCC's, but the eligibility criteria are different because the CCMHC credential is a specialized certification. These criteria currently include at least sixty semester hours of graduate-level academic preparation from an accredited institution; two years of postgraduate degree work experience as a mental health counselor, at least 1,500 clock hours of counseling experience supervised by a CCMHC or a person with a similar credential, letters of reference, and at least fifty hours per year of ongoing individual supervision. Payment of requisite fees, submission of a work sample (audio or videotape), and successful completion of the

NACCMHC examination are also required. Renewed certification as a CCMHC necessitates that CCMHCs participate in professional development activities and pay fees for recertification.

A new counselor professional certification has recently been created by the National Council for Credentialing of Career Counselors (NCCCC). The designation awarded is *Professional Career Counselor* (PCC). NCCCC's process is closely related to NBCC's because PCC certification is a second tier to certification as a NCC. The eligibility criteria include NCC status, an advanced degree in counseling, a supervised practicum that includes career counseling, relevant professional work experience as a career counselor, letters of reference, completion of a personal statement explaining the basis for seeking certification, successful completion of the NCCCC examination, and payment of fees. Continuing professional development activities and fee payment are required for recertification.

A professional certification older than these is that offered by the Commission on Rehabilitation Counselor Certification (CRCC). CRCC was created through the collaborative efforts of the American Rehabilitation Counseling Association (ARCA), a division of AACD, and the National Rehabilitation Association (NRA). CRCC has eight different eligibility categories because, unlike other specialties in counseling, some educational institutions offer baccalaureate degree programs in rehabilitation counseling. Therefore, in order to equate minimum eligibility criteria, work experience requirements vary as a function of the particular academic degree the candidate holds and the program from which the degree was received. For example, rehabilitation counselor graduates from CORE-accredited programs need not have postgraduate degree work experience, whereas graduates with a master's degree that is not in rehabilitation counseling must have a minimum of five years of work experience. In general, CRCC eligibility criteria include combinations of an appropriate degree, professional work experience, a supervised internship in rehabilitation counseling, payment of fees, and successful completion of the CRCC examination. The designation given is *Certified Rehabilitation Counselor* (CRC).

Another credential that is potentially applicable to professional counselors is that of the AAMFT. AAMFT does not provide certification per se, but rather has a clinical membership category. Eligibility criteria for the designation *AAMFT Clinical Member* are similar to those for certification processes and include graduation from a graduate-level program composed of experiences as identified in the AAMFT program accreditation standards. The criteria also include at least two hundred hours of supervised experience in marriage and family counseling,

1,500 hours of work experience in marriage and family counseling, evidence of having worked with at least fifty different families, and two years of postgraduate degree work experience supervised by a clinical member of AAMFT.

Certification is an aspect of professionalism potentially applicable to all professional counselors regardless of their work locations. There are other important professional credentials, however, that are available only to counselors in particular locations. One of the newest of these is registry.

Registry

The term *registry* is the most frequently misused term in any discussion of professional credentialing. A registry is a *noun* literally meaning a list of names. Thus, it is appropriate to write of a *registering* process, which results in a registry, rather than of a "registry" process. A registry, as used in the counseling profession, is a publicly distributed list of names of persons who have met some identified set of minimum qualifications (Loesch & Vacc, 1985).

Registries are a common by-product of certification processes. For example, NBCC, NACCMHC, and CRCC each publish a registry of the professional counselors they have certified. Although registries such as these are available to the public, they are more frequently used by professionals such as potential employers, who are interested in the professional credentials of counselors. Registries are important, therefore, because they serve a public relations function for counselors and the counseling profession.

Development of a registry is sometimes used as an alternative to counselor licensure. For example, North Carolina has a registry law as opposed to a counselor licensure law. North Carolina counselors fulfilling specified minimum requirements may be placed on the state's registry and, as a result, may present themselves as *Registered Professional Counselors* (RPCs). The criteria for inclusion on the North Carolina Registry include residency, a master's degree in counseling from an accredited institution, two years of postgraduate degree work experience, letters of reference, payment of fees, and successful completion of an examination.

Registering processes, such as the one used in North Carolina, are similar, at a theoretical level, to certification processes at a theoretical level because they are both title control processes. That is, they restrict who may use a title but not who may engage in an activity. For example, the North Carolina law stipulates specifically that many persons may hold themselves out as counselors, but that only those listed on the Registry may present themselves to the public as *Registered Professional Counselors.*

Although registering typifies a geographically restricted professional credential, registering as a primary professional credential is relatively rare. In fact, North Carolina is currently the only state having a registry law. Licensure, also a geographically restricted professional credential, is more common, and the number of state licensure laws appears to be increasing rapidly.

Licensure

In 1977 the (former) U.S. Department of Health, Education, and Welfare defined *licensure* as:

> [T]he process by which an agency of government grants permission to an individual to engage in a given occupation upon finding that the applicant has attained the minimal degree of competency necessary to ensure that the public health, safety, and welfare will be reasonably well protected. (p. 4)

Licensure in the counseling profession refers to laws implemented by various states to regulate the practice of counseling in those states. Because licensure laws literally control who may provide counseling services and under what conditions, they are often referred to as *practice acts* (Shimberg, 1981). Licensure laws are also title control acts, however, because they regulate the title *licensed counselor.*

There is one common exception to licensure laws as primary practice control legislation. Each of the United States has an agency (usually the state's DOE) that regulates the practice of school counseling through *school counselor certification* legislation. Such legislation is actually a practice act because it controls who may function as a school counselor. Confusion arises, however, because the term "certification" is usually not used for practice control legislation and because school counselor certification legislation typically does not have the requirements that are used in most licensure legislation, for example, successful completion of an examination. Thus, school counselor certification processes do not fall appropriately into the general categories of either "certification" or "licensure" as the terms are commonly used in the counseling profession (Wittmer, 1985b).

There are three major licensure classifications in the counseling profession. The first is licensure as a *psychologist.* Each of the fifty states and the District of Columbia have licensure laws for psychologists (Sweeney, 1983). The majority of states regulate both the title and (counseling) functions of psychologists. Other states have what may be called *certification licensure laws* because they regulate only who may use the title psychologist. A few other states have nonstatutory processes that are coordinated by their state psychological associations rather than state agencies. The trend in psychologist licensure, however, is toward the regulation of both title and functions (Sweeney, 1983).

Individual licensure laws for psychologists are extremely varied among the states, but a few trends can be identified. For example, almost all states require a doctoral degree from an accredited program in psychology or one that is "primarily psychological in nature." Additionally, professional work experience as a psychologist, an in-state residency period, supervised experience, payment of fees, letters of reference, and the successful completion of an examination are typically required (Wayne, 1982).

A second licensure classification is *marriage* and *family therapist* (or *counselor*), as currently licensed in eight states: California, Florida, Georgia, Michigan, New Jersey, Nevada, North Carolina, and Utah. In each state the legislation regulates both the title and the functions of the therapist. Marriage and family therapists licensure laws are often similar to those for psychologists. Eligibility criteria usually include a residency requirement, supervised experience, graduation from an accredited program, payment of fees, postgraduate degree professional work experience, references, and successful completion of an examination. The primary differentiating aspect is the requirement of a master's degree from an AAMFT-accredited program or a program of studies that would fulfill the AAMFT accreditation requirements. A second major factor is the (typical) requirement of five years of postgraduate degree professional work experience under the supervision of a licensed marriage and family therapist. Because the AAMFT requirements for clinical membership surpass the licensure requirements in most states, AAMFT clinical member status is often reciprocal with licensure (Kosinski, 1982).

Sixteen states currently have *counselor licensure laws,* which is the third classification. These states are Alabama, Arkansas, Florida, Georgia, Idaho, Maryland, Mississippi, Missouri, Montana, North Carolina, Ohio, Oklahoma, South Carolina, Tennessee, Texas, and Virginia. In eight of the states, the designation awarded is *Licensed Professional Counselor* (LPC). In Florida, the designation is *Mental Health Counselor* (MHC). The counselor licensure laws in each of these states regulate both the title and the functions of the counselor.

Professional counselor licensure requirements are essentially a synthesis of those used for licensure of psychologists and marriage and family therapists. They include such things as a minimum of a master's degree from an accredited program, letters of reference, residency requirements, payment of fees, postgraduate degree work experience, supervised experience, and successful completion of an examination. The primary difference between licensure as a professional counselor and other licensures is the nature of the accreditation for the academic program from which the counselor's degree is obtained. In general, the academic program accreditation requirements for licensure as a professional counselor are more localized. For example, for licensure as a psychologist, graduation from an APA-accredited program is a common stipulation. Licensure as a professional counselor, however, typically requires graduation from a program (only) accredited by the state in which licensure is sought. This does not mean that the accreditation requirements are less stringent, only that they are more geographically restricted.

Accepted Practices in Certification, Registry, and Licensure

The commonalities among certification, registry, and licensure have come to be accepted practices for the awarding of these types of professional credentials. The individual manifestations of these accepted practices provide a convenient method for comparisons among the processes. The following list is presented for that purpose; it was derived from the works of Forster (1977), Gross (1978), Loesch (1984), Loesch and Vacc (1985), Phillips (1982), Matarazzo (1977), Shimberg (1981, 1982), USDHEW (1977), Wayne (1982), Wittmer (1985a, 1985b), and Wittmer and Sweeney (1983).

Governance. The management agency of a credentialing process reflects the geographic region covered by the process. For example, licensure is an activity that is managed at the state level, while certification processes are typically national (or international) in scope and therefore are managed by national (but nongovernmental) agencies such as professional organizations. Relatedly, licensure boards are typically composed of professionals from within a state, whereas certification boards typically include professionals from larger geographic areas.

Area of Impact. Generally, licensure stops at the state boundary whereas certification is *carried with* the professional. Exceptions are made where reciprocity agreements are in effect.

Volunteerism. All professional credentials are technically voluntary because counselors don't necessarily have to have them to do some types of counseling. Restrictions placed on specific professional counseling activities and/or titles, however, imply that counselors *need* certain credentials to have choices about professional endeavors in which they may be interested.

Academic Preparation. All processes of individual credentialing require a specified minimum academic background, which is stated typically in terms of degrees held. Scrutiny of the requirements, however, reveals that they are actually specified in terms of particular academic experiences. Thus, persons who do not hold stipulated degrees may sometimes still be eligible for a credential if they have had the appropriate academic experiences.

Supervised Training Experience. All certification, registry, and licensure processes require supervised experience before the respective credential will be awarded. The most common type of required supervised experience is a minimum number of *contact hours* with clients, typically ranging from approximately 300 to 1,500 hours. Additionally, most processes require some minimum number of hours of supervision.

Professional Experience. Most individual credentialing processes require relevant professional work experience before the respective credential is awarded. The amount of work experience required, however, varies as an inverse function of the length of the supervised experience included in a candidate's academic preparation program.

Residency. All licensure and registry processes have a minimum residency requirement because they are (typically) geographically restricted; residency requirements for certification processes are rare.

Work Samples. A few individual credentialing processes require samples of applicants' work before the credential may be awarded. Typical samples include live demonstration, videotape, or a combination of these.

Personal Characteristics. All individual credentialing processes require that applicants provide information relative to their personal characteristics, usually through the provision of letters of reference. A few processes have other specific personal requirements such as a prohibition against credentialing a person who has a criminal record.

Examinations. Successful completion of an examination is required in all individual credentialing processes. Some agencies develop their own examinations, while others use examinations developed by professional testing companies.

Fees. All certification, registry, and licensure processes have required fees, typically for: (1) an initial application, (2) an examination, and (3) renewal of the credential.

Renewal. All individual credentialing processes have requirements for continuing professional development activities prior to continuation of the respective credential. Persons completing approved activities are awarded *continuing education units* (CEUs) toward a minimum number to be completed in a specified period of time (for example, 100 CEUs in five years for NCCs).

Reciprocities. Reciprocity is a process wherein one credentialing agency accepts the credential of another agency as equivalent to its own. Reciprocity agreements among states in regard to licensure as a professional counselor are fairly common, but reciprocities among licensure and certification agencies are rare. There are also partial reciprocities. For example, some states use NBCC's examination for professional counselor licensure; successful performance on the examination, as defined by the individual state, is acceptable for the state's professional counselor licensure process.

Although this list of accepted practices allows a general comparison of individual credentialing processes, persons interested in any particular credential should contact the appropriate credentialing agency to obtain the most accurate and current information.

COUNSELING AND THE LAW

There is no specific body of law that applies exclusively to the counseling profession, and there are few legal statutes or court cases of record pertaining directly to counseling. The result has been some confusion, and in a few cases anxiety, about the legal boundaries within which counselors may practice. Although literally all facets of law have at times affected counselors, most of the legal concern for counselors is in regard to liability.

Professional liability issues in the counseling profession relate to the possibility for counselors to cause harm to their clients. Legal matters involving counselor harm to clients include (alleged) infliction of: (1)

mental distress, (2) defamation of character, (3) sexual harassment, (4) negligence, (5) misrepresentation of professional service, and (6) battery. Additionally, the counselor's *duty to warn* has the potential for legal ramifications and becomes important in cases where a client threatens to inflict harm to others or self.

Liability cases against counselors are adjudicated in state courts. Because of the relatively few cases that have been brought against professional counselors, legal precedents for such cases are few. Typically, the cases have involved consideration of legal decisions rendered for psychologists or psychiatrists. Because counselors are distinct from psychologists and psychiatrists, however, such precedents are often only tangentially applicable.

Privileged communication is another important legal concern for counselors. In general, privileged communication is a legal concept that means that counselors are protected by law from disclosing information that they have obtained through their interactions with their clients. Technical, legal definitions of this term, in the few states where it exists for counselors, vary greatly, however. This issue is complicated because it involves a delicate balance between the client's right to privacy and the needs of society to know certain information. There are a few circumstances, however, in which the counselor *must* divulge information about a client, such as when the counselor: (1) is acting in a court-appointed capacity; (2) believes the client intends suicide, or (3) is being sued by a client. Additionally, counselors must divulge client information when a client is using insanity as a legal defense, a client under the age of majority reveals being a victim of a crime such as child abuse or rape, the client obviously needs psychiatric hospitalization, criminal action is involved, or the intention to commit a crime is evident (Corey, Corey, & Callanan, 1984).

Professional counselors currently are susceptible to an upsurge in legal actions because of the increasing recognition being given to them through credentialing activities. The counseling profession has taken steps to assist counselors involved in litigation, however, primarily through two means. First, *legal defense funds* have been developed and maintained by professional counseling organizations. Second, *professional liability insurance* has, through insurance agencies that are working in collaboration with professional organizations, become readily available to professional counselors. Thus, as the legal threats to counselors have increased, so have the sources of assistance.

Liability, privileged communication, and other legal concerns are realities for professional counselors. Those who seek counseling services typically reveal personal, intimate, and sometimes painful details of their lives. The manner in which a counselor responds in providing counseling services to clients forms the basis for any potential legal actions. Generally, a counselor's actions that are in accord with high standards of professionalism will less likely result in legal action and if questioned, will be much easier to defend.

ETHICAL CONSIDERATIONS IN COUNSELING

Professional ethical conduct is defined as voluntary adherence to standards of right or wrong that have been established by a profession. Therefore, a profession's *ethical code* dictates what is theoretically, morally, and logically expected from those working within the profession.

The Ethical Standards of AACD (see Appendix A) have been developed, refined, and systematized by its member professionals based on their many years of experience. These ethical standards, and others like them, apply to professionals, not to the persons they serve. Moreover, they specify only desirable and undesirable behaviors; they do not specify the penalties for ethical misconduct. Implicit in all ethical standards is the assumption that it is the responsibility of all counseling professionals to monitor both their own ethical behaviors and those of their peers.

The Ethical Standards of AACD contain a preamble and seven sections. Section one, General, addresses professional responsibilities to both clients and the setting in which services are provided, as well as ethical behavior with professional colleagues. It also addresses professional qualifications, service fees, and various types of discrimination. Relatedly, section two, Counseling Relationship, covers counselors' responsibilities within counseling relationships, including respecting clients' integrities and promoting their welfare. Confidentiality, professional consultation with colleagues, imminent danger to clients or others, management of records, and counselor responsibilities to inform clients or others are also covered in this section.

Section three, Research and Publication, addresses the ethical considerations for measurement and evaluation conducted by counselors. Topics such as counselors' obligations to inform clients of the purposes and uses of test information, public statements about test data, and the use of only methods that are psychometrically appropriate are covered. Special considerations for assessment of minority persons and the use of assessments in research with human subjects are also addressed in this section.

The fourth section, Consulting, refers to the consultation relationship between two professional counselors, or a counselor consulting with a business, group, or social unit. Private Practice, section five, covers ethical practices in initiating counseling, partnerships, corporations, fees, and other professional obligations pertaining to private practice business matters. Counselors' obligations with regard to presenting their own professional competencies to clients as well as to others with whom they work are covered in the sixth section, Personnel Administration. The last section, Preparation Standards, delineates responsibilities with regard to professional preparation for the provision of counseling services. It also relates ethical behaviors to AACD/CACREP's Standards for Preparation.

A profession is only as good as the behavior of its members. In the counseling profession, appropriate behavior is guided by an adherence to the ethical standards. Because the counseling profession is service-oriented, the fundamental premise of its ethical standards is the protection of the rights and welfare of service recipients. Because counselors engage in a variety of activities other than direct service provision, ethical standards encompass all types of professional involvement.

As noted above, compliance with the ethical standards is voluntary because they are not legal statutes and because monitoring ethical behavior is a responsibility of all counseling professionals. Professional organizations, such as AACD, assist in monitoring this process by providing means for the review of alleged ethical misconduct, the development of new ethical standards, and the dissemination of training materials and other pertinent information.

THE FUTURE IS NOW

Although credentialing has received the most professional attention in recent years, other topics are also important professional concerns. These topics are no less significant; indeed, many of them previously have been areas of primary professional emphasis. Because they have longer histories of professional attention, and therefore established professional involvements, they are currently less conspicuous. Nonetheless, they are important. These topics may be divided into two general categories for discussion purposes: *service recipients* and *professional activity trends*.

The evolution of the counseling profession is a reflection of an ever-increasing number of groups that have received counseling services. Indeed, the counseling profession now provides services for literally every facet of society. This diversity is exemplified in the following paragraphs.

Ethnic and Cultural Minorities

The case for professional attention to counseling for ethnic and cultural minorities (see Chapter 6) was effectively presented by Vacc and Wittmer (1980) when they stated:

> [H]elping professionals may hold the key to the process of reducing, if not eliminating, the social and emotional barriers which prevent many of America's subgroup members from becoming secure American citizens. To do this, helping professionals must make a concerted effort to understand cognitively the different subgroup members found among their clientele, an understanding that is over and above affectual understanding. (p. 6)

Older Persons

The need for counseling services for older persons has been identified by Myers and Loesch (1981) who wrote:

> Rapid and continuing increases in the numbers of older persons (i.e., over age 60) in the U.S. have focused attention on their need for effective professional social services. This need is particularly evident within the counseling profession since the desire, indeed demand, for counseling services for older persons is experiencing a parallel increase. (p. 21)

The response of those in the counseling profession has been multifaceted and pervasive. For example, opportunities for students to work with older persons as a part of professional training, though still limited, are increasing (Myers, 1983).

Women

Members of the counseling profession also have been particularly attentive to the specific counseling needs of women. Whiteley (1978) accented the current perspective when she wrote:

> [T]he purpose of therapy [for a woman] is no longer helping the woman understand, accept, and properly adjust to her "femininity." . . . Instead . . . [counseling is] helping women to examine the consequences for them personally of the conditioning of the culture, to discover their own individuality . . . to experience and nurture their own power and potency as a person . . . and, finally, to support women in whatever efforts they may wish to make in redefining the sex roles they have in their relationships with others. (p. 36)

Persons With Handicaps

Public Law 94-142 (see Appendix H), which provides for appropriate educational experiences for schoolchildren with handicaps, has had an impact in the counseling profession as well as in the American educational system, specifically, that (school) counselors are to be consulted in the development of educational programs for persons with handicaps (Perry, 1982). Concurrently, this impact has brought about realization of the need for more and better counseling services for persons with handicaps. Although primarily the province of rehabilitation counselors, many other counseling professionals now attend to the needs of persons with handicaps in their various counseling specialties.

Persons Who Are Abused

The substantial number of persons who are physically, sexually, or verbally abused has not gone unnoticed by the counseling profession, which is moving rapidly to provide appropriate and necessary counseling services, such as medical, environmental, and psychological assistance, for abused persons (Burcky, 1981). Although these services are not yet as comprehensive or as extensive as they should be, the counseling profession is making significant strides in providing such services.

These are a few of the many, many subgroups who are currently receiving professional counseling services. They were presented here because they typify the diversity of persons who need and receive those services. Other equally deserving groups of persons can easily be identified by reading recent issues of professional journals, such as the *Journal of Counseling and Development* (formerly the *Personnel and Guidance Journal*), and readers are directed to the professional literature for specific information on counseling services for other groups (see Appendix G).

By 1986 AACD's total membership had exceeded 46,000, the largest ever. More important, in the several preceding years, AACD's membership was increasing at the fastest rate ever. The largest and most rapidly increasing membership of AACD are but two of the indications of improving professional orientation among counselors. This improvement is attributable primarily to the many positive trends currently in evidence in the counseling profession. A few of the other trends are described in the following paragraphs.

Political Action

Perhaps the greatest change in the counseling profession over the past few years has been the rapid and extensive involvement of counselors in political activities. The basis for this involvement was summarized effectively by Solomon (1982):

> Counselors and other human service providers are in a pivotal position to communicate the concerns of people they serve effectively to policy makers at local, state, and national levels of government. They are in an even better position to help shape legislative initiatives, bills, and laws to more appropriately address counseling issues that directly impact the counseling profession as well as the people they serve. Most of the political successes that affect the counseling profession will depend largely on counselors themselves. (p. 580)

In brief, counseling professionals have realized that they can be a viable political force and that it is in their own best interests to initiate political action rather than waiting to have political action imposed upon them. Again, professional organizations such as AACD are coordinating these efforts.

Family Counseling

The changing nature of the American family is a concern to the counseling profession, and in response there have been rapid increases in both counselor training for and provision of family counseling services. Although this trend has not yet established a clear pattern, it is evident that an emphasis is emerging. Professionals in a variety of settings and with a variety of professional orientations, as well as counselor educators, are working together to develop the most appropriate system for the delivery of this important counseling service. Professional organizations are also contributing to this development by providing pertinent materials and coordinating professional development activities.

Professional Development

Continuing professional development through participation in activities such as workshops, seminars, and conventions has always been an integral part of professionalism for counselors. Credentialing has further increased interest in such activities, primarily in response to requirements for the renewal of credentials.

Consultation

Historically, the counseling profession focused extensively on the provision of direct services to clients. This focus continues. Counselors have also realized that their effectiveness can be extended greatly by providing consultation services to other helping professionals. Thus, consultation has become a major focus in both counselor preparation and practice, and the subject of a considerable number of professional development activities (see Chapter 3).

Business and Industry

The expansion of counseling services into the realm of business and industry is one of the most recent trends in the counseling profession (Lewis & Hayes, 1984). Smith, Piercy, and Lutz (1982) presented an explanation of both the rationale for this expansion and the nature of the services rendered:

> [M]ore corporations have begun to realize the effects that mental health problems have on the work life of the employee as related to absenteeism, turnover, and reduced productivity. . . . [C]ounselors have been employed in training and development, career development, employee assistance, and other related HRD [human resource development] functions in business and industry. . . . Key components of HRD include counseling (often within the company's employee assistance program), training and development (involving human relations training and technical update), and career development. Consultation, employee relations, performance, appraisal, organizational development, and research are among other activities included in HRD. (p. 108)

Primary Prevention

Another major trend in the counseling profession is the increasing emphasis on *primary prevention* instead of *remedial intervention.* In essence, primary prevention is the attempt to stop problems before they begin. Shaw and Goodyear (1984) captured the essence of primary prevention when they wrote:

> It is increasingly clear that our more traditional methods of individual, family, or group counseling are unlikely to reach any significant proportion of the population. The time-worn analogy used to contrast remedial with primary prevention approaches is that in which the helper must choose between attempting to rescue drowning people floating by in the current or going upstream to find out who is throwing them in. (p. 445)

Primary prevention approaches involve counselors working with relatively large groups of people, usually over relatively extended time periods. They are also approaches that can be used in literally any setting where professional counseling services are provided.

Multicultural Counseling

The counseling profession is, and desires to be, an integral part of the worldwide community. This orientation is manifested in multicultural counseling activities (which are explored in greater depth in Chapter 6). This trend has followed a pattern typical of others in the profession including the development of both a strong knowledge base and a set of uniquely applicable skills. Collectively, the result has been an increased appreciation and greater understanding of the need for and potential benefits of multicultural counseling among counselors.

Computers and High Technology

The counseling profession, along with everyone and everything else, is enmeshed in high technology. Within the profession, computers have received the most attention, primarily because of the growing accessibility of microcomputers to counselors.

The uses of computers in the counseling profession may be divided into two categories: *computer-managed counseling* (CMC) and *computer-assisted counseling* (CAC) (Walz, 1984). CMC refers to the use of computers (and other technology) to relieve counselors as much as possible of burdensome work (for example, record keeping and scheduling) so that they have more time to devote to their clients. CAC refers to the use of computers and other technology in actual counseling processes. CMC has been openly welcomed in the counseling profession. CAC has received a mixed reception; some believe it is "the wave of the future" whereas others view it as depersonalization of the counseling process. In either event, there is no doubt that computers and other technology are a rapidly growing part of the counseling profession.

Unfortunately, space limitations allow only this sample of the many, many important professional activities currently receiving attention in the counseling profession. It should be remembered, however, that all activities within the profession are important and significant because people's needs are being met by them.

PROFESSIONAL ORIENTATION REVISITED

Counseling is a true profession because its members hold a professional orientation. Professional counselors seek continually to act in the best interests of their clients and to improve themselves in as many ways as possible. The counseling profession reflects this perspective by attempting to provide effective services to as many people, with as many alternatives, and in as many circumstances, as possible. As the preceding discussions exemplify, the counseling profession uses a collective effort to attempt to better the world in ways and areas that are appropriate to its spheres of influence and operation.

Each counselor who holds and acts in accord with a professional orientation makes a significant contribution to this collective effort. Professionalism is idealized in many ways and at many levels, but it can be operationalized only by individual counselors. Fortunately, when counselors do behave as professionals, the benefits are both personal and societal.

REFERENCES

Burcky, W. (1981). The battered wife: Past, present, and future. *AMHCA Journal, 3,* 72–78.

Corey, G., Corey, M., & Callanan, P. (1984). *Issues and ethics in the helping professions* (2nd ed.). Monterey, CA: Brooks/Cole.

Forster, J. R. (1977). What shall we do about credentialing? *Personnel and Guidance Journal, 55,* 573–576.

Gross, S. J. (1978). The myth of professional licensing. *American Psychologist, 33,* 1009–1016.

Ivey, A. E. (1982). Credentialism: Protection for the public or the professional? In E. L. Herr & N. W. Pinson (Eds.), *Foundations for policy in guidance and counseling* (pp. 131–154). Washington, DC: American Personnel and Guidance Association.

Kosinski, F. A., Jr. (1982). Standards, accreditation, and licensure in marriage and family therapy. *Personnel and Guidance Journal, 60,* 350–352.

Lewis, J. A., & Hayes, B. A. (1984, December). Options for counselors in business and industry. *Counseling and Human Development, 17* (4), 1–8.

Loesch, L. C. (1984). Professional credentialing in counseling—1984. *Counseling and Human Development, 17,* 1–11.

Loesch, L. C., & Vacc, N. A. (1985). *National Counselor Certification Examination preliminary technical manual.* Alexandria, VA: National Board for Certified Counselors and American Association for Counseling and Development.

Matarazzo, J. D. (1977). Higher education, professional accreditation, and licensure. *American Psychologist, 32,* 856–859.

Myers, J. M. (1983). Gerontological counseling training: The state of the art. *Personnel and Guidance Journal, 61,* 398–401.

Myers, J. M., & Loesch, L. C. (1981). The counseling needs of older persons. *The Humanist Educator, 20,* 21–35.

Pennell, N. Y., Proffitt, J. R., & Hatch, T. D. (1971). *Accreditation and certification in relation to allied health manpower.* Washington, DC: U.S. Department of Health, Education and Welfare, Public Health Service. Cited in B. Shimberg (no date), *The relationship of accreditation, certification, and licensure.* Princeton, NJ: Educational Testing Service.

Perry, L. (1982). *Special populations: The demands of diversity.* In E. L. Herr & N. M. Pinson (Eds.), *Foundations for policy in guidance and counseling* (pp. 50–69). Alexandria, VA: American Association for Counseling and Development.

Phillips, B. N. (1982). Regulation and control in psychology: Implications for certification and licensure. *American Psychologist, 37,* 919–926.

Shaw, M. C., & Goodyear, R. K. (1984). Introduction to the special issues on primary prevention. *Personnel and Guidance Journal, 62,* 444–445.

Shimberg, B. (1981). Testing for licensure and certification. *American Psychologist, 36,* 1138–1146.

Shimberg, B. (1982). *Occupational licensing: A public perspective.* Princeton, NJ: Educational Testing Service.

Smith, R. L., Piercy, F. P., & Lutz, P. (1982). Training counselors for human resource development positions in business and industry. *Counselor Education and Supervision, 22,* 107–112.

Solomon, C. (1982). Special issue on political action: Introduction. *Personnel and Guidance Journal, 60,* 580.

Sweeney, T. J. (1983). *Licensure in the helping professions.* In J. McFadden & D. K. Brooks, Jr. (Eds.), *Counselor licensure action packet* (pp. 117–126). Alexandria, VA: American Association for Counseling and Development.

U.S. Department of Health, Education and Welfare. (1977). *Credentialing health manpower.* Washington, DC: Author.

Vacc, N. A., & Wittmer, J. (1980). *Prologue.* In N. A. Vacc & J. Wittmer (Eds.), *Let me be me: Special populations and the helping professional* (p. 5). Muncie, IN: Accelerated Development.

Walz, G. R. (1984). Role of the counselor with computers. *Journal of Counseling and Development, 63,* 135–138.

Wayne, G. (1982). An examination of selected statutory licensing requirements for psychologists in the United States. *Personnel and Guidance Journal, 60,* 420–426.

Whiteley, R. M. (1978). Counseling women in groups. In L. W. Harmon, J. M. Birk, L. E. Fitzgerald, & M. F. Tanney (Eds.), *Counseling women* (pp. 34–58). Monterey, CA: Brooks/Cole.

Wittmer, J. (Ed.). (1985a). *Accreditation procedures manual and application for counseling and related educational programs.* Gainesville, FL: Council for the Accreditation of Counseling and Related Educational Programs.

Wittmer, J. (1985b). Counselor credentialing in America. In T. Husen & N. Postlethwaite (Eds.), *The International Encyclopedia of Education* (pp. 1087–1088). London: Pergamon Press.

Wittmer, J., & Sweeney, T. (1983). Counselor education and the psychology of more: A response. *Counselor Education and Supervision, 22,* 287–289.

EPILOGUE

You, the reader, now have a clear notion about what the counseling profession is today. You know that counseling has emerged in less than a century from an occupation to a full-fledged profession, guided by national standards, and beginning to achieve consistent public recognition. You know that today's professional counselor works with a myriad of client populations, using a variety of technologies to enhance human development and intervene in problem situations. You know that the counselor, whether working with an individual, leading a group, interpreting a test, or consulting with an organization, understands the need to preserve individual dignity and promote development within a social and cultural context.

You also know, however, that the counseling profession is fluid and dynamic. Historically, counselors have learned to respond to the changing priorities of their clients, developing fresh approaches and technologies as they were needed to address new issues. Because continued change and renewal will be essential if the profession is to live up to its promise, we believe it is important to project into the future and make some estimations at this point about the counselors of tomorrow. What characteristics are likely to be important for these counselors? What skills and attitudes will they need if they are to meet challenges that are, as yet, unknown?

1. Tomorrow's counselors will need a strong sense of professional identity.

Counselors of the future can be expected to graduate from nationally accredited counseling programs, to be licensed or certified as counselors, to read literature intended for professional counselors, and to be recognized as members of a separate mental health specialty. But a sense of professional identity requires more than training and public recognition. It also depends on a shared vision and a shared sense of tradition. Counselors have been unique among helping professionals because of their focus on working with healthy populations, their ability to understand organizational contexts, their expertise in carrying out preventive and educational interventions, and their responsiveness to social change. Tomorrow's counselors will be successful only to the degree that they cherish this uniqueness and maintain what should be a leadership position in the field of human development.

2. Tomorrow's counselors will need the ability to work with diverse populations and settings.

The counselor of the future will deal with a broad range of concerns, persons, and situations and will therefore need to use models that transcend individual differences. The helping professions have evolved gradually from an assumption that what worked with White, middle-class, English-speaking males would work with everyone to a focus on searching for methods of meeting the special needs of minorities. The next stage in this evolution will involve developing intervention models that take into account the nature of individual-environment interactions and recognize the effects of gender, culture, and socioeconomic factors on these interactions.

These helping models must also be broad enough to transcend the work setting. Counselors have moved in recent years from an identification with the educational institutions to a concentration on community agencies to an interest in business and industry as appropriate settings for counseling. In all likelihood, tomorrow's counselors will find still new environments in which to serve. They will be ready for these new challenges only if they have succeeded in devising a professional identity capable of spanning a variety of settings.

3. Tomorrow's counselors will need a developmental orientation.

The counseling profession has traditionally focused its attention upon the promotion of human development. Recently, this focus has become even clearer, with professional organizations moving to include the words "counseling and development" in their titles and counselors coming to appreciate a lifespan approach that has brought new recognition to the concerns of people of all ages. Counseling is not a service limited to individuals whose life progress has somehow slowed or taken a detour, or even to those who are very young. Counseling today seeks to promote the human development of all persons under a wide variety of circumstances over the course of the entire lifespan from birth to death.

Counselors of the future will need to be life-skills trainers more than therapists. They will draw on a large body of data about human development, acknowledging crisis as a prelude to creation and taking the importance of preventive interventions for granted.

4. Tomorrow's counselors will need a holistic, interdisciplinary orientation.

A focus on development brings with it a concentration on physical as well as mental health and on environmental as well as intrapsychic phenomena. Counselors who are interested in promoting their clients' development will need to base their interventions on the recognition that affect, cognition, and behavior are inseparable and are as much affected by social and biological factors as by psychological ones. Tomorrow's counselors will need to be comfortable dealing with the innovative concepts of other fields, including biology, sociology, anthropology, economics, and political science along with education and psychology.

5. Tomorrow's counselors will need to involve themselves with their clients' environments.

Professionals are now at the point of recognizing the importance of environmental influences on human development. Increasingly, counselors have become interested in studying social systems, from the family to the organization to the society as a whole. This trend is likely to continue as counselors recognize the difficulties inherent in attempting to bring about change with the very limited tools of individual assessment and counseling. What many term an "ecological approach" can move from the realm of study to that of action only when counselors change their own perceptions of reality, making automatic cognitive connections between environmental conditions and individual behaviors and thus being quick to recognize social and political factors that might place their clients at risk.

6. Tomorrow's counselors will need to be "developmentally advanced."

There is virtually no possibility that the counselors of the future will have a set of specific guidelines to follow in dealing with all situations. These counselors, like the ones who came before them, will have to cope with a broad range of complex client concerns that may be difficult to predict. The only kind of person who can be at ease with such uncertainty is one who is at a relatively advanced stage of moral, intellectual, and social development and who can therefore make decisions from the vantage point of his or her unique commitment. Because such individuals are developed, and not simply born, the counseling profession will need to make human development a conscious preoccupation, not just for its clients, but for its practitioners as well.

APPENDIX A
ETHICAL STANDARDS OF THE AMERICAN ASSOCIATION FOR COUNSELING AND DEVELOPMENT

PREAMBLE

The Association is an educational, scientific, and professional organization whose members are dedicated to the enhancement of the worth, dignity, potential, and uniqueness of each individual and thus to the service of society.

The Association recognizes that the role definitions and work settings of its members include a wide variety of academic disciplines, levels of academic preparation and agency services. This diversity reflects the breadth of the Association's interest and influence. It also poses challenging complexities in efforts to set standards for the performance of members, desired requisite preparation or practice, and supporting social, legal, and ethical controls.

The specification of ethical standards enables the Association to clarify to present and future members and to those served by members, the nature of ethical responsibilities held in common by its members.

The existence of such standards serves to stimulate greater concern by members for their own professional functioning and for the conduct of fellow professionals such as counselors, guidance and student personnel workers, and others in the helping professions. As the ethical code of the Association, this document establishes principles that define the ethical behavior of Association members.

SOURCE: Copyright AACD. Reprinted with permission. No further reproduction authorized without further permission of AACD.

Approved by Executive Committee upon referral of the Board of Directors, January 17, 1981.

SECTION A: GENERAL

1. The member influences the development of the profession by continuous efforts to improve professional practices, teaching, services, and research. Professional growth is continuous throughout the member's career and is exemplified by the development of a philosophy that explains why and how a member functions in the helping relationship. Members must gather data on their effectiveness and be guided by the findings.
2. The member has a responsibility both to the individual who is served and to the institution within which the service is performed to maintain high standards of professional conduct. The member strives to maintain the highest levels of professional services offered to the individuals to be served. The member also strives to assist the agency, organization, or institution in providing the highest caliber of professional services. The acceptance of employment in an institution implies that the member is in agreement with the general policies and principles of the institution. Therefore the professional activities of the member are also in accord with the objectives of the institution. If, despite concerted efforts, the member cannot reach agreement with the employer as to acceptable standards of conduct that allow for changes in institutional policy conducive to the positive growth and development of clients, then terminating the affiliation should be seriously considered.
3. Ethical behavior among professional associates, both members and nonmembers, must be expected at all times. When information is possessed that raises doubt as to the ethical behavior of professional colleagues, whether Association members or not, the member must take action to attempt to rectify such a condition. Such action shall use the institution's channels first and then use procedures established by the state Branch, Division, or Association.
4. The member neither claims nor implies professional qualifications exceeding those possessed and is responsible for correcting any misrepresentations of these qualifications by others.
5. In establishing fees for professional counseling services, members must consider the financial status of clients and

locality. In the event that the established fee structure is inappropriate for a client, assistance must be provided in finding comparable services of acceptable cost.
6. When members provide information to the public or to subordinates, peers or supervisors, they have a responsibility to ensure that the content is general, unidentified client information that is accurate, unbiased, and consists of objective, factual data.
7. With regard to the delivery of professional services, members should accept only those positions for which they are professionally qualified.
8. In the counseling relationship the counselor is aware of the intimacy of the relationship and maintains respect for the client and avoids engaging in activities that seek to meet the counselor's personal needs at the expense of that client. Through awareness of the negative impact of both racial and sexual stereotyping and discrimination, the counselor guards the individual rights and personal dignity of the client in the counseling relationship.

SECTION B: COUNSELING RELATIONSHIP

This section refers to practices and procedures of individual and/or group counseling relationships.

The member must recognize the need for client freedom of choice. Under those circumstances where this is not possible, the member must apprise clients of restrictions that may limit their freedom of choice.

1. The member's *primary* obligation is to respect the integrity and promote the welfare of the client(s), whether the client(s) is (are) assisted individually or in a group relationship. In a group setting, the member is also responsible for taking reasonable precautions to protect individuals from physical and/or psychological trauma resulting from interaction within the group.
2. The counseling relationship and information resulting therefrom be kept confidential, consistent with the obligations of the member as a professional person. In a group counseling setting, the counselor must set a norm of confidentiality regarding all group participants' disclosures.
3. If an individual is already in a counseling relationship with another professional person, the member does not enter

into a counseling relationship without first contacting and receiving the approval of that other professional. If the member discovers that the client is in another counseling relationship after the counseling relationship begins, the member must gain the consent of the other professional or terminate the relationship, unless the client elects to terminate the other relationship.
4. When the client's condition indicates that there is clear and imminent danger to the client or others, the member must take reasonable personal action or inform responsible authorities. Consultation with other professionals must be used where possible. The assumption of responsibility for the client(s) behavior must be taken only after careful deliberation. The client must be involved in the resumption of responsibility as quickly as possible.
5. Records of the counseling relationship, including interview notes, test data, correspondence, tape recordings, and other documents, are to be considered professional information for use in counseling and they should not be considered a part of the records of the institution or agency in which the counselor is employed unless specified by state statute or regulation. Revelation to others of counseling material must occur only upon the expressed consent of the client.
6. Use of data derived from a counseling relationship for purposes of counselor training or research shall be confined to content that can be disguised to ensure full protection of the identity of the subject client.
7. The member must inform the client of the purposes, goals, techniques, rules of procedure and limitations that may affect the relationship at or before the time that the counseling relationship is entered.
8. The member must screen prospective group participants, especially when the emphasis is on self-understanding and growth through self-disclosure. The member must maintain an awareness of the group participants' compatibility throughout the life of the group.
9. The member may choose to consult with any other professionally competent person about a client. In choosing a consultant, the member must avoid placing the consultant in a conflict of interest situation that would preclude the consultant's being a proper party to the member's efforts to help the client.
10. If the member determines an inability to be of profes-

sional assistance to the client, the member must either avoid initiating the counseling relationship or immediately terminate that relationship. In either event, the member must suggest appropriate alternatives. (The member must be knowledgeable about referral resources so that a satisfactory referral can be initiated). In the event the client declines the suggested referral, the member is not obligated to continue the relationship.

11. When the member has other relationships, particularly of an administrative, supervisory and/or evaluative nature with an individual seeking counseling services, the member must not serve as the counselor but should refer the individual to another professional. Only in instances where such an alternative is unavailable and where the individual's situation warrants counseling intervention should the member enter into and/or maintain a counseling relationship. Dual relationships with clients that might impair the member's objectivity and professional judgment (e.g., as with close friends or relatives, sexual intimacies with any client) must be avoided and/or the counseling relationship terminated through referral to another competent professional.
12. All experimental methods of treatment must be clearly indicated to prospective recipients and safety precautions are to be adhered to by the member.
13. When the member is engaged in short-term group treatment/training programs (e.g., marathons and other encounter-type or growth groups), the member ensures that there is professional assistance available during and following the group experience.
14. Should the member be engaged in a work setting that calls for any variation from the above statements, the member is obligated to consult with other professionals whenever possible to consider justifiable alternatives.

SECTION C: MEASUREMENT AND EVALUATION

The primary purpose of educational and psychological testing is to provide descriptive measures that are objective and interpretable in either comparative or absolute terms. The member must recognize the need to interpret the statements that follow as applying to the whole range of appraisal techniques including test and nontest data. Test results constitute only one of a variety of pertinent sources of information for personnel, guidance, and counseling decisions.

1. The member must provide specific orientation or information to the examinee(s) prior to and following the test administration so that the results of testing may be placed in proper perspective with other relevant factors. In so doing, the member must recognize the effects of socioeconomic, ethnic and cultural factors on test scores. It is the member's professional responsibility to use additional unvalidated information carefully in modifying interpretation of the test results.
2. In selecting tests for use in a given situation or with a particular client, the member must consider carefully the specific validity, reliability and appropriateness of the test(s). *General* validity, reliability and the like may be questioned legally as well as ethically when tests are used for vocational and educational selection, placement, or counseling.
3. When making any statements to the public about tests and testing, the member must give accurate information and avoid false claims or misconceptions. Special efforts are often required to avoid unwarranted connotations of such terms as *IQ* and *grade equivalent scores.*
4. Different tests demand different levels of competence for administration, scoring, and interpretation. Members must recognize the limits of their competence and perform only those functions for which they are prepared.
5. Tests must be administered under the same conditions that were established in their standardization. When tests are not administered under standard conditions or when unusual behavior or irregularities occur during the testing session, those conditions must be noted and the results designated as invalid or of questionable validity. Unsupervised or inadequately supervised test-taking, such as the use of tests through the mails, is considered unethical. On the other hand, the use of instruments that are so designed or standardized to be self-administered and self-scored, such as interest inventories, is to be encouraged.
6. The meaningfulness of test results used in personnel, guidance, and counseling functions generally depends on the examinee's unfamiliarity with the specific items on

the test. Any prior coaching or dissemination of the test materials can invalidate test results. Therefore, test security is one of the professional obligations of the member. Conditions that produce most favorable test results must be made known to the examinee.

7. The purpose of testing and the explicit use of the results must be made known to the examinee prior to testing. The counselor must ensure that instrument limitations are not exceeded and that periodic review and/or retesting are made to prevent client stereotyping.
8. The examinee's welfare and explicit prior understanding must be the criteria for determining the recipients of the test results. The member must see that specific interpretation accompanies any release of individual or group test data. The interpretation of test data must be related to the examinee's particular concerns.
9. The member must be cautious when interpreting the results of research instruments possessing insufficient technical data. The specific purposes for the use of such instruments must be stated explicitly to examinees.
10. The member must proceed with caution when attempting to evaluate and interpret the performance of minority group members or other persons who are not represented in the norm group on which the instrument was standardized.
11. The member must guard against the appropriation, reproduction, or modifications of the published tests or parts thereof without acknowledgment and permission from the previous publisher.
12. Regarding the preparation, publication and distribution of tests, reference should be made to:
    a. *Standards for Educational and Psychological Tests and Manuals,* revised edition, 1974, published by the American Psychological Association on behalf of itself, the American Educational Research Association and the National Council on Measurement in Education.
    b. The responsible use of tests: A position paper of AMEG, APGA, and NCME, *Measurement and Evaluation in Guidance,* 1972, 5, 385-388.
    c. "Responsibilities of Users of Standardized Tests," APGA, *Guidepost,* October 5, 1978, pp. 5-8.

SECTION D: RESEARCH AND PUBLICATION

1. Guidelines on research with human subjects shall be adhered to, such as:
   a. *Ethical Principles in the Conduct of Research with Human Participants,* Washington, D.C.: American Psychological Association, Inc., 1973.
   b. Code of Federal Regulations, Title 45, Subtitle A, Part 46, as currently issued.
2. In planning any research activity dealing with human subjects, the member must be aware of and responsive to all pertinent ethical principles and ensure that the research problem, design, and execution are in full compliance with them.
3. Responsibility for ethical research practice lies with the principal researcher, while others involved in the research activities share ethical obligation and full responsibility for their own actions.
4. In research with human subjects, researchers are responsible for the subjects' welfare throughout the experiment and they must take all reasonable precautions to avoid causing injurious psychological, physical, or social effects on their subjects.
5. All research subjects must be informed of the purpose of the study except when withholding information or providing misinformation to them is essential to the investigation. In such research the member must be responsible for corrective action as soon as possible following completion of the research.
6. Participation in research must be voluntary. Involuntary participation is appropriate only when it can be demonstrated that participation will have no harmful effects on subjects and is essential to the investigation.
7. When reporting research results, explicit mention must be made of all variables and conditions known to the investigator that might affect the outcome of the investigation or the interpretation of the data.
8. The member must be responsible for conducting and reporting investigations in a manner that minimizes the possibility that results will be misleading.
9. The member has an obligation to make available suffi-

cient original research data to qualified others who may wish to replicate the study.
10. When supplying data, aiding in the research of another person, reporting research results, or in making original data available, due care must be taken to disguise the identity of the subjects in the absence of specific authorization from such subjects to do otherwise.
11. When conducting and reporting research, the member must be familiar with, and give recognition to, previous work on the topic, as well as to observe all copyright laws and follow the principles of giving full credit to all to whom credit is due.
12. The member must give due credit through joint authorship, acknowledgment, footnote statements, or other appropriate means to those who have contributed significantly to the research and/or publication, in accordance with such contributions.
13. The member must communicate to other members the results of any research judged to be of professional or scientific value. Results reflecting unfavorably on institutions, programs, services, or vested interests must not be withheld for such reasons.
14. If members agree to cooperate with another individual in research and/or publication, they incur an obligation to cooperate as promised in terms of punctuality of performance and with full regard to the completeness and accuracy of the information required.
15. Ethical practice requires that authors not submit the same manuscript or one essentially similar in content, for simultaneous publication consideration by two or more journals. In addition, manuscripts published in whole or in substantial part, in another journal or published work should not be submitted for publication without acknowledgment and permission from the previous publication.

SECTION E: CONSULTING

Consultation refers to a voluntary relationship between a professional helper and help-needing individual, group or social unit in which the consultant is providing help to the client(s) in defining and solving a work-related problem or potential problem with a client or client system. (This definition is adapted from Kurpius, DeWayne. Consultation theory and process: An integrated model. *Personnel and Guidance Journal,* 1978, 56.

1. The member acting as consultant must have a high degree of self-awareness of his-her own values, knowledge, skills, limitations, and needs in entering a helping relationship that involves human and-or organizational change and that the focus of the relationship be on the issues to be resolved and not on the person(s) presenting the problem.
2. There must be understanding and agreement between member and client for the problem definition, change goals, and predicated consequences of interventions selected.
3. The member must be reasonably certain that she/he or the organization represented has the necessary competencies and resources for giving the kind of help that is needed now or may develop later and that appropriate referral resources are available to the consultant.
4. The consulting relationship must be one in which client adaptability and growth toward self-direction are encouraged and cultivated. The member must maintain this role consistently and not become a decision maker for the client or create a future dependency on the consultant.
5. When announcing consultant availability for services, the member conscientiously adheres to the Association's *Ethical Standards.*
6. The member must refuse a private fee or other remuneration for consultation with persons who are entitled to these services through the member's employing institution or agency. The policies of a particular agency may make explicit provisions for private practice with agency clients by members of its staff. In such instances, the clients must be apprised of other options open to them should they seek private counseling services.

SECTION F: PRIVATE PRACTICE

1. The member should assist the profession by facilitating the availability of counseling services in private as well as public settings.
2. In advertising services as a private practitioner, the member must advertise the services in such a manner so as to accurately inform the public as to services, expertise,

profession, and techniques of counseling in a professional manner. A member who assumes an executive leadership role in the organization shall not permit his/her name to be used in professional notices during periods when not actively engaged in the private practice of counseling.

The member may list the following: highest relevant degree, type and level of certification or license, type and/or description of services, and other relevant information. Such information must not contain false, inaccurate, misleading, partial, out-of-context, or deceptive material or statements.

3. Members may join in partnership/corporation with other members and-or other professionals provided that each member of the partnership or corporation makes clear the separate specialties by name in compliance with the regulations of the locality.
4. A member has an obligation to withdraw from a counseling relationship if it is believed that employment will result in violation of the *Ethical Standards*. If the mental or physical condition of the member renders it difficult to carry out an effective professional relationship or if the member is discharged by the client because the counseling relationship is no longer productive for the client, then the member is obligated to terminate the counseling relationship.
5. A member must adhere to the regulations for private practice of the locality where the services are offered.
6. It is unethical to use one's institutional affiliation to recruit clients for one's private practice.

SECTION G: PERSONNEL ADMINISTRATION

It is recognized that most members are employed in public or quasi-public institutions. The functioning of a member within an institution must contribute to the goals of the institution and vice versa if either is to accomplish their respective goals or objectives. It is therefore essential that the member and the institution function in ways to (a) make the institution's goals explicit and public; (b) make the member's contribution to institutional goals specific; and (c) foster mutual accountability for goal achievement.

To accomplish these objectives, it is recognized that the

member and the employer must share responsibilities in the formulation and implementation of personnel policies.

1. Members must define and describe the parameters and levels of their professional competency.
2. Members must establish interpersonal relations and working agreements with supervisors and subordinates regarding counseling or clinical relationships, confidentiality, distinction between public and private material, maintenance, and dissemination of recorded information, work load and accountability. Working agreements in each instance must be specified and made known to those concerned.
3. Members must alert their employers to conditions that may be potentially disruptive or damaging.
4. Members must inform employers of conditions that may limit their effectiveness.
5. Members must submit regularly to professional review and evaluation.
6. Members must be responsible for inservice development of self and-or staff.
7. Members must inform their staff of goals and programs.
8. Members must provide personnel practices that guarantee and enhance the rights and welfare of each recipient of their service.
9. Members must select competent persons and assign responsibilities compatible with their skills and experiences.

SECTION H: PREPARATION STANDARDS

Members who are responsible for training others must be guided by the preparation standards of the Association and relevant Division(s). The member who functions in the capacity of trainer assumes unique ethical responsibilities that frequently go beyond that of the member who does not function in a training capacity. These ethical responsibilities are outlined as follows:

1. Members must orient students to program expectations, basic skills development, and employment prospects prior to admission to the program.
2. Members in charge of learning experiences must estab-

lish programs that integrate academic study and supervised practice.
3. Members must establish a program directed toward developing students' skills, knowledge, and self-understanding, stated whenever possible in competency or performance terms.
4. Members must identify the levels of competencies of their students in compliance with relevant Division standards. These competencies must accommodate the para-professional as well as the professional.
5. Members, through continual student evaluation and appraisal, must be aware of the personal limitations of the learner that might impede future performance. The instructor must not only assist the learner in securing remedial assistance but also screen from the program those individuals who are unable to provide competent services.
6. Members must provide a program that includes training in research commensurate with levels of role functioning. Para-professional and technician-level personnel must be trained as consumers of research. In addition, these personnel must learn how to evaluate their own and their program's effectiveness. Graduate training, especially at the doctoral level, would include preparation for original research by the member.
7. Members must make students aware of the ethical responsibilities and standards of the profession.
8. Preparatory programs must encourage students to value the ideals of service to individuals and to society. In this regard, direct financial remuneration or lack thereof must not influence the quality of service rendered. Monetary considerations must not be allowed to overshadow professional and humanitarian needs.
9. Members responsible for educational programs must be skilled as teachers and practitioners.
10. Members must present thoroughly varied theoretical positions so that students may make comparisons and have the opportunity to select a position.
11. Members must develop clear policies within their educational institutions regarding field placement and the roles of the student and the instructor in such placements.
12. Members must ensure that forms of learning focusing on self-understanding or growth are voluntary, or if required

as part of the education program, are made known to prospective students prior to entering the program. When the education program offers a growth experience with an emphasis on self-disclosure or other relatively intimate or personal involvement, the member must have no administrative, supervisory, or evaluating authority regarding the participant.
13. Members must conduct an educational program in keeping with the current relevant guidelines of the Association and its Divisions.

APPENDIX B
ETHICAL GUIDELINES FOR GROUP LEADERS OF THE ASSOCIATION FOR SPECIALISTS IN GROUP WORK

PREAMBLE

One characteristic of any professional group is the possession of a body of knowledge and skills and mutually acceptable ethical standards for putting them into practice. Ethical standards consist of those principles which have been formally and publicly acknowledged by the membership of a profession to serve as guidelines governing professional conduct, discharge of duties, and resolution of moral dilemmas. In this document, the Association for Specialists in Group Work has identified the standards of conduct necessary to maintain and regulate the high standards of integrity and leadership among its members.

The Association for Specialists in Group Work recognizes the basic commitment of its members to the Ethical Standards of its parent organization, the American Personnel & Guidance Association and nothing in this document shall be construed to supplant that code. These standards are intended to complement the APGA standards in the area of group work by clarifying the nature of ethical responsibility of the counselor in the group setting and by stimulating a greater concern for competent group leadership.

The following ethical guidelines have been organized under three categories: the leader's responsibility for providing information about group work to clients, the group leader's responsibility for providing group counseling services to clients, and the group leader's responsibility for safeguarding the standards of ethical practice.

SOURCE: Copyright AACD. Reprinted with permission. No further reproduction authorized without further permission of AACD.

Approved by the ASGW Executive Board, November 11, 1980.

A. RESPONSIBILITY FOR PROVIDING INFORMATION ABOUT GROUP WORK AND GROUP SERVICES

A-1. Group leaders shall fully inform group members, in advance and preferably in writing, of the goals in the group, qualifications of the leader, and procedures to be employed.

A-2. The group leader shall conduct a pre-group interview with each prospective member for purposes of screening, orientation, and insofar as possible, shall select group members whose needs and goals are compatible with the established goals of the group; who will not impede the group process; and whose well-being will not be jeopardized by the group experience.

A-3. Group leaders shall protect members by defining clearly what confidentiality means, why it is important, and the difficulties involved in enforcement.

A-4. Group leaders shall explain, as realistically as possible, exactly what services can and cannot be provided within the particular group structure offered.

A-5. Group leaders shall provide prospective clients with specific information about any specialized or experimental activities in which they may be expected to participate.

A-6. Group leaders shall stress the personal risks involved in any group, especially regarding potential life-changes, and help group members explore their readiness to face these risks.

A-7. Group leaders shall inform members that participation is voluntary and that they may exit from the group at any time.

A-8. Group leaders shall inform members about recording of sessions and how tapes will be used.

B. RESPONSIBILITY FOR PROVIDING GROUP SERVICES TO CLIENTS

B-1. Group leaders shall protect member rights against physical threats, intimidation, coercion, and undue peer pressure insofar as is reasonably possible.

B-2. Group leaders shall refrain from imposing their own agendas, needs, and values on group members.

B-3. Group leaders shall insure to the extent that it is reasonably possible that each member has the opportunity to utilize group resources and interact within the group by minimizing barriers such as rambling and monopolizing time.

B-4. Group leaders shall make every reasonable effort to treat each member individually and equally.

B-5. Group leaders shall abstain from inappropriate personal relationships with members throughout the duration of the group and any subsequent professional involvement.

B-6. Group leaders shall help promote independence of members from the group in the most efficient period of time.

B-7. Group leaders shall not attempt any technique unless thoroughly trained in its use or under supervision by an expert familiar with the intervention.

B-8. Group leaders shall not condone the use of alcohol or drugs directly prior to or during group sessions.

B-9. Group leaders shall make every effort to assist clients in developing their personal goals.

B-10. Group leaders shall provide between-session consultation to group members and follow-up after termination of the group, as needed or requested.

C. RESPONSIBILITY FOR SAFEGUARDING ETHICAL PRACTICE

C-1. Group leaders shall display these standards or make them available to group members.

C-2. Group leaders have the right to expect ethical behavior from colleagues and are obligated to rectify or disclose incompetent, unethical behavior demonstrated by a colleague by taking the following actions:

(a) To confront the individual with the apparent violation of ethical guidelines for the purposes of protecting the safety of any clients and to help the group leader correct any inappropriate behaviors.

(b) Such a complaint should be made in writing including the specific facts **and dates** of the alleged violation and all relevant supporting data. The complaint should be forwarded to:

> The Ethics Committee,
> c/o The President
> Association for Specialists in Group Work

5999 Stevenson Avenue
Alexandria, Virginia 22304

The envelope must be marked "CONFIDENTIAL" in order to assure confidentiality for both the accuser(s) and the alleged violator(s). Upon receipt, the President shall (a) check on membership status of the charged member(s), (b) confer with legal counsel, and (c) send the case with all pertinent documents to the chairperson of the ASGW Ethics Committee within ten (10) working days after the receipt of the complaint.

(c) If it is determined by the Ethics and Professional Standards Committee that the alleged breach of ethical conduct constitutes a violation of the "Ethical Guidelines," then an investigation will be started within ten (10) days by at least one member of the Committee plus two additional ASGW members in the locality of the alleged violation. The investigating committee chairperson shall: (a) acknowledge receipt of the complaint, (b) review the complaint and supporting data, (c) send a letter of acknowledgment to the member(s) of the complaint regarding alleged violations along with a request for a response and relevant information related to the complaint and (d) inform members of the Ethics Committee by letter of the case and present a plan of action for investigation.

(d) All information, correspondence, and activities of the Ethics Committee will remain confidential. It shall be determined that no person serving as an investigator on a case have any disqualifying relationship with the alleged violator(s).

(e) The charged party(ies) will have not more than 30 days in which to answer the charges in writing. The charged party(ies) will have free access to all cited evidence from which to make a defense, including the right to legal counsel and a formal hearing before the ASGW Ethics Committee.

(f) Based upon the investigation of the Committee and any designated local ASGW members one of the following recommendations may be made to the Executive Board for appropriate action:
1. Advise that the charges be dropped.

2. Reprimand and admonishment against repetition of the charged conduct.
3. Notify the charged member(s) of his/her right to a formal hearing before the ASGW Ethics Committee, and request a response be made to the Ethics Chairperson as to his/her decision on the matter. Such hearing would be conducted in accordance with the APGA Policy and Procedures for Processing Complaints of Ethical Violations, "Procedures for Hearings," and would be scheduled for a time coinciding with the annual APGA convention. Conditions for such hearing shall also be in accordance with the APGA Policy and Procedures document, "Options Available to the Ethics Committee, item 3."
4. Suspension of membership for a specified period from ASGW.
5. Dismissal from membership in ASGW.

APPENDIX C
CODE OF ETHICS FOR CERTIFIED CLINICAL MENTAL HEALTH COUNSELORS OF THE AMERICAN MENTAL HEALTH COUNSELORS ASSOCIATION

PREAMBLE

Certified Clinical Mental Health Counselors believe in the dignity and worth of the individual. They are committed to increasing knowledge of human behavior and understanding of themselves and others. While pursuing these endeavors, they make every reasonable effort to protect the welfare of those who seek their services or of any subject that may be the object of study. They use their skills only for purposes consistent with these values and do not knowingly permit their misuse by others. While demanding for themselves freedom of inquiry and communication, certified clinical mental health counselors accept the responsibility this freedom confers: competence, objectivity in the application of skills and concern for the best interests of clients, colleagues, and society in general. In the pursuit of these ideals, clinical mental health counselors subscribe to the following principles:

PRINCIPLE 1. RESPONSIBILITY

In their commitment to the understanding of human behavior, clinical mental health counselors value objectivity and integrity,

---

SOURCE: Board of Licensed Professional Counselors in Virginia, *Code of Ethics for Certified Clinical Mental Health Counselors,* pp. 13-19. Copyright by the Board of Licensed Professional Counselors. Reprinted by permission.

This Code is an adaptation of the code of the Board of Licensed Professional Counselors in Virginia.

and in providing services they maintain the highest standards. They accept responsibility for the consequences of their work and make every effort to insure that their services are used appropriately.

a. Clinical mental health counselors accept ultimate responsibility for selecting appropriate areas for investigation and the methods relevant to minimize the possibility that their finding will be misleading. They provide thorough discussion of the limitations of their data and alternative hypotheses, especially where their work touches on social policy or might be misconstrued to the detriment of specific age, sex, ethnic, socioeconomic, or other social categories. In publishing reports of their work, they never discard observations that may modify the interpretation of results. Clinical mental health counselors take credit only for the work they have actually done. In pursuing research, clinical mental health counselors ascertain that their efforts will not lead to changes in individuals or organizations unless such changes are part of the agreement at the time of obtaining informed consent. Clinical mental health counselors clarify in advance the expectations for sharing and utilizing research data. They avoid dual relationships which may limit objectivity, whether theoretical, political, or monetary, so that interference with data, subjects, and milieu is kept to a minimum.
b. As employees of an institution or agency, clinical mental health counselors have the responsibility of remaining alert to institutional pressures which may distort reports of counseling findings or use them in ways counter to the promotion of human welfare.
c. When serving as members of governmental or other organizational bodies, clinical mental health counselors remain accountable as individuals to the Code of Ethics of the National Academy of Certified Mental Health Counselors.
d. As teachers, clinical mental health counselors recognize their primary obligation to help others acquire knowledge and skill. They maintain high standards of scholarship and objectivity by presenting counseling information fully and accurately, and by giving appropriate recognition to alternative viewpoints.
e. As practitioners, clinical mental health counselors know that they bear a heavy social responsibility because their recommendations and professional actions may alter the lives of

others. They, therefore remain fully cognizant of their impact and alert to personal, social, organizational, financial or political situations or pressures which might lead to misuse of their influence.
f. Clinical mental health counselors provide reasonable and timely feedback to employees, trainees, supervisors, students and others whose work they may evaluate.

PRINCIPLE 2. COMPETENCE

The maintenance of high standards of professional competence is a responsibility shared by all clinical mental health counselors in the interest of the public and the profession as a whole. Clinical mental health counselors recognize the boundaries of their competence and the limitations of their techniques and only provide services, use techniques, or offer opinions as professionals that meet recognized standards. Throughout their careers, clinical mental health counselors maintain knowledge of professional information related to the services they render.

a. Clinical mental health counselors accurately represent their competence, education, training and experience.
b. As teachers, clinical mental health counselors perform their duties based on careful preparation so that their instruction is accurate, up-to-date and scholarly.
c. Clinical mental health counselors recognize the need for continuing training to prepare themselves to serve persons of all ages and cultural backgrounds. They are open to new procedures and sensitive to differences between groups of people and changes in expectations and values over time.
d. Clinical mental health counselors with the responsibility for decisions involving individuals or policies based on test results should know and understand literature relevant to the tests used and testing problems with which they deal.
e. Clinical mental health counselors/practitioners recognize that their effectiveness depends in part upon their ability to maintain sound interpersonal relations, that temporary or more enduring aberrations on their part may interfere with their abilities or distort their appraisals of others. Therefore, they refrain from undertaking any activity in which their personal problems are likely to lead to inadequate professional services or harm to a client, or, if they are already engaged in such activity when they become aware of their

personal problems, they would seek competent professional assistance to determine whether they should suspend or terminate services to one or all of their clients.

PRINCIPLE 3. MORAL AND LEGAL STANDARDS

Clinical mental health counselors' moral, ethical and legal standards of behavior are a personal matter to the same degree as they are for any other citizen, except as these may compromise the fulfillment of their professional responsibilities, or reduce the trust in counseling or counselors held by the general public. Regarding their own behavior, clinical mental health counselors should be aware of the prevailing community standards and of the possible impact upon the quality of professional services provided by their conformance to or deviation from these standards. Clinical mental health counselors should also be aware of the possible impact of their public behavior upon the ability of colleagues to perform their professional duties.

a. To protect public confidence in the profession of counseling, clinical mental health counselors will avoid public behavior that is clearly in violation of accepted moral and legal standards.
b. To protect students, counselors/teachers will be aware of the diverse backgrounds of students and, when dealing with topics that may give offense, will see that the material is treated objectively, that it is clearly relevant to the course, and that it is treated in a manner for which the student is prepared.
c. Providers of counseling services conform to the statutes relating to such services as established by their state and its regulating professional board(s).
d. As employees, clinical mental health counselors refuse to participate in employer's practices which are inconsistent with the moral and legal standards established by federal or state legislation regarding the treatment of employees or of the public. In particular and for example, clinical mental health counselors will not condone practices which result in illegal or otherwise unjustifiable discrimination on the basis of race, sex, religion or national origin in hiring, promotion or training.
e. In providing counseling services to clients clinical mental health counselors avoid any action that will violate or diminish the legal and civil rights of clients or of others who may be affected by the action.

f. Sexual conduct, not limited to sexual intercourse, between clinical mental health counselors and clients is specifically in violation of this code of ethics. This does not, however, prohibit the use of explicit instructional aids including films and video tapes. Such use is within accepted practices of trained and competent sex therapists.

PRINCIPLE 4. PUBLIC STATEMENTS

Clinical mental health counselors in their professional roles may be expected or required to make public statements providing counseling information, professional opinions, or supply information about the availability of counseling products and services. In making such statements, clinical mental health counselors take full account of the limits and uncertainties of present counseling knowledge and techniques. They represent, as objectively as possible, their professional qualifications, affiliations, and functions, as well as those of the institutions or organizations with which the statements may be associated. All public statements, announcements of services, and promotional activities should serve the purpose of providing sufficient information to aid the consumer public in making informed judgments and choices on matters that concern it.

a. When announcing professional services, clinical mental health counselors limit the information to: name, highest relevant degree conferred, certification or licensure, address, telephone number, office hours, cost of services, and a brief explanation of the types of services offered but not evaluative as to their quality of uniqueness. They will not contain testimonials by implication. They will not claim uniqueness of skill or methods beyond those available to others in the profession unless determined by acceptable and public scientific evidence.
b. In announcing the availability of counseling services or products, clinical mental health counselors will not display their affiliations with organizations or agencies in a manner that implies the sponsorship or certification of the organization or agency. They will not name their employer or professional associations unless the services are in fact to be provided by or under the responsible, direct supervision and continuing control of such organizations or agencies.
c. Clinical mental health counselors associated with the development or promotion of counseling devices, books, or other

products offered for commercial sale will make every effort to insure that announcements and advertisement are presented in a professional and factually informative manner without unsupported claims of superiority. Such claims must be supported by scientifically acceptable evidence or by willingness to aid and encourage independent professional scrutiny or scientific test.

d. Clinical mental health counselors engaged in radio, television or other public media activities will not participate in commercial announcements recommending to the general public the purchase or use of any proprietary or single-source product or service.

e. Clinical mental health counselors who describe counseling or the services of professional counselors to the general public accept the obligation to present the material fairly and accurately, avoiding misrepresentation through sensationalism, exaggeration or superficiality. Clinical mental health counselors will be guided by the primary obligation to aid the public in forming their own informed judgments, opinions and choices.

f. As teachers, clinical mental health counselors ensure that statements in catalogs and course outlines are accurate, particularly in terms of subject matter to be covered, bases for grading, and nature of classroom experiences. As practitioners providing private services, CMH counselors avoid improper, direct solicitation of clients and the conflict of interest inherent therein.

g. Clinical mental health counselors accept the obligation to correct others who may represent their professional qualifications or associations with products or services in a manner incompatible with these guidelines.

PRINCIPLE 5. CONFIDENTIALITY

Clinical mental health counselors have a primary obligation to safeguard information about individuals obtained in the course of teaching, practice, or research. Personal information if communicated to others only with the person's written consent or in those circumstances where there is clear and imminent danger to the client, to others or to society. Disclosures of counseling information are restricted to what is necessary, relevant, and verifiable.

a. All materials in the official record shall be shared with the client who shall have the right to decide what information may be shared with anyone beyond the immediate provider of service and to be informed of the implications of the materials to be shared.
b. The anonymity of clients served in public and other agencies is preserved, if at all possible, by withholding names and personal identifying data. If external conditions require reporting such information, the client shall be so informed.
c. Information received in confidence by one agency or person shall not be forwarded to another person or agency without the client's written permission.
d. Service providers have a responsibility to insure the accuracy and to indicate the validity of data shared with their parties.
e. Case reports presented in classes, professional meetings, or in publications shall be so disguised that no identification is possible unless the client or responsible authority has read the report and agreed in writing to its presentation or publication.
f. Counseling reports and records are maintained under conditions of security and provisions are made for their destruction when they have outlived their usefulness. Clinical mental health counselors insure that privacy and confidentiality are maintained by all persons in the employ or volunteers, and community aides.
g. Clinical mental health counselors who ask that an individual reveal personal information in the course of interviewing, testing or evaluation, or who allow such information to be divulged, do so only after making certain that the person or authorized representative is fully aware of the purposes of the interview, testing or evaluation and of the ways in which the information will be used.
h. Sessions with clients are taped or otherwise recorded only with their written permission or the written permission of a responsible guardian. Even with guardian written consent one should not record a session against the expressed wishes of a client.
i. Where a child or adolescent is the primary client, the interests of the minor shall be paramount.
j. In work with families, the rights of each family member should be safeguarded. The provider of service also has the responsibility to discuss the contents of the record with the parent

and/or child, as appropriate, and to keep separate those parts which should remain the property of each family member.

PRINCIPLE 6. WELFARE OF THE CONSUMER

Clinical mental health counselors respect the integrity and protect the welfare of the people and groups with whom they work. When there is a conflict of interest between the client and the clinical mental health counselor employing institution, the clinical mental health counselors clarify the nature and direction of their loyalties and responsibilities and keep all parties informed of their commitments. Clinical mental health counselors fully inform consumers as to the purpose and nature of any evaluative treatment, educational or training procedure, and they freely acknowledge that clients, students, or subjects have freedom of choice with regard to participation.

a. Clinical mental health counselors are continually cognizant both of their own needs and of their inherently powerful position vis-à-vis clients, in order to avoid exploiting the client's trust and dependency. Clinical mental health counselors make every effort to avoid dual relationships with clients and/or relationships which might impair their professional judgment or increase the risk of client exploitation. Examples of such dual relationships include treating an employee or supervisor, treating a close friend or family relative and sexual relationships with clients.
b. Where clinical mental health counselors' work with members of an organization goes beyond reasonable conditions of employment, clinical mental health counselors recognize possible conflicts of interests that may arise. When such conflicts occur, clinical mental health counselors clarify the nature of the conflict and inform all parties of the nature and directions of the loyalties and responsibilities involved.
c. When acting as supervisors, trainers, or employers, clinical mental health counselors accord recipients informed choice, confidentiality, and protection from physical and mental harm.
d. Financial arrangements in professional practice are in accord with professional standards that safeguard the best interests of the client and that are clearly understood by the client in advance of billing. This may best be done by the use of a

contract. Clinical mental health counselors are responsible for assisting clients in finding needed services in those instances where payment of the usual fee would be a hardship. No commission or rebate or other form of remuneration may be given or received for referral of clients for professional services, whether by an individual or by an agency.

e. Clinical mental health counselors are responsible for making their services readily accessible to clients in a manner that facilitates the client's ability to make an informed choice when selecting a service provider. This responsibility includes a clear written description of what the client may expect in the way of tests, reports, billing, therapeutic regime and schedules.

f. Clinical mental health counselors who find that their services are not beneficial to the client have the responsibility to make this known to the responsible persons.

g. Clinical mental health counselors are accountable to the parties who refer and support counseling services and to the general public and are cognizant of the indirect or long-range effects of their intervention.

h. The clinical mental health counselor attempts to terminate a private service or consulting relationship when it is reasonably clear to the clinical mental health counselor that the consumer is not benefiting from it. If a consumer is receiving services from another mental health professional, clinical mental health counselors do not offer their services directly to the consumer without informing the professional persons already involved in order to avoid confusion and conflict for the consumer.

PRINCIPLE 7. PROFESSIONAL RELATIONSHIP

Clinical mental health counselors act with due regard to the needs and feelings of their colleagues in counseling and other professions. Clinical mental health counselors respect the prerogatives and obligations of the institutions or organizations with which they are associated.

a. Clinical mental health counselors understand the areas of competence of related professions and make full use of other professional, technical, and administrative resources which best serve the interests of consumers. The absence of formal relationships with other professional workers does not relieve clinical mental health counselors from the responsibility of securing for their clients the best possible professional service; indeed, this circumstance presents a challenge to the professional competence of clinical mental health counselors, requiring special sensitivity to problems outside their areas of training, and foresight, diligence, and tact in obtaining the professional assistance needed by clients.

b. Clinical mental health counselors know and take into account the traditions and practices of other professional groups with which they work and cooperate fully with members of such groups when research, services, and other functions are shared or in working for the benefit of public welfare.

c. Clinical mental health counselors strive to provide positive conditions for those they employ and that they spell out clearly the conditions of such employment. They encourage their employees to engage in activities that facilitate their further professional development.

d. Clinical mental health counselors respect the viability, reputation, and the proprietary right of organizations which they serve. Clinical mental health counselors show due regard for the interest of their present or prospective employers. In those instances where they are critical of policies, they attempt to effect change by constructive action within the organization.

e. In the pursuit of research, clinical mental health counselors give sponsoring agencies, host institutions, and publication channels the same respect and opportunity for giving informed consent that they accord to individual research participants. They are aware of their obligation to future research workers and insure that host institutions are given feedback information and proper acknowledgment.

f. Credit is assigned to those who have contributed to a publication, in proportion to their contribution.

g. When a clinical mental health counselor violates ethical standards, clinical mental health counselors who know firsthand of such activities should, if possible, attempt to rectify the situation. Failing an informal solution, clinical mental health counselors should bring such unethical activities to the National Academy of Certified Clinical Mental Health Counselors.

PRINCIPLE 8. UTILIZATION OF ASSESSMENT TECHNIQUES

In the development, publication, and utilization of counseling assessment techniques, clinical mental health counselors follow relevant standards. Individuals examined, or their legal guardians, have the right to know the results, the interpretations made, and where appropriate, the particulars on which final judgment was based. Test users should take precautions to protect test security but not at the expense of an individual's right to understand the basis for decisions that adversely affect that individual or that individual's dependents.

a. The client has the right to have and the provider has the responsibility to give explanations of test results in language the client can understand.
b. When a test is published or otherwise made available for operational use, it should be accompanied by a manual (or other published or readily available information) that makes every reasonable effort to describe fully the development of the test, the rationale, specifications followed in writing items, analysis or other research. The test, the manual, the record forms and other accompanying material should help users make correct interpretations of the test results and should warn against common misuses. The test manual should state explicitly the purposes and applications for which the test is recommended and identify any special qualifications required to administer the test and to interpret it properly. Evidence of validity and reliability, along with other relevant research data, should be presented in support of any claims made.
c. Norms presented in test manuals should refer to defined and clearly described populations. These populations should be the groups with whom users of the test will ordinarily wish to compare the persons tested. Test users should consider the possibility of bias in tests or in test items. When indicated, there should be an investigation of possible differences in validity for ethnic, sex, or other subsamples that can be identified when the test is given.
d. Clinical mental health counselors who have the responsibility for decisions about individuals or policies that are based on test results should have a thorough understanding of coun-

seling or educational measurement and of validation and other test research.

e. Clinical mental health counselors should develop procedures for systematically eliminating from data files test score information that has, because of the lapse of time, become obsolete.

f. Any individual or organization offering test scoring and interpretation services must be able to demonstrate that their programs are based on appropriate research to establish the validity of the programs and procedures used in arriving at interpretations. The public offering of an automated test interpretation service will be considered as a professional-to-professional consultation. In this the formal responsibility of the consultant is to the consultee but his/her ultimate and overriding responsibility is to the client.

g. Counseling services for the purpose of diagnosis, treatment, or personalized advice are provided only in the context of a professional relationship, and are not given by means of public lectures or demonstrations, newspapers or magazine articles, radio or television programs, mail or similar media. The preparation of personnel reports and recommendations based on test data secured solely by mail is unethical unless such appraisals are an integral part of a continuing client relationship with a company, as a result of which the consulting clinical mental health counselor has intimate knowledge of the client's personal situation and can be assured thereby that his written appraisals will be adequate to the purpose and will be properly interpreted by the client. These reports must not be embellished with such detailed analyses of the subject's personality traits as would be appropriate only for intensive interviews with the subjects.

PRINCIPLE 9. PURSUIT OF RESEARCH ACTIVITIES

The decision to undertake research should rest upon a considered judgment by the individual clinical mental health counselor about how best to contribute to counseling and to human welfare. Clinical mental health counselors carry out their investigations with respect for the people who participate and with concern for their dignity and welfare.

a. In planning a study the investigator has the personal responsibility to make a careful evaluation of its ethical acceptability,

taking into account the following principles for research with human beings. To the extent that this appraisal, weighing scientific and humane values, suggest a deviation from any principle, the investigator incurs an increasingly serious obligation to seek ethical advice and to observe more stringent safeguards to protect the rights of the human research participants.
b. Clinical mental health counselors know and take into account the traditions and practices of other professional groups with members of such groups when research, services, and other functions are shared or in working for the benefit of public welfare.
c. Ethical practice requires the investigator to inform the participant of all features of the research that reasonably might be expected to influence willingness to participate, and to explain all other aspects of the research about which the participant inquires. Failure to make full disclosure gives added emphasis to the investigator's abiding responsibility to protect the welfare and dignity of the research participant.
d. Openness and honesty are essential characteristics of the relationship between investigator and research participant. When the methodological requirements of a study necessitate concealment or deception, the investigator is required to insure as soon as possible the participant's understanding of the reasons for this action and to restore the quality of the relationship with the investigator.
e. In the pursuit of research, clinical mental health counselors give sponsoring agencies, host institutions, and publication channels the same respect and opportunity for giving informed consent that they accord to individual research participants. They are aware of their obligation to future research workers and insure that host institutions are given feedback information and proper acknowledgment.
f. Credit is assigned to those who have contributed to a publication, in proportion to their contribution.
g. The ethical investigator protects participants from physical and mental discomfort, harm and danger. If the risk of such consequences exists, the investigator is required to inform the participant of that fact, secure consent before proceeding, and take all possible measures to minimize distress. A research procedure may not be used if it is likely to cause serious and lasting harm to participants.
h. After the data are collected, ethical practice requires the

investigator to provide the participant with a full clarification of the nature of the study and to remove any misconceptions that may have arisen. Where scientific or humane values justify delaying or withholding information, the investigator acquires a special responsibility to assure that there are no damaging consequences for the participants.

i. Where research procedures may result in undesirable consequences for the participant, the investigator has the responsibility to detect and remove or correct these consequences, including, where relevant, long-term after effects.

j. Information obtained about the research participants during the course of an investigation is confidential. When the possibility exists that others may obtain access to such information, ethical research practice requires that the possibility, together with the plans for protecting confidentiality, be explained to the participants as a part of the procedure for obtaining informed consent.

APPENDIX D
RESPONSIBILITIES OF USERS OF STANDARDIZED TESTS

American Association for Counseling and Development

INTRODUCTION

During the past several years, individual APGA members have been under increasing pressure from their various constituencies to define, provide and employ safeguards against the misuse of standardized tests. APGA as an organization has also been challenged by individuals and agencies to provide leadership in the face of growing concern about the effects of testing on clients of all ages and all subpopulations, and in all settings.

At the 1976 APGA convention, the board of directors requested action on the development of a statement on the responsible use of standardized tests. A committee representing all APGA divisions and regions spent two years studying the issues and developing the following statement.

To furnish perspective for the work of this committee, a review of relevant literature was conducted and each member of the committee received copies of numerous position papers, reports, articles and monographs that added to understanding the issues and the consequences of alternative principles.

Among these papers were the interim report of the 1975-76 APGA Committee on Standardized Testing; the 1972 APGA/

Source: American Personnel & Guidance Association, *APGA Policy Statement: Responsibilities of Users of Standardized Tests.* Copyright 1980 by American Personnel & Guidance Association. Reprinted by permission.

Originally published in Guidepost, October 5, 1978. Reprinted by the Association for Measurement and Evaluation in Guidance, a division of the American Personnel and Guidance Association. Additional copies may be ordered from APGA Publication Sales, Two Skyline Place, Suite 400, 5203 Leesburg Pike, Falls Church, VA 22041.

AMEG Statement on the Responsible Use of Tests; position papers of individual divisions and of other professional organizations such as the American Psychological Association, the American Educational Research Association and the National Council on Measurement in Education; journal articles; and conference presentations.

The committee's statement is intended to be sensitive to current and emerging problems and concerns that are generic to all APGA divisions/regions and to address these problems and concerns with principles that are specific enough to serve as a template to develop division/region statements addressed to the specific disciplines/settings of individual divisions/regions.

Target Audience

The statement is intended to present the position and address the needs of the professional members of APGA divisions and regions. Although this position may provide guidance for test developers, teachers, administrators, parents, press or the general public, it is not designed to represent these audiences. The statement is built on the assumption that test data of themselves are neutral and that guidelines are needed to promote constructive use of tests.

Organization and Focus

The statement is organized into eight sections: Introduction, Decision Rules, Test Selection, Qualifications of Test Users, Test Administration, Scoring of Tests, Test Interpretation and Communication. Each section is directed toward the various uses and decisions that must be made by the test user (e.g., whether to test, which test(s) to use, what data to obtain, how to interpret, etc.). The committee developed a classification system for the uses of standardized tests and treated only those issues that fit into the use classification scheme.

The next step was to define issues related to the classification system. Issues were sought from individuals, professional statements, literature and the popular press. Issues were examined in terms of their relevance to APGA members and to their importance in terms of the possible consequences to the person(s) tested.

Only the principles underlying each issue are specified. These principles are appropriate as standards for all APGA divisions and regions. Divisions and regions are encouraged to develop their own statements, expanding on each principle with specific procedures and examples and appropriate to their members. The principles are grouped around similar issues and are indexed for easy reference.

DECISION RULES

In human service agencies, decisions about client needs may be made on the basis of direct observation or historical information alone. Further refinement of direct observation and historical data can often be obtained by employing standardized tests.

Deciding whether to test creates the possibility of three classes of errors relative to the agency functions of description, diagnosis, prescription, selection, placement, prediction, growth evaluation, etc.

First, a decision not to test can result in misjudgments that stem solely from inadequate data.

Second, tests may be used well, producing data that could improve accuracy in decisions affecting the client but that are not utilized.

Third, tests may be misused through inappropriate selection, improper administration, inaccurate scoring, incompetent interpretation or indiscriminate, inadequate, or inaccurate communication.

To reduce the chance for errors, the responsible practitioner will always determine in advance why a given test should be used. This provides protection and benefits for both the client and the agency. Having a clearly developed rationale increases the probable benefits of testing by indicating how a particular set of information, when used by an individual or set of individuals, will contribute to a sounder decision without prejudice to either the client or the agency.

The guidelines that follow are intended to provide decision rules to help agencies and practitioners avoid charges of irresponsible practice.

Defining Purposes for Testing

1. Decide whether you will be testing to evaluate individuals, groups or both.
2. Identify your interests in the particular target population in terms of the agency's purposes and capabilities.
3. Determine limits to diagnosis, prediction or selection

created by age, racial, sexual, ethnic or cultural characteristics of those to be tested.
4. Develop specific objectives and limits for the use of test data in relation to each of the component service areas of placement/selection, prediction (expectancies), description/diagnosis and growth studies (assessing change over time).

A. Placement. If the purpose is selection or placement (selection is a simple in-out sort of placement), the test selector and interpreter must know about the programs or institutions in which the client may be placed and be able to judge the consequences of such placement or exclusion for the client.

B. Prediction/expectancies. If the purpose is prediction, the persons deciding to test and/or interpret the results must understand the pitfalls of labeling, stereotyping and prejudging people. Ways to avoid these potentially invidious outcomes should be known.

C. Description/diagnosis. If the purpose is diagnosis or description, the selector or interpreter should understand enough about the general domain being measured to be able to identify those aspects adequately measured and those not.

D. Growth/change assessment. If the purpose is to examine growth, the person designing the study and interpreting the results needs to know the many problems associated with such measurement:

1. the unreliability of change measures;
2. the pitfalls in using norms as reference points;
3. the associated problems of articulation and comparability;
4. the limitations of scoring scales, such as grade equivalents, that may not have the comparable meaning which they appear to have at different scale levels.

Determining Information Needs

1. Assess the consequences for the clients of both testing or not testing.
2. Determine what decisions can be made with existing information to avoid unnecessary data-gathering efforts.
3. Limit data gathering to those functions or aptitude, achievement, interests/attitudes/values and perceptual-

motor skills that are directly relevant in making decisions about delivery of services to a particular individual or group.
4. Identify whether the test being considered can provide acceptable levels of precision (reliability) for the decision being made.
5. Identify whether the data obtained can be cross-validated against other available data as a part of the decision-making process.
6. Determine the amount and form of data to be shared on the basis of maximum relevance to the agency's purposes and capabilities.

Identifying Users of Test Information

1. Data should be prepared so that they can be comprehended by the persons using the data for decision-making.
2. Limit access to users specifically authorized by the law or by the client.
3. Identify obsolescence schedules so that stored personal test data may be systematically reclassified and relocated to historical files or destroyed.
4. Process personal data used for research or program evaluation so as to assure individual anonymity.

QUALIFICATIONS OF TEST USERS

All professional personnel and guidance workers should have formal training in psychological and educational measurement and testing. Nevertheless, it is unreasonable to expect that this training necessarily makes one an expert or even that an expert always has all the knowledge and skill appropriate to any particular situation. Thus, questions of user qualifications should always arise when testing is being considered.

Those who participate in any aspect of testing should be qualified to do so. Lack of proper qualifications leads to misuse, errors and sometimes damage to clients. Each professional is responsible for making judgment on this matter in each situation and cannot leave that responsibility either to clients or to those in authority.

In many instances information or skills that may be lacking can be acquired quite readily by those with a background of professional training and experience. In all instances it is incumbent upon the individual to obtain that training or arrange for proper supervision and assistance when engaged in, or planning to engage in, testing.

The requisite qualifications for test users depend on four factors: (1) the particular role of the user; (2) the setting in which the use takes place; (3) the nature of the test; and (4) the purpose of the testing.

These factors interact with each other but may nevertheless be considered separately for the purposes of these standards.

Roles of Test Users, Selectors, Administrators, Scorers and Interpreters

A test user may play all of these roles or any subset of them when working with other professional personnel. In some situations each role may be the responsibility of a different person. The knowledge and skills that pertain to these roles are listed under the sections so headed. The general principle is that the test users should engage in only those testing activities for which their training and experience qualify them.

Settings and Conditions of Test Use

Counselors and personnel workers should assess the quality and relevance of their knowledge and skills to the situation before deciding to test or to participate in a testing program.

Characteristics of Tests

Tests differ in many ways, and users need to understand the peculiarities of the instruments they are using.

Purposes of Testing

The purpose of the testing dictates how the test is used and thus may influence requisite qualifications of users beyond those entailed by their testing roles. Technically proper use for ill-understood purposes may constitute misuse.

TEST SELECTION

Tests should be selected for a specific measurement purpose, use and interpretation. The selection of tests should be guided by information obtained from a careful analysis of the following major considerations:

What are the characteristics of the population to be tested?
What knowledge, skills, abilities or attitudes are to be assessed?
What are the purposes for testing?
How will the test scores be used and interpreted?

When complete answers to these questions have been obtained, selection or development of tests should be directed toward obtaining measures that are congruent with the stated needs for assessment in terms of the purposes, content, use, interpretation and particular characteristics of the individuals who are to be tested.

Selection of tests must also be guided by the criteria of technical quality recommended by the measurement profession and published by APA/AERA/NCME in "Standards for Educational and Psychological Tests" (1974). Full recognition and analysis of these considerations should become the focus of a process to select appropriate tests. The responsible test selector will:

Select Appropriate Tests

1. Select tests that have been demonstrated, to the satisfaction of professional specialists, as appropriate for the characteristics of the population to be tested.
2. Select tests that are within the level of skills of administration and interpretation possessed by the practitioner.
3. Determine whether a common test or different tests are required for the accurate measurement of groups with different characteristics.
4. Recognize that different tests for cultural, ethnic and racial groups constitute inefficient means for making corrections for differences in prior life experiences, except where different languages are involved.
5. Determine whether persons or groups that use different languages should be tested in either or both languages and in some instance by prior testing for bilingualism.

Relate Evidence or Validity to Particular Usage

1. Apply tests or selection only when they show predictive

validity for the specific tasks or competencies needed in an educational or employment assignment to maintain legal prescriptions for non-discriminatory practices in selection, employment or placement.
2. Determine validity of a test (whether the test measures what it claims to measure) through evidence of the constructs used in developing the measures, the correlation of the test performance with another appraisal of the characteristics being measured, or the predictions of specified behavior from the test performance.
3. Determine that the content of the test has high congruence with the users' definition of the knowledge and skills that are the desired criteria of human performance to be appraised.
4. Confirm that the criteria of human performance to be appraised are contained in the tasks and results of the testing procedure.

Employ User Participation in Test Selection

Actively involve the persons who will be using the tests (administering, scoring, summarizing, interpreting, making decisions) in the selection of tests that are congruent with the locally determined purposes, conditions and uses of the measurement.

Select Tests to Satisfy Local Use

1. Give specific attention to how the test is designed to handle the variation of motivation among persons taking the test, the variation or bias in response to the test content and the effects of the presence or absence of guessing in the responses to the test questions.
2. Determine whether tests standardized for nationwide use show evidence that such tests yield comparable results for individuals or groups with cultural differences.
3. Identify and analyze the effects of working speed and language facility in relation to the criteria of human performance that are expected to result from the test.

Consider Technical Characteristics of Tests

1. Select only published or locally developed tests that have documented evidence of the reliability of consistency of the measure.

2. Select tests that have documented evidence of the effectiveness of the measure for the purpose to be served: placement/selection, prediction (expectancy), description/diagnosis, or growth studies (change over time). A test is rarely equally effective for the four common test uses.
3. Consider the procedures used in standardization and norming for relevance to the local population and the desired use and interpretation.
4. Use separate norms for men and women only when empirical evidence indicates this is necessary to minimize bias.
5. Determine the degree of reliability (or validity) demanded of a test on the basis of the nature of the decisions to be based on test scores.
6. A test for final diagnosis or selection requires a higher degree of reliability than an initial screening test.
7. Explicitly list and use the ease and accuracy of the procedures for scoring, summarizing and communicating test performance as criteria for selecting a test.
8. Recognize that the technical characteristics and norms of standardized tests may vary when used with different populations. The selection process should include trial administrations to verify that the test is functioning with the technical characteristics and desired results for the local population and local uses.

Practical constraints of cost, conditions and time for testing must be considered but not used as the primary criteria for test selection.

TEST ADMINISTRATION

Test administration includes all procedures that are used to ensure that the test is presented consistently in the manner specified by the test developers and used in the standardization and that the individuals being tested have orientation and conditions that maximize opportunity for optimum performance.

Standardized tests should provide manuals giving specific directions for administering, scoring and interpreting tests. Tests developed for a specific local purpose, use or population should be administered in a prescribed and consistent manner to obtain optimum performance from the individuals being tested. Effective administration of tests requires that the administrator have knowledge and training with the instruments and the processes of presentation.

Orientation

1. Inform testing candidates, relevant institutions or agencies and the community about the testing procedure. The orientation should describe the purposes and contents sampled by the test, how it is administered and how the scores will be reported and used.
2. Provide annual training for test administrators by qualified professional specialists if your agency or institution uses tests or sponsors testing programs.
3. Routinely review the test materials and administration conditions well in advance of the time for testing so that full preparation will ensure standardized administration and recognition of any irregularities that may occur.
4. Ensure that the orientation is sufficient to make the test relevant for the individual or group being tested before beginning test administration.
5. Ensure that all persons being tested have the specified practice with sample problems or test taking skills prior to their performance on the test.
6. Demonstrate the techniques and requirements for marking machine-scorable answer sheets. Check all individuals taking a test for competency in the techniques of recording their answers prior to the specific period of testing.

Qualifications of Test Administrators

1. Administer standardized tests only if you are qualified by training and experience as competent to administer particular tests.
2. Know the exact population and procedures used in standardizing the test and determine that the test is appropriate for the local population that is to be tested.
3. Acquire extensive training required to administer, score or interpret tests requiring test-specific training.

Giving Directions

1. Administer standardized tests with the verbatim instructions, exact sequence and timing and the identical materials that were used in the test standardization.

2. Present all tests (whether standardized, published or locally constructed) in an identical manner to ensure that the test is a fair and comparable demonstration of the performance of each individual taking the test.

Recognize that taking a test may be a new and frightening experience or stimulate anxiety or frustration for some individuals. Communicate to the examinees that they should attempt each task with positive application of their skills and knowledge and the anticipation that they will do their best.

Testing Conditions

1. Devote concentrated attention to observing the condition and reactions of the individuals being tested. Observe those being tested and identify environmental, health or emotional conditions that should be recorded and considered as invalidating elements for the test performance.
2. Possess and demonstrate clear verbal articulation, calmness and positive anticipation, empathy for social identification with the examinees, and, impartial treatment for all being tested.
3. Determine whether the testing environment (seating, work surfaces, lighting, heating, freedom from distractions, etc.) is conducive to the best possible performance of the test-takers.
4. Administer tests in physical facilities and psychological climates that allow each individual being tested to achieve optimum performance.
5. Record any deviation from standardized test administration procedure (such as used to accommodate handicapping conditions) and make it a permanent attachment to the test score or record.
6. Develop and complete for each test a systematic and objective procedure for observing and recording the behavior of those being tested (and recording conventional or deviant conditions of testing). Attach this record to the test scores of the persons tested.
7. Provide a written record of any circumstances that may have increased or reduced the opportunity of an individual being tested to demonstrate his or her best performance.
8. Accept responsibility for seeing that invalid or question-

able test scores are not recorded, or not recorded without written qualification of the conditions that may have affected optimum test performance.
9. Arrange assistance from trained personnel in providing uniform conditions and in observing the conduct of the examinees when large groups of individuals must be tested.

Professional Collaboration

Recognize that in institutional settings, and wherever skill and knowledge can be pooled and responsibility shared, it is the qualifications of the team as a whole that count rather than those of individuals. However, coordination and consistency must be maintained.

TEST SCORING

The measurement of human performance depends on accurate and consistent application of defined procedures for crediting the responses made by persons being tested. The procedures for scoring and recording test performance must be continuously audited for consistency and accuracy.

1. Routinely rescore a sample of the test answer sheets to verify the accuracy of the initial scoring.
2. Employ systematic procedures to verify the accuracy and consistency of machine scoring of answer sheets.
3. Obtain a separate and independent verification that appropriate scoring rules and normative conversions are used for each person tested.
4. Verify as accurate the computation of raw scores and the conversion of raw scores to normative or descriptive scales prior to release of such information to the tested person or to users of the test results.
5. Routinely check machine or manual reports of test results for accuracy. The person performing this task must be qualified to recognize inappropriate or impossible scores.
6. Develop and use systematic and objective procedures for observing and recording the conditions and behaviors of persons being tested and make this a part of the scores or test results that are reported.
7. Clearly label the scores that are reported and the date that a particular test was administered.

TEST INTERPRETATION

Test interpretation encompasses all the ways we assign value to the scores.

A test can be described as a systematic set or series of standard observations of performances that all fall in some particular domain. Typically each observation yields a rating of the performance (such as right or wrong and pass or fail), then these ratings are counted and this count becomes the basis of the scores. Such scores are usually much more stable than the result of any single performance. This score reliability creates the possibility of validity greater than can be obtained from unsystematic or nonaggregated observations.

The proper interpretation of test scores starts with understanding these fundamental characteristics of tests. Given this, the interpretation of scores from a test entails knowledge about (1) administration and scoring procedures; (2) scores, norms, and related technical features; (3) reliability; and (4) validity.

Adequate test interpretation requires knowledge and skill in each of these areas. Some of this information can be mastered only by studying the manual and other materials of the test; no one should undertake the interpretation of scores on any test without such study.

Administration and Scoring

Standard procedures for administering and scoring the test limit the possible meanings of scores. Departures from standard conditions and procedures modify and often invalidate the criteria for score interpretation.

1. The principles in the section on administration and scoring need to be understood by those engaged in interpretation.
2. Ascertain the circumstances peculiar to the particular administration and scoring of the test.
    A. Examine all reports from administrators, proctors and scorers concerning irregularities or conditions, such as excessive anxiety, which may have affected performance.
    B. Weigh the possible effects on test scores of examiner-examinee differences in ethnic and cultural background, attitudes and values in light of research on

these matters. Recognize that such effects are probably larger in individual testing situations.
   C. Look for administrators' reports of examinee behavior that indicate the responses were made on some basis other than that intended — as when a student being tested for knowledge of addition-number-facts adds by making tallies and then counting them.
3. Consider differences among clients in their reaction to instructions about guessing and scoring.
4. Recognize or judge the effect of scorer biases and judgment when subjective elements enter into scoring.

Scores, Norms, and Related Technical Features

The result of scoring a test is usually a number (or a set of numbers) called a raw score. Raw scores taken by themselves are not usually interpretable. Some additional steps must be taken.

The procedures either translate the numbers directly into descriptions of their meaning (e.g., pass or fail) or into other numbers called derived scores (e.g., standard scores) whose meaning stems from the test norms.

To interpret test scores, these procedures and the resulting descriptions or derived scores need to be thoroughly understood. Anything less than full understanding is likely to produce at least some, and probably many, serious errors in interpretation. The following are imperatives for interpreting tests:

1. Examine the test manuals, handbooks, users' guides and technical reports to determine what descriptions or derived scores are produced and what unique characteristics each may have.
2. Recognize that direct score interpretations such as mastery and nonmastery in criterion-referenced tests depend on arbitrary rules or standards.
   A. Report number or percent of items right in addition to the indicated interpretation whenever it will help others understand the quality of the examinee's test performance.
   B. Recognize that the difficulty of a fixed standard, such as 80 percent right, will vary widely from objective to objective. Such scores are not comparable in the normative sense.
   C. Recognize that when each score is classified as pass-

fail, mastery-nonmastery or the like, that each element is being given equal weight.
3. Use the derived scores that fit the needs of the current use of the test.
    A. Use percentile ranks for direct comparison of individuals to the norm or reference group.
    B. Use standard scores or equal unit scaled scores whenever means and variances are calculated or other arithmetic operations are being used.
4. Recognize that only those derived scores that are based on the same norm group can be compared.
5. Consider the effect of any differences between the tests in what they measure when one test or form is equated with another, as well as the errors stemming from the equating itself.

    Give greater credence to growth or change shown by the same test (including level and form) than to equated measures except where practice effects or feedback have destroyed the validity of a second use.
6. Evaluate the appropriateness of the norm groups available as bases for interpreting the scores of clients.
    A. Use the norms for the group to which the client belongs.
    B. Consider using local norms and derived scores based on these local norms whenever possible.
7. Acquire knowledge of specific psychological or educational concepts and theories before interpreting the scores of tests based on such knowledge.

Reliability

Reliability is a prerequisite to validity. Generally, the greater the number of items the greater the reliability of the test. The degree to which a score or a set of scores may vary because of measurement error is a central factor in interpretation.

1. Use the standard error of measurement to obtain a rough estimate of the probable variation in scores due to unreliability.
2. Use the reliability coefficient to estimate the proportion of score variance that is not due to error.
3. Consider the sources of variance attributable to error in

the particular reliability indexes reported in relationship to the uses being made of the scores.
   4. Assess reported reliabilities in light of the many extraneous factors that may have artificially raised or lowered these estimates, such as test speededness, sample homogeneity or heterogeneity, restrictions in range and the like.
   5. Distinguish indexes of rater reliability (i.e., of objectivity) from test reliability.

Validity

Proper test interpretation requires knowledge of the validity evidence available for the test as used. Its validity for other uses is not relevant. The purpose of testing dictates how a test is used. Technically proper use for ill-understood purposes may constitute misuse. The nature of the validity evidence required for a test is a function of its use.

Prediction — developing expectancies: The relationship of the test scores to an independently developed criterion measure is the basis for predictive validity.

1. Consider both the reliability and the relevance of the criterion measures used.
2. Use cross-validation data to judge the validity of predictions.
3. Question the meaning of an apparently valid predictor that lacks both construct and content validity. Assess the role of underlying and concomitant variables.
4. Consider the validity of a given measure in the context of all the predictors used or available. Does the measure make an independent contribution to the prediction over and above that provided by other measures?
5. Consider the pitfalls of labeling, stereotyping and prejudging people. The self-fulfilling prophecies that may result are often undesirable.

Placement/selection: Predictive validity is the usual basis for valid placement. Consider the evidence of validity for each alternative (i.e., each placement) when inferring the meaning of scores.

1. Obtain adequate information about the programs or insti-

tutions in which the client may be placed in order to judge the consequences of such placement.
2. Estimate the probability of favorable outcomes for each possible placement (e.g., both selection and rejection) before judging the import of the scores.
3. Consider the possibility that outcomes favorable from an institutional point of view may differ from those that are favorable from the examinees' point of view.
4. Examine the possibility that the clients' group membership (race, sex, etc.) may alter the reported validity relationships.
5. Use all the available evidence about the individual to infer the validity of the score for that individual. Each single piece of information about an individual, (e.g., test score, teacher report, or counselor opinion) improves the probability that proper judgments and decisions can be made.
   A. Test scores should be considered in context; they do not have absolute meaning.
   B. Single test scores should not be the sole basis for placement or selection.

Description/diagnosis: Distinguish between those descriptions and diagnoses using psychological constructs that can be validated only indirectly and those for which content specifications suffice.

1. Identify clearly the domain specified by those asserting content validity. Assess the adequacy of the content sampling procedures used in writing and selecting items.
2. Identify the dimensions of the construct being measured when multiple scores from a battery or inventory are used for description.
   A. Examine the content validity and/or the construct validity of each score separately.
   B. Consider the relative importance of the various subtests, parts, objectives or elements yielding separate scores and judge the weight they each should be given in interpretation.
   C. Recognize that when scores are summed or averaged, their weight is a function of their variances.
   D. Recognize that when each score is classified as pass-fail, mastery-nonmastery or the like, each element is being given equal weight.

3. Examine the completeness of the description provided, recognizing that no set of test scores completely describes a human being.

Growth — Studies of change: Valid assessment of growth or change requires both a test having descriptive validity and a procedure for establishing that the scores obtained differ from those that might arise when no change has occurred.

1. Report as possibilities all the interpretations the study or evaluation design permits. Point out those interpretations that are precluded by the design used.
    A. When standard procedures such as the RMC models (see Tallmadge, G.K., and Horst, D.P., A procedural guide for validating achievement gains in educational projects; Mountain View, Calif: RMC Research Corp., Dec. 1975) for measuring growth in achievement are employed, use the descriptions of strengths and weaknesses provided.
    B. Look for naturally occurring control groups not part of design whenever possible.
2. Consider the strengths and weaknesses of the particular tests used with respect to this use.
    Consider the possibility of floor or ceiling effects, the content changes level to level, the adequacy of articulation in multilevel tests, the comparability of alternate forms, the adequacy of the score-equating across forms, and the comparability of timing of the testing to that of the norming.
3. Recognize the unreliability of individual score differences as measures of change.
4. Recognize the limitations of scoring scales such as grade equivalents that may not have the comparable meaning they appear to have at different levels of the scale.
5. Recognize the need for equal interval scales when trying to assess the amount of change.

COMMUNICATING TEST RESULTS

Communication consists of reporting data in such a way that it is comprehensible and informative. The responsible practitioner reports test data with a concern for the user's need for information and the purposes of evaluating the significance of the information.

There must also be a concern for the right of the individual tested to be informed regarding how the results will be used for his or her benefit (informed consent), who will have access to the results (right to privacy), and what safeguards exist to prevent misuse.

Where standardized test data are being used to enhance decisions about an individual, the practitioner's responsibilities are as follows:

Know the Manual

1. Become thoroughly familiar with the publisher's manual before attempting to "explain" any results.
2. Develop skills needed to communicate results of tests, using concepts that are frequently misunderstood before communicating results to clients, the public, or other recipients of the information.

Know the Limits

1. Inform the person receiving the test information that "scores" are approximations, not absolutes, and indicate the SEM or the margin of error in some other way, such as by reporting score intervals rather than points.
2. Candidly discuss with the person receiving the test information any qualifications necessary to understand potential sources of bias for a given set of test results relative to their use with a specific individual.
3. Emphasize that test data represent just one source of information and should rarely, if ever, be used alone for decision making.

Informed Consent

1. Inform the person receiving the test information of any circumstances that could have affected the validity or reliability of the results.
2. Inform the examinee of what action will be taken by the agency and who will be using the results.
3. Obtain the consent of the examinee before using test

results for any purpose other than that advanced prior to testing.

Right to Privacy

Inform the examinee of steps to be taken to correct any erroneous information that may be on file as a result of testing.

Where standardized test data are being used to describe groups for the purpose of evaluation, the practitioner's responsibilities are as follows:

Background Information

1. Include background information to improve the accuracy of understanding about any numerical data.
2. Identify the purposes for which the reported data would be appropriate.

Politics

Be aware that public release of test information provides data for all kinds of purposes and that some of these may be adverse to the interests of those tested.

Averages and Norms

1. Clarify in particular that "average" on a standardized test is a range, not a point, and typically includes the middle 50 percent of the group being considered.
2. Qualify all group data in terms of the appropriateness of the norms for that group.

Agency Policies

1. Work for agency test-reporting policies designed to strengthen and protect the benefits of the groups being measured.
2. Work within the agency to establish procedures for periodic review of internal test use.

APPENDIX E
CREDENTIALING INFORMATION

Information on counselor certifications can be obtained from:

National Board for Certified Counselors, Inc.
5999 Stevenson Avenue
Alexandria, VA 22304

National Council for Credentialing of Career Counselors
c/o NBCC
5999 Stevenson Avenue
Alexandria, VA 22304

National Academy for Certified Clinical Mental Health Counselors
5999 Stevenson Avenue
Alexandria, VA 22304

Commission on Rehabilitation Counselor Certification
162 North State Street
Suite 317
Chicago, IL 60601

American Association for Marriage and Family Therapy
1717 K Street, N.W.
Suite 407
Washington, DC 20006

Information on program accreditations and licensures for counselors and psychologists, respectively, can be obtained from:

American Association for Counseling and Development
5999 Stevenson Avenue
Alexandria, VA 22304

American Psychological Association
1200 Seventeenth Street, N.W.
Washington, DC 20036

APPENDIX F
COUNSELING-RELATED ORGANIZATIONS

American Association for Counseling and Development
5999 Stevenson Avenue
Alexandria, VA 22304

Divisions:
American College Personnel Association
Association for Counselor Education and Supervision
National Career Development Association
Association for Humanistic Education and Development
American School Counselor Association
American Rehabilitation Counseling Association
Association for Measurement and Evaluation in Counseling and Development
National Employment Counselors Association
Association for Multicultural Counseling and Development
Association for Religious and Value Issues in Counseling
Association for Specialists in Group Work
American Mental Health Counselors Association
Public Offender Counselor Association
Military Educators and Counselors Association

American Psychological Association
Division 17/Counseling Psychology
1200 Seventeenth Street, N.W.
Washington, DC 20036

American Association for Marriage and Family Therapy
1717 K Street, N.W.
Suite 407
Washington, DC 20006

American Orthopsychiatric Association
19 W. 44th Street
New York, NY 10036

American Educational Research Association
Division H/Counseling and Human Development
1230 17th Street, N.W.
Washington, DC 20036

American Vocational Association
1025 15th Street, N.W.
Washington, DC 20005

APPENDIX G
RELEVANT PROFESSIONAL PUBLICATIONS

Journals of the American Association for Counseling and Development:

> Journal of Counseling and Development
> Journal of College Student Personnel
> Counselor Education and Supervision
> Vocational Guidance Quarterly
> Journal of Humanistic Education and Development
> The School Counselor
> Elementary School Guidance and Counseling Journal
> Rehabilitation Counseling Bulletin
> Measurement and Evaluation in Counseling and Development
> Journal of Employment Counseling
> Journal of Multicultural Counseling and Development
> Counseling and Values
> Journal for Specialists in Group Work
> Journal of Offender Counseling
> American Mental Health Counselors Association Journal

Counseling-related journals of the American Psychological Association:

> American Psychologist
> Journal of Counseling Psychology
> The Counseling Psychologist
> Journal of Consulting & Clinical Psychology
> Journal of Personality & Social Psychology

Other relevant journals:

Counseling and Human Development
Exceptional Children
Journal of Vocational Behavior
Journal of Community Psychology
American Journal of Community Psychology
American Journal of Orthopsychiatry
Community Mental Health Journal
Journal of Marriage and Family Counseling
Journal of Marriage and the Family
American Educational Research Journal
Review of Educational Research
Phi Delta Kappan
Journal of Humanistic Psychology

APPENDIX H
EDUCATION FOR ALL HANDICAPPED CHILDREN ACT, PL 94-142: A SUMMARY

HISTORY

On November 29, 1975, President Ford signed the Education for All Handicapped Children Act (PL 94-142). This act extends the existing education of the handicapped and adds some important new dimensions. PL 94-142 was enacted as a result of congressional findings which included: (1) that there are over 8 million handicapped children in the United States today, (2) that the special education needs of such children are not being fully met, (3) that more than half of the handicapped children in the United States do not receive appropriate education services enabling them to have full equality of opportunity, (4) that 1 million of the handicapped children are entirely excluded from public school systems, (5) that there are children in the public education system whose handicapping conditions have not yet been diagnosed, (6) that parents have been forced to provide, at their own expense, education for their handicapped children outside the public school, and (7) that technology for educating handicapped children is available and all that is lacking is the necessary funding, (8) that state educational agencies (SEA) and local educational agencies (LEA) have the responsibility to provide education for all handicapped children, and (9) that it is in the national interest that the federal government assist the state and local efforts to provide programs to meet the educa-

---

Source: From "Education for all Handicapped Children Act" by Joseph Ballard, *Public Law, 94-142,* 1980 (Rev. Ed.) pp. 2-13. Copyright 1980 by The Council for Exceptional Children. Reprinted with permission.

tional needs of handicapped children in order to assure equal protection of the law.

Handicapped children are defined by PL 94-142 as mentally retarded, hard of hearing, deaf, speech impaired, visually handicapped, seriously emotionally disturbed, orthopaedically impaired, or other health impaired, or children with specific learning disabilities who by reason thereof require special education and related services. The definition given to specific learning disabilities is: "those children who have a disorder in one or more of the basic psychological processes involved in understanding or in using language spoken or written, which disorder may manifest itself in imperfect ability to listen, think, speak, read, write, spell, or do mathematical calculations." This term does not include children who have learning problems which are primarily the results of visual, hearing, or motor handicaps, of mental retardation, of emotional disturbance, or of environmental, cultural, or economic disadvantage.

MAJOR PROVISIONS OF PL 94-142

In order for a state to become eligible for the funding, the state must demonstrate to the Commissioner of Education that the following conditions are met:

1. A Free, Appropriate Public Education Must be Assured to All Handicapped Children

States accustomed to providing only caretaking facilities for their institutionalized multiply and severely handicapped citizens will now find it important to provide educational facilities within state institutions for children ages three to twenty-one. Children who have not received an educational program which fits their particular need to children who have gone undiagnosed but remained in the public school classroom must receive attention under PL 94-142.

Children with difficult and/or unexplained handicaps are often removed from our public educational process, and the parent is then left with the staggering expense of a residential or day school which can provide some education for their handicapped child. With the passage of PL 94-142, there exists for parents a set of procedures through which they can demand justice for their child.

2. Least Restrictive Environment or Alternative (LRE)

Educators throughout the country are struggling to define least restrictive alternatives or least restrictive environments. LRE is commonly associated with the concept of "mainstreaming." There are some great differences when one considers the multiply severely handicapped child for whom the least restrictive environment may be a self-contained classroom within a public school building, as well as the child with a mild handicap who spends some time in a resource room. There are many facets to examine when considering the least restrictive environment for a child who is handicapped. It does tend to enforce consideration of the particular program provided by those educators dealing with the child. In this sense, it encourages the spirit of the law. Much work will be given in a short period of time to determine least restrictive alternatives for all handicapped children.

3. Individual Education Plan

The Individual Education Plan (IEP) which must be furnished and maintained for each handicapped child through his local educational agency is a central issue of the entire PL 94-142. This individualized education plan is required to be on record with each state office of education. Although no guidelines or format have yet been developed for the IEP, it is meant to plan and track the progress of each child throughout his years of education. This educational plan is to be developed jointly with the educational and support staff involved with the child, the parent, and sometimes the child. The educational plan shall include according to the law: (a) a statement of the present levels of educational performance of the child, (b) a statement of annual goals including short-term instructional objectives, (c) a statement of the specific educational services to be provided each child and the extent to which the child will be able to participate in regular education programs, and (d) a date for initiation and anticipated duration of the services as well as evaluation procedures and schedules for determining, on at least an annual basis, whether instructional objectives are being achieved.

These plans are to be on file for all children in both public and private educational institutions. A properly developed educational plan with long-term and short-term goals should assure a free appropriate education for all and education within the least restrictive environment. The plan will furnish a method of validation of the educational process for the handicapped child.

4. Confidentiality of Student Information

Section 617 (c) of PL 94-142 provides that the secretary of education shall assure "the protection of the confidentiality of any personally identifiable data, information, and records collected or maintained by the commissioner and by state and local educational agencies pursuant to the provisions of this act." The Buckley Amendment deals strongly with the confidentiality of all records. Guidelines controlling the management of information by school districts have been incorporated into common practice in many states. The rules and regulations governing special education in Illinois were recently updated and provide stringent requirements to guard the confidentiality of student records. Records are now open to parents and/or to students over eighteen. Since students and parents now have recourse against records they deem to be incorrect or worse, school districts are attempting to record only factual, verified information. The ACT specifically decrees that information collected by the state or federal offices of education will be protected to assure confidentiality.

5. Due Process

If parents are not satisfied that a free, appropriate education is being provided to their handicapped child, they have the right to an impartial due process hearing. Disagreements regarding identification, evaluation, and educational placement may also be resolved at a due process hearing.

APPENDIX I
COMMONLY USED ASSESSMENT TOOLS & TEST PUBLISHERS

American College Test
American College Testing
 Program
P.O. Box 168
Iowa City, Iowa 52240

Bender Visual Motor Gestalt Test
American Orthopsychiatric Association, Inc.
1790 Broadway
New York, New York 10019

California Psychological Inventory
Consulting Psychologists Press, Inc.
577 College Avenue
Palo Alto, California 94306

California Test of Mental Maturity
CTB/McGraw-Hill
Del Monte Research Park
Monterey, California 93940

California Test of Personality
California Test Bureau
Del Monte Research Park
Monterey, California 93940

Career Counseling Personal Data Form
Martin M. Bruce
340 Oxford Road
New Rochelle, New York 10804

Columbia Mental Maturity Scale
Harcourt Brace Jovanovich, Inc.
757 Third Avenue
New York, New York 10017

Cooperative School and College Ability Tests
Cooperative Test Division
Educational Testing Service
Princeton, New Jersey 08540

Edwards Personal Preference Schedule
Psychological Corporation
304 East 45th Street
New York, New York 10017

Edwards Personality Inventory
Science Research Associates, Inc.
P.O. Box 10021
1450 Page Mill Road
Palo Alto, California 94303

Graduate Record Examinations Aptitude Test
Educational Testing Service
Princeton, New Jersey 08540

Henman Nelson Tests of Mental Ability
Houghton-Mifflin Company
2 Park Street
Boston, Massachusetts 02107

Iowa Test of Educational Development
Science Research Associates
259 East Erie Street
Chicago, Illinois 60611

Kuder General Interest Survey
Science Research Associates, Inc.
259 East Erie Street
Chicago, Illinois 60611

Kuder Occupational Interest Survey
Science Research Associates, Inc.
259 East Erie Street
Chicago, Illinois 60611

Metropolitan Achievement Tests
Harcourt Brace Jovanovich, Inc.
757 Third Avenue
New York, New York 10017

Miller Analogies Test
Psychological Corporation
304 East 45th Street
New York, New York 10017

Minnesota Multiphasic Personality Inventory
Psychological Corporation
757 Third Avenue
New York, New York 10017

Minnesota Vocational Interest Inventory
Psychological Corporation
304 East 45th Street
New York, New York 10017

Myers-Briggs Type Indicator
Consulting Psychologists Press, Inc.
577 College Avenue
Palo Alto, California 94306

Omnibus Personality Inventory
Psychological Corporation
304 East 45th Street
New York, New York 10017

Otis Lennon Mental Ability Test
Harcourt Brace Jovanovich, Inc.
757 Third Avenue
New York, New York 10017

Peabody Picture Vocabulary Test
American Guidance Service, Inc.
720 Washington Avenue, S.E.
Minneapolis, Minnesota 55414

Scholastic Aptitude Test (College Board)
College Entrance Examination Board
Educational Testing Service
Princeton, New Jersey 08540

Self Explorations Inventory
Psychological Publications Press
8830 West McNichols Road
Detroit, Michigan 48221

Sequential Test of Educational Progress
Cooperative Test Division
Educational Testing Service
Princeton, New Jersey 08540

Sixteen Personality Factor Questionnaire
Institute for Personality and Ability Testing
P.O. Box 188
Champaign, Illinois 61820

Stanford-Binet Intelligence Scale
Houghton-Mifflin Company
One Beacon Street
Boston, Massachusetts 02107

Strong Vocational Interest Blank
Stanford University Press
Stanford, California 94305

Thematic Apperception Test
Harvard University Press
79 Garden Street
Cambridge, Massachusetts 02138

Wechsler Adult Intelligence Scale
Psychological Corporation
304 East 45th Street
New York, New York 10017

Wechsler Intelligence Scale for Children
Psychological Corporation
304 East 45th Street
New York, New York 10017

Wechsler Preschool and Primary Scale of Intelligence
Psychological Corporation
304 East 45th Street
New York, New York 10017

NAME INDEX

Adler, A., 62, 87
Alberti, R.E., 23, 28
Allen, M., 67, 88
Allinsmith, W., 16, 28
Allport, G. W., 16, 20, 28, 40, 65, 87
Alschuler, A., 23, 28
Alyn, J. H., 157, 161
American Personnel and Guidance Assoc., 24, 28, 273, 276
American Psychological Association, 24, 28, 272, 276
Anastasi, A., 37, 67, 87, 265, 276
Angeles, P. A., 235, 245
Anthony, L., 222, 245
Antholz, M.B., 197, 201, 214
Anton, J. L., 293, 299
Archer, J., Jr., 157, 161
Arendt, H., 16, 28
Argyle, M., 234, 235, 245
Asarnow, J., 120, 128
Aubrey, R., 87, 88
Ausubel, D. P., 19, 28
Axelrod, S., 13, 14, 30, 187, 210

Babcock, R. J., 202, 209
Bagoon, S. R., 157, 165
Baker, J. R., 220, 245
Balaban, R. M., 287, 299
Bales, R. F., 142, 143, 161
Bandura, A., 52, 88, 119, 120, 126, 180, 209
Barry, R., 14, 19, 28, 29
Barshay, H., 228, 245
Beck, A., 53, 88
Becker, L. A., 157, 161
Bednar, R. L., 140, 150, 151, 152, 153, 160, 161, 162, 165
Benefield, W., 5, 34

Benjamin, D., 120, 128
Benne, K. D., 142, 162
Benner, H., 62, 89
Berenson, B., 99, 127
Bergland, B. W., 181, 209
Berne, E., 63, 88
Bersoff, D. N., 298, 299
Bessell, H., 23, 29
Best, J. W., 280, 299
Blake, W., 238, 245
Blanchard, K. H., 140, 145, 164
Blau, P. M., 183, 209
Bloch, S., 147, 162
Blocher, D., 16, 19, 29
Block, D., 123, 126
Bloom, B., 16, 29
Bloom, L. J., 157, 163
Bloomfield, M., 7, 29
Blustein, D. L., 157, 162
Bonney, W. C., 141, 143, 144, 162
Bordin, E. S., 13, 20, 29, 184, 209
Borg, W. R., 280, 299
Borow, H., 168, 182, 209
Bottoms, J. E., 203, 214
Bowlby, J., 55, 56, 88
Brabeck, M., 87, 88
Brammer, L. M., 98, 126
Brewer, J. M., 6, 29
Brill, A. A., 184, 209
Bronowski, J., 216, 245
Bruner, J. S., 16, 29
Buhler, C., 15, 29, 67, 88
Burck, H. D., 286, 299
Burcky, W., 324, 328
Buros, O. K., 264, 276
Burton, A., 231, 245
Bustad, J. W., 183, 209

Callanan, P., 320, 328

399

NAME INDEX

Campbell, N., 79, 88
Campbell, R. E., 196, 209
Canino, G., 224, 234, 245
Canino, I. A., 224, 234, 245
Capuzzi, D., 157, 162
Carey, R., 202, 210
Carkhuff, R., 17, 23, 29, 97, 98, 99, 102, 104, 127, 129
Carlozzi, A., 79, 88
Carter, J. A., 126, 127, 297, 299, 300
Cartwright, D., 131, 138, 141, 145, 162
Cattell, R., 67, 88
Cellini, J. U., 196, 209
Chapman, A., 19, 32
Chapman, W., 195, 210
Chelune, G. J., 240, 245
Chiroboga, D., 192, 212
Christie, S. G., 123, 128
Clarke, D. L., 157, 162
Cobb, J., 237, 249
Coche, E., 152, 162
Cohen, M., 218, 232, 245
Cole, N. S., 240, 245
Coleman, J. S., 16, 29
Coles, R., 226, 245
Comas, Diaz, L., 157, 162
Combs, S., 13, 20, 29
Conant, J., 15, 16, 29
Conyne, R. K., 131, 132, 162
Corazzini, J. C., 140, 165
Cordes, C., 270, 272, 277
Corey, G., 113, 119, 120, 127, 148, 163, 320, 328
Corey, J., 12, 30
Corey, M., 320, 328
Cormier, L. S., 104, 106, 107, 109, 110, 111, 112, 126
Cormier, W. H., 104, 106, 107, 109, 110, 111, 112, 126
Corsini, R., 147, 163
Cramer, S. H., 169, 170, 176, 184, 194, 211
Cremin, L., 6, 30
Crites, J. O., 176, 189, 206, 209, 210
Cronbach, L., 265, 277
Crouch, E., 147, 162

Daley, P. C., 157, 163
D'Andrea, M., 79, 88
Davis, A., 16, 30
Davis, J., 6, 30
Deffenbacher, J. L., 157, 163
Dickson, W. J., 287, 300
Dies, R. R., 152, 154, 162
Dinkmeyer, D., 23, 30, 62, 88, 140, 165

Dixon, D. N., 52, 106, 107, 108, 122, 127, 128
Dobbert, M. L., 291, 299
Dollard, J., 52, 88
Donner, L., 238, 246
Draguns, J. G., 240, 241, 245
Dreikurs, R., 62, 88
Drier, H., 172, 213
Drum, D. J., 140, 163
Dudley, G. A., 192, 210
Dulit, E., 74, 88
Dymond, R. F., 12, 34

Egan, G., 45, 88, 103, 109, 127
Ellis, A., 17, 30, 53, 62, 88, 122, 127
Ellis, D. G., 130, 163
Ellis, E. M., 157, 163
Ells, K., 13, 35
Emmons, M. L., 23, 28
Enderlein, T., 184, 211
Eng, J. E., 203, 210
Erickson, V. L., 75, 89
Erikson, E., 12, 16, 18, 20, 27, 30, 63, 64, 89, 192
Evans, H., 62, 89
Evans, R., 65, 89

Farb, P., 219, 221, 224, 246
Faris, E., 220, 246
Farwell, G., 19, 33
Fast, J., 239, 246
Field, F. L., 17, 35
Fischer, K., 37, 89
Fisher, B. A., 130, 163
Flam, L., 219, 246
Foley, J. D., 8, 35
Forster, J. R., 317, 328
Forsyth, D. R., 150, 163
Foulks, E. F., 224, 246
Foulkes, S. H., 136, 155, 163
Fox, W. M., 68, 89
Frankl, V., 12, 30, 62, 67, 89
Freud, A., 58, 89
Freud, S., 22, 30, 57, 60, 61, 89
From, F., 237, 246
Fromm, E., 62, 89

Gall, M. D., 280, 299
Gallessich, J., 125, 127
Gardner, H., 40, 89
Gardner, J., 16, 30
Gassel, I., 219, 246
Gazda, G. M., 132, 134, 135, 139, 140, 144, 146, 148, 161, 163, 164
Gelatt, H. B., 181, 193, 202, 210
Gelso, C. J., 126, 127

NAME INDEX

Gershaw, N. J., 161, 164
Gershenfeld, M. K., 139, 165
Gibbs, J., 40, 89
Gilligan, C., 61, 79, 89, 91
Ginsburg, S., 13, 14, 30, 187, 210
Ginzberg, E., 7, 8, 10, 13, 30, 187, 210
Glanz, E., 17, 30
Glasser, W., 17, 30
Glover, J. A., 106, 107, 108, 122, 127
Goethals, G., 16, 28
Goetz, J. P., 291, 299
Goldman, L., 279, 280, 285, 299
Goldstein, A. P., 96, 97, 128, 161, 164
Good, R., 184, 196, 211
Goodman, M., 155, 164
Goodman, P., 16, 30
Goodyear, R. K., 326, 329
Gordon, T., 23, 30
Godedman, L., 157, 162
Gottdanker, J. S., 203, 210
Gough, H., 236, 246
Gould, R., 192, 210
Goulding, M., 119, 127
Goulding, R., 119, 127
Greeley, A. M., 239, 246
Greenberg, L. S., 117, 127
Greenson, R. R., 229, 230, 246
Greenwood, D. J., 218, 246
Gribbons, W. D., 184, 210
Griffith, A. R., 173, 210
Gross, H. S., 238, 246
Gross, M. L., 237, 246
Gross, S. J., 317, 328
Gysbers, N. L., 169, 175, 208, 210

Haan, N., 74, 91
Hagan, E. P., 265, 277
Hampden-Turner, C., 226, 246
Hansen, J. C., 142, 164
Hansen, L. S., 169, 197, 201, 210, 211, 214
Hanssol, R. O., 227, 249
Harlow, H., 55, 90
Harlow, M., 55, 90
Harmon, L. W., 279, 280, 299
Harold, M., 270, 277
Harren, V. A., 176, 181, 213
Harrington, M., 16, 31
Harris, M., 221, 247
Harrison, D. K., 239, 246
Hartman, J. J., 139, 151, 152, 153, 164
Hatch, T. D., 303, 329
Hathaway, B., 270, 277
Havighurst, R., 12, 15, 16, 18, 20, 31, 33, 64, 90
Hayes, B. A., 326, 328
Hayes, R., 27, 31, 41, 62, 79, 87, 89, 90
Healy, C. C., 205, 211
Hearn, M. T., 111, 127
Hempel, C., 40, 90
Hendricks, G., 68, 90
Herbert, M. R., 238, 246
Herma, J., 13, 14, 30, 187, 210
Herr, E. L., 169, 170, 176, 184, 194, 196, 211
Hersey, P., 140, 145, 164
Hersh, R., 75, 93
Hickey, J., 79, 91
Hill, C.E., 297, 299, 300
Hills, J. R., 179, 211
Hilton, T. J., 175, 211
Hipple, J., 157, 164
Hirschman, C., 222, 247
Hofferth, S. L., 222, 247
Hoggart, R., 183, 211
Holland, J. L., 13, 31, 185, 186, 197, 211
Hollingshead, A. B., 12, 31, 183, 211
Hollis, J. U., 24, 31
Hollon, S., 121, 178
Horney, K., 219, 247
Hosford, R. E., 52, 90
Hotelling, K., 157, 164
Howe, L. W., 23, 34
Howes, R. J., 148, 164
Hummel, R., 17, 31
Hunt, C., 84, 94
Hunt, J., 16, 31
Hunter, J. E., 240, 249
Hurst, J. C., 287, 300

Inhelder, B., 12, 311
Ivey, A. E., 87, 90, 101, 108, 110, 111, 127, 289, 290, 300, 302, 304, 328

Jacobson, E., 49, 90
Jensen, M. A. C., 144, 166
Jepsen, D. A., 193, 211
Jessor, R., 183, 209
Johnson, D. A., 203, 214
Johnson, D. W., 140, 164
Johnson, F. P., 140, 164
Johnson, R. H., 201, 212
Johnson, V., 49, 92
Jones, B., 172, 213
Jordaan, J. P., 189, 214
Jordan, W. D., 220, 247
Jourard, S., 67, 90, 227, 247
Jung, C., 62, 90

Kadushin, K. C., 237, 247
Kagan, N., 79, 90
Kanfer, F. H., 96, 97, 128
Kardiner, A., 237, 247
Karon, B. P., 216, 247
Katz, M., 16, 31, 179, 195, 209, 212
Katz, R. C., 227, 247
Kauffman, K., 79, 91
Kaufman, M. A., 202, 209
Kaul, T. J., 140, 150, 151, 152, 153, 160, 161, 162
Kees, W., 235, 248
Kegan, R., 2, 31, 44, 85, 91
Kehas, C., 16, 31
Keierleber, D. L., 169, 210
Kelly, G. A., 20, 31
Kendall, P., 121, 128
Kenney, J., 41, 90
Kerr, B. A., 107, 128
Kiesler, D. J., 231, 250
King, P. T., 17, 31, 84, 91
Kingdom, M. A., 157, 165
Kirschenbaum, H., 23, 34
Kissen, M., 155, 156, 165
Kitchener, K., 84, 91
Kitson, H. D., 7, 31
Kivlighan, D. M. J., 140, 165
Klaurens, M. K., 197, 201, 214
Klein, S., 157, 162
Kluckhohn, C., 219, 247
Kluckhohn R., 221, 247
Knatterud, G. L., 238, 246
Knefelkamp, L., 84, 91
Knowdell, R. L., 203, 212
Knott, J. E., 140, 163
Knowles, H., 131, 138, 139, 165
Knowles, M., 131, 138, 139, 165
Kohlberg, L., 15, 23, 31, 32, 40, 44, 74, 75, 79, 91, 93
Kosinski, F. A., Jr., 316, 328
Kramer, E., 157, 162
Kravitz, D. A., 150, 153, 160, 165
Krumboltz, J., 17, 32, 180, 212
Kuhn, D., 79, 91
Kuhn, T. S., 40, 91
Kurpius, D. J., 109, 120, 123, 125, 128, 129

Lambergt, H., 79, 91
Langer, J., 38, 40, 41, 42, 43, 71, 74, 91, 92
Larsen, M. J., 139, 164
Larson, D., 161, 165
Lasch, C., 6, 32
Laswell, H. D., 122, 128
Laurin-Frenette, N., 222, 247

Lawler, E. E., 179, 212
Lazarus, A. A., 23, 32
Lazerson, A., 37, 89
Lebra, T. S., 228, 237, 247
LeCompte, M. D., 291, 299
Lenneberg, E., 56, 92
Lerner, R. M., 205, 214
Levine, M., 280, 300
Levinson, D., 62, 64, 92, 192, 212
Lewin, K., 20, 32
Lewis, J. A., 26, 32, 287, 300, 326, 328
Lewis, M. D., 26, 32, 287, 300
Liam, P., 207, 212
Lidz, T., 218, 223, 247
Lindeman, R. E., 189, 214
Linder, R., 202, 212
Lipiec, K., 157, 162
Lippitt, R., 146, 166
Lipscomb, W. D., 243, 248
Lipsett, L., 183, 212
Little, W., 19, 32
LoCascio, R., 184, 212
Loesch, L. C., 310, 312, 317, 328, 329
Loevinger, J., 57, 58, 65, 79, 92
Lohnes, P. R., 184, 210
Long, T. E., 196, 211
Lorenz, K., 55, 92
Lowenthal, M. F., 192, 212
Luft, J., 132, 138, 140, 143, 145, 146, 149, 165
Lutz, P., 326, 329
Lynd, H. M., 12, 32
Lynd, R. J., 12, 32

Mackin, R. K., 201, 212
Mackinnon, R. A., 234, 248
Magoon, T. M., 197, 203, 211, 212
Mahdavi, E., 120, 129
Mahoney, M. J., 120, 121, 128
Marrow, A. J., 289, 300
Maslow, A. H., 12, 16, 20, 32, 30, 67, 92, 185, 212, 218, 221, 223, 248
Masters, W., 49, 92
Matarazzo, J. D., 317, 329
Mathay, E. R., 202, 212
Mathews, K. E., Jr., 227, 249
Mathewson, R., 15, 16, 18, 32, 33
May, R., 17, 33
Mayer, R., 40, 75
McClelland, D., 16, 33, 226, 231, 248
McCloskey, G., 184, 176, 211
McDaniels, C., 169, 170, 171, 213
McFadden, J., 243, 248

NAME INDEX

McGovern, T. V., 140, 165
McGrath, J. E., 150, 153, 160, 165
Mead, G. H., 20, 33
Meeker, M., 13, 35
Meichenbaum, D. H., 53, 92, 120, 128
Melnick, J., 140, 162
Mentkowski, M., 84, 92
Meyerson, L., 17, 33
Michael, J., 17, 33
Michels, R., 234, 248
Miller, C. H., 5, 6, 33
Miller, G. P., 202, 210
Miller, N., 52, 88
Miller-Tiedeman, A., 192, 214
Mitchell, A. M., 172, 213
Mitchell, J. V., 264, 277
Moeser, M., 84, 92
Montagu, A., 216, 248
Moore, E. J., 169, 210
Moreno, J. L., 23, 33
Morran, D. K., 109, 120, 128, 135, 160, 166
Morrill, W. H., 287, 300
Mosak, H., 63, 92
Mosher, R. L., 23, 33, 75, 92, 94
Mounin, G., 234, 248
Mumford, L., 5, 33
Munsterberg, H., 7, 33
Muro, J. J., 140, 165, 166
Myers, J. M., 323, 329
Myers, R. A., 189, 214
Myrick, R. D., 201, 212

Nachman, B., 13, 29, 184, 209
Napier, R. W., 139, 165
Nelson, R. C., 199, 213
Nichols, M. P., 157, 163
Noam, G., 40, 93
Nuttall, E. V., 289, 290, 300

Ochanine, D., 227, 248
Oetting, E., 286, 287, 300
O'Farrell, M. K., 297, 299, 300
Offer, D., 241, 248
O'Hara, R. P., 191, 214
Olmedo, E. L., 240, 248
Oppenheimer, B., 147, 165
Overton, W. F., 37, 39, 40, 93
Ovesey, L., 237, 247

Page, R. C., 157, 165
Page, J. D., 241, 248
Paolitto, D., 75, 93
Parnes, H. S., 183, 209
Parsons, F., 7, 33, 176, 213, 215, 248

Pavlov, I., 46, 92
Peatling, J. H., 192, 213
Peck, R. F., 16, 33
Pedersen, P. B., 241, 248
Pelto, G. H., 240, 248
Pelto, P. J., 240, 248
Pennell, N. Y., 303, 329
Perls, F. S., 17, 33, 117, 118, 129
Perry, L., 324, 329
Perry, W. G., Jr., 81, 92
Peters, H., 19, 33
Peters, T. J., 122, 129
Pew, W., 62, 88
Phillips, B. N., 317, 329
Phillips-Jones, L., 172, 213
Philosophy of Science and Counseling Research, 200, 300
Piaget, J., 12, 15, 18, 20, 31, 33, 69, 70, 74, 93
Piercy, F. P., 326, 329
Pitz, G. F., 176, 181, 213
Proctor, W. M., 5, 33, 34
Proffitt, J. R., 303, 329

Racker, H., 231, 248
Raush, H. L., 280, 300
Rayman, P., 207, 212
Rayner, R., 48, 95
Reese, K. H., 157, 164
Reese, H. W., 37, 39, 40, 93
Reibstein, J., 147, 162
Reimer, J., 75, 93
Reisor, J. S., 157, 161
Richards, F., 67, 95
Richardson, B. Z., 227, 249
Richardson, K., 57, 93
Riesman, D., 12, 34
Roberts, L., 183, 213
Robinson, S. E., 122, 125, 128
Roe, A., 13, 34, 189, 213
Roethlisberger, F. J., 287, 300
Rogers, C. R., 12, 34, 67, 69, 93, 98, 102, 129, 227, 247
Rogoff, B., 54, 93
Rose, G. S., 140, 165
Rosenberg, B., 147, 163
Rubin, R., 52, 93
Ruesch, J., 230, 235, 248
Rutan, J. S., 134, 165

Sabshim, M., 241, 248
Salter, A., 48, 93
Sanborn, M. P., 296, 300
Sarason, S., 10, 11, 12, 34
Sattler, J. M., 57, 93
Scharf, P., 79, 91

NAME INDEX

Scheflen, A. E., 229, 234, 249
Scheler, M., 228, 249
Schlossberg, N. K., 192, 213
Schmidt, F. L., 240, 249
Schmidt, J. A., 198, 213
Schmidt, J. S., 199, 214
Schmidt, L. D., 108, 129
Schneider, J., 79, 90
Schwartz, B. D., 154, 155, 164, 165
Scriven, M., 290, 300
Segal, S. J., 13, 29, 124, 209
Sennett, R., 237, 249
Sharey, J., 40, 93
Shaw, M. C., 326, 329
Sheats, P., 142, 162
Sherif, M., 150, 165
Sherman, S. E., 227, 249
Shertzer, B., 15, 34
Shimberg, B., 309, 315, 317, 329
Shoben, E. J., 220, 249
Shostrom, E. L., 98, 126
Silver, S., 120, 129
Simon, S. B., 23, 34
Singer, E., 229, 249
Skinner, B. F., 50, 93
Slepitza, R., 84, 91
Smith, E. J., 143, 164
Smith P., 161, 166
Smith, R. L., 326, 329
Snow, L. J., 157, 166
Snygg, D., 13, 20, 29
Solomon, C., 325, 329
Spears, D., 57, 93
Spitz, R., 55, 94
Sprafkin, R. P., 161, 164
Sprinthall, N. A., 23, 33, 75, 92, 94, 280, 300
Steiner, G., 232, 234, 249
Stephenson, B., 84, 94
Stewart, D. A., 227, 249
Stewart, R., 157, 163
Stini, W. A., 218, 246
Stockton, R., 135, 166
Stone, G. L., 120, 121, 129
Stone, S. C., 15, 34
Stone, W. N., 134, 165
Storr, A., 218, 249
Stotland, E., 227, 249
Strait, M., 84, 92
Strang, R., 19, 34
Strong, S. R., 52, 94, 108, 129
Super, D. E., 10, 13, 14, 16, 34, 35, 169, 176, 188, 189, 190, 191, 213, 214
Sullivan, H. S., 12, 13, 20, 34, 64, 94
Sweeney, T. J., 315, 316, 317, 329

Swensen, C. H., 79, 81, 94
Szalita, A. B., 227, 249

Taft, R., 237, 249
Tate, R., 67, 95
Tennyson, W. W., 197, 201, 214
Thass-Theinemann, T., 226, 249
Thompson, A. S., 189, 214
Thoresen, C. E., 17, 32
Thorndike, E. L., 49, 94
Thorndike, R. H., 265, 277
Thurnher, M., 192, 212
Tiedeman, D. V., 17, 35, 191, 210, 213, 214
Tinbergen, N., 55, 94
Truax, C., 94, 129
Tuckman, B. W., 144, 166
Turiel, E., 23, 32
Turkington, C., 275, 277

Uhlemann, M. R., 111, 127
U. S. Dept. of Health, Education, and Welfare, 315, 317, 330
U.S. National Advisory Commission on Civil Disorders, 219, 221, 249

Vacc, N. A., 312, 317, 323, 328, 330
Van Kaam, A., 12, 17, 35
Varenhorst, B., 202, 210
Villemez, W. J., 222, 249
Vondracek, F. W., 205, 214
Vontress, C. E., 222, 239, 241, 244, 249, 250
Vygotsky, L., 53, 54, 94

Walker, L., 74, 94
Walker, L. J. S., 157, 166
Walz, G. R., 327, 330
Wantz, R., 24, 31
Ward, G., 79, 88
Warner, R. W., 143, 164
Warner, W. L., 13, 35
Wasserman, E., 75, 91
Watchel, P. L., 234, 250
Waterman, R. H., 122, 129
Watson, J. B., 47, 48, 94, 95
Watts, A. G., 193, 214
Wayne, G., 316, 317, 330
Weinhold, B., 68, 90
Weinstein, E., 196, 197, 214
Weisser, R. J., Jr., 109, 110, 111, 112, 127
Weitz, A., 184, 196, 211
Welch, I., 67, 95
Welfel, E., 87, 88
Werbel, W. S., 130, 163

Werner, H., 44, 95
Wertsch, J., 54, 93
Wessler, R., 79, 92
Wexler, D. A., 120, 121, 129
White, R., 146, 166
White, R. W., 13, 16, 35
Whiteley, J., 75, 89
Whiteley, R. M., 323, 330
Wilborn, B. L., 140, 166
Wilcock, R. C., 183, 209
Williamson, E. G., 7, 8, 35
Wills, J., 157, 165
Winter, J., 199, 214
Wittmer, J., 305, 315, 317, 323, 330
Wolf, B., 14, 19, 28, 29

Wollman, M., 203, 214
Wolpe, J., 17, 35, 48
Wong, M. G., 222, 247
Wood, S., 275, 277
Wrenn, C. G., 5, 16, 34, 35
Wylie, R. C., 16, 35

Yalom, I. D., 143, 144, 147, 155, 166
Young-Eisendrath, P., 81, 84, 95
Yulis, S., 231, 250

Zander, A., 131, 134, 135, 138, 145, 151, 153, 162, 166
Zetzel, E. R., 225, 250
Zimet, C. N., 135, 166

SUBJECT INDEX

Accreditation
  defined, 303
  information on, 387
  origin of counselor, 305
  procedures, 305-309
  standards, 305
Age of psychotherapy, 11
American Association for Counseling and Development (AACD), 13, 24, 206, 243, 273, 276, 304-306, 310-312, 321-322, 324-325
American Association of Marriage and Family Therapists (AAMFT), 308, 313-314, 316
American College Personnel Association (ACPA), 13, 305-306
American Educational Research Association (AERA), 271
American Mental Health Counselors Association (AMHCA), 14, 305-306, 312
American Personnel and Guidance Association (APGA), see American Association for Counseling and Development (AACD)
American Psychological Association (APA), 13, 24, 206, 271, 276, 307, 308
American Rehabilitation Counselors Association (ARCA), 13, 305
American School Counselor Association (ASCA), 13, 306
Analytic psychology, 61-62
Anxiety
  behavioral view of, 48, 53
  career development and, 170
  existential-humanistic view of, 115
  psychoanalytic view of, 57-60
  structural view of, 70-71, 75
  trait theory view of, 67

Appraisal
  defined, 251-252
  ethical issues involved in, 338-342, 363-364, 367-386
  formal, 254-256
  informal, 265-269
  process of, 253-256
  reasons for, 252-253
  test bias in, 269
  tools and test publishers, 396-398
Association for Counselor Education and Supervision (ACES), 13, 305
Association for Humanistic Education and Development (AHEAD), 13
Association for Measurement and Evaluation in Counseling and Development (AMECD), 13, 305, 310, 311
Association for Measurement and Evaluation in Guidance (AMEG), see Association for Measurement and Evaluation in Counseling and Development (AMECD)
Association for Multicultural Counseling and Development (AMCD), 13-14, 243, 305
Association for Non-White Concerns in Personnel and Guidance (ANWC), see Association for Multicultural Counseling and Development (AMCD)
Association for Religious Values in Counseling (ARVIC), 14
Association for Specialists in Group Work (ASGW), 14, 305, 348-352

Behaviorism
  applications to counseling of, 8-9,

SUBJECT INDEX

17, 51-52, 119-122
classical conditioning and, 46-49
described, 44-51
key concepts of, 41-42, 44-47, 49-51
mediation and cognition in, 52-53, 119-120
operant conditioning and, 49-51, 120
origins of, 46-48
problem solving and, 49, 54
psychometrics and, 8-10
social learning theory and, 52
Behavioral counseling
anxiety hierarchy, 49
assertiveness training, 23, 48, 120, 158-159, 161, 170, 203
aversive counterconditioning, 49, 120
behavior modification, 51
bibliotherapy, 52
biofeedback, 23, 51
career counseling and, 180
computer-assisted instruction, 51
deep muscle relaxation, 48
extinction, 51, 120
flooding, 52
goals in, 42
group work and, 155
implosion therapy, 52, 120
overcorrection, 50
paradoxical intention, 52
programmed instruction, 51
reciprocal inhibition, 17, 48
reinforcement schedules, 51
relaxation response, 48
research methodology in, 293-294
sensate focus, 49
sexual arousal, 49
successive approximations, 51
systematic desensitization, 49, 120
therapeutic techniques of, 121-122
thinning, 51
time-out, 50
Boulder conference, 14

Career counseling
career development as outcome of, 170
competencies for counselors, 173-174
defined, 170-172
early history, 6-8, 13
occupational information in, 194-197
tests for use in, 262-263
Career development

choice theory, viii, 174-193
defined, 167-168
exploration techniques to promote, 197-204
history of, viii, 13, 14, 19
lifespan human development and, 168, 187-193, 205, 207-208
life-style and, 167, 169
Career guidance, see career counseling
Caring, 96, 122
Certification
Certified Rehabilitation Counselor (CRC), 313
Clinical Mental Health Counselor (CMHC), 312-313
defined, 309
history of counselor, 310-312
information on, 387
marriage and family counselor, 313-314
National Certified Counselor (NCC), 312
procedures for counselor, 311-314
Professional Career Counselor (PCC), 313
registry and licensure compared to, 317-319
school counselor, 315
Character type
analytic psychology and, 61-62
career development and, 184-187
individual psychology and, 62-63
psychoanalysis and, 59-61
trait theory and, 65, 67
Clinical psychology, 4, 10, 24
Cognition
language and, 233
mediation and, 52-54
stages of development and, 43-44, 70-74
structuralism and, 43
Commission on Rehabilitation Counselor Certification (CRCC), 310, 311
Community counseling, 287
Consultation
compared with counseling, 122, 325
ethical conduct in, 322, 337-338, 342-343
human relations core for, 123-124
skills core for, 124-125
social influence core for, 124
theory core for, 125
types of, 125
Continuing education units (CEUs),

SUBJECT INDEX

319
Council for the Accreditation of Counseling and Related Educational Programs (CACREP)
  accreditation procedures of, 306-307
  organizational structure of, 305-306, 311
  origin of, 305
  Standards for Preparation of the, vii, 312, 322
Council of Guidance and Personnel Associations (CGPA), see American Association for Counseling and Development (AACD)
Counseling
  abused persons, 324
  appraisal and, 252
  as the natural facilitation of development, 2-4, 85-86
  behaviorism and, 7-10, 12, 23
  client-centered, 10-12, 20, 21, 69
  developmental psychology and, 18-20, 81, 332
  directive, 8
  eclecticism and, 87, 244
  ego development and, 79
  ethical development and, 81, 84-85
  handicapped persons, 324
  humanistic psychology and, 12
  marriage and family, 325
  older persons and, 323
  origins of, 11
  political action and, 324-325
  professional organizations and, 13-14, 388-389
  professionalization of, 2
  psychoanalysis and, 7, 12, 17, 57
  rehabilitation, 10
  stimulation of development and, 19, 79, 332
Counseling psychology, 206, 307
Counselor characteristics
  client centered therapy and, 69
  cognitive development and, 74, 332
  cultural influences on, 224
  effective cross-cultural counseling and, 236
  ego development and, 79, 81, 332
  Gestalt therapy and, 117
  group leadership and, 145-146, 154
Counselor education
  as skill training, 23
  as the stimulation of human development, 333-334
  ethical behavior and, 345-347, 354-356, 358, 360, 362
  preparation standards for, viii, 312, 322
Counselor's role
  in industry, 173, 326
  in schools, 173
  professional identity and, viii, 331-332
Cross-cultural counseling
  career development and, 204-205
  client experience of, 239-240
  defined, 215-216
  differing views on, 240-242
  need for, 215, 323, 327
  role of language in, 231-235
  transference and countertransference in, 227, 229-231
Culture
  cross-cultural counseling and, 216, 332
  ethnicity and, 220-221
  race and, 219, 220
  social class and, 221-225
  types of, 216-221

Deliberate psychological education, 23, 75
Diagnosis
  appraisal and, 252
  cultural influences on, 224, 236-239, 241

Ego psychology, 19, 20, 61-65, 79-81
Empathy, 98-101, 116, 227-228, 236
Empiricism
  human development and, 39-40
  traditional research and, 282-284
Employee assistance programs, 242, 326
Ethical behavior
  codes of, 311, 321, 334-386
  counseling relationship and, 336-342
  group work and, 148-149, 337, 348-352
  mental health counselors and, 353-366
  of using interpreters, 233-234
  research and, 298
  sexual conduct and, 338, 350, 357
  testing, test results, and, 271, 272-273, 275-276, 367-386
Existential psychology, see humanistic psychology

Field theory, 20
Future, counseling in the, 87, 160-161, 207-208, 244, 298-299, 322-327

Gender issues
  assertiveness training and, 158, 203
  career development and, 202, 203, 204, 207
  counseling and, 323, 332
  group work and, 157
  human development and, 60-61
  test bias and, 269-270
Genuineness, 102-104
Gestalt therapy, 17, 116-118
"Giving psychology away," 22, 23, 161
Group
  appraisal, 255, 267
  defined, 130-131
  development, 143-144
  leadership, 144-145
Group work
  benefits of, 137
  career counseling and, 180, 202, 207
  code of ethics for, 348-352
  group guidance, 10, 134
  key concepts of, 138-149
  lifespan human development and, 135, 157-158
  methodology and, 149-152
  models of, 161
  origins of, 22-23, 62
  peer counseling as, 52
  self-help and, 23
  teacher/parent effectiveness training in, 23
  theoretical orientations to, 154-155
  types of, viii, 131-132, 134-135
Guidance
  counseling and, 11
  group work and, 10
  social reform movements and, 4-5
  origins of, 5-7
  vocational, see career counseling

Hawthorne Effect, 150, 287
Helping relationship
  behavioral view of the, 119-120
  characteristics of the, 96-98
  client-centered view of, 116-117
  cognitive-behavioral view of the, 119-122
  cross-cultural views of the, 241
  cultural influences on the, 225-236
  Gestalt view of the, 117-118
  human relations core of the, 98-104
  humanistic view of the, 115-116
  psychoanalytic view of the, 114-115
  skills core of the, 108-112
  social influence core of the, 104-108
  theory core of the, 112-122
  Transactional analysis view of the, 118-119
Hierarchy of needs, 2, 68-69, 183, 185, 218, 221, 222, 233
Holism, 2, 14, 20, 62, 192, 207, 231, 291, 332
Human development
  approaches to, viii, 40-44
  behavioral view of, 40, 53
  career development and, 168-170, 207
  cognitive, 70-74, 192
  counseling and, viii, 12-13, 14-15, 19, 36-44, 332
  critical periods and, 55
  culture and, 216-218
  decision theory and, 179, 193-196
  dichotomies of, 36-39
  group work and, 155
  heritability and, 56
  humanistic view of, 68-69
  key concepts of, 36-44
  lifespan, 15, 19-20, 62-63, 85, 135
  maturational view of, 40
  moral, ethical, and ego, 74-85
  object relations and, 85-86
  opposing views of, 39-40
  organicism and, 39-40
  paradigms of, 40
  psychoanalytic view of, 59-61
  psychosocial view of, 15, 63-64, 192
  stages in, 38-39, 43-44
  structural view of, 40, 69-71
  tasks and career development, 201
  tasks and education, 15, 64
Humanistic education, 23
Humanistic psychology
  client-centered counseling and, 69
  group work and, 155
  key concepts of, 12, 67
  origins of, 12, 14, 62-63, 67

Identity crisis, 64
Individual psychology, 62-63
Interviews, types and use of, 268-269, 287-288

SUBJECT INDEX

Knowledge
  behaviorism and, 41-42
  maturationism and, 42-43
  structuralism and, 43-44

Language
  cross-cultural counseling and, 231-235
  cultural origins of, 218
  nonverbal difficulties in, 234
  para-, 234
  social class differences in use of, 222
  verbal difficulties in, 232-234
Law of Effect, 49-50
Licensed Professional Counselor (LPC), 316
Licensure
  appraisal and, 252
  as a counselor, 315-317
  as a marriage and family counselor, 316
  as a psychologist, 315-316
  defined, 315
  information on, 387

Maturationism
  analytic psychology and, 61-62
  basic concepts of, 42-43, 54
  counseling goals of, 42
  different approaches to, 55-69
  ethology and, 55-56
  genetic factors and, 56
  humanistic psychology and, 67-69
  individual psychology and, 62-63
  interpersonal relations and, 65
  psychoanalysis and, 57-61
  psychosocial development and, 63-64
  trait theory and, 65, 67
Meaning-making, 54, 62, 69, 85
Mental health
  an age of, 12
  counselors and ethical behavior, 353-366
  cross-cultural definitions of, 241
  industrialization and, 3
  prevention and, 158-159
Mental Health Counselor (MHC), 316
Military Educators and Counselors Association (MECA), 14
Moral development
  cognitive development and, 74-79
  counselors and, 333
  psychoanalysis and, 60-61
  stimulation of, 75-76, 332-333
Moral education, 23, 75-76
Multicultural counseling, see cross-cultural counseling

National Academy for Certified Clinical Mental Health Counselors (NACCMHC), 310, 311, 313
National Association of Counseling and Guidance Trainers (NACGT), see Association for Counselor Education and Supervision (ACES)
National Board for Certified Counselors (NBCC), viii, 252, 310, 311, 312
National Career Development Association (NCDA), 7, 13, 206, 208, 305
National Catholic Guidance Conference (NCGC), see Association for Religious Values in Counseling (ARVIC)
National Certified Counselor (NCC), 312
National Council for Accreditation of Teacher Education (NCATE), 308
National Council for Credentialing of Career Counselors (NCCCC), 313
National Defense Education Act (NDEA), 15, 215
National Employment Counselors Association (NECA), 13
National Rehabilitation Association (NRA), 313
National Vocational Guidance Association (NVGA), see National Career Development Association (NCDA)
National Training Laboratories (NTL), 23

Personality
  as learning, 52
  dynamics of, 57
  structure of, 57-59, 61-69
  tests of, 263-264
  theories and career counseling, 184-187
Prevention, 158, 326
Public Offender Counselors Association (POCA), 14
Problem solving, 53, 58, 73, 121, 161, 181
Professional liability
  defined, 319

SUBJECT INDEX 411

duty to warn and, 320, 337-338, 340-341, 345-346, 349, 360, 365
privileged communication and, 336-337, 342, 349, 358-359, 366, 371, 385-386
Profession
defined, 27-28, 301, 327-328
Professional Career Counselor (PCC), 313
Professionalism
defined, 302-303
organizations and, viii, 13-14, 388-389
publications and, 390-391
Psychoanalysis
career counseling and, 184
character types and, 59-61
cognition and, 57-58
conscious, preconscious, and unconscious in, 58-59
defense mechanisms in, 58-59
dynamics of personality in, 57
extensions and adaptations of, 61-65
group work and, 155
humanistic psychology and, 67-69
id, ego, and superego in, 57-59
identification and, 58
importance of early development in, 59
key concepts of, 57-61
perspective on sexual development, 60-61
resistance in, 42, 114-115
stages of development in, 59-61
therapeutic goals of, 42-43
therapeutic techniques of, 114-115
trait theory and, 65-67
transference and countertransference in, 115, 229-231
Public Law, 94-142, 324, 392-395

Rational-emotive therapy, 17, 62, 122
Reality therapy, 17
Records
data collected in, 267-268
ethical behavior in keeping, 336-337, 358-360
purposes for use of, 267
Research
action, 289-291
basic and applied, suggestions regarding, 284-285
evaluation and, 286-298

claimed contributions of, 278-279
ethical issues in, 298, 338, 341-342, 354, 359, 364-366, 367-386
ethnographic approaches to, 291-293
follow-up studies in, 294-296
in group work, 152-154, 160
limitations of traditional, 282-284
longitudinal studies in, 296-297
professional publications of counseling, 390-391
traditional types of, 280-284
using case studies in, 297-298
validity of, 150-151
Registry
defined, 314
in North Carolina, 314-315
Respect, 101-102

Self-concept, 13, 15, 20, 69, 179, 190, 192, 199, 201
Self-actualization, 67-69
Social work, 10, 24, 252
Standards
of preparation for counselors, viii, 312
ethical, see Ethics
Structuralism
counseling goals of, 44
cognitive development and, 43, 70-74
dynamics of development in, 70-71
key concepts of, 43-44
moral, ethical, and ego development and, 74-86
stages of development in, 43, 71-86
Student Personnel Association for Teacher Education (SPATE). see Association for Humanistic Education and Development (AHEAD)

Tests
access to results of, 273-274
achievement, 258-259
aptitude, 259-260
cultural/ethnic/gender bias in, 269-271
ethical use of, 271-273, 275-276, 338-340, 355, 363-364, 367-386
group, viii, 255, 261
individual, viii, 255, 261
intelligence, 9, 56, 260-261, 270
interest, 262-263

limitations of, 274-275
personality, 263-264
predictability of, 8
reliability of, 256, 381-382
selection and use of, 256-258
sources of data on, 264
standardized, 258-264
standards for the use of, 271-273
test publishers and, 396-398
validity of, 8, 256, 383
Technology and the counselor, 180, 207, 275, 327
Trait theory, 7-9, 66-67, 168, 176-178, 181-182
Transactional analysis, 63, 116, 118-119
Transpersonal psychology, 68

Values clarification, 23, 179-180, 199, 201, 202
Veterans Administration, 11
Vocational counseling, *see* career counseling
Vocational development, *see* career development
Vocational guidance, *see* career counseling
Vocationalism, 14
Vocation Bureau, 7

Wellness, 20

Zone of mediation, 85
Zone of proximal development, 54

THE BOOK MANUFACTURE

An Introduction to the Counseling Profession was typeset at Kachina Typesetting, Inc., Tempe, Arizona. Printing and binding was by Braun-Brumfield, Inc., Ann Arbor, Michigan. Cover design was by John Goetz, Chicago, Illinois. Internal design was by F. E. Peacock Publishers' art department. The typeface is Optima.